Rethinking In[...] [...]

Mabel Moraña and Bret Gustafson (eds.)

Washington
University in St.Louis

SOUTH BY
MIDWEST

Rethinking Intellectuals in Latin America

Mabel Moraña and Bret Gustafson (eds.)

Iberoamericana • Vervuert • 2010

Library of Congress Cataloging-in-Publication Data

Rethinking intellectuals in Latin America / Mabel Moraña and Bret Gustafson, editors.
    p. cm. -- (South by midwest ; 2)
    Includes bibliographical references and index.
    ISBN 978-1-936353-01-9 (Iberoamericana Vervuert Publishing Corp.)
    -- ISBN 978-8484894933 (Iberoamericana) -- ISBN 978-3-86527-560-8 (Vervuert)
    1. Intellectuals--Political activity--Latin America. 2. Latin America--Intellectual life.
    I. Moraña, Mabel. II. Gustafson, Bret Darin, 1968-
    F1408.3.R442 2010
    980--dc22

                                                                        2010022844

ISBN 978-84-8489-493-3 (Iberoamericana)
ISBN 978-3-86527-560-8 (Vervuert)
ISBN 978-1-936353-01-9 (Iberoamericana Vervuert Publishing Corp.)

info@ibero-americana.net
www.ibero-americana.net

Depósito Legal: M-28091-2010

Diseño de la cubierta: Carlos Zamora
Impreso en España
Este libro está impreso íntegramente en papel ecológico sin cloro

CONTENTS

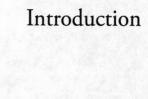

Introduction

Rethinking Intellectuals in Latin America: Questions and Problems

Mabel Moraña

The first *South by Midwest* International Conference on Latin America, which took place in St. Louis in November 2006, was planned as an introduction to the study of Latin American societies as they appear at the beginning of the 21st-century: as a complex and heterogeneous arrangement of social actors and political projects severely impacted by the effects of neoliberalism and globalization. By the turn of the 20th century, the emergence of the so-called "Latin American pink tide," the conflictive encounter of social movements and traditional politics, the increase of urban and border violence and the surfacing of new forms of hegemony and marginalization became some of the most notorious phenomena in the rapidly changing Latin American scenery. For many, this panorama triggered a wave of uncertainty and cynicism about the region while it inspired in others a theoretical and epistemological search for new models of social and political analysis. During the discussions that took place in 2006, now compiled in the book *Cultura y cambio social en América Latina* (Iberoamericana/Vervuert, 2008), it soon became apparent that while current realities surpass the parameters of "modern" concepts such as nation, identity, citizenship, governability, consensus, and the like, it is part of the paradoxical nature of our time that "old categories do not die; instead they stick around, generating influence anxiety" (Moulthrop 269).

It is perhaps emerging from these feelings of concern and uneasiness regarding the real nature and challenges of our work that the theme selected for the second *South by Midwest* international conference in November 2008 focused on a topic that complements the first (*culture and social change*) and is crucial to the social sciences and, in a more general sense, to the configuration of social consciousness and the interdisciplinary analysis of collective imaginaries: the *role of intellectuals* and the definition of *intellectual practices* in peripheral societies.

Both the conference and the resulting book which is now offered to the reader constitute an attempt to reflect on a variety of intertwined notions and practices relating to the processes of production and dissemination of knowledge in the Latin American region. One of the premises of this reflection is the need to define the *locus of enunciation* of intellectual discourses as a primarily *ideological* – and not only *geocultural* – location, but also as a strategic position for the elaboration of cultural policies and political projects. It also entails a reflection on the significance and transformation of cultural and political institutions as well as on the increasing role that the media and virtual technologies play in our contemporary world.

Without a doubt, the first challenge in approaching these issues is the demarcation and definition of the elusive and ambivalent *intellectual* function, which assumes distinct and specific modalities in Latin American society since the emergence of the Creole *letrado* until today.[1] The relationship between power / knowledge and in particular the degree of autonomy or *organic* association between intellectual

---

1. For different attempts to define intellectual practices see, in addition to the classical studies by Weber, Gramsci, and Said, Buci-Glucksmann, Fischer, and Maldonado. For illuminating studies on the history and role of intellectuals in Latin American history see, among many others, Rama, Ramos, Miller and Altamirano. About intellectual work in present (Latin American) scenarios, see Arditi, García Canclini, Lechner, Brunner, and Mansilla. Miller recalls Bauman's useful distinction between intellectuals as "legislators" of opinion (a term used by Rousseau and mainly applicable to European civil societies) and intellectuals as "interpreters." As Miller explains, "the interpreter role is dependent on the recognition of equality between different traditions [...] it is an active intervention in the sense of an act of constructing meaning." For Miller, in 20th-century Spanish America intellectuals have rather adopted a "strategy of mediation": "They tried to act as 'go-betweens' in multiple ways, mediating between elites and masses, nations and peoples, and Latin America and the developed world" (133). Miller elaborates on these functions and

work and State institutions has always constituted a key element in the development of critical thought from colonial times to the present. Nowadays, the articulation of intellectual work to the cultural market and to academia, as well as the connections between "high" culture, mass media and popular culture, adds new facets to the development of critical thinking and to the production and dissemination of knowledge, particularly in peripheral societies.

How do we define, then, within the current conditions of cultural production, "intellectual work"? How does this category adapt to the accelerated process of transformation of our world, deeply impacted not only by the influence of technology but also by the emergence of new sensibilities and new forms of social and political agency? What are the elements that the notion of "intellectual work" still mobilizes in cultural and political debates, and which are the connotations that can be considered obsolete under current circumstances? Even more importantly, what role do intellectual practices play in the social transformations of postcolonial societies, where vast sectors of the population still suffer social marginalization, racial discrimination and political exclusion? Let's examine some of the basic issues related to this topic.

Traditionally, the work of scholars, pedagogues, political activists, community leaders, cultural advisors, artists, writers, filmmakers and even scientists and religious leaders has been identified as *intellectual labor*. In spite of their different approaches to society and culture these activities have in common the predominant exercise of critical analysis, educational attitudes, creativity, philosophical speculation and ideological inquiry.[2] At the same time, it is commonly assumed that

on the particular role intellectuals have been able to adopt in Latin America, given the specific form that modernity has assumed in the region.

2. There is an extensive bibliography on the definition of intellectuals and the historical transformation of intellectual functions. One of the most influential works published on this topic in the last 15 years is Edward Said's *Representation of the Intellectual*, in which the author discusses many classical approaches to this topic (Benda, Shils, Gellner, et al.). In Latin America, Ángel Rama's elaboration on transculturation, and his book *The Lettered City*, have been highly influential in the field and have triggered multiple debates on the role of Latin American intelligentsia in relation to modernization processes, to what Rama defines as the "real city," to the place of writing in contemporary culture, and to the connections between high and popular culture in peripheral societies.

diverse forms and degrees of *intellectuality* are present in every manifestation of human / rational behavior.[3] Therefore, it is obvious that
the intellectual function is not only the privilege of a selected elite but
it is disseminated at all levels in contemporary society. Our topic covers, then, an ample spectrum, from the general human faculty to analyze, interpret, and critique the world, to the specialized and often
professionalized forms of social, cultural and political *intervention*.

I believe it is particularly this idea of *intervention* (of *involvement,
interference* and *disruption,* and also the notion of intellectual work as a
critical interruption of dominant discourses) that we would like to
emphasize and explore in this book. In other words, the ways in which
intellectual practices register, organize and challenge knowledge and
experience, as well as the manner in which intellectual work produces
an effect of ideological (conceptual, ethical, philosophical) *interpellation*. Intellectual work, then, is here understood as a practice that has
as much to do with reflection and analysis as with mobilization,
activism, and the articulation of political actors and public resources.
At the same time, it must be recognized that if the work of intellectuals is often identified as being tightly connected to the interpretation
of traditions and the exploration of *the real* (historical circumstances,
concepts, and events), it is also undoubtedly related to the exercise
of imagination and the production of innovative thought. The role of
myth, the invention of ideological (philosophical and political) systems, and the elaboration of utopia all result from the direct application of intellectual energy to our understanding of the world.

INTELLECTUAL *AFFAIRES*

In order to initiate our reflection about modern and postmodern
intellectuals, we could start by suggesting that the history of intellectual work could be traced as the route that connects two or three significant cultural *affaires* that took place, in turn, in France, the United

---

3. Gramsci is just one of the many authors that recognize that while all human
beings are intellectuals, not all of them have the function of intellectuals in society.
So, while it is possible to speak of "intellectuals" it would be a mistake to speak of
"non-intellectuals" since this kind of individual does not exist.

States, and Latin America. Although these affairs emerge from very different cultural and political circumstances, they connect, in different but representative manners, political, ethical and social issues that are crucial for the understanding of intellectual practices.

The first event would be the well-known *Dreyfus Affair*, initiated with the letter that Emile Zola wrote to the president of France in 1898 denouncing the anti-Semitic persecution of Captain Alfred Dreyfus. This letter triggered a chain of public reactions and declarations, in which the word "intellectual" became popularized as the term that served to identify a distinctly critical and belligerent group that came together to confront official policies in which culture, ethics, and ideology clearly intertwined.

This *affaire*, which exemplifies the involvement of intellectuals in political matters, initiates "*la trahison des clercs*" analyzed by Julien Benda in his classic and controversial book of the same title which, published in 1928, included a visionary study of the values and behavior of French and German *intelligentsia* during World War II.[4] From its opening lines, this book, considered to this day as a pivotal work for the study of the relations between power, culture, race, and nationalism, sets the tone for the long and convoluted debate that has been taking place around the role of intellectuals in modern times:

> We are to consider those passions termed political, owing to which men rise up against other men, the chief of which are racial passions, class passions and national passions (Benda 3).

4. As it is well known, the Dreyfus Affair was initiated with Emile Zola's letter addressed to Félix Faure, President of France, and published in *L'Aurore litteraire* on January 13, 1898. The letter was given the title "J'accuse" by George Clemenceau, director of the newspaper. It constituted a protest against the violation of legal procedures against Dreyfus, a French Jewish military officer, and was followed by a declaration signed by a number of writers, scholars, and scientists. Some of these figures were the writers Anatole France and Marcel Proust, historians like Lanson and Seignobos, classicists such as Victor Bérard, etc. This declaration, titled "Un protestation," is referred to by Clemençeau as the expression of a group of "intellectuals," thus giving the term a specific and at the same time very comprehensive meaning. However, critics agree that the word "intellectual" had been already in use as a noun in the English language since the XVIth century. According to Maldonado, in Spanish, A. Ayala seems to be considered the first in using this term in 1848 (Maldonado 13). For more information about the Dreyfus Affair, see Reinach. On intellectual history and its connections with Latin American culture see, among others, Gutiérrez Girardot.

At the end of the 20th-century although in a very different cultural and ideological environment, during the *Sokal Affair*, the concept of intellectuality touched one of its possible limits: one that has to do with the processes of professionalization and the compartmentalization of knowledge at the centers of intellectual and academic production in Western societies.[5] Alan Sokal, professor of Physics at New York University, submitted in 1996 an article titled "Transgressing the Boundaries: Towards a Transformative Hermeneutics of Quantum Gravity" to *Social Text*, a specialized journal published by Duke UP, which did not have at the time a peer review process in place. The article, purposely plagued with false data and superficial ideological concepts, was published in May of 1996 in a special issue of the journal titled "Science Wars." The article, defined as "a hodgepodge of unsupported arguments, outright mistakes and impenetrable jargon, designed to 'test' its host journal's intellectual integrity" (Sokal, *The Sokal Hoax* 1) exposed the weakness of the academic establishment at least in some of its most reputed mechanisms: the production and reproduction of intellectual knowledge.

If in the *Dreyfus Affair* what we see at play is the Enlightened tradition in which Reason functions as the honorable tribune from which social justice and critical judgment should be exercised, the *Sokal Affair* exemplifies the misleading seductions of "arrogant reason" which is often considered a characteristic feature of postmodern times. Within this context, the boundaries between fiction and scholarship have been blurred: the coherence of discourse distracts from its connectedness with truth and reality, and intellectual production escapes every possible system of quality control, as if scholarship constituted a self-preserved and self-legitimized commodity that circulates freely within the limits of the cultural and intellectual markets.

In the space / time of our own field of study, no reflection on intellectual practices could leave aside the *Padilla Affair*, one of the thorns in the side of leftist ethics in Latin America. This affair, in which ideological issues and intellectual freedom collided with particular vigor in

5. At the time of the publication, Professor Sokal announced in *Lingua Franca* the nature of this paper, which was intended as a way of testing the academic standards of scholarly publications. On the impressive amount of articles and debates generated by the Sokal Affair see: http://www.physics.nyu.edu/faculty/sokal/.

post-revolutionary Cuba, confronted intellectuals around the world with a moral dilemma that polarized the effervescent cultural and political scene of the '70s – the conflict between power and intellectual production – and, for that reason, it has remained as an iconic moment of Latin America's contemporary history.[6]

In reference to the influence of State politics on cultural institutions, twenty years after the circumstances that surrounded the *Caso Padilla*, the American sociologist James Petras offered in 1990 a strong criticism of the work and orientation of Latin American intellectuals. According to Petras, both the dictatorships that devastated Latin America in the '70s and part of the 80s and U.S.-based cultural and political agencies had managed to inhibit and domesticate Latin American intellectuals, who had succumbed, since the 1980s, to the defeat of leftist movements in the region and the effects of neoliberalism.[7] Petras' position, which reopened the topic of the intellectual's political engagement and the conflict between national politics and freedom of expression, also gave evidence of the transformation of Latin America's cultural and ideological scene toward the end of the 20th century, and of the advent of a new era in which most of the philosophical and professional configurations of the Latin American intellectual field were rapidly acquiring a new face.

New scenarios / New problems

Although the above-mentioned intellectual *affaires* are, in many ways, paradigmatic moments in the cultural history of Western intellectuals and expose most of the ethical and ideological tensions that traverse this field, they are obviously representative of the privileged and protected space of the *lettered city*. They leave aside other manifestations of intellectual work, particularly those that challenge the

---

6. Heberto Padilla (1932-2000) was a Cuban poet and writer. Though an early supporter of the Cuban revolution, he was imprisoned by the Castro regime in 1971 – an event which sparked international outrage – and later emigrated to the U.S. after his release in 1980.

7. James Petras' opinions were answered by Carlos Vilas, Benjamin Arditti, F. J. Hinkelammert, among others. In this respect see also Mansilla.

values, traditions and forms of intervention that are characteristic of modernity and were institutionalized during that time.

In addition to the well-known power struggles that are inherent to the *lettered* intellectual field, we must recognize that today, both in academia and in more informal cultural environments, we face unseen cultural challenges and social transformations which are closely connected to the pluralization of cultural markets, the impact of globalization on regional cultures, and the advancement of communications since the last decades of the 20th century. These challenges derive, to a great extent, from the activation of social sectors whose cultures were suppressed or marginalized for centuries as a result of external or internal colonialism and have now acquired political cohesiveness and worldwide visibility.

For this reason, more than a historiographical purpose, what guides our reflections in this book is the attempt to focus on the transformations that impact both the production of knowledge and the exercise of critical thought in peripheral societies at the beginning of the 21st century. We are particularly concerned with the processes of recognition, development, and dissemination of alternative models of knowledge in Latin America, where vast sectors of the population still exist at the margins of dominant cultures and occupy a disadvantaged position with respect to hegemonic epistemologies and the corresponding institutional establishment. Our purpose is to explore how social change translates into cultural, intellectual, and educational languages, and how the desires, needs and expectations of heterogeneous constituencies find representation in intellectual practices.

A number of factors have impacted Latin American societies since the last decades of the 20th century, and have considerably modified the relations between intellectuals and political power and the production of critical thought in the region.

One of these factors is the activation of the *public sphere*, both in connection to the re-emergence of populist movements and as a consequence of the action developed in the region by social movements, NGOs, etc. At this level, one of the most conspicuous facts is the utilization of non-traditional channels of organization and communication by communities and political groups whose actions have been taking place outside of the parameters of modern institutions and political parties. In many cases, even the language used by these new subjects has also been substantially modified. Their discursive strategies have ceased to reproduce in a mechanical and predictable way the concepts that characterized the political language of modernity (*nation, identity, citizenship, progress, consensus*) and have instead started to mobilize new values, goals and epistemic categories that were displaced for centuries from the public arena.

Another important element in current scenarios is the modification of the political and ideological composition of national governments, particularly in the countries in which new leftist movements have gained access to power. I am referring for instance to the leadership of women and ethnic minorities in central government, and the presence of militants of leftist movements that were declared illegal by repressive regimes a few decades ago and who now hold official political and diplomatic positions. These changes give evidence of the exhaustion of traditional politics and at the same time, of an obvious degree of domestication of the left, that has unwound its political *ethos* within the limits of electoral democracy. This situation has also modified public expectations, methods of communication and political interactions, all of which have a notorious impact on the work and positioning of public intellectuals, scholars, educators, journalists, and the like.

A third point involves the emergence of what we could call postnational scenarios, such as those created by the flux of migration, the importance of ecological issues, the application of flexible regimes of labor, the transnationalization of markets, the accelerated relocation of material and symbolic commodities, and the proliferation of virtual and provisional forms of social *affiliation*, that defy the *modern* conceptual and ideological parameters of representation and interpretation of social processes particularly in peripheral societies, and call for the elaboration of new approaches to these changing realities.

Fourth, as a result of the dynamics that have been outlined thus far, it is obvious that intellectual work functions at the intersection of a series of ideological positions, cultural backgrounds and transdisciplinary orientations that often translate into oppositional categories: humanism vs. technocracy, academicism vs. deformalization of knowledge, preeminence of the *lettered city* vs. audio-visual communication, etc. As diverse and conflictive as these alternatives are, they combine in hybrid intellectual practices which are defined across cultural and disciplinary boundaries.

Finally, with the substantial modification of national cultures, the work of intellectuals has also diversified. While some of them still hold an organic role as members of the *lettered city*, others function in the public arena with a higher degree of autonomy from State institutions. The definition of local or regional agendas as well as the awareness about issues such as global integration, cultural homogenization, etc., often counterbalances the unified and centralized notion of national culture and allows for the elaboration of specific agendas that represent a variety of interest groups that otherwise would not have been sufficiently visible at a national level. More often than not, new forms of intellectual work coexist with traditional roles due to the impact of the market in the production and dissemination of cultural production, the competitive nature of higher education increasingly configured as an entrepreneurial enterprise, and also as a result of globalization and the transnationalization of symbolic commodities. In many cases, the State continues to exist as an "empty signifier" whose former power and prestige has been transferred to the realm of non-official institutions. However, the State often retains control over education and communications as well as over the configuration and implementation of cultural politics.

Under these circumstances, and within the framework of neoliberal politics, it would be naïve to assume that the State can still function according to the paternalist and protectionist model it held during modernity, when, among its many functions, it constituted the nucleus for the production and administration of *national identity* and the warranty of social welfare. But it would be equally wrong to disregard the variable degrees in which those functions, although undoubtedly diminished, still influence the daily life of Latin American societies and their collective imaginaries. Although intellectual practices exist today more than ever, disseminated in civil society, and the intellectual, as an enlightened elite defined by humanistic and universal values is a species that faces the risk of a rapid extinction, it would be excessive to consider that intellectual work is now a direct emanation of society. In some domains more than others, intellectual mediation is still the instance in which the formalization and distribution of knowledge is implemented, although this process is often subsumed in the vast domain of market relations, thus giving the illusion of a wide cultural democratization and total and "naturalized" access to cultural commodities.

ISSUES AT PLAY

Taking into consideration this complex scenario in which the continuity of modern categories and models of intellectual intervention combine with the new factors at play in Latin American societies, we identified a series of issues that deserve particular attention and could be instrumental in the reinterpretation of the role intellectual practices can play in the following decades. These problems were elaborated, in part, both at the *South by Midwest* international symposium that took place in St. Louis in 2008 and at the sessions organized under the title *"Intelectuales latinoamericanos y la aldea global [I and II]"* held in Rio de Janeiro at the LASA conference in June 2009. Other aspects have been addressed in articles requested from scholars for inclusion in this book. Some of these issues are:

- The definition of intellectual practices in connection with academia (research and pedagogical activities), with political action within or outside of State institutions and also in connection to the creation of specific spaces of community mobilization. In this sense, and in addition to the configuration of intellectual fields *á la Bourdieu*, we would like to understand the common *processes of popular intellectualization* in society. In other words, we are particularly concerned with the discursive and rhetorical strategies that contribute to the construction of meaning and connect, at this level, with discourses of power and resistance. This includes the linguistic machinery that propels populism and feeds democracy, and the textuality that supports demagogy and "legitimizes" authoritarianism. How do these processes contribute to the construction of leadership and general constituencies, to the legitimization of State policies, and to the elaboration of national- popular subjectivities?

- What is the articulation between national cultures and intellectual practices?[8] How can the action of intellectuals contribute

8. Regarding the ties of intellectuals with national institutions, Said considers that intellectuals' position has shifted all over the world, from an attitude of loyalty and patriotic consensus to a more skeptical and even belligerent posture. Also in

to the understanding of the debated relation between *globality* and *locality*, and to the design of regional, local and sectorial agendas that could complement or counterbalance transnational fluxes of economic, financial, political, and cultural power?

• In this direction, what are the tensions between *immanence* and *transcendence* in the configuration of *the political*, between universalism and particularism, between contingency and totalization, and how do these polarizations affect intellectual production?

It is obvious that any evaluation of intellectual practices today entails a critique of the universalist and at the same time exclusionary premises that provided a basis for both the project of modernization and the implementation of (neo)liberalism in peripheral societies. Only through this critique would it be possible to recognize the place that alternative models of knowledge and intellectual practices could have within new social and political scenarios. And it is obvious that this recognition should emerge not from multiculturalist claims related to fashionable – politically correct or populist – ideological perspectives that leave intact the Occidentalist basis of society, but from the understanding that the political should not get diluted in the diversified offering of postmodern cultural marketing and that, as Zizek has warned, the urgency of the economic is replaced by the seduction of the symbolic. In other words, intellectual work should refine its ideological and theoretical approaches in order to assure that a focus on *inequality* does not disappear in the vain and superficial celebration of *difference*. But these problems also imply a reflection on *postmodern* conditions of intellectual production. In this sense,

connection to the national question, in an interview conducted by Silvia Sigal, Alain Touraine indicates that one of the main roles of both Latin American and European intellectuals has been the creation of a myth of integration of three themes that are key in contemporary societies: modernization, nationalism, and class. His opinion that most themes and approaches in the Latin American intellectual field remain almost invariable between the 50s and the 80s should be qualified, I believe, in current scenarios. However, he recognizes that the myths of unification and the references to totalizing categories have disappeared from intellectual debates in the region.

- Is Latin America's subordinate position altered in any way in the "wired" world? Does virtual integration as well as spatial and temporal simultaneity necessarily imply communicative democratization, universal access to information and knowledge, equal resources and equal opportunities, or do these conditions just instate new forms of hegemony and marginalization across the world and with them, new modalities of expertise, exclusion and illiteracy?[9]

- How do these new forms of technological prevalence connect to the realms of passion, affect and desire, so often invoked in relation to the configuration of the market, the increase of violence and the emergence of new (postmodern) subjectivities, which are not necessarily determined by rigid categories of nationhood, religion, ethnic, class, or gender identity?

- How does intellectual work illuminate the processes of social and self-recognition in relation to the dynamics of migration, exile, economic diaspora and other forms of nomadic existence and reterritorialization that characterize contemporary societies?

- What are the connections between aesthetic / symbolic *representation* and political / ideological *representativity*? This problem, extensively discussed in the 80s and 90s as a result of the preeminence of testimonial discourse, is still current during the decline of this genre. Whose voice speaks for the dispossessed, the victims, the marginalized, the subaltern? How is this ventriloquism legitimized? Is it part of the intellectuals' mission to constitute a public voice, to administer the community's collective memory, to decode societies' political unconscious? Does political *representativity* strengthen, limit or condition in any way the autonomy and vigor of intellectuals' critical judgment?[10]

9. On the connections between technocracy and intellectual work see Fischer.
10. Regarding the interconnections of politics and intellectual work in Latin America see Hofmeister and Mansilla.

- Is it possible to generate emancipated knowledge in spite of the existence of hegemonic models of thought and social action that have systematically excluded dominated cultures? How can subaltern epistemological and political paradigms surpass their passive role of primarily constituting repositories of archaic memories and cultural archives? Is it possible to produce decol-onized knowledge within Western societies where most intellec-tuals have an organic mission or have been, in variable degrees, co-opted by the ideological apparatus of the State?[11] And, in this process, how can "new" and "old," central and peripheral, hegemonic and subaltern forms of knowledge be productively articulated? Or is a universal, relativistic and all-encompassing conception of knowledge in order here, in which all categories could be absorbed and all positions negotiated?

- How can the crisis and decentering of writing (a crisis that is well-known in the field of Anthropology) be incorporated in this panorama? How does the predominance of audio-visual cultures, the eloquence of oral histories, and the ephemeral forms of virtual representation destabilize the predominance of the *lettered city*?[12]

- What space is occupied nowadays by non-traditional intellectu-als whose epistemological paradigms collide with dominant models of knowledge and representation (indigenous or Afro-Hispanic intellectuals, for instance, who question the dominant "Latino" component in "*Latino*américa," as suggested by Wal-ter Mignolo in *The Idea of Latin America*, for instance)? Today, what is the place and function of *Creole intellectuals* who have incorporated and disseminated European and Anglo-Saxon cul-tures within and about Latin American societies since the "dis-covery"? From new perspectives, how can we elaborate the legacy and "the burdens of modernity"? How do we articulate global and local knowledge? How can local and regional wis-

---

11. See, for instance, Vilas, Arditi, and Hinkelammert.

12. On the significance of oral history in Latin America see Mignolo, "El potencial epistemológico."

dom be secured and defended without falling into the traps of fundamentalism, thus replicating the same excesses and exclusionary strategies we are trying to combat?

In addition to these problems and questions, many of the articles included in this book also focus on the key role racial factors play in the construction and dissemination of knowledge, and on the importance of ethnicity in the construction of modern and postmodern concepts of citizenship and in the definition of political agency. All forms of discrimination as well as all modalities of ethnic and cultural miscegenation undoubtedly connect with colonialism, and with the perpetuation of *coloniality* in modern times, so this continues to be a crucial problem that still needs historical and philosophical elaboration.[13]

The issues mentioned above are also connected to one of the most persistent concerns of Latin American intellectuals: the need to understand the politics of culture – the politics *in* culture – and the urgency to produce emancipated knowledge in peripheral, neocolonial societies. These issues are present in the uses of language and discourse, in the universalist ethics of Human Rights, in the intricacies of power and resistance, in the voices of organic, public and "informal" intellectuals, in populism, community organizations and social movements. The studies included in this book elaborate on these topics across the boundaries of disciplinary fields to interrogate social and political scenarios where traditions remain deeply rooted in collective imaginaries, while new social behaviors work toward the transformation of political and economic structures. Without a doubt, due to the changing nature of our cultures and the deep changes we are witnessing both at social and political levels in Latin America, all the answers that we seem to find to our questions today are necessarily provisional and subject to reconsideration. This book is intended as a modest but passionate contribution to this process of recognition and understanding.

We would like to acknowledge the support received from different sources for the organization of the *South by Midwest* International Conference on Latin American Cultural Studies (St. Louis, November

---

13. A contribution to the elaboration of (post)colonial issues in Latin America is the collection of essays included in *Coloniality at Large: Latin America and the Postcolonial Debate*, Mabel Moraña, Enrique Dussel and Carlos A. Jáuregui, eds.

2008), for the organization of the LASA sessions (Rio de Janeiro, June 2009) and for the publication of this book: The Dean of Humanities, the International and Area Studies Program, the Center for the Humanities, the Department of Anthropology and the Department of Romance Languages and Literatures at Washington University, St. Louis. We thank them all for their generous contributions to this project. We are very grateful to the scholars who participated in this book for their generous intellectual contributions and for their patient cooperation with all aspects related to the preparation of this work. Finally, we would like to express our gratitude to the translators of the articles, Barbara Corbett, Rosalía Bermúdez, and Gonzalo Aguiar, and to those who contributed to the preparation of the manuscript, particularly Gonzalo Aguiar and Alejandra Aguilar.

WORKS CITED

ALTAMIRANO, Carlos. *Intelectuales. Notas de investigación*. Buenos Aires: Grupo Editorial Norma, 2007.
—, dir. *Historia de los intelectuales en América Latina*. Buenos Aires: Katz, 2008.
ARDITI, Benjamín. "Intelectuales y política." *David y Goliath* 56 (1990): 27-35.
ARROSA SOARES, María Susana. "Os intelectuais e a questão cultural." *Os intelectuais nos processos políticos da América Latina*. Comp. Maria Susana Arrosa Soares. Porto Alegre: Editora da Universidade Federal do Río Grande do Sul, 1985. 146-50.
BENDA, Julien. *The Treason of the Intellectuals*. London: Norton, 1980.
BUCI-GLUCKSMANN, Christine. "Los intelectuales y el Estado." Arrosa Soares 118-23.
BRUNNER, José Joaquín. "La función utópica de los intelectuales." Arrosa Soares 22-31.
FISCHER, Frank. *Technocracy and the Politics of Expertise*. London: Sage, 1990.
GARCÍA CANCLINI, Néstor. "Campo intelectual y crisis socio-económica." Arrosa Soares 151-62.
GELLNER, Ernest. "La trahison de la trahison des clercs." *The Political Responsibility of Intellectuals*. Eds. Ian Maclean, Alan Montefiore, and Peter Winch. Cambridge, U.K., and New York: Cambridge UP, 1990. 17-27.

GRAMSCI, Antonio. *Gli intelettuali e l'organizzazione della cultura*. Turín: Einaudi, 1949.

GUTIÉRREZ GIRARDOT, Rafael. *El intelectual y la historia*. Caracas: Fondo Editorial La Nave Va, 2001.

HINKELAMMERT, F. J. "La libertad académica bajo control en América Latina." *Nueva Sociedad* 107 (May-June 1990): 131-137.

HOFMEISTER, Wilhelm and H.C. F. MANSILLA, eds. *Intelectuales y política en América Latina. El desencantamiento del espíritu crítico*. Santa Fe, Argentina: Homo Sapiens, 2003.

LECHNER, Norbert. "Intelectuales y política: nuevo contexto y nuevos desafíos." *Los intelectuales y los dilemas políticos en el siglo XX*. Eds. Laura Baca Olamendi and Isidro H. Cisneros. Vol 2. México: FLACSO/Triana, 1997. 411-7.

MALDONADO, Tomás. *¿Qué es un intelectual? Aventuras y desventuras de un rol*. Barcelona: Paidós, 1995.

MANSILLA, H.C.F. "Intelectuales y política en América Latina. Breve aproximación a una ambivalencia fundamental." *Intelectuales y política en América Latina. El desencantamiento del espíritu crítico*. Eds. Hofmeister and Mansilla. 17-44.

MATO, Daniel, comp. *Estudios y otras prácticas intelectuales latinoamericanas en cultura y poder*. Caracas: CLACSO, 2002.

—, comp. *Cultura, política y sociedad. Perspectivas latinoamericanas*. Buenos Aires: CLACSO, 2005.

MIGNOLO, Walter. "El potencial epistemológico de la historia oral: Algunas contribuciones de Silvia Rivera Cusicanqui." Mato, *Estudios* 201-212.

—. *The Idea of Latin America*. Malden, MA: Blackwell, 2005.

MILLER, Nicola. *In the Shadow of the State. Intellectuals and the Quest for National Identity in Twentieth-Century Latin America*. London: Verso, 1999.

MORAÑA, Mabel, ed. "Negociar lo local. La 'marea rosa' en América Latina o, ¿qué queda de la izquierda?" *Cultura y cambio social en América Latina*. Madrid / Frankfurt: Iberoamericana / Vervuert, 2008. 113-34.

—, Enrique DUSSEL and Carlos A. JÁUREGUI, eds. *Coloniality at Large. Latin America and the Postcolonial Debate*. Durham: Duke UP, 2008.

MOULTHROP, Stuart. "No War Machine." *Reading Matters: Narrative in the New Ecology of Media*. Eds. Joseph Tabbi and Michael Wutz. Ithaca: Cornell UP, 1997. 269-92.

PETRAS, James. "Los intelectuales en retirada." *Nueva Sociedad* 107 (May-June 1990): 92-120.

—. "Una pequeña parte de la lucha." *Nueva Sociedad* 123 (January-February 1993): 165-9.

—. "The Metamorphosis of Latin America's Intellectuals." *Latin American Perspectives* 17.2 (1990): 102-112.

RAMA, Ángel. *La ciudad letrada.* Hanover: Ediciones del Norte, 1984.

RAMOS, Julio. *Desencuentros de la modernidad en América Latina: literatura y política en el siglo XX.* México: FCE, 1989.

REINACH, Joseph, comp. *Histoire de l'affaire Dreyfus.* 7 vols. Paris: Revue Blanche et Fasquelle, 1901-1911.

SAID, Edward W. *Representations of the Intellectual.* London: Vintage, 1994.

SHILS, Edward. *Los intelectuales y el poder.* México: DIMELISA, 1972.

—. *Los intelectuales en las sociedades modernas.* Buenos Aires: Tres Tiempos, 1974.

SIGAL, Silvia. "América Latina y sus intelectuales. Conversación con Alain Touraine." Web. <http://bibliotecavirtual.clacso.org.ar/ar/libros/critica/nro13/SIGALpdf>.

SOKAL, Alan. "Transgressing the Boundaries: Towards a Transformative Hermeneutics of Quantum Gravity." *Social Text* 46/47 (Spring/Summer 1996): 217-252.

—. "A Physicist Experiments with Cultural Studies." *Lingua Franca.* 5 Jun. 1996. Web. <http://www.physics.nyu.edu/faculty/sokal/lingua_franca_v4/lingua_franca_v4.html>.

—. *The Sokal Hoax: The Sham That Shook the Academy.* U of Nebraska P, 2000.

VILAS, Carlos M. "Sobre cierta interPETRASción de la intelectualidad latinoamericana." *Nueva Sociedad* 107 (May-June 1990): 121-130.

WEBER, Max. *El trabajo intelectual como profesión.* Barcelona: Bruguera, 1983.

I. Intellectual Roots in Latin America

Intellectuals and *Mestizaje:* Inca Garcilaso, Blas Valera and the Organic Function of Colonial *Letrados*[1]

José Antonio Mazzotti

Introduction

This essay proceeds on the premise that several of the most important concepts fueling discussions of indigenous movements today – notions such as ethnic nationalism, epistemological rupture, and *suma kawsay* ("good living" in Quechua) – become even more powerful and persuasive when understood from the perspective of history's *longue durée*. With this in mind, what I propose to do in this essay is explore the writings of two major intellectual figures from the early colonial period who also wielded arguments of indigenous vindication, and underscore those elements within their writings that constitute colonial antecedents to elements of contemporary discourse on indigenous rights.

To begin with, it is important to acknowledge that the role of cultural critic and interpreter of social trends has historically been tied in an intimate way to the exercise of power. Certainly the principal protagonists of nation-formation in early 19th-century Latin America were prominent Creole elites like Andrés Bello, Simón Rodríguez and Domingo Sarmiento. Looking back to the 18th century, we encounter

1. Translated by Barbara J. Corbett.

a figure like the Creole scholar Pedro de Peralta, who as a loyal and devoted advisor to several viceroys, was able to produce an ethnocentric poem in celebration of Lima's "Creole grandeur" and several detailed proposals on how to improve his native city. Retreating even further back into the 16th century, we find the example of Bartholomew de las Casas, an intellectual figure whose legal and historical works had tremendous influence over the political decisions of the Spanish king and the Council of Indies. For the purposes of this essay, the critical element to underscore about these well-known intellectual elites is that the power of their symbolic and political agency was directly tied to their cultural and socio-economic status.

This essay examines a different *breed* of colonial scholar; that is, the *mestizo* or bicultural professionals of learned discourse who occupied a mediating position within the pre-Enlightened social hierarchy. For those scholars who assumed representation of a non-elite ethnic group, the peculiarly colonial notion of *caste* defined the nature and limits of intellectual agency. Even as definitions of caste gave way to the scientific discourse of race in the 18th century, the same reality of mixed cultural origin continued to define and limit one's intellectual influence, and would continue to do so right through the 19th century. In the 16th and early 17th centuries, however, the notion of race was still largely understood in cultural and ethnic terms. In 1611, for example, Covarrubias could discuss the characteristics of the Moorish and Jewish "races" without ever mentioning skin color or phenotype (f. 155v).

In marked contrast to the privileges enjoyed by Spaniards and Creoles of that era, mestizos found themselves at an enormous disadvantage. As the offspring of mixed race unions, and usually illegitimate, American mestizos of the mid-16th century were regularly denied any meaningful social mobility. Their lives were highly circumscribed by a series of strict legal codes. At best they could aspire to become master artisans (silversmiths, cobblers, bricklayers, etc.), but they were prohibited from holding any public office. They were not allowed to carry firearms, administer a *repartimiento de indios* (an allotment of Indian labor), or force Indians to work for them. Studies by Rosenblat (160-190), Konetzke (230-23), López Martínez (15-21) and Hemming (ch. XVII) offer abundant evidence of these limitations. During the first decades after the Conquest, mestizos *were* permitted to enter

the different religious orders. Over time, however, after Church officials and Spanish elites repeatedly accused *mestizo* priests of improper
behavior (generally blamed on their indigenous blood) and excessive
toleration of native idolatries, many religious orders became more
racially-exclusive in membership.

Be that as it may, in the first decades after the Conquest, some
mestizos did manage to become part of the educated colonial elite.
Although not "intellectuals" in the modern sense of the term, these
learned churchmen, lawyers and historians nonetheless fulfilled within
their own societies some of the "organic" functions that Gramsci
ascribed to intellectuals.[2] In particular, two colonial scholars of
Andean birth, Inca Garcilaso de la Vega and Blas Valera, offer clear
examples of the variety and effectiveness of mestizo intellectual strategies during the viceroyalty of Francisco de Toledo (1569-1581), the
era historians generally recognize as the consolidation of Spanish colonial rule in the Andes. During these years, in an effort to justify and
solidify their dominion, the Spanish Crown and viceregal authorities
began to disseminate an official image of the Inca Empire as illegitimate and tyrannical; an image deliberately aimed at squashing any
perceived notions about the benevolence of Incan rule. At the same
time, bureaucratic Crown policies also targeted the entrenched power
of the conquerors, whose heroic image had been seriously tarnished by
the *encomendero* rebellion that wreaked havoc in the Andean countryside from 1540 to 1550. As a direct result of these historiographical
and legislative initiatives, social opportunities for mestizos were even
further blocked or restricted, especially in the case of those relatively
well-positioned children of unions between Spanish conquerors and
Incan princesses (as was the case with Inca Garcilaso). As for the
indigenous population, Spanish officials began forcefully relocating
native communities into *reducciones de indios* in order to facilitate the
operations of the colonial *mit'a*, the forced labor draft for the mines. It
was the colonial *mit'a* which eventually spelled the end of a system of
agrarian production that had managed to feed over six million people

2. Gramsci was obviously referring to the role of the modern intellectual who
functions within, and on behalf of, a particular class configuration. However, I
believe that the role played by certain learned men in the early modern period can
be seen as analogous. See Gramsci and Martínez Lorca.

during the time of the Inca, a population that began to disappear by the tens of thousands in the first decades of Spanish colonial rule.

Because of their relatively privileged status as mestizo colonial scholars, Inca Garcilaso and Blas Valera share parallel, albeit different, life histories. They never actually met in person. Inca Garcilaso left Peru as a young man in 1560, never to return to the New World; Blas Valera, on the other hand, spent most of his adult life in the New World, working as a Jesuit priest in Lima, Cuzco, Potosí and other highland communities before being condemned to prison in 1586. The exact reasons for his imprisonment remain unclear. Refuting previous claims that Valera was jailed for having been discovered in a flagrant act of fornication, Sabyne Hyland suggests that Valera was jailed for staunchly defending Incan religion and criticizing Spanish colonial administration (Ch. 1). In any case, after spending eight years in prison, Valera was sent to Spain, where he apparently died as a result of wounds suffered during the 1596 British sack of Cádiz. Not long thereafter, the Jesuit Pedro Maldonado de Saavedra handed over Valera's "tattered papers" to Inca Garcilaso, who would subsequently cite them at length in his *Royal Commentaries*, published in 1609.

Both Garcilaso and Valera were closely aligned with the Jesuits, a religious order already experiencing tremendous conflicts with the Spanish court in Madrid and the viceregal authorities in Peru. As a result of this shared affiliation, these two mestizo historians became engaged in the scholastic debates over the search for "the common good." This expression and variations of it appear numerous times in the *Royal Commentaries,* both in Garcilaso's own narrative voice and in the lengthy quotations he cites from Valera's writings.

"THE COMMON GOOD" AND A MESTIZO POLITICAL AGENDA[3]

As we all know, the notion of "the common good" permeates political writings from the Renaissance period. From Erasmus' *Institutio Principis Christiani* in 1516 to Pedro de Ribadeneyra's *Príncipe cristiano* nearly eighty years later, the idea of *bonus communis* was

---

3. Much of what follows is partially based on my forthcoming essay in Spanish entitled "Garcilaso y el 'bien común': mestizaje y posición política."

unanimously held to constitute the ultimate end of all political work-
ings, and was eventually wielded explicitly by writers like Ribadeneyra to counter Machiavelli's doctrine of the "Reason of State."

Inca Garcilaso's particular use of the term "common good" was also
steeped in a long scholastic tradition stretching back to at least the
treatises of Saint Thomas Aquinas, who had adapted the Aristotelian
doctrine of *Ética Nicomaquea* and *Politics* to his own understanding
of Christian morality. Aquinas believed that a just order – one that
attended to the basic necessities of the population while pursuing spiritual salvation for all – was the very manifestation of God's kingdom
on earth. This, he argued, was the true end of all politics. As Martínez
Barrera notes in regard to Aquinas' vision, "the ultimate common
good...is God [himself]" (73).

In the Thomist scholastic tradition, the grand social edifice necessarily rests upon the union of humanity with the moral imperative of
the common good. Politics and ethics are indivisible; the primacy
of the individual over the collective was not part of God's divine plan
at creation, nor is it reflected in the daily life of humans: "For Saint
Thomas, to say *human* and to say *moral* is exactly the same thing"
(Martínez Barrera 74).

In the teachings of Saint Thomas, the utopian vision of the common good can only be realized under a government that follows the
teachings of Christ, or those ideas that would later became known as
philosophia Christi.[4] According to this doctrine, only a sovereign who

4. Arocena offers the following definition of *philosophia Christi*: "Humanism
aspired to the revitalization of Christianity, which was struggling at the time under
the weight of strict rituals of crass superstition, an increasingly-secularized Church,
and external signs of a lifeless faith. This aspiration found its articulation in the postulates of '*philosophia Christi*,' a philosophy geared more to concrete, lived experiences than to the subtleties of speculation. In particular, it demanded that one
become conscious of being a Christian and then acting accordingly. The norms of
behavior had to once again emerge from the simple words of the gospels themselves,
stripped of the complex garments with which they had been covered and even dis-
figured by scholastic teachings. In order for the world to be transformed, argued the
Humanists, in order for Christianity to become a happy reality on earth, there was
no need for wise treatises that failed to address either Christ or his apostles; all that
was needed was for preachers in their sermons and teachers in their classrooms to
spread the truths proclaimed in the gospels, with no additions or ornaments, and
for these truths to be the inspiration for the conduct of the prince" (30).

acts in the best interests of his subjects deserves to embody the divine charge. Sovereignty legitimately resides in a royal authority if, and only if, that royalty fulfills the mission of realizing the common good. Otherwise, his reign is nothing more than tyranny, and his subjects have the right to dethrone and even eliminate him, but only if doing so serves the common good and does not bring about a new tyranny.[5]

With the emergence of the Counter Reformation in mid-16th century Spain, the ideals of high scholasticism and neo-Thomism came once again into vogue and had a profound effect upon debates about the justice of Conquest in the New World and the sovereign's duty to improve the lives of his new American subjects. Spanish neo-scholastics repeatedly evoked the Thomist social edifice to argue for the incorporation of the indigenous masses into the great universalizing project of the Counter Reformation. Obviously, their utopian projects were never realized; for despite the efforts of such leading Spanish theologians and political philosophers as Francisco de Vitoria, Melchor Cano, Francisco Suárez and Juan de Mariana, the idea of creating, as Maravall put it, "a new State, a new world and a new man," (51) was unrealistic from the start, both because the Crown had little or no control over the Spanish authorities in the New World and because the Spaniards had no real knowledge of the indigenous population.

In any case, one of the fundamental principles of 16th-century neo-scholasticism was the idea of *pacto subjectionis* introduced by the Jesuit Francisco Suárez. According to this principle, universal happiness could only be achieved through a pact of mutual consent between a king and his vassals. In his *De iuramento fidelitatis*, for example, Suárez, who was one of the most influential political thinkers of his time, insisted that both parties (king and vassals) had to commit to the principle of monarchical sovereignty, but only if there were no transgressions of the pact and only as long as the well-being of the vassals was not threatened by tyrannical actions on the part of the king (see esp. 42-50). Suárez clearly stipulated the right of vassals at any time to rebel against a transgressing power, but only as a last alternative when all attempts at remaking the political arrangement had failed.[6] Súarez was not alone in envisioning a social pact between king and vassals;

---

5. See Aquinas 267-71 and Mariana 1, 110-15.
6. See Ch. 4, "Verdadera doctrina sobre el tiranicidio."

the Jesuit Juan de Mariana would echo many of the same arguments in his *Del Rey y de la institución real.*

THE PRESENCE OF VALERA IN INCA GARCILASO

Upon its arrival in Peru in 1568, the Jesuit order enthusiastically began its work of evangelizing the population and educating Creole, mestizo and indigenous elites. The growing influence of the Jesuits had become evident by the early 1580s when they convened and chaired the 3rd *Concilio Limense* (1582-83). Their cultural predominance meant that the theological doctrines of Suárez, so important in Jesuit teachings, would also come to hold a prominent place in the thinking of Creole and mestizo scholars. This was particularly so after the Jesuits reached an agreement with viceregal authorities in Peru to make attendance at the Jesuit College of San Pablo a prerequisite for further study at the University of Lima or San Marcos (Martin 33).[7]

This Jesuit influence in the latter half of the 16th century is important to acknowledge because of the obvious affinity for this religious order that Inca Garcilaso expresses throughout his writings, notwithstanding the fact that he had left Peru eight years before the Jesuits even arrived. Nonetheless, his own ideas were informed by and coincident with many Jesuit teachings. There is even evidence to suggest that upon his arrival in Spain, Garcilaso immediately fell under the influence of the Company; during his first years in the Andalusian town of Montilla (where he ended up living for more than thirty years), it seems that Garcilaso regularly attended the Jesuit church of Santiago.

More importantly, Garcilaso developed friendships with some of the most notable Jesuits in Spain, especially those in Córdoba. In his various writings, Garcilaso makes references to conversations and correspondence with the likes of Juan de Pineda, Francisco de Castro, Pedro Maldonado de Saavedra, Bernardo de Aldrete and other Jesuit theologians, and his comments reveal relationships of mutual appreciation. One of the Jesuits whose presence is of fundamental importance within the *Royal Commentaries* is Blas Valera. As mentioned previously,

---

7. See also Coello de la Rosa on the presence of Creoles and mestizos in the Jesuit order of Peru in the 16th and 17th centuries.

the two Peruvian mestizos apparently never met; however, Garcilaso claims that Valera's "tattered papers" were given to him in 1597, shortly after the death of this renowned mestizo scholar from the Andean region of Chachapoyas, mortally wounded in the 1596 British sack of Cádiz.[8] It bears mentioning here that, with the discovery of the so-called Naples manuscripts several years ago, scholars began to question the veracity of Garcilaso's account of Valera's death and of his [Garcilaso's] having received Valera's papers in 1597.[9]

These debates aside, what matters for the purposes of this essay is to note that in the sections of the *Royal Commentaries* that Garcilaso dedicates to the nature of Incan political rule (particularly the first sixteen chapters of Book V in Part One), he relies upon lengthy quotations from Blas Valera to provide the descriptive details. Within these cited fragments from the "tattered papers," Valera makes explicit and repeated mention of the idea of "the common good" as it existed under Incan rule. Likewise, in this and many other sections of the text, the voice of the narrator Garcilaso also evokes the fundamental principle of "the common good" as a hallmark of Incan administration.[10]

---

8. In Part One, Book I, Ch. VI of the *Royal Commentaries*, Garcilaso defers to the authority of the mestizo Jesuit for his explanation of the origins of the name "Peru." He writes, "I can refer here to the authority of another distinguished religious man from the blessed Company of Jesus called Father Blas Valera, who wrote the history of that empire [Peru] in the most elegant Latin, but could have written it in many other languages since he was gifted in many. Much to the dismay of my homeland, which was not lucky enough to have the history of its republic penned by that man, his papers were lost in the ruin and siege of Cádiz carried out by the British in the year 1596, and he died shortly thereafter. After the siege, I was able to obtain the remnants of what remained of his papers, but felt the greatest pain and shame for those which were lost, [whose contents] one can only gather from those that were found. The remnants were so tattered that the greatest and most important parts were missing. [The remnants] were given to me by the reverend Father Pedro Maldonado de Saavedra, native of Seville and of the same religious order" (First Part f. 5v).

9. See Laurencich, ed.; Laurencich; and Hyland Chs. 9 and 10.

10. Let us not forget that Garcilaso's views were informed by many other writings, especially those by the so-called "chroniclers" of the pre-Toledan period who praised the benevolence of Incan rule and the admirable aspects of Incan imperial administration. In Ch. 52 of his *Crónica del Perú*, for example, Pedro de Cieza de León writes that "truly, few nations have there been in the world, in my view, that have had a better government than the Incas" (Cieza 161). At other points in his

For his part, Garcilaso utilizes various expressions to refer to the idea of "the common good" as accepted and practiced by the Incas. Even a brief perusal of the *Royal Commentaries* provides ample evidence of Garcilaso's use of terms like "*huaccha cuyac*," or "lover of the poor" to characterize the ideal of "common good" that he posits as the ordaining principle of political administration for the former governors of Cuzco. For example, in Part One, Book I, Chapter XXI entitled "The teachings the Inca [Manco Capac] gave to his vassals," the narrator states that the first Inca, when it came time to designate the *curacas*, or chieftains, who would oversee the communities newly-assimilated into the empire, selected "those who had worked hardest to domesticate the Indians; [those who] showed themselves to be the most congenial, the kindest and most pious, the most friendly to the common good" (f. 20). From the very beginning of the Incan monarchy, then, this imperative infused the design of all governing bodies, from the superior commanders to the lower-level bureaucrats, defining – not just the governing Inca – but the Incan state itself, as the agent of the fulfillment of "the common good."

This imperative was not limited to the Incan authorities; as the following passage from Book II, Chapter XIII of the First Part makes clear, the general population was also assimilated to the ideal:

> For those laws to be adhered to with love and respect, it was also very important that the people understood them to be of divine origin. Because they ignorantly believed that their Kings were sons of the Sun, and that the Sun was their god, they felt that all common orders from the King, and especially those laws he made for the common good, were divine commandments.

Throughout the *Royal Commentaries*, then, Garcilaso emphasizes the importance of "the common good" to various aspects of Incan political life, presenting the Incan Empire, not as just another utopia, but a utopia in the neo-scholastic mold. There are countless illustrations of

---

Crónica, however, Cieza de León condemns the Incas as practitioners of demonology and human sacrifice, but still bitterly criticizes the actions of the conquerors. On both these points, Garcilaso distances himself from Cieza de León and fervently identifies instead with Valera's views.

this imaging in the pages of the *Royal Commentaries*, but in the interest of the public good, I will refrain from enumerating all the passages, many of which are already well known.[11] What is critical to recognize, however, is that the first sixteen chapters of Book V of the First Part offer ample evidence, not only of the influence of Blas Valera in Garcilaso's text, but also of the important relationship between Blas Valera and Francisco Falcón, yet another Jesuit whose writings had apparently served as an important source for Valera. After exploring these linkages, I will turn to the notion of "the common good" as it emerges in

11. A few examples will suffice. Part One, Book II, Ch. XX ("The great province of Chucuitu agrees to peace; many other provinces do the same"): "The Inca was welcomed with great joy and fanfare in Cuzco, where he remained for several years overseeing the government and *common welfare* of his vassals" (emphasis added). Part One, Book III, Ch. XVII ("Of the pacification [by the Inca Cápac Yupanqui] of five large provinces without other events"): "[The Inca] ordered that great aqueducts be constructed to water the fields, he ordered many bridges to be built over the rivers and large streams for safe pedestrian passage, he ordered new roads to be opened between the provinces so that everyone in the Empire could communicate with each other: in sum, he did everything he deemed best for the *common good and benefit* of his vassals and for his own grandeur and majesty" (emphasis added). Part One, Book IV, Ch. X ("Different ways of succession to power") recounts the case of the *curaca* don García during the early years after the Conquest: "The curaca of the community was called don García. When he realized he was close to death, he called together his four sons and the noblemen of his community and told them in the way of a final testament that they must follow the doctrine of Jesus Christ which they had newly received, that they must always give thanks to God for having sent them this doctrine, and that they must serve and respect the Spaniards for having delivered the doctrine." In particular, he told them that they must serve their master [their new curaca] with much love and that he would be very lucky to be their new lord. Lastly he told [the noblemen] that, since according to the customs of our land, as you well know, the most virtuous and magnanimous of my sons is to inherit my position, I entrust you to choose which of them seems the most so, and if none of them seems so, then I order that they be disinherited and that you elect one of yourselves to look after our honor, health, and well-being; for I wish more for the *common good* of all than for the particular fortune of my sons" (emphasis added). Part One, Book VI, Ch. XXIII ("Toast one another, and under what order"): "And let it be noted that the Inca did not invite every curaca to his table (although he did [invite] all the captains) but only those particular ones who were most magnanimous with his vassals and most committed to the common good, for this was the objective they all sought to attain, as much the *curacas* and all the Ministers of War and Peace as the Inca himself" (emphasis added). Examples like these abound in the text.

the Second Part of the *Royal Commentaries* in order to better understand its centrality to Inca Garcilaso's political vision.

As mentioned previously, Valera performed years of evangelizing
work in many different Andean cities, including Cuzco and Potosí,
before the Jesuit order condemned him to prison, for reasons that
remain unclear. Without entering into detail on the legal proceedings
against him, there is evidence to suggest that his radical opinions criticizing Spanish viceregal administration and praising the Incan political system played a central part in the conflicts he experienced with his
religious superiors, and of course, with civil authorities. Blas Valera,
the elusive author of the *Historia Occidentalis,* the text that Garcilaso
relied upon so heavily for his depiction of Incan social well-being, may
well have been the author of yet another fundamental work of Andean
historiography, the *Relación de las costumbres antiguas de los naturales
del Pirú* (*Account of the ancient customs of the native peoples of Peru*) by
the so-called Anonymous Jesuit.[12] Even if the veracity of the *Historia
Occidentalis* is questioned because we only know of its existence via
the word of Garcilaso, there can be little doubt as to the existence
of the *Relación,* even if the Anonymous Jesuit is not Valera. Certainly
there are many similarities between the *Relación* and the *Royal Commentaries* in terms of the descriptions of Incan religiosity. In particular,
the idea that the Incas believed in an invisible supreme deity who del-
egated roles to a group of lesser deities appears in the *Relación,* and was
the most likely source for Garcilaso's description in the *Royal Commentaries* of the secondary chambers in the Incan Temple of the Sun,
or *Coricancha,* in Cuzco. In his text, Garcilaso explains that each of
these rooms was dedicated to a specific divinity like the Moon, the
Rainbow, or Lightning, and that each of these lesser divinities held
a specific place within the Incan pantheon.[13] This is not the only

12. Porras was inclined to identify the Anonymous Jesuit as Blas Valera, in
accordance with the dominant tendency in Peruvian historiography (462). Durand,
however, raised serious doubts about Valera's authorship, suggesting instead that the
anonymous author of the *Relación* was another priest called Luis López.

13. According to the Anonymous Jesuit: "The sun told [the natives] that he was
the son of the great Illa Tecce, and that the physical light that he had was the aspect
of divinity granted to him by Illa Tecce so that he could order and govern the days,
seasons, years and summers, as well as the kings, kingdoms, lords and other things.
To the moon, who was the sister and wife of the sun, Illa Tecce had also given an

argumentative coincidence between Garcilaso's text and the *Relación;* both texts also insist that the Incas did not practice human sacrifice. According to the Anonymous Jesuit, this argument was based upon a lost work entitled *Apología pro Indis* by Francisco Falcón.[14]

THE IMPORTANT AND FORGOTTEN ROLE OF FRANCISCO FALCÓN

In the *Historia Occidentalis* by Blas Valera one finds a most clear and compelling argument about the just policies of Incan administration. However, it would seem that a true appreciation of Valera's text requires us to go back and examine the writings of the Spanish-born scholar Francisco Falcón, who lived in Lima in the mid-16th century and served as a *Procurador de Indios*, or defense attorney in cases involving indigenous individuals or communities. In a little known text from 1567 entitled *Representación de los daños y molestias que se hacen a los indios*, Falcón criticizes key features of viceregal policy towards the indigenous population, especially the system of *corregimientos* and the excessive collection of tribute. Falcón goes on to propose an alternative series of protectionist measures to be enacted over the natives. Throughout his text, the theme of tribute forms the epicenter of a much broader debate about the realization of "the common good." The critique of the tribute system that Falcón lays out in his *Representación* was to become a cornerstone of Valera's argument against viceregal administration in *Historia Occidentalis*; and since Garcilaso subsequently relied so heavily upon Valera, echoes of Falcón's critique are present in the *Royal Commentaries* as well.

In proposing an alternative to the viceregal policies of tribute collection, Falcón suggests that an Incan tributary system be established,

---

aspect of divinity and made her goddess of the sea and the winds, of queens and princesses, of childbirth, and she was made queen of the heavens. They called the moon *Coya*, which means queen. The morning star was made goddess of maidens and princesses, author of the flowers of the field, and mistress of the dawn, the twilight, and clouds; and that she spread dew onto the earth when she shook out the locks of her hair, and for this they called her Chasca" (136). There are evident similarities between this passage and the description of the Incan pantheon found in Book II of the First Part of the *Royal Commentaries*.

14. See Hampe.

one based upon the practices Incan royalty used on their subjects before the conquerors arrived. One of the criteria that Falcón proposes is that there be no forced labor in the mines, but that natives who volunteered to work in the mines be well-compensated. In general, however, Falcón downplays the importance of mining work and is instead a strong proponent of increased agricultural production, extolling the virtues of the Inca Empire for being more interested in the well-being of its subjects than in profits garnered from mining. This particular argument will be echoed repeatedly by both Valera and Garcilaso. Falcón proceeds to denounce the excessive burdens of the Spanish viceregal tribute system, arguing that any careful comparison of the two tributary systems would certainly favor the former governors of Peru. To make the viceregal system more palatable, he strongly suggests that tribute be paid through the performance of only one kind of service; demanding multiple services, he argues, destroys natural liberty.[15]

In another section of his essay, Falcón proposes that the salary of *corregidores* be paid directly from Crown coffers rather than from tribute revenues, since *corregidores* serve the interest of the Crown much more than they do the interests of Indians. Other arguments in Falcón's *Representación* cut to the very heart of debates on the legitimacy of Spanish rule over the Indies, raising the question of the "right of conquest" and whether or not the war against the Indians was just. At one point he argues that Pope Alexander VI had granted the King of Spain the concession over the New World in 1494 in order to facilitate the evangelization of its peoples through the image of an Emperor among kings, not to promote the image of a king who simply replaces the native governors.[16]

15. Falcón writes that: "you cannot burden the Indians with more tribute than they were burdened with by their lords during the time of the infidels" (144). Furthermore, that "in the days of the Incas, no Indian was compelled to hand over any part of his wealth to the Inca or to any other lord; he was only obligated to work the lands that were specified by [the Inca], to take care of his livestock and to serve him, his judges and his *curacas*, each one with the kind of work he knew best, whether it be making clothes, constructing buildings, mining different metals, making plates and cups of gold, or things of wood or earthenware, or by sharing some of the fruits of his harvest and livestock" (144).

16. In effect, after questioning the very political title of the Spanish king based on what he considers to be an unjust war, Falcón offers his thoughts on the papal

Given the breadth of his critique, one would have to include Falcón's *Representación* in the "pro-indigenous spirit" that Lohmann Villena (23) has argued characterized the 1560s. However, there is one very significant difference between Falcón's writings and the ideas of Las Casas, also writing in the 1560s. Paradoxically, Falcón, the *Procurador de Indios* whose job it was to defend Indians, is an explicit and passionate defender of the *encomienda* as a protective institution for indigenous peoples; that is, a defender of the *encomienda* as a system regulated by Christian principles and dedicated to the task of evangelization. He even suggests that *encomenderos* should not live in the vicinity of their Indians so as not to interfere with the daily lives of the *encomendados*, except to make sure to station priests among their Indians at all times.[17]

Garcilaso only explicitly mentions Falcón once in the *Royal Commentaries*. In Book I, Chapter XXIII of the Second Part he refers to him as "the Aragonese Falconio" and attributes to him the authorship of a lost work entitled *De libertate indorum servanda*. Garcilaso claims, via Valera once again, that this lost text contained the famous Cajamarca dialogue that he [Garcilaso] had previously presented. Despite this brief mention by Garcilaso, it is clear that Falcón's characterization of the many virtues of Incan administration, a characterization that is echoed in Blas Valera, has much in common with what we find in other sources on the Incas. In fact, the image seems to coincide pretty well with the historical portrait of Incan tribute poli-

concession: "as to the second title, conceded to the Castilian monarchs by Pope Alexander VI, it is well-known that by that concession, [the Pope] was not granting them dominion over the kingdoms and the properties of the natives of these lands. And even though the concessions state that [the Spaniards] are lords over all these lands and their jurisdictions, it is understood that this was for the purposes of evangelization and that the sovereignty of these kingdoms still belongs to the natural lords as part of an empire. Therefore, [the concession] did not deprive the natural lords or their legitimate successors of their sovereignty or their wealth or the wealth of all the rest [of the people]. These things could not be taken from them, nor should one believe that this was the intention of the Pope" (136-37).

17. "…one can infer how carefully and what a Christian spirit the titles over the Indians were granted, calling them *encomiendas*, which is the same as saying safekeeping, so that those that have [*encomiendas*] understand that they were created more for the benefit of the *encomendados* than for the *encomenderos*" (138).

cies outlined by Franklin Pease in his celebrated article "Garcilaso andino" (see Works Cited).

CONCLUSIONS

Having completed this brief overview of the positions taken by Garcilaso and Valera on such issues as tribute, *encomienda* and the common good, some preliminary conclusions are in order.

In the first place, mestizo scholars who engaged in the debates about viceregal policies towards the Indians argued from an "organic" position based upon their ethnic origins. Inca Garcilaso and Blas Valera represented a sector of the New World *intelligentsia* that tried to rearticulate social relations with the dominant Spanish and Creole elites, proclaiming themselves unique spokesmen for the project of defending the indigenous population. At the same time, in defending the *encomienda* system, seemingly retrograde and feudalistic, they were positioning themselves against administrative centralism and the growing consolidation of colonial bureaucracy under the Viceroy Toledo.

No doubt their wielding of a type of "strategic essentialism" *avant-la-lettre* enabled these two mestizo scholars to authorize themselves as true intermediaries between the Indians and the Spaniards. This mediating position was predicated upon their knowledge of indigenous languages and the oral traditions of the oppressed peoples; in other words, upon their alternative epistemological knowledge. At the same time, however, Garcilaso, Valera and others (including someone like Guaman Poma who was of indigenous origin but culturally mestizo) appropriated the art of writing to defend their respective agendas. In doing so, they inaugurated one of the most interesting chapters in the construction of the Latin American *lettered city*. By this I mean the subversion of the ultimate purposes of the domination of writing over native oralities and cosmovisions, the opening up of fissures between the walls of the *lettered city* and the immense "oral village" that surrounds it.[18]

18. In his analysis of a particular sector of 20th-century Latin American narrative, Carlos Pacheco coined the phrase "oral village" to complement Ángel Rama's notion of the lettered city.

Looking ahead to the 20th century, the intellectual positioning of modern intellectuals is often radically different from that of scholars like Garcilaso, Valera, and Guaman Poma. In speaking of the role of the modern intellectual, Mariátegui writes in 1925 that:

> Intellectuals, in general, tend to be averse to any discipline, program or system. Their psychology centers on the individual and their way of thinking is heterodox. Most importantly, their sense of individuality is exuberant and boundless. The individuality of intellectuals almost always makes them feel superior to common rules. Because of this, intellectuals most often have a sense of disdain for politics; to them, politics is a game for bureaucrats and charlatans (154).

I should clarify that Mariátegui was referring here to Creole intellectuals of his day. At other moments and in other texts, however, his support of *indigenismo* and his defense of other mestizo intellectuals makes it clear that he held a broader, more varied, opinion of intellectuals than the stern critique in the above quotation indicates. In any case, much has changed since 1925, and even if Mariátegui's description still rings true for some of today's evasive intellectuals and academics, the examples of Garcilaso and Valera offer a very different model, one centered on the mediating, organic and strategic function of the mestizo intellectual.

In recent years, we have seen the emergence of strong indigenous movements in Latin America and the development of indigenous intellectual elites who have entered the academic and professional fields in unprecedented numbers. Indigenous groups in Bolivia have established several important cultural and research centers including the PROEIB, dedicated to training indigenous professionals, Silvia Rivera Cusicanqui's Workshop on oral traditions, and the *Fundación Tierra*. These initiatives reflect the opening up of cultural and educational spaces unimaginable in the 16th century, when the mestizos and indigenous populations were largely self-taught and attendance at a university was a far greater privilege than it is today. Despite the centuries-long processes of cultural secularization that separate the mestizo scholars of the 16th century from indigenous intellectuals of the 21st century, important points of continuity remain: the demand for the material improvement of living conditions for indigenous peoples, the revalorization of man's relationship with nature, and the preoccupation with the survival of native cultural traditions and epistemological concepts.

Hopefully, this essay will serve as a reminder of the importance of examining the colonial antecedents of contemporary discourse on indigenous intellectuals and movements. When viewed only from an external perspective or solely in reference to contemporary theoretical frameworks like multiculturalism and postmodernity, the emergence of indigenous intellectuals in Latin America today and their discourses of indigenous vindication cannot be fully appreciated.

WORKS CITED

AQUINAS, Saint Thomas. *Saint Thomas Aquinas on Law, Morality, and Politics.* Ed. William P. Baumgarth and Richard Regan S. J. Indianapolis: Hackett, 1988.

AROCENA, Luis. *El Inca Garcilaso y el humanismo renacentista.* Buenos Aires: Bartolomé U. Chiesino, 1949.

CIEZA DE LEÓN, Pedro de. *Crónica del Perú. Primera Parte.* 1553. Lima: Peisa, 1984.

COELLO DE LA ROSA, Alexandre. "De mestizos y criollos en la Companía de Jesús (siglos XVI-XVII)." *Revista de Indias* LXVIII 243 (2008): 37-66.

COVARRUBIAS HOROZCO, Sebastian de. *Tesoro de la lengva castellana, o española.* Madrid: L. Sánchez Impressor del rey n.s. 1611.

DURAND, José. "Blas Valera y el Jesuita Anónimo." *Estudios Americanos* 109-11 (1961): 73-94.

FALCÓN, Francisco. "Representación hecha por el Licenciado Falcón en Concilio Provincial, sobre los daños y moléstias que se hacen a los índios." *Informaciones acerca de la religión y gobierno de los incas.* 1567. Ed. Horacio Urteaga y Carlos A. Romero. Lima: Imprenta y Librería Sanmarti y Cía., 1918. 133-176.

GARCILASO DE LA VEGA, Inca. *Primera Parte de los Commentarios Reales, qve tratan del origen de los Yncas, Reyes que fveron del Perv, de su idolatria, leyes, y gouierno en paz y en guerra: de ſus vidas y conquiſtas, y de todo lo que fue aquel Imperio y ſu Republica, antes que los Eſpañoles paſſaran a el.* Lisboa: Imprenta de Pedro Crasbeeck, 1609.

—. *Historia General del Perú. Segunda Parte de los Commentarios Reales.* Córdoba: Por la Viuda de Andrés Barrera, 1617.

46 JOSÉ ANTONIO MAZZOTTI

46JOSÉ ANTONIO MAZZOTTI

GRAMSCI, Antonio. *Gli intellettuali e l'organizzazione della cultura*. Roma: Editori Riuniti, 1971.

HAMPE MARTÍNEZ, Teodoro. "Una polémica versión de la conquista del Perú: ¿es auténtica la *Relación* de Francisco de Chaves (1533)? In *Guaman Poma y Blas Valera: tradición andina e historia cultural*. Ed. by Francesca Cantú. Rome: Antonio Pellicani Editore, 2001. 343-364.

HEMMING, John. *La conquista de los incas*. 1970. México: FCE, 1982.

HYLAND, Sabine. *The Jesuit and the Incas. The Extraordinary Life of Father Blas Valera, S. J.* Ann Arbor: U of Michigan P, 2003.

JESUITA ANÓNIMO (attributed to Blas Valera). *Relación de las costumbres antiguas de los naturales del Pirú. Tres relaciones de antigüedades peruanas*. 1880. Asunción: Guaranía, 1950. 133-203.

KONETZKE, Richard. "El mestizaje y su importancia en el desarrollo de la población hispanoamericana durante la época colonial. (Conclusión)." *Revista de Indias* VII 24 (1946): 215-237.

LAURENCICH-MINELLI, Laura. "Los documentos Miccinelli (Siglo XVII): Dos curiosos testigos sobre una utópica reducción 'Inca'/Jesuita en la provincia peruviana. *Sublevando el Virreinato. Documentos contestarios a la historiografía tradicional del Perú Colonial*. Ed. Laura Laurencich Minelli and Paulina Numhauser. Quito: Ediciones Abya-Yala, 2007. 301-338.

LAURENCICH-MINELLI, Laura, ed. *Exsul Immeritus Blas Valera Populo Suo et Historia et Rudimenta Linguae Peruanorum*. Bologna: CLUEB, 2007.

LOHMANN VILLENA, Guillermo. "El Licenciado Francisco Falcón (1521-1587): vida, escritos y actuación de un Procurador de los Indios". *Anuario de Estudios Americanos* 27 (1970): 131-194.

LÓPEZ MARTÍNEZ, Héctor. *Rebeliones de mestizos y otros temas quinientistas*. Lima: Imprenta Gráfica Villanueva, 1971.

MARAVALL, José Antonio. *Carlos V y el pensamiento político del Renacimiento*. Madrid: Instituto de Estudios Políticos, 1960.

MARIANA, Juan de. *Del rey y de la Institución de la Dignidad Real*. 1599. 2 vols. Madrid: Imprenta de la Sociedad Literaria y Tipográfica. 1845.

MARIÁTEGUI, José Carlos. *La escena contemporánea*. Lima: Amauta, 1925.

MARTIN, Luis. *The Intellectual Conquest of Peru. The Jesuit College of San Pablo, 1568-1767*. New York: Fordham UP, 1968.

MARTÍNEZ BARRERA, Jorge. "El bien común político según Santo Tomás de Aquino." *Thémata Revista de filosofía* 11 (1993): 71-99.

MARTÍNEZ LORCA, Andrés. *El problema de los intelectuales y el concepto de cultura en Gramsci*. Prólogo de José Luis Aranguren. Málaga: Universi-dad de Málaga, 1981.

MAZZOTTI, José Antonio. *Actas del congreso internacional El Inca Garcilaso entre varios mundos*. Ed. Gerhard Penzkofer and José Morales Saravia. Würzburg University, September 2008. Forthcoming.

PACHECO, Carlos. *La comarca oral: la ficcionalización de la oralidad cultural en la narrativa latinoamericana contemporánea*. Caracas: La Casa de Bello, 1992.

PEASE, G.Y., Franklin. "Garcilaso Andino." *Revista Histórica* XXXIV (1984): 41-52.

PORRAS BARRENECHEA, Raúl. *Los cronistas del Perú (1528-1650) y otros ensayos*. Prologue by Franklin Pease G. Y. Lima: Banco del Crédito del Peru, 1986.

RAMA, Ángel. *La ciudad letrada*. Hanover: Ediciones del Norte, 1984.

RIBADENEYRA, Pedro de. *Tratado de la religión y virtudes que debe tener el príncipe cristiano para governar y conservar sus Estados. Contra lo que Nicolás Machiavelo y los políticos de este tiempo enseñan*. Amberes: Empresa Plantiniana, 1597.

ROSENBLAT, Ángel. *La población indígena y el mestizaje en América*. 2 vols. Buenos Aires: Nova, 1945.

SUÁREZ, Francisco. *De Iuramento Fidelitatis Regis Angliae*. Madrid: Consejo Superior de Investigaciones Científicas, 1978.

BLACK, FAMOUS, AND OUT OF PLACE: AN ALTERNATIVE INTELLECTUAL IN EARLY NINETEENTH-CENTURY MONTEVIDEO

William G. Acree, Jr.

In stark contrast to the second half of the nineteenth century when people from the old colonial castes made their mark in the world of writing, being an intellectual in Latin America prior to 1850 meant almost always being white.[1] And since intellectual life came with its share of public prestige and was so often interwoven with affairs of the state, those who had traces of mixed blood opted more often than not to pass for white when possible. This was certainly the case in the Banda Oriental – today's Uruguay – and the larger region of the Río de la Plata. In 1830, when Uruguay's first constitution took effect and when the region's budding written culture was gaining legitimacy, roughly thirty percent of the population in both Montevideo and Buenos Aires consisted of people of African descent (Andrews, *Afro-Argentines* 4-6; *Afro-Latin America* 41; Goldberg). The indigenous inhabitants in Uruguay would soon be all but eliminated, while in Argentina immigration in later years successfully "whitened" Buenos Aires and neighboring provinces. But on both sides of the Plata River from the wars of independence through the end of a long period of civil war in 1852,

---

1. Of course a handful of indigenous intellectuals, women, and Afro-descendants such as Felipe Guaman Poma de Ayala (Adorno) and Ursula de Jesús (van Deusen) stood out in colonial America, but such figures are exceptional.

Afro-descendants played key roles as soldiers, *pregoneros* (town criers), artisans, clothes-washers, musicians, poets, and even intellectuals.

Jacinto Ventura de Molina was one of these. He was black and proud of it, became famous in 1820s and 1830s Montevideo, and, as an intellectual of African descent, was certainly out of place. Though biographical studies of his life have recently been published (Acree; Acree and Borucki; Gortázar), a few essential details of his life story are in order here. He was born to Juana del Sacramento and Ventura de Molina in 1766 along the frontier separating the Spanish and Portuguese empires in America, what is today the border between Uruguay and Brazil. His mother had been an African slave in Brazil before escaping to territory occupied by the Spanish in the Banda Oriental, while his father, as Jacinto later wrote, had been born somewhere along the Middle Passage from Africa's Gold Coast most likely to Montevideo. In 1762 his father had saved the life of his master, the Spanish brigadier José Eusebio de Molina, who was a military commander in the struggle to settle Colonia del Sacramento. As a reward, Ventura was offered his freedom, and when he decided to stay on with his master, the Spaniard promised to serve as the caretaker for Jacinto, who was born free. This care included most importantly for Jacinto private tutors, nightly reading practice, and enrollment in a convent school in Montevideo, which he attended with some of the city's future leading white men of letters.

Over the seventy-five years he lived, Jacinto became a transformational alternative intellectual in early nineteenth-century Montevideo. He exercised this transformational character through writing and oratory, which we will explore below. But first, a few theoretical caveats are important to address. Jacinto wrote some poetry based on religious topics and praising royal figures, like the wife of Brazil's first emperor, and there is evidence that he liked to draw, though he was not very good at it. What allows for qualifying him as an intellectual *per se*, however, was his constant engagement in the public sphere through writing and as a lawyer, his involvement with issues that concerned black "nations" in Montevideo,[2] laws, public moral codes, and his

2. For a concise description of forms of community organization, including black "nations," among Afro-descendants in Argentina (as well as Uruguay), see ch. 8 in Andrews, *Afro-Argentines.*

petitions to and quarrels with royal officials, religious authorities, and members of the Uruguayan state. In other words, his public employment as a man of letters who manipulated codes of the lettered city made him an intellectual, though his white peers were not comfortable recognizing him as such.

Secondly, Molina's case requires thinking about the concepts of intellectual and political frontiers in new ways. Categories of dominant and subaltern, lettered and unlettered, architect of power through writing or author of resistance, while useful in some circumstances, do not adequately fit his position in Uruguayan society or speak to the complex shifts in power that resulted from the movement for independence, a decade of Luso-Brazilian occupation of the Banda Oriental, and then independence with Argentine and British intervention.[3] He was certainly excluded at times from fields of power, though not always. In fact, he took great pride in his relationship with Carlos Federico Lecor (leader of the occupying forces of the Banda Oriental) and the protection he received from Emperor Pedro I, and at the end of his life the Uruguayan state recognized him as a *Licenciado* and *Defensor de pobres* (Defender of the Poor).[4] Approaching some of these complexities can help us understand just what it meant to be black, famous, and out of place.

RACE AND WRITING

In a September 1823 issue of the Montevidean newspaper *Los amigos del pueblo,* the editors praised one of "el negro Molina's" recent compositions, remarked that he was "well-known in the republic of negro letters," and informed readers that copies of the text and its "curiosities" would be for sale at the Librería Yáñez, one of the city's few bookstores.[5] This positive assessment is the first mention of

3. Mabel Moraña questions such binary categories around the period of independence, specifically as they relate to Simón Bolívar, and concludes that "they do not represent by any means separate ideological or autonomous spaces" (32).

4. *Licenciado* or doctor was the title used by those who had earned a degree in law.

5. My thanks to Wilson González Demuro for sharing this issue of the newspaper with me. All translations of Spanish to English in this article are my own.

Molina I have come across in this sort of public forum. Some sixty years later the prolific Uruguayan chronicler Isidoro de María included a chapter on Jacinto in his *Montevideo antiguo*, which appears to be the last comment on Molina by someone who knew him. De María mixed praise with ridicule. He relates that he had read some of Molina's many "aimless writings" and that the poor Molina's clothes often had holes or patches. But "if he was lacking in color [whiteness]," concludes de María, "his courteous manners and honorable behavior were like those of any white man" (240-42).

These two remarks loosely frame the range of opinions of contemporaries regarding this alternative intellectual. Of course, there were others who did not interpret positively by any means the idea of a black man mingling in the world of writing or Molina acting as a lawyer for black nations. In fact, fear of blacks gaining too much influence or banding together to carry out repeat episodes of the Haitian revolution was widespread among white Creoles all across Latin America. Moreover, though not voiced explicitly, this fear may have been one reason for shunning Molina's writings and poking fun at his petitions, though Molina himself did not threaten to use race as a mobilizing force.[6] A handful of views illustrate the uneasiness (or downright alarm) others felt toward Molina.

In 1832, the then celebrated and now canonical Argentine man of letters, Florencio Varela, had signed with Uruguayan officials documents recognizing Molina as a *Licenciado*, but the following year opposed allowing a naturalist by the name of Carlos Orviñeta to take samples of Molina's writing to display in Italy. Perhaps Varela, like a certain J. Oyuela who relates this incident to General Manuel Oribe, was afraid of the possibility of the "impertinent writings of an old Ethiopian" representing Uruguayan intellectuals abroad (Acree and Borucki 200-01).[7] In April 1834, two officials mocked one of Molina's requests on behalf of the black nation *Congos de Gunga*, calling

6. On the fear the Haitian revolution instilled across America, see Geggus; on the interesting case of how the *pardo* (or mulatto) José Padilla invoked race, see Helg.

7. Roughly sixty percent of Molina's extant writings as well as correspondence with contemporaries and their remarks about him and his role as an author can be found in Acree and Borucki, hence the references to the texts in this edition. A second, revised edition of these writings is forthcoming with Iberoamericana / Vervuert.

him "unlettered" (*iletrado*) for having written the request on unofficial paper (without the proper stamps) and inventing words to make fun of his ornate style of exposition (Acree and Borucki 126-27). One anonymous author scribbled on a printed loose leaf of Molina's poetry: "Verses of *tío* Jacinto... a black who said he was a doctor of law, and all of us older gentlemen led him to believe this was in fact true" (Molina, *Loose-leaf*). A last example of some of the harsh criticism he received appears in a poem penned by another anonymous author. "Let it go, filthy and crazy black / ... / work in your calling of shoemaker / ... / stop writing your brash compositions / that serve no purpose other than for a good laugh" (Acree and Borucki 203). As is evident from these opinions of contemporaries, race and writing were no easy mix.

Molina himself understood his blackness to be inseparable from his calling as a writer. He was aware that his early education was unique for an Afro-descendant, and this led in part to the religious sense of obligation to learning and educating others of African ancestry (Acree, "Jacinto"). He was a proud student, too, recalling in his autobiographical writings that "no child in schools in Rio Grande, Santa Teresa, Montevideo or Buenos Aires was ahead of me in the subjects of doctrine, math, reading, or knowledge of proper punctuation (periods, commas, semicolons, question marks, exclamation marks)" (Acree and Borucki 62). During his adolescence, he remembers as well the lawyer Antonio Escarranea who heard of Molina's talent for copying documents. Once he verified that Jacinto was black, Escarranea decided to provide him with "drafts of all the methods for writing memorials and political expositions... [and] a summary of laws and books where I could study these" (Acree, "Jacinto"). José de Molina's defense of the young Jacinto learning to read, which scandalized more than one of the Spaniard's friends, also left lasting impressions on the young boy. On one occasion the minister of naval forces was visiting José de Molina's house and saw Jacinto writing. The minister proceeded to ask the Spaniard if he was 'crazy,' especially since issues of slavery and education were being debated in Cádiz. José de Molina gave his friend a cold look and did not say a word, which led the minister to conclude that the Spaniard "was in a bad mood" and that it would be better to see him another day (Acree and Borucki 67-68).

It is no surprise, then, that Jacinto began writing on behalf of others, notably Afro-descendants, at a young age. As early as 1804 he worked as a ghostwriter of sorts. One known example is a petition he wrote on behalf of the free black Juan Colorado who was engaged in a land dispute with a neighbor (Molina, *Petición*). Given Molina's involvement in black militias around this period it is likely that he wrote for other blacks in Buenos Aires and Montevideo, though similar documents have not yet been discovered. In the 1820s and 1830s he composed many legal documents as a scribe and lawyer. One of these was the 1823 last will and testament of María Castro, member of the black *Cofradía de San Benito de Palermo*. Another was a court case where he defended "*la morena*" and widow Teresa Mojica against unfair claims to her inheritance made by a stepson. In the same year of 1834 Molina represented the free black woman María Guardado, who had been accused of robbery (Acree and Borucki 214, 222-33).

As he became more active publicly in the 1820s and 1830s, Molina's pride in writing and speaking for black communities increased. On March 2, 1833, he delivered what was the "keynote" speech for the election of a new princess of the Urid Uryola nation in Montevideo. His "rare discourse," as he called it, began with an unidentified yet telling quote of how he envisioned the role of his speech: "He consoled them with his first words and was sensitive to their needs with his speech." Ironically the aforementioned María Guardado (accused of robbery) was being elected as princess, and Molina defended her in the speech as "*la morena* of greatest political merit... the most pious woman, the most charitable toward your companions." Later in the speech he drew attention to his role as a black intellectual: "Listen well to a speech by a man of your color... I speak among you, black men and women, as white *letrados* do among their kind.... Be attentive, for I aim to educate and entertain you." He went on to note that his writings have suffered a sort of criticism not experienced by "any other *letrado*," and gave a summary history of Afro-descendants in the Bible as a display of his erudition (Acree and Borucki 119-22).

Molina was even more involved in the affairs of the *Congos de Gunga* nation throughout the decade of 1830. From 1832 to 1834 he wrote a string of petitions to Uruguayan officials requesting permission for the members to have their "*sala de nación,*" or house where they could congregate, and to hold *candombes* on weekends and on

January 6, when San Baltasar was honored. The *candombes* were dance parties where tight collective bonds formed, and where members of the *Congos de Gunga* as well as other nations were able to tap into their African roots (Andrews, "Remembering Africa"). Special meaning was derived from these gatherings during the celebration of San Baltasar, the Afro-descendant king among the Magi. That Molina led the effort to convince the state to allow the *Congos de Gunga* to continue with their *candombes* is one clear sign of how he had become a spokesperson for blacks in the city, a voice of collective conscience. One example will prove the point. In the printed petition that he composed to members of the legislature on behalf of the hierarchy of the Congos de Gunga, he opens with three adjectives meant to grant legitimacy to the request: "Jacinto de Molina, free black, *Americano*, and *Licenciado en Derechos.*" The text weaves the collective voice of *Congo de Gunga* officials with that of Molina the black intellectual to argue that the *candombes* are peaceful public gatherings in "known houses" and with religious and charitable objectives. The gatherings help teach proper behavior and religious piety. Moreover, the colonial state allowed them, so it is only fitting for a new, liberal republican government to grant the same permission to the Congos de Gunga. Molina's sole voice ends the petition with a reference to the possibility of "fomenting education among the sad black folk" and reminding his readers of his titles or, put differently, his official status as intellectual: "As is evident from my exposition here, it is not in vain that I possess among my titles that of *Escritor de Cámara*" (Acree and Borucki 139-42).

However, Jacinto's popularity among black communities was undoubtedly a double-edged sword. In 1832, Uruguayan authorities named him *Defensor de negros* (Defender of the Blacks) "considering the scarcity of men of letters currently found in the Republic, and considering that citizens of color will benefit enormously from an eloquent and philanthropic advocate of their rights" (Acree and Borucki 204-207). What this meant in reality was that the state was validating a position he had held in various contexts since at least the early 1800s: that of mediator between people of African descent and people in positions of power, first as a literate black soldier in the king's army, and later under the rule of Luso-Brazilian occupying forces in the 1820s. Yet the more support he garnered from fellow Afro-descendants, and the more his fame as a mediator spread, the more criticism of him and his work grew in quantity and severity. Put differently, he became more and more out of place. Ironically, though, this public profile also contributed to making Molina a transformational figure.

MOLINA AS A TRANSFORMATIONAL FIGURE

Like many polemical, alternative intellectuals, Jacinto de Molina's writing and public persona had consequences that at the time he neither understood nor intended, though most likely would have welcomed. His endless stream of letters to royal officials, the Uruguayan state and its representatives, and high-ranking members of the Church, forced them all to take notice of him and his ability to manipulate codes of writing. And by taking notice of this alternative intellectual, members of the lettered city had to consider individuals, groups, and particular grievances mentioned in Molina's texts. Simply put, Jacinto was a transformational figure not only for other Afro-descendants in the region, but also for reconceptualizing – if not reconfiguring – intellectual and political frontiers.

First, we have seen examples of how some of his contemporary intellectuals reacted to his engagement in the sphere of letters. At the least, these variations in reception point to Molina "shaking up" the field of intellectual exchange. Some white intellectuals did not know how to respond to Molina's barrage of writing. The Basque artist Juan Manuel Besnes e Irigoyen, who drew the only known portrait of Jacinto, wrote a caption below the image that embodies the mixed feelings stirred by Molina. After labeling this alternative intellectual as "an indefatigable and original writer on all subjects," Besnes concludes the biographical note stating that the "new literary genre with Molina's name will make him at least as famous as Dulcinea del Toboso" (Acree and Borucki 209-10). This was not the nicest of compliments, but the fact that this artist completed a serious portrait of Molina out of all Afro-descendants in the city speaks to his presence in intellectual circles. On the other hand, a handful of prominent white intellectuals and statesmen helped protect Molina and promote his causes, and thus participated in reconceptualizing intellectual frontiers. One of these was the priest and first director of Montevideo's public library, Dámaso Larrañaga. Jacinto recounts Larrañaga dictating to him

responses to criticism, which the priest with failing eyesight would later sign. Another was the lawyer and politician Joaquín Sagra y Périz,
who was in part responsible for hiring him as sacristan in the Hospital
de Caridad, and who helped preserve some of the thousands of pages
of Molina's manuscripts and letters.

Molina himself took his role among intellectuals very seriously. He
defended this role to Carlos Federico Lecor and the Brazilian emperor
in 1828: "At no previous moment has there been a black man whose
name was supported by your Excellency with more enthusiasm than
mine in this country. But it is also true that no other black man in this
country has experienced the acrimonious disdain I have for the sole
reason of my distinguished birth and surname" (Acree and Borucki
189-90). By "birth" Jacinto here refers to having been born free to
black parents. This pride in his blackness and humility shows clearly
in an 1833 letter to Pope Gregory 16: "My blackness, my indigent
condition, have earned me the singular grace of ending my days hap-
pily in the clergy. I am an example for those of my color in the areas of
education, comportment, study, and reflection" (Acree and Borucki
162). The key point here is the idea of Molina as a unique figure who
could set an example for other Afro-descendants and transform, even
in minor ways, their relationships with the state and mainstream white
intellectuals.

In the second place, it is hard to imagine that in light of all Molina
wrote against the slave trade and the institution of slavery, his words
and presence did not weigh heavily on the minds of those involved in
the final negotiations leading to abolition in Uruguay in the early
1840s (Borucki, *Abolicionismo*; Borucki et al.). At present there is no
direct evidence of the impact he had on bringing an end to slavery, but
the logic of his arguments is worth highlighting, as is the fact that he
directed these to the same reading public of the majority of his writings - Church and State leaders (including the Pope), military officials,
and white intellectuals. Jacinto wrote of slavery being contrary to
nature and humanity, and he supported his claims with references
to religious authorities, Montesquieu, and other philosophers, despite
considering most philosophers sophists. His greatest moral defense
against slavery, though, came from his devout Catholicism and his
vision of slavery as a violation of all things predicated by the Church:
"Can the Church say with conviction during the baptism of black

children that 'he is a slave who belongs to Don Fulano?' And if it is possible here in Uruguay, then why not in Rome, Paris, Madrid, Naples, or Lisbon, too?" (Acree and Borucki 238). In other writings Jacinto argued that it was no more right to enslave blacks than whites, and since these are not made slaves, then blacks should neither be bought nor sold. It was this very notion of human property that outraged Molina: "Oh how many unhappy souls have suffered the perversity and gross arrogance of those men who have no other claim to ownership of slaves than the fear of losing this property?" For him slavery went hand in hand with the unwillingness to provide for the education of Afro-descendants: "Not teaching blacks to read or write is so terrible and contrary to religion. From this principle stems the idea of blacks – even those born in the Republic – not being men in the eyes of the Republic, religion, or the Church" (Acree and Borucki 238-40). Sadly, Molina, who was a staunch royalist throughout his life, was the most outspoken proponent of the republican principle of educating Uruguay's Afro-descendants.

This is where his dreams for founding a school and monastery for blacks come into play. His proposals for the creation of these institutions circulated among state officials and are some of the most direct evidence of Molina interpellating the state regarding the wellbeing of people of African descent in Uruguay. In petition after petition to the kings of Spain and Portugal, the Pope, the emperor of Brazil and his wife, and Uruguayan authorities, Jacinto detailed his idea of building the *Colegio María Rufina Campana*, named after his first wife who died illiterate, but who loved hearing Jacinto read to her, and a monastery where blacks would be trained under his direction as the lead priest. The establishment would be built on the outskirts of the growing Montevideo by the very students who would populate it, thus reducing costs, and it would occupy six full blocks. "This idea," wrote Jacinto, "is the singular work of the intellect of a black man, and I do not know of any other who has proposed a similar one in the universe." He went further in the letter he wrote to the Pope asking for support for the idea: "María Rufina Campana, the name of the school, or university of arts and sciences, the first for blacks in all the world. Oh admiration of the entire universe!" (Acree and Borucki 146-64; Molina, *Letter*). These dreams of Molina did not become reality, but his campaign on their behalf did force others to consider the plans, however outlandish they may have seemed. In fact, some of his detractors in the 1830s were quicker to label Molina 'crazy' following his proposal for the Colegio María Rufina Campana.

A last arena where Molina was a transformational figure is among other Afro-descendants. Just how influential Molina was for others "of his color," as he hoped to be, is open to further research. But like his presence in the minds of leaders debating abolition, it is safe to assume that his role as a writer and lawyer, as an outspoken and out-of-place intellectual, did serve as an example for other Afro-descendants. As a young boy Jacinto knew how to read from age five and he writes of being told to help another young black by the name of Joaquín learn to read (Acree and Borucki 75). We have seen how different black nations in Montevideo entrusted him with their representation to the state, so it is easy to imagine how such a figure could have been a source of pride for many - one of 'them' who could navigate the legal system and had 'their' interests at heart. As one of few publicly known Afro-descendants who could write during the first third of the century, Jacinto would have been esteemed by members of these nations as a man of letters, which equated to a man of certain importance. Moreover, his status as an intellectual lent legitimacy to his voice as a representative of the 'negro-literary republic' and black communities in the city. We also know that Jacinto frequently attended the theater, in particular the one run by the *Hermandad de la Caridad* where several black actors performed (Borucki, "Tensiones raciales"). What is less clear is the type of interactions Jacinto had with these actors or how he was seen, for example, by his fellow soldiers when he served in black militias. These are both areas where more research can shed light on the dynamic roles Afro-descendants played in intellectual life in early nineteenth-century Latin America. Again, such roles may not fit easily with our traditional understanding of common intellectual behavior, but there is no doubt that blacks enriched the field of intellectual exchange in numerous ways.

Molina did just this from the early 1800s up to the last years before his death in 1841. From his criticism of slavery to his advocacy on behalf of black nations and poor residents of the city – both black and white – he was a transformational figure whose intellectual activity, often verbose compositions, and peculiar personality elicited at times strong reactions and vehement critiques. By 1835 he was a well-known person in lettered circles as well as in black communities. After this year his voice seems to disappear, perhaps because he suffered from illness or no longer was physically capable of writing. Whatever the explanation may be, the trajectory of his life can help us draw conclusions about alternative intellectuals in the broader context of early nineteenth-century Latin America.

CONCLUSIONS

As is the case with many alternative intellectuals prior to the twentieth century, Molina's legacy was buried for close to a hundred years in archives. Isidoro de María had access to some of the manuscripts in the late 1800s, and the female writers for the paper *La cotorrita: órgano especial del sexo bello* (The Little Parrot: Mouthpiece of the Fairer Sex) make reference to Molina as a chronicler of the festivities in honor of San Baltasar in their issue for January 6, 1877. But his work seems to have gone largely unnoticed until Ildefonso Pereda Valdés published in 1941 a copy of the printed document requesting the *sala de nación* for the Congos de Gunga. The majority of Molina's manuscripts were not 'recovered' until the 1990s, when they were sold to the *Biblioteca Nacional* in Montevideo, allowing for scholars to explore his work and unusual life. Situating his example in the larger regional context of the Río de la Plata in the early 1800s alongside figures such as Bartolomé Hidalgo, Francisco de Paula Castañeda, and Luis Pérez, can help to draw several broad conclusions about alternative intellectuals in this period.

Before turning our attention to those conclusions, however, a few words are necessary about these other figures whose roles and life stories have undergone or are undergoing a similar process of recovery. Bartolomé Hidalgo is the well-known author of gauchesque poetry – *cielitos* and *diálogos* – from the 1810s and early 1820s. Often recognized as the 'father' of this popular poetry, or at least one of the first to write in the style of gaucho speak, Hidalgo exercised a range of jobs, from barber to scribe to soldier to director of Montevideo's *Casa de Comedias* (Praderio xi-xxx), where he interacted with Joaquín Sagra y Périz and possibly with Molina. While a handful of his verses appeared in the voluminous anthologies of patriotic poetry in Argentina and

Uruguay (*La lira argentina* and *El parnaso oriental*), Hidalgo's name did not gain much of the currency it had in his own time until the early twentieth century. Francisco de Paula Castañeda and Luis Pérez were more popular than Hidalgo when alive, but have not received similar attention from academics. The Argentine Castañeda was a renegade priest who ran into trouble with both the Catholic Church and the Unitarian government of the 1820s. He wrote acidic newspapers like the *Despertador Teo-filantrópico* and *Doña María Retazos*, whose supposed female editor Castañeda invented. Many of his papers have not survived the passage of time, yet recent interest in the priest has renewed efforts to explore his polemical positions (Furlong). More prolific than Castañeda was Pérez, who published some thirty popular newspapers, many in the voice of gauchos, peasants, and blacks, from 1830 to 1834. Like Hidalgo, Pérez was a soldier in the 1810s whose writing was enthusiastically received. But Pérez, more than either Hidalgo or Castañeda, was a partisan whose politics ultimately led to his demise (Acree, "Gaucho Gazetteers"). Details of the lives of Hidalgo, Castañeda, and Pérez are sparse, just like those of Molina's life, but all of these men share things in common that speak to more general traits of alternative intellectuals.

First among these traits is that all four were intellectuals who wrote from marginal positions yet enjoyed close contact with people in positions of power before falling out of favor. In this sense they were anti-intellectuals of sorts. Hidalgo did enjoy the privilege of directing Montevideo's main theater, but his life as a writer was unconventional, at least for the standards of the early 1800s. He wrote a play that was performed in Montevideo in 1816, but he produced most of his poetry – what he is best known for – from the edges of the lettered city after moving to Buenos Aires and losing his connections to prominent actors on the political stage. We have seen how Molina was an out-of-place intellectual. His fall from the graces of intellectual circles took place after his death, when he could no longer respond to his critics to defend his reputation and name. Luis Pérez's ardent Federalism served him well during the early years of Juan Manuel de Rosas's governorship, when he had the support of many government officials. In later years Pérez butted heads with Pedro de Angelis, editor of state newspapers, which resulted in his imprisonment and apparent disappearance. His politics were also responsible for his accomplishments being disregarded by later generations determined to 'forget' all things associated with Rosas.

A second conclusion about these alternative intellectuals is that while they enjoyed high levels of fame during their lifetime, they spent their last days in poverty or were embroiled in political scandals like Castañeda and Pérez. Hidalgo died poor, despite the successful sale of many of his compositions. Molina died poor as well. He made several pleas for his protectors like Sagra y Périz to provide him with ink, pens, and paper, so he could continue to write in his last days, and he petitioned the Hospital de Caridad on numerous occasions for his supposedly unpaid salary. It is clear, then, that their celebrity status, albeit for being intellectual outsiders, and the commercial success of their intellectual production (in the case of Hidalgo and Pérez) was not enough to provide these men with comfortable last days.

Lastly, and tied to the issue of fame, much of what people like Molina or Hidalgo wrote and the circles where they operated were closely connected to popular classes, or at the very least linked popular classes to the state and state discourse. Molina's blackness made him an alternative intellectual by default, but it was the intellectual activity that he chose to pursue that allowed him to position himself as a voice of black communities among white lettered officials. Hidalgo, Castañeda, and Pérez did not face the same skin-deep discrimination (although Castañeda called Hidalgo the 'darkie' from Montevideo), yet the success of all three derived from their ability to mine popular discourse. This ultimately placed them in the similar position as mediators vis-à-vis the state or the Church, on the one hand, and peasants, artisans, and people from the countryside, on the other.

The capacity and will of Molina, Hidalgo, Castañeda, and Pérez to work in different registers and address different publics is something they share in common with alternative intellectuals of today and is indeed one of the factors leading to their categorization as 'alternative.' Jacinto de Molina, for his part, has shown us here how a black, famous, and out-of-place intellectual could indeed participate in the reconceptualization and reconfiguration of political and intellectual frontiers in early nineteenth-century Montevideo. He engaged the power of the state, but was never one its architects, and while he promoted the end of slavery and a better quality of life for Afro-descendants in Uruguay and elsewhere in America, he was not a reactionary author of resistance. It is here, in his skill at negotiating such differences and extremes, and in maneuvering between such different audiences, where we can see more clearly the meaning of alternative intellectual in early nineteenth-century America.

WORKS CITED

ACREE, William. "Gaucho Gazetteers, Popular Lite:^ture, and Politics in the Río de la Plata." *Studies in Latin American Popular Culture* 26 (2007): 197-215.

—. "Jacinto Ventura de Molina: A Black Letrado in a White World of Letters, 1766-1841." *Latin American Research Review* 44.2 (2009): 37-58.

ACREE, William, and Alex BORUCKI, eds. *Jacinto Ventura de Molina y los caminos de la escritura negra en el Río de la Plata.* Montevideo: Linardi y Risso, 2008.

ADORNO, Rolena. *Goman Poma: Writing and Resistance in Colonial Peru.* Austin: U of Texas P, 2000.

Amigos del pueblo, Los. 13 September 1823.

ANDREWS, George Reid. *Afro-Latin America, 1800-2000.* New York: Oxford UP, 2004.

—. *The Afro-Argentines of Buenos Aires, 1800-1900.* Madison: U of Wisconsin P, 1980.

—. "Remembering Africa, Inventing Uruguay: Sociedades de Negros in the Montevideo Carnival, 1865-1930." *Hispanic American Historical Review* 87.4 (2007): 693-726.

BORUCKI, Alex. *Abolicionismo y esclavitud en Montevideo tras la fundación republicana (1829-1853).* Unpublished book.

—. "Tensiones raciales en el juego de la representación. Actores afro en Montevideo tras la fundación republicana (1830-1840)." *Gestos* 42 (2006): 33-56.

BORUCKI, Alex, Karla CHAGAS, and Natalia STALLA. *Esclavitud y trabajo: un estudio sobre los afrodescendientes en la frontera uruguaya (1835-1855).* Montevideo: Pulmón, 2004.

CASTAÑEDA, Francisco de Paula. *Doña María Retazos.* With a preliminary study by Néstor T. Auza. Buenos Aires: Taurus, 2001.

DE MARÍA, Isidoro. *Montevideo antiguo: tradiciones y recuerdos,* Vol. 1 With a prologue by Juan E. Pivel Devoto. *Clásicos Uruguayos.* Vol. 23. Montevideo: Ministerio de Instrucción Pública y Previsión Social, 1957. 240-42.

FURLONG, Guillermo. *Vida y obra de Fray Francisco de Paula Castañeda: un testigo de la naciente patria argentina, 1810-1830.* San Antonio de Padua: Castañeda, 1994.

GEGGUS, David. "The Sounds and Echoes of Freedom: The Impact of the Haitian Revolution on Latin America." *Beyond Slavery: The Multilayered Legacy of Africans in Latin America and the Caribbean.* Ed. Darién J. Davis. Lanham, MD: Rowman & Littlefield, 2007. 19-36.

GOLDBERG, Marta B. "La población negra y mulata de la ciudad de Buenos Aires, 1810-1840." *Desarrollo Económico* 16.61 (1976): 75-99.

GORTÁZAR, Alejandro. *El licenciado negro: Jacinto Ventura de Molina.* Montevideo: Trilce, 2007.

HELG, Aline. "Simón Bolívar and the Spectre of 'Pardocracia': José Padilla in Post-Independence Cartagena." *Journal of Latin American Studies* 35.3 (2003): 447-71.

MOLINA, Jacinto Ventura de. *Letter to Joaquín Sagra y Périz.* Archivo General de la Nación, Uruguay. Ex Archivo y Museo Histórico Nacional, box 205, folder 7.

—. *Loose-leaf poetry.* Arhivo General de la Nación. Uruguay. Ex Archivo y Museo Histórico Nacional, box 205, folder 7.

—. *Petition of Juan Colorado to the Governor of Montevideo.* Archivo General de la Nación, Uruguay. Ex-Archivo General Administrativo, box 283, folder 3, doc. 12, July 12, 1804.

MORAÑA, Mabel. "Ilustración y delirio en la construcción nacional, o las fronteras de la *ciudad letrada.*" *Latin American Literary Review* 25.50 (1997): 31-45.

PEREDA VALDÉS, Ildefonoso. *Negros esclavos y negros libres: esquema de una sociedad esclavista y aporte del negro en nuestra formación nacional.* Montevideo: Imprenta "Gaceta Comercial," 1941. 157-61.

PRADERIO, Antonio. Prologue. *Obra completa.* By Bartolomé Hidalgo. Clásicos Uruguayos. vol. 170. Montevideo: Ministerio de Educación y Cultura, 1986. vii-lxxx.

VAN DEUSEN, Nancy E., trans. and ed. *The Souls of Purgatory: the Spiritual Diary of a Seventeenth-Century Afro-Peruvian Mystic, Ursula de Jesús.* Albuquerque: U of New Mexico P, 2004.

Triumph of the Will: Annihilation of Ariel in Manuel Gálvez's *Calibán*

Gonzalo Aguiar

Introduction

Regardless of one's ideological affiliations, any discussion of rightist intellectual practice in Latin America must include an overview of their work toward the stabilization of concepts such as 'nation,' 'culture,' and 'social change.' This is not simply a question of discursive and rhetorical strategies to differentiate themselves from others in the power struggle within the intellectual field. It implies a whole system of social, political, cultural, and economic networking designed to legitimize a concept of nation-state that reproduces the notion of Latin American countries as 'peripheral' societies. In other words, the role played by Latin American liberal politics in the late 19th century and early 20th century is reproduced, to a certain extent, by more conservative intellectual practices insofar as it involves the selective production and distribution of knowledge to highly stratified societies. The general trajectory of these practices is the generation of spaces of conformity within society and the categorization of dissidence as 'wrongful', 'evil', or anarchic.

In this chapter, I consider a historical case of the development of rightist political philosophy and practice by examining how intellectual work is transformed by imperatives other than the ones emanating from the particularities of a given discipline. The case is that of the Argentine writer Manuel Gálvez (1882-1962). Taking his early devotion to means and ends in intellectual life as my point of departure, I will show how this ideal was contested by his own depiction of Caliban at a later stage of his professional career. Caliban, as a "conceptual personage" (Jáuregui 313), is brought to life again by Gálvez in 1943 to critique the notion of restricted democracy upheld by the liberal elite, but also against the populist discourse which was pervading Argentina's political and social life in the 1930s and early 1940s.[1] For this reason, in this chapter I will touch on articulations between symbolic discourses and political representation and highlight Gálvez's historical case as an example of intellectual ethics that offers itself as a mediation between the two as a means of generating consensus across many different areas of cultural, political, and social life.

FROM ABSTRACT TRUTH TO SOCIOPOLITICAL KNOWLEDGE: ORTEGA'S INTELLECTUAL ETHICS

In "Carta a un joven argentino que estudia filosofía" (Letter to an Argentine Young Man Who Studies Philosophy), a 1924 letter published in his journal *El Espectador*, the Spanish philosopher José Ortega y Gasset (1883-1955) provided some acute observations regarding the state of the Argentine intellectual milieu at that time. Based on firsthand knowledge about the intricacies of those intellectual circles and their supposedly 'marketable' production for a broader audience, Ortega posits a number of sociological problems in face of Argentina's political instability.[2] Viewing the cultural situation in Argentina from a rather neocolonial viewpoint, the Spanish philosopher attempts to

---

1. See also Jáuregui's exhaustive work on "calibanesque insurgencies" (313) within the hegemonic arielist discourse during the first half of the 20ᵗʰ century. Through the discussion of figures such as Paul Groussac (1848-1929), Ruben Darío (1867-1916), José Martí (1853-1895), José Enrique Rodó (1872-1917), and Gálvez himself, Jauregui explores varying symbolic appropriations of Shakespeare's characters in *The Tempest* and their links to neocolonial or postcolonial (re)readings of Latin America as a space of theoretical reflection.

2. I return to this point below. Tulio Halperin Donghi's and José Luis Romero's classic studies are among the best written about the subject.

explain why the intellectual production of this country falls behind its European counterpart. Despite its brevity, Ortega's text offers itself as a grand statement on Latin American intellectual idiosyncrasy when faced with the task of solving social and cultural issues on a national scale. This is especially significant since the patriarchal voice implied in the text presupposes an asymmetric relation between speaker and addressee. Communication here is a one-way process in which, much like the Uruguayan thinker José Enrique Rodó's *Ariel* (1900), a *magister* disseminates knowledge for the benefit of a very attentive (and subordinated) disciple.[3] Unlike the earlier text, however, the letter leaves the actual recipient out from the text, thus explicitly erasing any marks of a concrete context of communication that may reduce the impact of the whole message to younger generations in the Latin American region.

This being said, it would be unfair to dismiss Ortega's arguments all at once. What is at issue here is whether or not this letter offers a concise introduction to some of the most difficult challenges Latin American intellectuals have faced during the rapid modernization of their nations at the turn of the 20th century. Whatever the answer may be, the "Carta" undeniably incorporates itself into this debate by calling for a more rigorous intellectual ethics for cultural elites in Latin America. As I will demonstrate later by using the example of Manuel Gálvez, the "Carta" is a key text for understanding the ideological implications deriving from an intellectual imperative that rapidly turns into an imperative of social order.

A close examination of the text would be useful for the purpose of my analysis. Briefly, the letter enumerates a number of obstacles that new generations will find in their way to a sense of fulfillment of their own intellectual potentialities. First, Ortega points out that sociocultural conditions in Argentina conspire against any attempt to produce a scientific discourse of its own. An emphasis on rhetorical shallowness coupled with intellectual narcissism is one of the problems that Ortega encounters when it comes to understanding the conditions of production of cultural elites in the region (68-9).

Secondly, the excessive aestheticization of both literary and 'scientific' works only denotes a blatant dependency on Europe's philosophical

---

3. In reference to the complex relationship between master and disciple in Rodó's text, see González Echevarría.

tradition that goes beyond the political emancipation obtained in the nineteenth century: "You are more sensitive than accurate," Ortega maintains, "and while this does not change you will depend completely on Europe on an intellectual level" (69).[4] As a result, this situation is a good example of the extent to which Latin American countries are feminized in Ortega's discourse, since they lack a "*viril apetito de perforación*" (a virile appetite for perforation) in order to resume a wholly new intellectual enterprise for their countries.

Finally, Ortega's reformation of the Argentine intellectual field would include the fostering of an inner discipline that at times is handicapped by the country's social and political turmoil.[5] Here the Spanish author is clearly revealing his own opinion on such a troubling subject. Ideologically affiliated with the "*Generación del 98*", a group of Spanish artists and intellectuals who hoped for the restoration of Spain's image after losing its last colonies around the world, Ortega is proving himself to be extremely wary of any reformation involving the State and its institutions (70). Given the fact that Ortega himself has been studied from the point of view of his fluctuating political ideas ranging from liberalism and conservatism to close associations with fascism, it is no wonder to see him adopting a radical perspective regarding the limits of democracy. As Andrew Dobson has remarked on this issue, "Ortega is perfectly happy to place the nation above the institutions of the state" (97). This ultimately serves as a clever justification for an ideological balance between man and mass in (Western) society, which is at the very core of Ortega's political ideas.[6]

---

4. All translations from Spanish or Portuguese are the author's.

5. Despite objections by Altamirano and Sarlo about the instrumentality of "intellectual field" to refer to Argentina's cultural circumstances around the celebration of the *Centenario* (13), for the sake of clarity I would like to keep the concept throughout this article. Bourdieu's understanding of the term differs considerably from that of Latin Americanists insofar as the use of "intellectual field" by the former implies a European setting – such as Paris, "capital of the 19th century" – displaying an 'organic' development as society. For an extensive treatment of this subject, see Bourdieu's *The Rules of the Art.*

6. In fact, Dobson is prompted to point out "two nodal points of Ortega's political thought [that] come into conflict: the desire to see a modernized Spain, and the requirement of a society in which all individuals have a guaranteed, inviolable private space – the former implies control, the latter, the lack of it" (69).

A LABOR OF LOVE: POLITICS, NATIONALISM, IMMIGRATION, AND OTHER MAJOR INTELLECTUAL DISPUTES

Despite lacking conceptual density with regard to the major problems already being discussed in Latin America at that time, Ortega's text is an adequate point of departure for my own reflections about Manuel Gálvez as a professional man of letters. His intellectual performance was particularly relevant throughout the celebration of the *Centenario* in 1910 (commemoration of Argentina's first century of independence) until his own decline in the 1940s during Juan Domingo Perón's first administration. Most importantly, his life and works illuminate to a great extent the role played by intellectuals in the organization of ideological principles for a nation in search of its own cultural archive. For that reason, I will map some of his best-known writings by following the implications of Ortega's assertion that intellectual discipline requires a 'disinterested' attitude towards the fulfillment of a respectable position in society. This opinion was contested by Manuel Gálvez himself; ironically enough, he was a notorious supporter of the ideology of *hispanismo*, a philosophical trend that claimed the necessity of restoring Spanish roots to a continent which had lost its 'true' identity.[7] Consequently, I will finally focus my analysis in *Calibán*, a 1943 play by Gálvez which was long underestimated by critics and writers alike. Considered by many as mere propaganda material from a writer who happens to be highly disillusioned with local political issues, this play is by all means a 'cheap' version of political as well as sociocultural dilemmas that Gálvez was used to placing in writings from his earlier nationalistic period. Yet *Calibán* encapsulates an intellectual trajectory characterized by the all-encompassing ambition of putting Argentina back on its feet.

This article aims to provide not only a conceptual basis to discuss Caliban's genealogy in the light of Gálvez's own contribution to the ongoing debate on such a theorized trope in Latin American thought. It also attempts to demonstrate the validity of this dramatic character

---

7. See Shumway 287. For a discussion of the new politics of Hispanism in academia – particularly related to the current trend of Transatlantic Studies – see Trigo in this volume.

to a number of arguments focused on exploring ethical ideologies coupled with metaphorical uses of literature. In other words, it is the ultimate testimony from a writer who has failed to keep abreast of political events as Ortega prescribed in his aforementioned text.[8] Regardless of earlier ideological affiliations, here Gálvez acknowledges the fact that the 'arielist spirit' has no use for containing the uncontrollable advent of the masses in a populist government. Caliban is identified as a symbol of populism controlled by the contingent and dangerous rule of the masses, as 'perverted' democracy that goes against Rousseau's "general will."[9] Such straightforward content is conveyed in the typical tone of a pamphleteer interested in getting everybody's attention for political reasons. There is no doubt, as I hope to prove later in this article, that Gálvez's attitude has to do with a sense of failure in his own intellectual work when it is seen from a rather idealistic point of view. Therefore, one should ask whether the ethics of writing itself is being put into question by the same writer who, many years ago, endowed his profession with a status never reached before.[10] By being forced to comply with a political machine always ready to draw upon intellectual reputation, Gálvez finally acknowledges the contingent nature of his work when it comes to understanding all the political and social changes that his country underwent during the first decades of the 20th century. It is my contention that this problem situates Gálvez as the perfect illustration of a conservative intellectual working alongside the State for good; and this is so after a life spent in the intellectual arena to work for improving the status of his profession.

---

8. Julien Benda has set the standard for the subject of 'detached' intellectuals acting in politically troubled times.

9. Actually this is what Gálvez means in his essay "El espiritu de aristocracia" (The Spirit of Aristocracy), which revolves around the idea that democracy can be enjoyed only by people of merit: "Democracy does not pursue equality in ignorance, misery, or vulgarity. A true democrat, yearning for the perfection of humankind, aspires to equality in excellency" (20).

10. For an analysis of the relationship between literature and the ethics of writing, see Aníbal González. See Dalmaroni ("Providencia") for a divergent perspective than that provided by Julio Ramos' classic study on intellectuals and the State at the turn of the 20th century. See also Rama and Jitrik for illuminating studies on the role played by *políticos letrados* in the configuration of the "lettered city" (Mabel Moraña in this volume).

This dramatic shift in Gálvez's career did not happen by chance. Born to a traditional and prosperous family in the provincial city of Paraná, Argentina (they later moved to Santa Fe, another province in Argentina's countryside), Gálvez fostered Catholic values and a conservative viewpoint during his formative years. This was particularly evident after his return from a trip to Europe in 1905. Around that time, Gálvez had experienced a crisis of faith that ended up being one of the most significant moral grounds for his literary work. From that moment on, the Argentine writer intended to rewrite the history of his country based on a nationalistic sentiment that impinged on hot topics such as immigration, peripheral capitalism, widespread materialism, and the present condition of a population devoid of any sense of spirituality. This is to say that his passion for a 'better' Argentina, which ultimately is a nationalistic discourse shared alongside figures such as Ricardo Rojas in *La restauración nacionalista* (1910) and Leopoldo Lugones in conferences at Odeón theatre in Buenos Aires entitled *El payador* (1916), entails not only a belief in values rooted in 'land', 'blood', or 'race.' At the same time, it provides a conceptual understanding of how an intellectual constructs his/her object of knowledge by utilizing scientific as well as aesthetic data in order to channel a preexisting idea of what a nation should be.

Even though Gálvez was very much an intellectual of his own (Quijada 7, 51), soon he became a notorious spokesperson for the *Generación del Centenario*, a movement of young writers and critics alike who longed for reconstituting an ideal of nation. In Quijada's words, Gálvez represented Argentina's *zeitgeist* insofar as he:

[C]ried out for the necessity of reconquering the country's spiritual life by means of education of citizens, study of the collective soul, and the implication of ideal travels [*viajes ideales*]. He feared the disappearance of the love of one's country because a certain type of Argentine was arising from massive inmigration, a type who was no longer a genuine product of the soil, the race, and the setting. (24)

The *Centenario* intellectuals, without being overtly optimistic about the immigrant situation in Argentina, are otherwise hopeful that education and state control would rectify the wrong path that the liberal oligarchy in power had taken in sociopolitical issues concerning the nation's welfare. In a number of writings Gálvez insisted upon restoring national values to a country increasingly affected by the premises of the world market. What is striking about Gálvez's work, however, is that his cultural nonconformity gains momentum at a time when he struggled to make a living out of his image as a 'traditional' intellectual. Despite not agreeing with some of the legislative measures of the liberal oligarchy, Gálvez was always careful in crafting an intellectual persona who enjoyed close contact with people in positions of power. This fact speaks eloquently about his commitment to preserve traditional values for a nation in need of establishing its own cultural repository. He was mainly affected by an increasingly rationality of labor encouraged by state policies, which in its turn would affect the relation among social classes. Accordingly, this would suppose the emergence of radical movements that have changed the face of Argentina's politics since.

It is worth remembering that Argentina entered into a new stage of industrialization from 1880 on due to the expansion of world capitalism, which gave the country a privileged situation as a provider of raw materials. The urban oligarchy, more than the provincial one, was the actual beneficiary of the new market conditions since the former controlled the port of Buenos Aires (in this way maintaining a close relationship with the ups and downs of the world market) while the latter tended to consider themselves as a conservative group of families deeply rooted in local traditions. These traditions, being somewhat inherited from the time the nation belonged to the Viceroyalty of the Río de la Plata, were cultivated as a badge of honor among the latifundist elite who owned vast extensions of land in the provinces of Argentina. With the arrival of over 6 million immigrants between 1871 and 1914 to Argentine soil (Lewis 55; Fishburn 47), the liberal proclamation of encouraging the populating of the country with European peoples was called to a halt around the turn of the 20th century. The Residential Law (1902), which was passed in Congress during Julio A. Roca's second term in office, proved to be a repressive mechanism destined for containing social demands mostly inspired by radical ideologies imported from Europe. This law aimed to prevent social distress among the working classes by simply evicting from national soil any *"extranjero cuya conducta pueda comprometer la seguridad nacional, turbar el orden público o la tranquilidad social"* (any foreigner whose conduct might compromise national security, disturb public order or social tranquility) (quoted in Quijada 15).

It was not so long until the liberal oligarchy realized that it was impossible to resolve the problem of incorporating immigrant masses and their descendants to the body politic by just outlawing the 'unwanted.' The ruling elite were surely at pains to deal with these social issues until the Sáenz Peña Law was signed in 1912. This law was intended to give, among other social reforms, electoral power to those sectors of the population formerly underrepresented because of their immigration status.[11] The Radical Party, opposed to the oligarchy in power, took advantage of the political situation created by this law and developed a sophisticated electoral machine which resulted in the election of Juan Hipólito Yrigoyen to the presidential office in 1916. Thus, the undisputed hegemony of the *Generación del 80* in the affairs of the nation was finally interrupted mainly because of the influence exerted by a huge constituency represented by the middle class.[12]

It is not difficult now to appreciate Manuel Gálvez's *El diario de Gabriel Quiroga* in light of the social forces at work in Argentina's political scenario. Published in 1910 as part of the intellectual efforts of a group of writers committed to rewriting the nation's past, the book expresses the author's viewpoint thinly disguised as Gabriel Quiroga's, a fictional character which represents a new type of intellectual emerging from the literary *modernismo* at the turn of the century (Gramuglio 29). In this respect, Quiroga's opinions enact some of the most important issues regarding the reorganization of the nation according to nationalist values. At odds with a positivism that continued to inform philosophical approaches to reality by ruling elites in Latin America, Quiroga vindicates in his "political book" (73) a humanist perspective on society.[13] This book surely meant to be a 'ground zero' for a nation deeply embedded in cosmopolitan as well as materialist values. Quiroga, whose 'editor' of his book (Gálvez himself) named him as a true "patriot" (73), is determined to turn certain social principles upside down in order to draw a line between what is good for the

---

11. It should be noted here that "women remained disenfranchised" (Lewis 77) throughout this historical process.

12. See Romero 328-39.

13. For an excellent approach to this subject, see Oscar Terán.

country and what is not. By stating that "*gobernar es argentinizar*" (to govern is to Argentinize) (117), for instance, Quiroga is clearly inverting the traditional motto set forth by Argentine liberals around mid-nineteenth century. From the former "*gobernar es poblar*" (to govern is to populate or people) to the imperative of educating masses in traditional values encouraged by Quiroga, the book asserts the necessity of revaluating Argentina's cultural landscape after a series of political-economic measures imposed during its rapid modernization.

For this reason, Quiroga advocates for a return to an 'original' state in which provincial life – characterized by Catholicism, uncorrupted by foreign values, and deeply committed to preserving local history – should be a model for the whole nation. Both writers and intellectuals are here of the utmost importance if they are to perform the kind of reformation suggested by Gálvez / Quiroga. Based on a commonplace notion which considers the young poet in Buenos Aires as an irremediable bohemian who spent his life in cafés, theaters and boarding-houses, Quiroga believes that "people from the provinces have a spiritual depth which men from Buenos Aires lack" (147).[14] This ultimately places the provincial intellectual in a privileged position as mediator vis-à-vis the state as long as they keep their 'ideals' away from more 'mundane' values. As the editor of Quiroga's writings says, "Gabriel, as I said before, lacks any ambition and disdains easy triumphs in life; and if he has relinquished his right to not publish this book – although he asserts quite the opposite – it is because he is expecting to make a contribution to his country's self-understanding, thus furthering its perfection through the path of the Ideal" (77-8). In this way, as Gálvez does as well in his novel *La maestra normal* (1914), Argentine intellectual production is directly linked to rethinking national spaces and restoring a sense of the past with which to counter the threat posed by the United States' pervasive influence across the Western world.[15] This looking back to the cultural memory

14. Gálvez's novel *El mal metafísico* is full of references illustrating such statements about idyllic life in the countryside in opposition to the corruption reigning in Buenos Aires.

15. See Culasso for a specific analysis of how spaces are treated in Gálvez's novels, especially in *La maestra normal*. Additional sources about his 'anachronic' literary realism are Dalmaroni ("Identidades") and Goldchluk.

of Argentina's countryside represents as well a correction to the Sarmentine dictum which favored European immigration to Argentina's coastal cities in the name of progress. Now civilization is reinterpreted as the residual effect of a massive affluence of foreign / alien people loosely subject to the laws of the host country. In Quiroga's words, *"en Buenos Aires hay civilización pero no cultura"* (in Buenos Aires there is civilization, but not culture) (98), which ultimately illustrates the point with regard to what is at stake in Gálvez's intellectual project.

Along with these fictional manifestoes – which helped in placing him in an influential position within Argentina's intellectual field in the 1910s and 1920s – Gálvez began writing a number of essays in which he explicitly adheres to Spain's supposedly spiritual legacy for the rest of the Hispanic world. In *El solar de la raza* (1913), for instance, Gálvez puts forth the 'Latin spirit' as a rhetorical device to harmonize different and contradictory discourses on whether Spain, as a former hegemonic entity, can provide Latin American nation-states anything in the realm of ideas. Gálvez carefully crafts his own answer by claiming that his admiration for Spain is "purely artistic and literary" (7); as such, he avoids implicating himself in a long dated debate of (post) colonial implications. In this book he reworks residual elements from the common Hispanic past in order to convey a new sense of 'being' Argentine. It is useful to bear in mind that Gálvez attempts to synthesize in *El solar* both conservative and liberal political viewpoints in order to suggest his project of a new kind of citizenship; that is, a project which is at odds with the cosmopolitan tendencies determining social habits and conduct in Argentine urban life. His dry prose attempts to make sense of this ideal by aiming to implicate the cultural elite in an intellectual struggle which must be furthered by the new generations to come:

Brava lucha es la nuestra. Tenemos que pelear lindamente – en los libros, en los diarios, en la cátedra, en todas partes – contra los calibanescos intereses creados que son los hábitos materialistas. Tenemos que predicar maniáticamente el amor a la patria, a nuestros pasajes, a nuestros escritores, a nuestros grandes hombres; desentrañar el idealismo y la originalidad de nuestro pasado, y enseñar cómo estas cualidades de la patria romántica y pobre pueden salvar, sin menoscabarla en su grandeza material,

a la actual patria viviente. Y tenemos, por último, que buscar por toda
la anchura de la tierra ejemplos de idealismo y tratar de crear, en el alma
de nuestros conciudadanos, la misma emoción purificadora que estreme-
ció a la nuestra. (16)[16]

In the same way as Ortega's claim that only intellectual elites are
capable of making substantial changes in the course of a nation's history (Castro-Gómez 102), Gálvez urges his fellow colleagues to reflect
on their own circumstances and propose a consensual definition of
what Argentina should be before the rest of the world.[17] His travels to
Spain in 1905 and 1910 were considered a point of departure for a
"work of evangelization" (Quijada 27) that continued throughout
Gálvez's life. As such, he combined a strong anti-imperialist sentiment against American policies regarding the Hispanic world with a
renewed faith in Catholic principles rooted in concepts such as land,
race, and civic spirituality. Furthermore, Gálvez demonstrates here his
conceptual ties with the *Generación del 98* as well as *arielismo* by calling for a 'spiritualization' of the nation which needs to be dated back
to the Greco-Latin civilization (*El solar* 13-21).

By the same token, Gálvez's ideological message attempts to reach
all levels of society and thus consolidate a national imaginary in which
intellectuals are highlighted by striving to fashion themselves as a disciplined and self-aware group in close contact with power. Much like
Eduardo Mallea's work on rediscovering the "invisible" Argentina by
means of a close look at the nation's 'real' values, Gálvez mystifies his
intellectual profile in order to establish himself as one of the members

---

16. "Ours is a brave struggle. We have to fight intensely – in books, papers, the
university, everywhere – against the calibaneseque interests of materialist habits. We
have to manically preach love for the fatherland, our landscapes, our writers, our
great men; to discover the idealism and originality of our past, and teach how these
qualities of the poor and romantic fatherland can save, without undermining its
material greatness, the living and present country. And we must, finally, seek across
the breadth of the Earth examples of idealism and try to create, in the soul of our
co-citizens, the same purifying emotion that makes our own tremble."

17. This is the very definition of a doctrine based on strong principles and supported by the largest members possible. In Alain Badiou's terms, an ethical ideology
constitutes "a consensual law-making concerning human beings in general, their
needs, their lives, and their deaths – and, by extension, the self-evident, universal
demarcation of evil, of what is incompatible with the human essence" (6).

of an elite destined to develop a 'true' mission in Argentina's future.[18] As a result, nationalist intellectual discourse on public affairs has no problem tailoring the State requirements for a sense of citizenship based on allegiance to common principles that are supposed to unite the nation under the same (ideological) flag.

IS CALIBAN STILL A SYMBOL FOR LATIN AMERICA?

While enough has been said to lend support to the contention that Gálvez's objectives are inextricably related to State policies during the first decades of the 20th century, it remains to be seen why this ambitious project failed the test of Argentine history throughout the 1930s and 1940s. A close analysis of Argentina's sociopolitical events during that time is undoubtedly beyond the scope of this article. But it is otherwise important to remember a few landmarks in the nation's history at that time in conjunction with Gálvez's identity discourse evolving from an earlier nationalism to a language verging on the coercive in his own version of the Shakespearean Caliban. As we shall see later, it is this significant shift in his intellectual performance which ultimately separates him from Ortega's ideas concerning the reflection on one's circumstances with a detached 'disinterestedness'.

When General José Félix Uriburu took power after deposing Yrigoyen from the presidential office in 1930, right-wing opponents and nationalists alike joined him with the hope of using "the state as a tool to enforce social harmony" (Lewis 84). Soon after the coup Uriburu blocked the Radical Party from elections in Buenos Aires province, thus allowing conservatives to take control of power on a national scale. This was the beginning of the *Década infame* (Infamous Decade) in which a cluster of right-wing political parties (known as

---

18. In Mallea's *Historia de una pasión argentina* (History of an Argentine Passion) there is a revealing passage which denotes a pessimistic analysis of the social compound in Argentina in the 1930s: "Our country's malaise is recent, it all started in the beginning of the 20th century. I have seen immigrant people before and after that. Similar to a deeply troubled human face, it is possible to study the history of our decadence as a fatherland, more than just simply a nation or a State" (21). For a useful comparison between Gálvez and Mallea and their respective intellectual backgrounds, see Cvitanovic.

Concordancia) was "in control of the political system from 1932 until 1943," mainly based on "fraud and force to rig elections and to maintain the appearance of a constitutional, representative form of government" (Lewis 85). This event inaugurated a series of unfortunate economic measures that troubled President Agustín P. Justo throughout his administration (1932-1938). Undoubtedly, the Great Depression had a lasting impact on Argentina's economy insofar as it produced social distress among the working classes. After winning the 1938 election by fraud, Roberto M. Ortiz and his Vice President Ramón Castillo alternated in the office until the former resigned in 1942, a period in which the outbreak of World War II forced Argentina to adopt a position regarding the conflict. During Ortiz's short term in office (1942-1943) the country remained neutral mainly because of its government ambiguity in relation to which side of the conflict would be more profitable to Argentina's economic interests (Lewis 90). As a suspicion about the intention of Castillo to join the military forces against the Triple Axis unfolded, concerns about the political feasibility of the government – represented in the act of both nationalists and Radicals joining forces against the regime – led to the military coup known as the "Revolución del 43" (the June Revolution).

Throughout this period Gálvez, aside from publishing his novels and essays, took an active part in the establishment of the Argentine Academy of Letters. This event helped consolidate his intellectual prestige among his peers, but at the same time it created new demands in light of political events which forced intellectuals to take sides in favor or against the ruling regime in the 1930s.[19] In Gálvez's case, the Irigoyen administration awakened his Catholic creed by acknowledging the fact that 'distributive justice' could also mean more popular participation in national affairs.[20] As Quijada maintains in his thor-

---

19. A radical example of the latter is the Argentine poet Leopoldo Lugones (1874-1938), thoroughly analyzed in Beired 51-5. See also Quijada for valuable information regarding Gálvez's intellectual disputes with Lugones on practically every single subject supported by the former (49).

20. David Rock explains how this Catholic perspective gave rise to an ethical ideology embedded in social ideas favoring State interventionism: "During the early twentieth century, Argentine Catholics were beginning to develop an organic vision of the nation as an aggregation of 'corporations.' Catholics upheld 'class harmony' and 'distributive justice,' in which both 'harmony' and 'justice' bore their original

ough study about the Argentine writer, this point is particularly relevant to understand some of the most twisted ideological positions that Gálvez had to adopt in order to meet different political, social and philosophical perspectives throughout his career (51). In other words, his inner need for social justice clashes with more conservative demands originated from his own elitist position in society, mostly inspired by his reading of French conservative philosopher Charles Maurras (1868-1952) (Beired 48-50; Quijada 47-8).

It was not until the 1930s that Gálvez radicalizes his opinions with the coming of a military intervention in the political arena in Argentina. Forced by recent local as well as international events – Yrigoyen being removed from office by a coup d'état (to which the writer himself lent support), a fascist movement on the rise in Italy and Germany, his public approval of Spanish Primo de Rivera's regime, and the like – Gálvez soon recognizes the importance of a corporative state for the sake of social order. In his remarkable book on authoritarian intellectuals from Argentina and Brazil in between the two World Wars, the Brazilian historian José Luis Bendicho Beired records an impressive amount of information on this particular subject. In stark contrast to the kind of intellectual that emerged from the printing press in the early 20th century, the new role played by the cultural elite has to do with a lobbyist-type action directly related to mechanisms of political power. As Beired reminds us, this is caused by a rejection of the restricted liberal model promulgated by the old oligarchies in favor of an authoritarian State based on economic protectionism and interventionist measures (105). In short, a corporative spirit among ruling elites was at the core of the new relationship established between rightist intellectuals and the State. This is precisely what the definition of "corporativism" entails according to Beired:

> Corporativism would fulfill the role of organizing society into non-competitive categories – or functional parts – which are integrated into a supportive whole. This way political as well as class conflicts are eradicated, favoring the foundation of social relations characterized by solidarity

Greek connotations of balance, measure, or proportion. Catholics rejected the *laissez-faire* state in favor of a modernized and idealized facsimile of the *ancien régime*: an interventionist government that in pursuit of 'justice' would promote social reform" (287).

and under the tutelage of a strong, authoritarian State, a kind of tutor which is able to impose direction and dispute any private interest. Only the exercise of authority will allow for a restoration of discipline, obedience, and hierarchy within a society corrupted by foreign influence. (104)

I think it is fair to say that, for Gálvez, many of these authoritarian aspects were not as exacerbated as in Lugones' famous speech "The Hour of the Sword".[21] His anti-Semitism and rejection of violence as a means of gaining power clearly indicates that a humanist Catholicism was still the foundational basis of his political creed. But *Calibán*, written in the aftermath of the *Década infame*, certainly is a prelude to his own 'hour of darkness' in face of the several frustrations he experimented with Argentina's political life in the course of his long and prolific life.

The 1943 play is loosely based on Shakespeare's plot. It only includes from the original story the highly symbolic couple composed of Calibán and Próspero, around which a group of characters bring to life a contemporary story centered on an undefined province of Argentina. Briefly, the play tells the political struggle between governor Próspero and Calibán, a rapacious character who intends to seize control of the province in order to satisfy his greed for power and money. The ironic point is that Calibán, born to an Indian father and a black woman, was raised by Próspero himself before the former betrays his 'master' by leading an insurrection under the guise of a political *caudillo*. While Próspero, due to his compassionate temperament, believes until the very last minute that his former protégé is after all a 'good savage' who may be redeemed because of his 'white' and 'liberal' upbringing, other characters surrounding him have a different idea in mind.

Anita, Próspero's wife, is relentless in judging Calibán as she remembers him as "that disgusting and wicked boy who looked like a monster and lived in this country house 20 years ago" (23). His 'disgusting'

21. "The 'Hour of the Sword' marked the conclusion of Lugones' long intellectual plunge from the anarchistic libertarianism of his youth, when he had also been an outstanding poet, into the pit of militarism and the incipient fascism of his later middle age" (Rock 298).

appearance points to a Lombrosian reference; thus, Próspero becomes a faulty character because it combines moral atrocities with a repulsive body. In Anita's view, Calibán is seen as "a little bit hunchbacked, cross-eyed, deformed, not tall, mulatto," who also happens to be a heavy drinker as well as a thief (24). Furthermore, Anita's racist perspective is fueled by a past episode in which she was approached by Calibán with overtly sexual intentions (30-1). Other characters in the play, like the Coronel (Colonel), Jefe de Policía (Police Chief), and Minister González, are instrumental in trying to bring Próspero to his senses before the fallout of his government happens. But nothing appears to change his mind until Calibán effectively takes power and Próspero is deposed after a series of failed attempts to persuade the masses not to follow their new 'charismatic' leader. As if an earlier Gálvez uttered the following words on the moral duties concerning intellectual work in society, Próspero reveals here his motives behind his decision to not take action against Calibán: "Neither law nor my own conscience yet authorize me to press charges against / to punish him" [Ni la ley ni mi conciencia me autorizan todavía a proceder contra él] (31).

In Gálvez's hands, this dialectical relation between master and slave, already studied in detail when it comes to examining the genealogical roots of this cultural concept, becomes one of a profound antagonism between different ways of doing politics in Latin America. Deeply embedded in recent political events, *Calibán*, properly subtitled *Tragicomedia de la Vida Política* (Tragicomedy of Political Life), explores this implication by employing propaganda techniques in order to make a hierarchical distinction among 'good' and 'bad' uses of politics. While Governor Próspero's coolness – appropriate for a traditionally 'wise' leader who is falling behind his own time – causes everyone else around him to experience anxiety or disappointment towards his faulty way of delivering justice, Calibán represents the populist tendency with his inflammatory speech delivered to both the people and his morally corrupted followers:

CALIBÁN. Desciendo de esclavos por mi madre, y por eso siento en mi corazón la esclavitud del pueblo. Yo vengo a libertar a la chusma de sus cadenas. Soy un símbolo, es cierto. Ustedes me siguen y me comprenden porque yo y ustedes estamos hechos de la misma materia. *Soy un símbolo porque represento y encarno los intereses morales y materiales de los últimos*

fondos de la sociedad... Triunfaremos porque tenemos razón, porque
necesitamos justicia y porque somos la mayoría. Ya no gobernará el frac
sino la alpargata. (37; emphasis added)[22]

[CALIBÁN. I was born to slaves on my mother's side, and that is why I
feel my people's slavery from the bottom of my heart. I come to release
the populace from their chains. It is true that I am a symbol. You follow
me and understand me because you and I are made of the same sub-
stance / matter. I am a symbol because I represent and embody moral
and material interests from the deepest pits of society. We shall triumph
because we are right, because we need justice and because we are majority. From now on the liberal politicians [the *frac*] do not rule the province
anymore. We do [the *alpargata*]]

At first glance, this rather polished speech by a supposedly 'inferior'
subject points to the propagandist nature spread throughout the play.
But if we look carefully to Calibán's words, its metonymic populism
encloses a self-conscious message which is part of the implied author's
strategy for undermining the validity of the whole political model.
More importantly, it conveys Gálvez's profound mistrust of the masses, a lack of faith in discourses of conciliation which might have given
some hope to a society in need of social justice. This is what González
implies in conversation with Próspero by the time both characters are
surrounded by popular forces:

> GONZÁLEZ. ...Ahora sabrá usted lo que es Calibán. Usted lo ha cono-
> cido en los libros. Ahora lo verá actuando en la vida real.
> PRÓSPERO. La vida de los libros es igual a la vida de la realidad. Por otra
> parte, usted se olvida que Calibán nació en mi casa y que yo le enseñé a
> leer.
> GONZÁLEZ. Me he referido al Calibán revolucionario y gobernante, al
> Calibán-símbolo. En cuanto al miserable degenerado a quien usted le
> enseñó a leer, ya verá cómo le corresponde. No hay mayor desagradecido
> que el pueblo" (63).
> [GONZÁLEZ. ...Now you will know what Calibán is made of. You
> have known him through books. Now you will see him performing in
> real life.

22. Jáuregui points outs similarities between this speech and Evita Perón's
rhetorical populism in addresses to the nation in the late 1940s (365).

PRÓSPERO. Life in books is similar to real life. On the other hand, you forget that Calibán was born in my house and that I taught him to read. GONZÁLEZ. I was referring to Calibán as a revolutionary and ruler, to Calibán as a symbol. Regarding the wretched degenerate you taught to read, you will see how he pays you back. There are no more ungrateful people than masses.]

In contrast with Próspero and González, Calibán's apotheotic moment as a character in the play comes from his mocking of republican institutions originated in the intellectual work of his 'masters' during the nation-building process in Latin America. Not only does he proclaim histrionically his triumph over Próspero by using a well-known formula in the Latin American emancipatory project: *¡Han triunfado el pueblo soberano y la verdadera democracia!* (the sovereign people and true democracy have triumphed!), but he also scorns the 'liberal' speech of his Minister Petroni (70), a venal bureaucrat who is a pitiful reminder of the way political practices are performed under these circumstances. Petroni's shallow rhetoric stands as a parodical remnant of an epoch in which politically savvy elites were able to construct a utopian society without taking much consideration of the real conditions of their nations.

Though I agree with Leonardo Senkman's assertion that the play is actually a metaphor of pro-fascist movements in Argentina (39), it is necessary to claim as well that Gálvez's faith in the group of nationalist colonels in power after 1943 implies a retroactive attitude towards his own accomplishments as a nationalist intellectual. The underlying assumption here is that Gálvez, by forcing his character Próspero to leave office even after Calibán's defeat at the hands of the military caste, recognizes the faulty nature of democratic institutions and acts accordingly. In this respect, the third and final act helps further this logic by letting González say that "Ethics has nothing to do with politics," as such supporting his view in favor of electoral fraud if that is essential for containing social demands from the masses (79). Similarly, a final speech from a colonel at the end of the play includes the political as well as the cultural implications of the new order established by military intervention:

CORONEL (a PRÓSPERO). Señor: voy a asumir el gobierno de la provincia...

Lamento que usted, que es un hombre honrado, no pueda volver al gobierno. Pero un interés superior lo exige. *Sus ideas liberales, señor, abrieron el camino a Calibán. El liberalismo trae fatalmente el libertinaje.* Sin quererlo, ha sido usted el cómplice de Calibán, ha hecho usted a la provincia un mal enorme que yo trataré de remediar... Han triunfado el order, la jerarquía y la disciplina, sin lo cual no hay grandeza ni moral verdaderas. (96-7; emphasis added)[23]

[CORONEL (to PRÓSPERO). Sir, I am going to assume the governor's position of this province... I regret that you, being an honest man, are not able to return to government. But a superior interest demands it so. His liberal ideas, sir, open the path to Calibán. Liberalism brings with it licentiousness. Unintentionally, you have been Calibán's accomplice, you have caused this province a great damage that I will try to solve... Order, hierarchy, and discipline have triumphed, without which there is no true greatness and morality.]

Without understanding the dialectical nature of the relation between Prospero and Caliban in the cultural processes in Latin America, the Colonel is indeed settling a binary opposition in which both symbolic entities are neither productive nor legitimate for the new Argentina that must rise from its own ashes. More importantly, it is instrumental in understanding Gálvez's compliance with a state of exception through which he redefines his whole intellectual career. Despite the brevity of his commitment with nationalist colonels in early 1940s, Gálvez's shifting ideological movements within his comprehensive nationalism ultimately depict the moral dilemmas (if any) faced by an intellectual in close contact with power.

---

23. In reality, these lines by the Colonel outline some of most relevant features of right-wing intellectuals, that is, ideological traditionalism, elitism, and a utopian tercerism. By *tercerismo* Marsal and Arent mean a third course of action for right-wing politicians other than both capitalism and communism. As such "the national ideology is presented as a realist and national policy, a 'realpolitik,' as an anti-ideology, identifying every other ideology as foreign, and their own, as a national synthesis" (*la ideología nacional es presentada como una política realista y nacional, una 'realpolitik', como una antiideología, identificando a toda otra ideología con lo foráneo, y a la propia con la 'síntesis nacional'*)" (25-6).

CONCLUSION

At this point one is reminded of Hernán Vidal's words about the intellectuals' enacting of fascist displays of power, the nature of which hints at what he calls a "radical scission" between the many different knowledges available in an otherwise free society: "Pro-fascist intellectuality's specific contribution to the legitimation of the regime will only happen with a radical scission between ideology and science which, in literary terms, is thematically, metaphorically and symbolically captured through scissions between human body and mind, emotion and reason, spirit and matter" (32). Certainly this phenomenon could not be avoided by Gálvez insofar as his Catholic roots prevented him from being at ease with this issue. Speaking in broader terms, this meant to him a relentless search for answers regarding the work of intellectuals in the elaboration of discourses of national identity. In a way similar to Ortega's ideas about the necessity of intellectual rigorousness in Latin America, Gálvez attempted to translate this imperative – 'translate' in its double sense of 'moving' and 'putting in other language's words' – to a corporatist ideology largely implicated in the political stabilization of Argentina. This situation forced him to occasionally twist his philosophical and political creed in order to meet the requirements of his own time. Hence his rather uncomfortable shift from an early call for intellectual discipline to a condition in which he discloses a transferential need for endowing intellectual power to military discipline.

WORKS CITED

ALTAMIRANO, Carlos, and Beatriz SARLO. *Ensayos argentinos. De Sarmiento a la vanguardia.* Buenos Aires: Ariel, 1997.

BADIOU, Alain. *Ethics: An Essay on the Understanding of Evil.* Trans. Peter Hallward. London & New York: Verso, 2002.

BEIRED, José Luis Bendicho. *Sob o signo da nova ordem: intelectuais autoritários no Brasil e na Argentina (1914-1945).* São Paulo: Loyola, 1999.

BENDA, Julien. *The Treason of the Intellectuals.* Trans. Richard Aldington. New York: William Morrow & Company, 1928.

BOURDIEU, Pierre. *The Rules of Art: Genesis and Structure of the Literary Field.* Stanford, CA: Stanford UP, 1995.

CASTRO-GÓMEZ, Santiago. *Crítica de la razón latinoamericana*. Barcelona: Puvill, 1996.

CULASSO, Adriana G. *Geopolíticas de ficción: espacio y sociedad en la novela argentina (1880-1920)*. Buenos Aires: Corregidor, 2006.

CVITANOVIC, Dinko. "Concepto y paradoja: los flujos barrocos del 98 en la Argentina." *Cuadernos Hispanoamericanos* 577-578 (1998): 215-37.

DALMARONI, Miguel. "Identidades nacionales y representación literaria: umbrales teóricos, textos argentinos y relecturas." *Literatura argentina y nacionalismo (Gálvez, Fogwil, Saer, Aira)*. Buenos Aires: Universidad Nacional de La Plata, 1995. 9-21.

—. "'La providencia de los literatos': escritores argentinos y Estado durante la modernización (1888-1917)." *Iberoamericana* 6.21 (2006): 7-24.

DOBSON, Andrew. *An Introduction to the Politics and Philosophy of José Ortega y Gasset*. Cambridge Iberian and Latin American Studies. Cambridge: Cambridge UP, 1989.

FISHBURN, Evelyn. *The Portrayal of Immigration in Nineteenth Century Argentine Fiction (1845-1902)*. Berlin: Colloquium Verlag, 1981.

GÁLVEZ, Manuel. *Calibán: tragicomedia de la vida política*. Buenos Aires: Edición del autor, 1943.

—. *El diario de Gabriel Quiroga: opiniones sobre la vida argentina*. Buenos Aires: Taurus, 2001.

—. *El espíritu de aristocracia y otros ensayos*. Buenos Aires: Agencia General de Librería y Publicaciones, 1924.

—. *El solar de la raza*. 5 ed. Madrid: Saturnino Calleja, 1920.

—. *Obras escogidas*. Madrid: Aguilar, 1949.

GOLDCHLUK, Graciela. "Un antinormalismo pedagógico: a propósito de *La maestra normal*, de Manuel Gálvez." *Literatura argentina y nacionalismo (Gálvez, Fogwil, Saer, Aira)*. Buenos Aires: Universidad Nacional de La Plata, 1995. 23-60.

GONZÁLEZ , Aníbal. " 'Press clippings' and Cortázar's ethics of writing." *Julio Cortázar: New Readings*. Ed. Carlos Alonso. Cambridge and New York: Cambridge UP, 1998. 237-57.

GONZÁLEZ ECHEVARRÍA, Roberto. "The Case of the Speaking Statue: Ariel and the Magisterial Rhetoric of the Latin American Essay." *The Voice of the Masters. Writing and Authority in Modern Latin American Literature*. Austin: U of Texas P, 1985.

GRAMUGLIO, María Teresa. *El diario de Gabriel Quiroga: opiniones sobre la vida argentina*. Buenos Aires: Taurus, 2001. 9-55.

HALPERIN DONGHI, Tulio. *Historia contemporánea de América Latina*. 2 ed. Madrid: Alianza, 1970.

JÁUREGUI, Carlos A. *Canibalia: canibalismo, calibanismo, antropofagia cultural y consumo en América Latina.* Madrid / Frankfurt: Iberoamericana / Vervuert, 2008.

JITRIK, Noé. "El *Facundo*: la gran riqueza de la pobreza." *Facundo o civilización y barbarie.* 1845. Caracas: Ayacucho, 1977. IX-LII.

LEWIS, David K. *The History of Argentina.* Westport and London: Greenwood P, 2001.

MALLEA, Eduardo. *Historia de una pasión argentina.* Buenos Aires: Sudamericana, 1961.

MARSAL, Juan F., and Margery J. ARENT. *La derecha intelectual argentina. Análisis de la ideología y la acción política de un grupo de intelectuales.* Buenos Aires: Instituto Torcuato Di Tella, 1970.

ORTEGA Y GASSET, José. "Carta a un joven argentino que estudia filosofía." *Meditación del pueblo joven y otros ensayos sobre América.* Madrid: Alianza, 1981. 67-73.

QUIJADA, Mónica. *Manuel Gálvez: 60 años de pensamiento nacionalista.* Buenos Aires: Centro Editor de América Latina, 1985.

RAMA, Ángel. *La ciudad letrada.* Hanover: Ediciones del Norte, 2002.

RAMOS, Julio. *Desencuentros de la modernidad en América Latina. Literatura y política en el siglo XIX.* México: FCE, 1989.

ROCK, David. "Intellectual Precursors of Conservative Nationalism in Argentina, 1900-1927." *The Hispanic American Historical Review* 67.2 (1987): 271-300.

ROMERO, José Luis. *Latinoamérica: las ciudades y las ideas.* Colombia: Universidad de Antioquia, 1999.

SENKMAN, Leonardo. "La representación ficcional del fascismo católico en Manuel Gálvez." *Sobre nazis y nazismo en la cultura argentina.* Ed. Ignacio Klich. College Park, MD: Hispamérica, 2002. 37-50.

SHUMWAY, Nicolás. "Hispanism in an Imperfect Past and an Uncertain Present." *Ideologies of Hispanism.* Ed. Mabel Moraña. Nashville: Vanderbilt UP, 2005. 284-99.

TERÁN, Oscar. "Ideas e intelectuales en la Argentina, 1880-1980." *Ideas en el siglo. Intelectuales y cultura en el siglo XX latinoamericano.* Ed. Oscar Terán. Buenos Aires: Siglo XXI, 2004. 13-95.

—. *Positivismo y nación en la Argentina.* Buenos Aires: Puntosur, 1987.

VIDAL, Hernán. "Hacia un modelo general de la sensibilidad social literaturizable bajo el fascismo." *Fascismo y experiencia literaria: reflexiones para una recanonización.* Ed. Hernán Vidal. Minneapolis: Institute for the Study of Ideologies and Literature, 1985. 1-63.

II. National Cultures and the
Challenges of Intellectual Work

The Professor and the Worker: Using Brazil to Better Understand Latin America's Plural Left[1]

John D. French

The decade following Hugo Chávez's 1998 election in Venezuela has seen left wing leaders reach the presidencies of a multitude of South American and Central American governments: Hugo Chávez, Lula, Tabaré Vázquez, Evo Morales, Rafael Correa, Daniel Ortega, Fernando Lugo, and, most recently, Mauricio Funes in El Salvador. This marks a dramatic political shift in the region's politics after three decades that included dictatorships, neoliberal restructuring, and a fragile but real process of democratization. Contemplating this turn to the left, Max Cameron, Eric Hershberg, and Jon Beasley-Murray asked in 2009: how are we to understand the "diverse parties, movements, and leaders of the Latin American Left" who have now risen to power? Introducing a *Third World Quarterly* special issue, they emphatically insist that we must think in terms of "left turns in the plural" that stem from "a multiplicity of disparate efforts" and currents (10).

1. Thanks are due to Bret Gustafson and Mabel Moraña for bringing together a stellar interdisciplinary group of Latin Americanists for the stimulating South-by-Midwest II Symposium on "Rethinking Intellectuals in Latin America" at Washington University in St. Louis on November 7-8, 2008. Their kind invitation allowed me to deepen my thinking on key issues that began at a May 2007 conference on "Political Imaginaries in Latin America: Reverberations on the Contemporary Left" sponsored by the Latin American programs of Indiana University and the University of Michigan.

As they note, the new leftist governments are "as heterogeneous in their politics as they are in their policies" while sharing a marked distance, in all their diversity, from North Atlantic liberalism. They specifically reject efforts "to identify and differentiate [left wing] political projects through dichotomies" (320, 323-5, 329) such as "social democratic" or "populist," which contrasts with Mexican intellectual Jorge Castañeda who emphatically defends "the adequacy of a dichotomous classification for the Latin American Left" in his coedited 2008 collection entitled *Leftovers: Tales of the Latin American Left* (Castañeda and Morales, 10).[2]

Nor do Cameron, Hershberg, and Beasley-Murray present the rise of the Lefts in Latin America as inevitable responses to, backlashes against, or repudiations of, neoliberalism. As I argued about Brazil in a 2005 article, the election of Lula in 2002 "was a defeat for neoliberalism and the Washington policy consensus of 1989, but the mass popular vote for Lula was not a conscious repudiation of those policies. Thus the election of Lula was not, as some have proclaimed, a vote for an alternative to neoliberalism" (French and Fortes). More broadly, we might heed similar warnings from James Dunkerley in 2007 against "rhetorical" explanations of the rise of Evo Morales based on "a model of dichotomous relations: international neoliberals v. exploited nationals; whites v. Indians; oligarchs v. subalterns; global models v. local experiences." Such generalizations, he insisted, are yet another indication of "an evident weakness of the Left when it indiscriminately deploys the term 'neoliberal model' as if that were everywhere a beast of self-evident characteristics." Emphasizing neoliberalisms in the plural, Bolivianist geographer Thomas Perrault has correctly emphasized that Latin America has experienced no "single, unitary, monolithic neoliberalism; there are, rather multiple, often contradictory neoliberalisms" (emphasis added) that can "best be thought of not as an end product, but as a variegated and highly contested process riven with internal contradictions."[3]

2. Castañeda's 2006 article in *Foreign Affairs*, which has proven influential in the Washington-New York corridor, championed what he called a "good" social democratic Left versus a "bad" populist Left. See French ("Understanding") for a detailed and wide-ranging critique.

3. I would go further and add that neoliberalism also needs to be understood as a utopia constituted by both a political and economic imaginary; indeed, several

This chapter places the upward trajectory of the Brazilian Left over the past thirty-five years of this century into regional perspective. If we are to understand the amazing success of the Brazilian Left that has thrived under the penumbra of Lula and his Workers' Party (PT), we must attend to the Left's trajectory since the late 1970s, its moment of maximal unity in the struggles against the military regime that ruled from 1964-1985. A contrast is drawn between the two historic leaders of the Brazilian Left of the 1970s – Fernando Henrique Cardoso (the professor) and Lula (the worker) – as exemplifying the fraught relationship between the intelligentsia and the popular classes. Over the following decades, they would diverge to the point in the 1990s where FHC was the presidential architect of Brazilian neoliberalism and Lula was its most visible opponent. These developments, it argues, are directly connected to the importance of linguistic and cultural capital as markers of distinction in Brazil, a society riven by hierarchies of class, education, color, gender, and origin. It then explores the relevance of this division, as well as class and generational identification, to Lula's triumphant reelection in 2006, despite dissent among important leftist sectors. The chapter ends by placing the Brazilian case into a broader regional perspective through a comparison with the trajectory of the Chilean and Peruvian Lefts.

THE BRAZILIAN LEFT IN REGIONAL PERSPECTIVE FROM 1980 TO 2002

To talk about a rise, resurgence, or reinvention of the Left raises the issue of the point of reference against which we are asked to judge the present. The relevant historical pivot can be found in the dramatic struggles that unified so much of Latin America in 1979-1980, among them the triumph of the Nicaraguan Revolution, the revolutionary explosions in Guatemala and El Salvador, and the strikes against foreign multinationals and the Brazilian military regime that originated in the industrial suburbs of São Paulo. The unity that marked this historical conjuncture can be clearly seen in the gathering of

scholars have noted that it was the political reforms associated with neoliberalism in Latin America that opened doors (inadvertently) for the success of the very forces that are currently repudiating the word, the ideal, and the outcomes. See also Jan French.

70,000 metalworkers in the Vila Euclides stadium in São Bernardo do Campo six days after El Salvadoran Archbishop Oscar Romero was gunned down in 1980 by right wing assassins in the cathedral of his nation's capital. The Catholic Bishop of ABC (the *municípios* of Santo André, São Bernardo do Campo, and São Caetano do Sul), Dom Claudio Hummes, was among those who spoke to the rally where workers had gathered to reaffirm their decision to strike indefinitely starting the next day. As he informed the crowd, the Council of Priests in the diocese had voted to support their movement "until the end, because we believe it is just. And we place the diocese at your service in every way," including the use of our churches, resources, and staff. As the newspaper reported, Bishop Hummes also recalled the assassination of the Archbishop of San Salvador "who died precisely for defending the cause of the people. And this should encourage you all the more," he went on, "to carry your struggle through to the end." Dom Hummes then asked the workers if they would like to pray the "Our Father" with him, and thousands of hands raised stayed upright throughout the prayer as they contemplated the imponderables of what would become the most extraordinary strike in Latin American history: the workers stayed out for forty-one days despite the occupation of the region by the Army, the closing of their union, mass beatings, and the arrest of their leaders – a degree of solidarity achieved without a single picket line! *("E Veio a Greve")*.

The Latin American and Latin Americanist critical intelligentsia has tended to shy away from this moment of maximal hope and utopian imagining which was followed so quickly by a dystopian regional impact of counter-revolutionary violence, foreign intervention, and defeat. In the recent past, this period has been addressed most explicitly through the study of trauma, memory, mourning and loss (be it in Chile, Argentina, Guatemala, or El Salvador).[4] Yet such pessimistic appreciations are far less convincing in the Brazilian case. In truth, Brazilians, and those who study Brazil, cannot possibly see the history of the last quarter century in stark and pessimistic terms.[5]

---

4. As a stimulating example, one might cite the thoughtful and deeply researched recent monographs by Steve Stern (2004, 2006).

5. Even the scale of the violence in Brazil is quite different, even if summed up across the twenty-one years of military rule: no more than four hundred politically-motivated deaths and disappearances (far fewer than were killed in the Mexican

It is not that Brazil did not suffer from a dictatorship, which began with U.S. support well before and lasted longer than other Latin American military regimes (1964-1985). Nor is it that tens of millions of Brazilians, of all social classes, did not struggle for democracy or that hundreds of thousands of Brazilians did come to embrace a socialist or revolutionary horizon as part of their struggle to overthrow the rule of the generals. The difference lies in the story of what happened once the country did achieve a democratic electoral system. Despite a post-1982 debt crisis that heralded two "lost" decades in terms of sustained economic growth or substantial social progress, the political story of Brazil's new democracy has not been one of defeat or marginalization of the Left. Instead, what we have seen has been a progressive deepening and broadening of the power of Brazil's various Lefts, and this creativity has been expressed in virtually all realms of national and international life. It was not mere vanity when Lula declared, in 2000 (Da Silva), that "the PT is the most important party of the Left in the world," having grown step by step (not sixteen steps at a time, he adds) to become a powerful and influential example of a Left that succeeded (*que deu certo*). Nor need we belabor the point by referencing the Brazilian example of internal party pluralism in the PT, the established tradition of inter-party unity on the Left, or the broader social innovations that have given the world "participatory budgeting,"[6] the Movement of Landless Rural Workers (MST),[7] and the World Social Forum, beacon of the alt-globalization movement.[8]

state of Guerrero alone in the 1970s, and this in the Latin American country that generously hosted one of the largest and most active communities of Latin American exiles during these years). See *Comissão de Familiares de Mortos e Desaparecidos Políticos* [Brazil]. Such factual observations about the most extreme form of political repression neither minimizes its significance nor should it be taken to obscure the underlying structural violence and repression characteristic of the Brazilian social order (our access to political and social police records from the 1920s through the 1980s is a unique plus for scholars of Brazil). On repression's origin, ubiquity, and impact in urban labor relations, see French ("Proclamando").

6. For good English-language introductions, see Baiocchi (2003, 2005) and Nylen.

7. In a recent review ("Review of"), I have offered a succinct analysis of where the MST fits within the Brazilian political scene.

8. For an inside view of the WSF, see the short book by Brazilian *petista* José Corrêa Leite with assistance from Carolina Gil.

In a real sense, Brazil stands as the prime example of a combative and democratic organized Left party that combines mass action with institutional participation and electoral success. Thus, the Brazilian trajectory since the 1970s is quite unlike Venezuela where the organized Left barely recovered from its defeats of the mid-1960s; nor does it share a great deal with Bolivia or Peru after the end of military regimes, where the organized Left briefly achieved electoral appeal or even reached power but saw their support collapse while the Left itself was reduced to disunity, dispersal, and loss of influence. And while contemporary Brazil, unlike Argentina, has not experienced a recent social explosion like 2001-02, with its notable creativity and innovation, Brazil in the 1990s did avoid the equivalent of the deeply-rooted hegemony of the extreme neoliberal vogue called *menemismo*.[9] In truth, the Brazilian Left could be said to share more with Mexico, especially given the centrality of newly-created leftist political parties (the PRD in Mexico and the PT in Brazil) whose presidential candidates have been serious electoral contenders since 1988-1989. Of course, this is not to overlook the *suigeneris* nature of the Mexican case, not to mention the creativity and impact of EZLN, and Brazil's democratization occurred at a very different pace and chronology that was not marked by a tripartite struggle for power between a defined Left, Right, and Center, as in Mexico. And of course, the Brazilian transition itself did not occur within the context of a decaying civilian authoritarian regime that grew out of the aftermath of a social revolution of a sort that Brazil has never experienced during its two centuries of independent existence.

INTELLECTUALS AND WORKERS: DYNAMICS OF INTER-CLASS RELATIONS IN SÃO PAULO

These comparative observations may be seen as a simple reiteration of the basic truth that national histories are distinct, despite our

9. In their interpretation of the slogan "*Que se vayan todos!*", Ariel C. Armony and Victor Armony advance a provocative hypothesis about how the discourse of *Menemismo* shaped the imaginary of middle class protests in 2001-02.

propensity for broad synthetic visions of the region. Yet it is precisely here that the call for a May 2007 workshop in Bloomington, Indiana on "Political Imaginaries in Latin America: Reverberations on the Contemporary Left" asked us to "reexamine the encounters between educated militants (university students, teachers, priests) and subaltern actors in order to shed light on how each understood and transformed the other. Specifically, we seek to understand the cultural contours of the transformative, utopian vision that emerged from these encounters." This avenue of inquiry allows us to understand the upward trajectory of the Brazilian Left over the past three decades. To begin, we need to return to the emblematic images that defined the fight for democracy: the massive stadium rallies of tens of thousands of metalworkers in 1979 and 1980. The emergence of Luis Inácio Lula da Silva, Brazil's current president, as a charismatic personality of unquestioned moral authority was linked to these events when workers repeatedly struck the foreign-owned automobile assembly plants in the suburban ABC region of Greater São Paulo. These strikes not only "infused extraordinary new energy into the labor movement," as Margaret Keck has written, "but fed the image of an increasingly powerful opposition within civil society to continued military rule" (266).

For many Brazilians, the demonstration of democratic freedom in ABC was so powerful that journalists began to talk about the "Republic of São Bernardo," the one free territory in a country ruled by a feared and stifling dictatorship. Occurring at a remarkable moment of generalized societal discontent with the military regime, even in the dominant class, the unprecedented images of plebiscitary assemblies with tens of thousands of workers was projected and further generalized through a mass media whose struggles to end prior censorship only succeeded as part of the negotiated *abertura* of the regime in 1979. Thus, people's eyes and imaginations were drawn to the stadium of Vila Euclides in São Bernardo, a municipal facility never referred to by its formal name, the Costa e Silva stadium, in honor of one of Brazil's post-1964 military dictators. What they saw or imagined was a "Theater of Democracy," with one individual, the thirty-four year-old Lula, playing the lead; a figure that seemed, with the more they heard, to personify something unimaginably new and democratic.

Having argued for the central importance of inter-class alliances in my first book on São Paulo's labor history up to 1950,[10] my new book entitled *Lula's Politics of Cunning: From Trade Unionism to the Presidency* engages directly with the inter-class dialogue as it played itself out between intellectuals and workers from the 1950s through the early 1980s.[11] In particular, I explore the relationship between "the Worker" (Lula) and "the Professor" Fernando Henrique Cardoso (FHC), the two central figures of the *paulista* left in the 1970s who will, by 2010, have served for sixteen consecutive years as Brazil's presidents (1994-2010). Here, I use as my starting point the multiple attempts by FHC to narrativize his relationship with Lula starting with his two memoirs from 2006, and then dipping back in time to his book-length interviews and biographies from the 1990s. As FHC told an interviewer in 1997, at a point when the president would not have imagined that Lula would ever be his successor (he beat Lula again in 1998): "It's difficult to combat Lula. It's as if I am fighting with my own shadow. I look at him and see my own history."[12]

The story of "The Professor and the Worker" is a conflicted one that alerts us to the importance of questions of linguistic capital as markers of social class and a hierarchy of worth. It should not entirely surprise us that FHC, in a recent public talk in Massachusetts, shared a Brazilian joke about George W. and Laura Bush having lunch with Lula during their trip to Brazil; the punch line: none of the three speak Portuguese! Even in his ghostwritten U.S. autobiography, FHC insisted on noting that Lula's "grammar was atrocious," though he graciously says that it is due to Lula's lack of education, and he begrudgingly references his successor's success, in passing, as a matter of having achieved a certain worldwide "celebrity." Indeed, these mildly disdainful comments are not unrelated to FHC's putdown, in the same book, of the DOPS police agents who briefly interrogated him in 1976 (his only experience with police repres-

---

10. "The restoration of democracy in Brazil and elsewhere on the continent in the 1980s highlights the importance of social and political alliances, placing the subject at the top of Latin Americanist research agendas" (282).

11. On the creative intelligentsia's engagement – in both theater and film – with workers between 1957 and 1981, see French, ("'They Don't Wear Black-Tie:'").

12. Cited in Leoni (334).

sion): "the two thugs . . . were barely capable of speaking correct Portuguese."[13]

In 2006, FHC reports having first met Lula in his think tank's offices in 1973, when Lula was a lowly first term member of the union *diretoria* accompanying its President Paulo Vidal. Having published about workers in the early 1960s, when he was director of a newly-formed Center for Industrial and Labor Sociology at USP, FHC reports that he interviewed Lula in 1973 "as I would have any other subject, treating him almost like the subject of a social science experiment." Five years later, he reports being surprised when "Lula quite literally summoned me to meet him in his union office" in São Bernardo do Campo.[14] In his 2006 Brazilian memoir, he describes this first meeting with Lula at the union's headquarters as "shocking . . . in the perceptions of a university professor educated within traditional formalities." (Cardoso and Setti, 84). In the English version, the scene in the union hall is described as intimidating, military-like in atmosphere, and bewildering, with men rudely barking orders. "Finally, I was escorted to a small smoky office where Lula sat, squinting, behind a wooden desk. Several burly men stood menacingly behind him, their arms folded. Lula regarded me for a long moment and then got right down to business" (Cardoso and Winter 136).

This is a central scene for FHC because it is the moment that he receives the support of Lula's union for his candidacy for the Senate (he was elected alternate and assumed the position in 1983 when its holder became Governor of São Paulo). It also opens a period of twenty months in which FHC will be in consistent and ongoing contact with Lula, including participating in a sequence of meetings in 1979 that will lead to the founding of the PT. Serious consideration of "The Professor and the Worker" speaks, in other words, to substantive political questions of continuity and discontinuity in the life of Brazil's single most important and influential Marxist intellectual. Coming from a family of nationalist military men, FHC (b. 1931) was a Communist Party member in his twenties (leaving in 1956), the leader of the influential Marx seminar at USP from 1958-1964, a figure critical of President João 'Jango' Goulart from the Left in 1961-64, and coauthor with

13. Cardoso and Winter (137, 117).
14. Cardoso and Winter (*Accidental* 136).

Enzo Faletto of the foundational text of the *dependencia* approach written while in exile in Chile in the mid-1960s. Forcibly retired from USP in 1969, FHC founded the leading opposition think tank CEBRAP where he served as the military regime's most cogent intellectual critic. As Margaret Keck reminds us in her book (*The Workers Party* 44), FHC was also the first to clearly articulate a credible new opposition strategy, what would today be called "building civil society," and he did so at a discouraging low point of opposition strength in 1973, at the height of the Brazilian "economic miracle" (1968-1974).

What makes FHC's retrospective storytelling all the more compelling is its patently conflicted and contradictory nature, which reflects the difficulties FHC has experienced in articulating a clear and convincing public answer, even to himself, as to why he did not join Lula in founding the Workers' Party (PT). I explore that first decision by FHC, with its intrinsic drama, because it sheds light on a sequence of subsequent political decisions through which FHC, and the party he founded (PSDB), came to define themselves as the dominant anti-leftist and anti-Lula force across the last twenty years of Brazilian democratic politics (Lula and the PSDB candidate squared off again in 2006). While FHC's decision in 1980 could be interpreted primarily as a question of political philosophy or opposition calculation, FHC's subsequent decisions have moved him further and further down a path towards becoming something different than what he had been. And this is true despite the overlay of verbal markers of "progressiveness" that have always characterized a Brazilian intelligentsia, most often drawn towards power but always desirous of maintaining external validation and internal prestige through proclaimed affiliations with advanced European thought (as with FHC's avowed "social democratic" politics).[15]

In this sense, I offer a surprisingly restrictive geographic answer to the question posed by the organizers of the Bloomington Indiana workshop, while speaking directly to the *South by Midwest* theme on "Rethinking Intellectuals in Latin America." What is the origin and fate of the political imaginaries of the 1960s and 1970s as they bear on inter-class encounters? The answer is to be found in the capital of São Paulo, a state with thirty five million residents, or, put most baldly and half-jestingly, the story of the past three decades of Brazilian politics can

---

15. This theme is more fully explored in French (2004).

be told in terms of what happened in the factories and union in ABC and the halls of the University of São Paulo. Indeed, it's by no means an irrelevant detail that the presidential candidate of the PSDB who Lula defeated in 2002, a one-time Maoist named José Serra, was a former student leader from USP. Not only that, but Serra's election as president of the National Union of Students in 1963 took place in the auditorium of the Santo André metalworkers union hosted by Marcos Andreotti, Lula's Communist trade union predecessor in ABC (French 2010).

In terms of USP (Brazil's equivalent of Harvard, Princeton, and Yale wrapped up in one in terms of prestige), the story can be narrowed further to a tale about the emergence of the new discipline of sociology in a department that produced FHC and a host of radical students who swarmed to São Paulo's factories (whether to study them or colonize them as radical missionaries). Moreover, several generations of scholarship on industrial workers in São Paulo came out of the USP sociology department as successive cohorts of intellectuals passed through various political conjunctures and styles of Marxist analysis between the mid-1950s and the early 1980s. Although the story has many levels of complexity, FHC's role retains its centrality in posing the biggest issues about "us and the other." Interviewed in 1971 by U.S. sociologist Joseph Kahl, FHC was quoted as saying: "The intellectuals in Latin America are important because they are the voices of those who cannot speak for themselves. Unlike the 'bureaucrats and politicians' who speak for the state, intellectuals can take a broader view and study poor people and their lives with the aim of discovering: 'What are the real possibilities for change, seen from the point of view of the people without power?'" (179).[16] Or, as FHC and his ghost writer (Cardoso and Winter 34) put it in his description of Lula's origin for his U.S. readers, what might it have been like to be part of "Brazil's neglected masses"? Or to have been "exposed [as was Lula] to the darkest, most hideous side of Brazilian poverty"?

So let us turn to the rural subaltern world from which tens of millions, including Lula and his family, migrated in search of a better life in the last fifty years. Lula was born in the rural *mestiço* hinterlands of Pernambuco, one of the historic centers of slaveholding northeastern

16. Kahl chose FHC's quote about the role of the intellectuals as the dedication of the book.

Brazil. Along with his mother and six of his seven siblings, Lula made a two-week trek southwards on the back of a truck, a ride so uncomfortable that it is known as the *pau de arara*, or parrot's perch (also the name for a particularly vile and well-established form of torture by Brazilian police). The destination of Lula's family was the jobs and hope that beckoned in São Paulo, where Lula was soon hustling for work in the streets.[17]

Given the significance of education as a marker for social class distinction in Brazil, it is important to contextualize Lula's level of educational achievement. Although Lula went part of a fifth year before dropping out to work, his profile was characteristic of the vast majority of the children of *paulista* workers who finished most if not all of the four years of primary school. As a researcher, I am lucky that in 1958 a USP sociologist undertook a rich ethnographic study of a primary school in a working class neighborhood in ABC, very close to where Lula's family lived at the same time (Pereira). Coming at a moment of stupendous in-migration and population growth, the state's public school system was entering into a downward spiraling crisis. Thus it is very likely that Lula, like the working class kids Luis Pereira studied, got, on average, only three of the four hours of daily instruction mandated by the state. The middle class teachers, who lived far away from the industrial frontier in ABC, felt disdain and prejudice towards their students, most of them the children of migrants, especially those from Minas and the Northeast who were most likely, like Lula, to be *mestiço* in origin and often black or brown in skin color. The teachers' performance was marked by frequent late arrivals, early departures, and a preference for gossiping together during class time, even putting aside the fact that so many regularly failed to show up to teach. Among the sharpest conflicts with the parents, or at least a tiny minority that was not entirely submissive (egged on by a local populist radio agitator turned politician), was their infliction of corporal punishment, although banned.

The figure of Lula thus stood in a very specific relationship to the racial, regional and educational hierarchies of a changing São Paulo, a city that was ninety percent white and overwhelmingly of European immigrant stock when he first arrived in the early 1950s. Like other

17. For wonderful extended interviews with Lula and his extended family, consult Paraná.

northeastern migrants, Lula was exposed to a barrage of racialized regionalist abuse, even in the factories where outright racism was common for those who were darker skinned. Indeed, even one of Lula's nicknames was *"Baiano,"* the ubiquitous racist label applied by Paulistas in an effort to stigmatize northeasterners by identifying them with the blackest state of their region, Bahia.

An important element of Lula's emerging appeal involved his ability to project elements of the private and the personal centrally into the public sphere where they gain a different valence. And here, the analysts can draw on the wealth of recent studies on gender and race, because their lives were shaped by the multiple hierarchies of subordination to which Brazil's working people were subjected, and to which they were subjected themselves. This points to a fundamental operative element of a gendered working class praxis and discourse: *fazendo-se respeitar*, which can be translated as "making yourself respected," the masculine ideal of imposing oneself in a violently hierarchical world that diminishes you and your manhood. Hence, the power that a discourse of dignity, the *resgate da dignidade* (the rescue or ransom of dignity), could play; indeed, this discursive element featured powerfully in Lula's discourse from the 1970s until today. And although Lula, like most of his fellow workers, never complained about his personal mistreatment (we're winners not whiners), the experience of a constantly reinforced social and cultural subalternization built up layers of resentment that would, in the end, find expression during the strikes when Lula's most aggressive oratory pledged, "we've been fucked over! We're going to apply the rod (*metendo pau*) to the bosses and the government! We're going to bring them to their knees!"

The end of the line of this thirty-year duet between USP intellectuals and São Paulo workers comes when a generation of Paulista intellectuals in the late 1970s, along with a handful from earlier generations, finally realized that it was time to listen![18] And thus was born a different configuration, and a new and different Left within the middle classes that was more socially open, less hidebound to past hierarchies of distinction, and more open to the idea that one might mix easily with and, more importantly, take leadership from those who do not

18. The landmark work of this leftist rethinking was by a veteran Marxist-Leninist New Left intellectual and former exile, Eder Sáder (1941-1988).

have your degrees, your vocabulary, or your conceptual universe of advanced Marxist thought. The time was coming to an end when a courageous intellectual opponent of the military regime, as late as 1994, famously declared that the choice in the election between FHC and Lula was a no-brainer: "You can vote for Jean Paul Sartre or you can vote for a plumber" (Medeiros 81-82).[19]

And what about the workers, or at least a worker (Lula), who had found his voice and managed to impose himself upon his superiors ("*fazendo-se respeitar*" in working class terminology)? The answer given would be to deny victimhood and reject the paternalistic condescension of social superiors that still marked FHC and other members of the educated elite in 2006 (indeed, I argue that Lula's heightened sensitivity to any hint of social superiority, once he gained a semblance of power, would play a key role in the unfolding of his subsequent political trajectory). Interviewed by Brazilian *Playboy* in August 2006, FHC was especially impatient in his criticism of Lula's failure to be a statesman, his lack of dignity, his populist traces. On the question of higher education, he sounded a condemnatory note based on a profoundly old-fashioned but deeply ingrained discourse of social superiority:

> You don't have to be a *doutor* [college graduate] to be the president of the Republic, but you also don't have to be an 'apologist' for ignorance, you needn't preach ignorance. It is better to have information, to have the capacity to form good judgments. I think that Brazilian society has had a certain tolerance with rusticness. The coarser [*bruto*] the better. . . [But] we live in a civilized society. The ideal is not to be coarse. It is the opposite: it is to be polished ("Fernando Henrique...").

HOPE, IDENTIFICATION, AND CRITIQUE: THE SUBALTERN, THE BRAZILIAN LEFTS, AND THE LULA GOVERNMENT

In 2009, the Brazilianist historian Joseph Love (305) asked: "In what ways does the Lula government represent a break with the past?" He began by noting that there are

---

19. The reference to Sartre is specific to FHC's biography since the young Marxist, having just returned from Paris, served as translator for Sartre and Simone de Beauvoir during their 1960 visit to São Paulo.

"many unique features of the Lula administration, beginning with the person of the President: He is the first head of state of a Latin American nation, and one of only a handful in world history, who can claim to be genuine members of the working class. Lula, moreover, has had less formal education than any previous president of Brazil, and is possibly – I emphasize this is conjecture – the least Caucasian president since Nilo Pecanha (1909-10)."

How does the combination of triply stigmatized features – manual labor, lack of education, and symbolic blackening (whether biological or in terms of his northeastern rural background) – play out in the politics of Lula's presidency? The dynamics of this symbolic and generational politics is well-captured by the 2005 documentary "Lula's Brazil: The Management of Hope," shot two years into Lula's first presidential term, by Uruguayan filmmaker Gonzalo Arijón. Elected in 2002, the former trade unionist maintained the neoliberal economic policies he had long opposed, including a fiscal austerity that precluded an immediate increase in social expenditures. By the time this 62-minute color film was released, Lula's administration had been devastated by a disgraceful 2005 corruption scandal that led to a barrage of resignations, talk of presidential impeachment, and a major drop in Lula's personal popularity. Rather than rendering the film irrelevant, subsequent developments underline its prescience in capturing the dynamics that led to Lula's stunning re-election in 2006 with 61% of the valid run-off vote.

So wherein does one find the hope referenced by the film's title? The answer begins to emerge when Chico Whitaker, one of the Brazilian architects of the World Social Forum (WSF), describes the extraordinary hope at Lula's 2003 inauguration as an emotion so powerful as to be painful. Sticking close to Lula's rhetoric, Brazil is described as a nation sundered by violent inequalities with 50 million at the top, fully integrated into the modern capitalist system, and 140 million poor on the bottom. Making use of Lula's campaign ads, Brazil is described not as a poor country but as a country with many poor people, while Lula declares that hunger is the result not of a lack of food but of a lack of shame on the part of those who govern the country.

From this opening, the film retraces Lula's personal trajectory while giving center stage to a dozen humble and eloquent voices from that "other Brazil, Lula's Brazil." We hear from the legendary cook at the São Bernardo metalworkers union, where Lula led famous strikes between 1978-1980, as well as from Gilberto dos Santos Souza, a rank-and-file autoworker and PT-member of African descent. Their words provide clear evidence of a powerful sense of identification that is bound up with Lula's origin in the misery of rural Pernambuco, where the film starts, through his migration to the big industrial city of São Paulo and eventual election as the country's first working class president. In Lula's hometown, we meet his cousin Antonio de Mello Ferreira (Lula's anti-hunger program 'is little but it helps,' he says) and accompany health workers who visit the homes of the rural poor to weigh malnourished children as part of the government's Zero Hunger campaign.

The film then moves to São Paulo where we visit squatters (*sem teto*) who have taken over an abandoned apartment building; families who mix struggle, resignation, and hope for their children while being helped by the government's hunger grants. It is in São Paulo, where so many millions flocked at mid-century, that Lula entered into the lowest part of the top 50 million as a worker in modern industry. After visiting the Daimler-Chrysler factory, we witness an extended barroom discussion among metalworkers who are proud that "one of their own" is running the country and doing so competently despite the predictions of economic disaster before his election. As they weigh their political disappointment against the fragility of hope, they show an acute awareness of the constraints on government action ('he'd like to move quickly but Brazilian voters didn't give him a congressional majority'). We then follow them on a march to Brasília for a minimum wage increase, a demand only partly met; at least this time, Gilson says, the police didn't beat us up and we marched right in to meet the president (we see their hearty exchange of hugs and greetings); besides, Lula promised to make up the rest of the increase before the end of his term.

The film then turns to the rural dimension of the balancing act involved with managing a country. It juxtaposes the critical views of rank-and-file members of the landless workers movement with those of large landowners who, as Whitaker notes, may not be part of Lula's base of support but whose fire power certainly cannot be ignored by the president. One landowner notes that Lula has been reasonable, lighting one candle to capitalism and one to socialism, but the government should stop nitpicking because Brazil's economy is sustained by the trade surpluses generated by Brazilian agribusiness; family farming may be a social priority, but it certainly is not an economic one.

The film thus sets up its overall objective: to "gauge the long and bumpy path ahead, a narrow path where hope and economic interests often clash." But is it really possible to "manage" hope under these tight constraints? Here, the film expresses the mature, critical, and balanced judgment that characterized the Brazilian Left in the middle of Lula's first term. We hear Frei Betto, a famous liberation theologian, who explains that one cannot demand results as if Lula had led a revolution when all he did was win an election, which allows at best for the conquest of small parcels of power. While recognizing Lula's limited space for maneuvering, Frei Betto expresses the hope that Lula will know how to conduct the process of change through paths unfamiliar to the Left. So here the film presents us with hope as trust in a politician to whom you are bound deeply, powerfully, and personally. While not abandoning radical desire, the mainstream of Brazil's Left understood that hope is something that cannot be allowed to be lost in a political war of maneuver. In the words of WSF (World Social Forum) leader Candido Grzyowski, Lula's government would do better if it were subject to more pressure from social movements paralyzed in the face of a government protected by its image. Or as Whitaker explains, 'a political victory helps. It is necessary but it is not the answer to our problems. We are all co-responsible for this government' and 'our civil society has to mobilize to confront this monster of inequality, and that development would be welcomed by Lula.'

The film also shows us the anger of disappointed hope when Lula spoke at the January 2005 WSF in Porto Alegre. Having been cheered in 2003, Lula's return is met by steady booing from a significant sector of the stadium audience who call him a "traitor" while chanting "Lula, how sad, a worker governing for the elites." This frustrated leftist hope would turn to rage, after the film was shot, when it became clear in mid-2005 that the PT was "just like any other party" in Brazil's notoriously corrupt political system. Indeed, the defections of voters furthest to the left frustrated Lula's effort to clinch his second term in the first round of the election on October 1, 2006. He fell short of the required 50% because nine million Brazilians, 9.5% of valid votes, gave their support to two politicians who had exited the PT in harsh protest against the government's inadequacies.[20]

Yet this WSF scene illustrates the complicated dynamics of hope since his critics are demanding an end to hope's betrayal and not all in the stadium are booing. Once Lula gets up to speak, we see the effectiveness of politics as embodied work done with words. In the face of hostile chants, Lula declares that hunger is a political and not a social problem, and criticizes Brazilians for looking northwards to Europe and the United States, and turning its back not only on South America but on Africa. "We are the second largest Black country after Nigeria," the Brazilian president declares, and this takes even his hecklers by surprise. As he reviews Brazil's leadership in the fight against the World Trade Organization, the applause grows as Lula's ends with his trademark "I am from a poor state, Pernambuco, and whoever doesn't die by the age of five is an untiring fighter." When next shown, Lula is on a panel at the Davos World Economic Forum with Bill Gates, where he is unceremoniously cut off after calling for hunger's elimination through an international campaign to be financed by a Tobin tax or a tax on arms sales.

From the depths of disappointment, despair, and anger in 2005, Lula swept the 2006 elections by building on the forms of hope captured in this movie: as identification, concrete benefits, faith, pragmatic calculation, and even hope as betrayal. Having seen Zero Hunger stumble, Lula's replacement *Bolsa Família* program was effectively and thoroughly implanted by 2006, with 11.1 million families receiving its benefits (he swept the poorest regions with 60-85% of the vote). Even the real value of the minimum wage was increased by a quarter in 2006 compared to 2002, as promised. And when leftist anger frustrated his first round victory, Lula not only won back those nine million votes, but even gained two and a half million from the first round total of his opponent (Hunter and Power). Lula, the untiring fighter, had once again won and, in his second term, faces the even stiffer challenge of growing hope as well as managing it.

20. For a persuasive analysis of those sectors of the Left that turned against Lula and the PT, see Fortes.

CONCLUSION

With a leadership born out of Latin America's most extraordinary strikes in 1979-1980, Lula went on to play a central role in the construction of a new trade union confederation, the CUT with 22 million current members, and founded an entirely new Workers' Party (the PT) that currently has a million members (at the height of the crisis in 2005, 400,000 PT members voted in the internal elections of a new party leadership). As early as 1990, political scientists of Latin America were well-aware that the PT represents a *sui generis* political experiment, a unique "mutational experience" in the words of Torcuato di Tella, whose success was likely to have a wide impact. Writing in 1998, the year Chávez was first elected, Kenneth Roberts was attentive to the centrality of the Brazilian Workers' Party experience to understanding the Lefts that were the focus of his monograph *Deepening Democracy?: The Modern Left and Social Movements in Chile and Peru.*

In characterizing the PT, Roberts judged the party to be what he called an organic rather than electoralist party of the Left, given its emergence from popular insurgencies and social movements and with a leadership drawn directly from them. The result, he suggests, is a "more open, inclusive, and pluralistic" structure with greater democratic participation at the grassroots" (75). In comparing the PT with the Peruvian PUM and the Chilean CP, Roberts notes that these vanguardist formations, despite having incorporating popular sector insurgencies into their ranks, had proven unable to "translate their strength in civil society into sustainable electoral success" after the end of authoritarian rule, unlike the "more 'organic' and heterogeneous Workers Party" in Brazil (271). The bridging of the divide between movement-parties and electorally-successful parties that occurred in Brazil, he suggested, is facilitated when "these organized social constituencies become linked to charismatic leaders with broad appeal, creating a hybrid between the organic model and the populist electoral model." Capable of aggregating "diverse and often atomized popular interests," the challenge is to avoid slipping into top-down "forms of mobilization that engender hierarchical control or displace the autonomous protagonism of organized popular sectors (76)."

The PT was central to the general reflections that Roberts offered on "the project of the Left as Latin America prepares to enter the twenty-first century." Contemplating the praxis of Latin American leftist parties under the "transnational neoliberal model of capitalist development," Roberts suggested that whatever emerged from such [leftist] experiments would differ markedly from social democracy as it has traditionally been conceived in Western Europe. More likely than a model of social democracy, with its tradition of centralized social and political organization and top-down reform, would be a process of decentralized bottom-up reform that would potentially build from municipal to national levels of power (276-77)." Having correctly identified the municipal path to power being pioneered during the 1990s by the PT in Porto Alegre, the *Frente Amplio* in Montevideo, and the PRD in Mexico City, he noted the PT's "conscious efforts to find political mechanisms that build bridges between diverse social movements and community organizations," as with participatory budgeting, while maintaining closer and more organic connection to organized labor. "The combination of effective political articulation and an organic party-society relationship has allowed the Brazilian Left to avoid the radical disjuncture between social movement and electoral strength that one finds in the Left in Peru and Chile, where vanguardist and electoralist orientations have predominated (277-78)." Perhaps, as we speak, the PT and its Latin American counterparts may have lessons to offer the U.S. as it contemplates a turn to the Left in a new post-neoliberal world.

WORKS CITED

ARIJÓN, Gonzalo. *Lula's Brazil: The Management of Hope*. Paris: Dissidents & Arte France. Distributed by First Run/Icarus Films, New York, 2005.

ARMONY, Ariel C. and Victor Armony. "Indictments, Myths, and Citizen Mobilization in Argentina: A Discourse Analysis." *Latin American Politics and Society* 47.4 (2004): 40-2, 46.

BAIOCCHI, Gianpaolo, ed. *Radicals in Power: The Workers' Party (PT) and Experiments in Urban Democracy in Brazil*. London, New York: Zed, 2003.

—. *Militants and Citizens: The Politics of Participatory Democracy in Porto Alegre*. Stanford: Stanford UP, 2005.

CAMERON, Maxwell A., Jon Beasley-Murray, and Erick Hershberg. "Latin American Left Turns: An Introduction." *Third World Quarterly* 30.2 (2009): 319-330.

CARDOSO, Fernando Henrique and Brian Winter. *The Accidental President of Brazil: A Memoir*. New York: Public Affairs, 2006.

CARDOSO, Fernando Henrique, and Ricardo A. Setti. *A Arte Da Política : A História Que Vivi*. Rio de Janeiro: Civilização Brasileira, 2006.

CASTANEDA, Jorge C. "Latin America's Left Turn." *Foreign Affairs* 85.3 (2006): 28-43

CASTAÑEDA, Jorge, and Marco A. Morales, eds. *Leftovers: Tales of the Latin American Left*. New York/London: Routledge, 2008.

COMISSÃO DE FAMILIARES DE MORTOS E DESAPARECIDOS POLÍTICOS [Brazil]. *Dossiê dos Mortos e Desaparecidos Políticos a Partir de 1964*. Recife: Companhia Editora de Pernambuco, Governo do Estado de Pernambuco, 1995.

CORRÊA LEITE, José, with assistance from Carolina Gil. *World Social Forum: Strategies of Resistance*. Translated by Traci Romine. Chicago, IL: Haymarket Books, 2005.

DA SILVA, Luis Inácio 'Lula'. "Lula: Somos O Mais Importante Partido de Izquerda No Mundo." *Caros Amigos* (2000).

DI TELLA, Torcuato S. *Latin American Politics: A Theoretical Framework*. Austin: U of Texas P, 1990.

DUNKERLY, James. "Evo Morales, the 'Two Bolivias' and the Third Bolivian Revolution." *Journal of Latin American Studies* 39 (2007): 141-42.

"E VEIO A GREVE: Uma Decisão Aprovada Por 82 Mil Metalúrgicos." *Jornal da Tarde*, 31 March 1980.

"FERNANDO HENRIQUE CARDOSO: Uma Conversa Franca com o Ex-Presidente [Entrevista Concedida a Reporter Fernando Barros de Mello e Edson Aran, Diretor de Redação]," *Playboy: A Revista do Homen [São Paulo, Brazil]*, 11 August 2006, 73-91.

FORTES, Alejandro. "In Search of a Post-Neoliberal Paradigm: The Brazilian Left and Lula's Government." *International Labor and Working-Class History* 75 (2009): 109-25.

FRENCH, Jan Hoffman. "Ethnoracial Identity, Multiculturalism, and Neoliberalism in the Brazilian Northeast." *Beyond Neoliberalism in Latin America? Societies and Politics at the Crossroads*, Ed. John Burdick, Kenneth M. Roberts, and Philip Oxhorn. New York: Palgrave Macmillan, 2009. 101-113.

FRENCH, John D. "How the Not-So-Powerless Prevail: Industrial Labor Market Demand and the Contours of Militancy in Mid-Twentieth Century São Paulo, Brazil." *Hispanic American Historical Review* 90.1(2010), 109-142.

—. "Proclamando Direitos, Metendo O Pau, e Lutando Pelos Direitos: A Questão Social Como Caso de Polícia, 1920-1964." *Direitos e Justiças No*

Brasil: Ensaios de História Social. Eds. Silvia Hunold Lara and Joseli Mendonça. Campinas: Editora da UNICAMP, 2006. 379-416.

—. *Drowning in Laws: Labor Law and Brazilian Political Culture*. Chapel Hill: U of North Carolina P, 2004.

—. "Review of *To Inherit the Earth: The Landless Movement and the Struggle for a New Brazil* by Angus Wright and Wendy Wolford (Oakland: Food First Books, 2003)." *Labor: Studies in Working Class History of the Americas* 4.1 (2007): 141-43.

—. "Understanding the Politics of Latin America's Plural Lefts (Chávez/Lula): Social Democracy, Populism, and Convergence on the Path to a Post-Neoliberal World." *Third World Quarterly* 30.2 (2009): 349-70.

—. *The Brazilian Workers' ABC: Class Conflicts and Alliances in Modern São Paulo*. Chapel Hill: U of North Carolina P, 1992.

—. "'They Don't Wear Black-Tie:'" Intellectuals and Workers in Modern São Paulo, 1958-1981." *International Labor and Working-Class History* 59 (2001): 60-80.

FRENCH, John D. and Alexandre FORTES. "Another World Is Possible: The Rise of the Brazilian Workers' Party and the Prospects for Lula's Government." *Labor: Studies in Working Class History of the Americas* 2.3 (2005): 23-4.

HUNTER, Wendy and Timothy J. POWER. "Rewarding Lula: Executive Power, Social Policy, and the Brazilian Elections of 2006." *Latin American Politics and Society* 49.1 (2007): 1-30.

KAHL, Joseph A. *Three Latin American Sociologists: Gino Germani, Pablo Gonzales Casanova, Fernando Henrique Cardoso*. Rutgers: Transaction Books, 1988.

KECK, Margaret E. "The New Unionism in the Brazilian Transition." *Democratizing Brazil: Problems of Transition and Consolidation*. Ed. Alfred Stepan. New York: Oxford UP, 1989.

—. *The Workers Party and Democratization in Brazil*. New Haven: Yale UP, 1992.

LEONI, Brigitte Hersant. *Fernando Henrique Cardoso: O Brasil do Possível*. Translated by Dora Rocha. Rio de Janeiro: Editora Nova Fronteira, 1997.

LOVE, Joseph L. "The Lula Government in Historical Perspective." *Brazil under Lula: Economy, Politics, and Society under the Worker-President*. Ed. Joseph Love and Werner Baer. New York: Palgrave Macmillan, 2009.

MEDEIROS, Alexandre. *Nos Bastidores da Campanha: Luiz Inácio Lula da Silva. Crônica de Um Sonho*. Rio de Janeiro: Editora Objetiva, 1994.

NYLEN, William R. *Participatory Democracy Versus Elitist Democracy: Lessons from Brazil*. New York: Palgrave Macmillan, 2003.

PARANÁ, Denise. *Lula, O Filho do Brasil. Edição Revista e Ampliada.* São Paulo: Editora Perseu Abramo, 2002.

PEREIRA, Luiz. *A Escola Num Área Metropolitana: Crise e Racionalização de Uma Empresa Pública de Serviços.* São Paulo: Pioneira, 1965.

PERRAULT, Thomas. "From the Guerra Del Agua to the Guerra Del Gas: Resource Governance, Neoliberalism, and Popular Protest in Bolivia." *Antipode* 38.1 (2006): 150-172.

ROBERTS, Kenneth M. *Deepening Democracy?: The Modern Left and Social Movements in Chile and Peru.* Stanford: Stanford UP, 1998.

SÁDER, Eder. *Quando Novos Personagens Entraram em Cena: Experiências e Lutas dos Trabalhadores Da Grande São Paulo, 1970-1980.* Rio de Janeiro: Paz e Terra, 1988.

STERN, Steve. *Remembering Pinochet's Chile on the Eve of London 1998: Vol. 1.* Durham: Duke UP, 2004.

—. *Battling for Hearts and Minds: Memory Struggles in Pinochet's Chile, 1973-1988.* Durham: Duke UP, 2006.

Cosmopolitan Theory and Anthropological Practice in Brazil

Jan Hoffman French

In relation to the theme of this volume – to inquire into transformations marked by knowledge-making projects and the role played by intellectuals – in this chapter I will focus on Brazilian anthropologists. In considering how impoverished or marginalized communities become integrated into global claims about the human condition, I analyze the efforts of Brazilian anthropologists on behalf of rural black communities in the northeastern backlands in light of cosmopolitan theory.

This chapter is based on research I conducted in Sergipe, the smallest state in Brazil and the northern neighbor of Bahia. Until 1823, Sergipe was part of Bahia, although in early colonial days it had been a captaincy in its own right. Even today there are some who believe that parts of Bahia should belong to Sergipe. In true boundary-setting practice, *sergipanos* insist that they are not like *baianos*. However, like Bahia, Sergipe shares an important geographic reality, a rainy coastal area, best-suited for sugar cane production, and a semi-arid interior, known as the *sertão*, where cattle raising is predominant. I carried out ethnographic research in the *sergipano* sertão not far from the point where Bahia, Sergipe, and Pernambuco converge. It was here that a large-scale messianic movement – the Canudos movement – arose and was then destroyed by government troops at the end of the 19th century.

It is also the region where the famous bandit Lampião and his band were captured and beheaded in 1938.

What follows is part of a larger book project about this region in which I develop a model for understanding how law can work to instigate revisions in ethnoracial identity and cultural practices. I focus on the two neighboring communities of the Xocó Indians and Quilombo Mocambo. Each was recognized and provided land within the last thirty years, the Xocó in 1979 under the Indian Statute of 1973 (full land title received in 1991) and Mocambo in 1997 under the 1988 Constitution's *quilombo* clause (full land title received in 2000).[1] My work addresses the ways that, in a place with many African-descended people, in a state that is largely nonwhite, these two *sertanejo* communities have asserted distinctive identities and rights to land. I am also interested in how they have succeeded with the crucial assistance of a number of forces, including NGOs, government lawyers, Catholic Church and political activists, and, most importantly for this chapter, anthropologists.

"COSMOPOLITAN HOPE" AND ANTHROPOLOGICAL PRACTICE

When I mention cosmopolitan theory to U.S. anthropologists I am generally told, "Anthropologists have always been cosmopolitan. So what's new?" Yet as I began to delve into the literature on cosmopolitanism, it occurred to me that the anthropologists I was talking to were referring to a preanalytic understanding of the concept. In the general sense, anthropologists from the global North travel and do their research at a variety of sites, speak multiple languages, and although traditionally concerned with cultural specificity and, more recently, with group rights, they have always debated and worked to reconcile that ostensible Boasian legacy with a universalistic concept

---

1. The *Quilombo* Clause (Transitory Article 68) provides that descendants/remnants (*remanescentes*) of *quilombo* (runaway slave/maroon) communities occupying their lands are recognized as owners, and the State shall issue them titles to the land. Consequently, the shortcut "*quilombo*" is used to designate a descendant of fugitive slave community, although technically there are no existing *quilombos*, since slavery was abolished in 1888.

of human rights (Engle). For example, there have been a number of recent attempts to resurrect the universalist aspects of Boas's career (see, e.g. Bunzl; Orta). Brazilian anthropologist Alcida Ramos ("Disengaging" 480) critiques these attempts with a sharp reproach that selective *ex post facto* readings of Boas's popular writings are being proposed now to show that "what for so many years lay dormant in the folds of anthropological memory, submerged by successive waves of theoretical novelties, reemerges as ancestral wisdom with the potential to rescue the discipline from a pending impasse." In a more fine-tuned analysis of the universalism of Boas, in this case in the context of the "failure of vernacular cosmopolitanisms," Charles Briggs (76, 78, 91) productively reflects on "the problem with Boas's notion of culture" which he states "lies not in its isolation from a broader critique of state and racial power," but rather "how [Boas] positioned 'culture' in relation to consciousness, science, colonialism, and cosmopolitanism" echoing through his commitment to rationality and modernity what Briggs calls "purifying practices."

Here I would like to investigate the role of anthropologists in *quilombo* and Indian recognitions in light of cosmopolitan theory. As such, I will focus on a theoretical development that might assist us in understanding the collaborative nature of, and the nature of collaboration in, the production of new ethnoracial identities in northeastern Brazil. New interest in theorizing cosmopolitanism in relation to anthropology has led to a burgeoning of literature (see e.g. Briggs; Friedman; Kahn; Kuper; Marsden; Notar; Tsing; Werbner) and the development of "Cosmopolitan Studies" as a field. For example, the St. Andrews' Social Anthropology department has a Center for Cosmopolitan Studies, and Keele University sponsored a high-level conference on cosmopolitanism and anthropology in 2006. Beth Notar provides a condensed history of cosmopolitanism from the Stoics through Kant to a revival in the 19th century and to a Hannah Arendt's vision of "a revival of cosmopolitan ideals as a way...to guard against the extreme fascism of WWII" (620). Most recently, the re-emergence of cosmopolitanism "as a topic of interdisciplinary study" may be seen as an "intellectual response to the perceived political dangers of isolationism, nationalism, [and] factionalism" (620). In its current permutation, cosmopolitanism is seen as a "continuous openness to the world" and a "capacity to interact across cultural lines" (618).

Moreover, Dorothy Hodgson (225) in a point particularly relevant to my field site sees a "dynamic relationship between cosmopolitan political projects such as the indigenous peoples' movement and the nation-states in which participants are inevitably located." In other words, what anthropologists have begun to discover is that backlanders in far reaches of the world are becoming cosmopolitans without going anywhere and that construction of new ethnoracial identities are an integral part of their cosmopolitanism.

A related trend that has attracted a fair amount of attention in U.S. anthropology is an interest in advancing a "critically engaged activist" practice (Hale; Speed), in its most sophisticated form. However, I believe that recent concerns with anthropological activism have short-circuited a full discussion of the role that requirements of "authentic" culture play in perpetuating an assumed dichotomy between cosmopolitanism (in its negative Bushite militaristic permutation [Briggs 94] or its positive universal human rights representation) and cultural specificity (in its negative relativistic version or its positive liberal multiculturalism variety). It is my goal to demonstrate that Brazilian anthropologists together with *quilombolas*[2] seeking government (and international) recognition are together constructing a form of cosmopolitanism that links universal expectations associated with human rights and an activist vision and politics of the Black Atlantic that draws on "subaltern cosmopolitan legality" (Santos and Rodríguez).

Boaventura de Souza Santos (Santos, "Toward;" Santos and Rodríguez Garavito) helps us understand cosmopolitanism in its counter-hegemonic form, as "animated by a redistributive ethos in its broadest sense, involving redistribution of material, social, political, cultural, and symbolic resources" (Santos and Rodríguez Garavito 29). For this, he explains, we need "alternative principles of law and politics" that "combine political mobilization with legal mobilization" (30). In fact, "subaltern cosmopolitan legality views law and rights as elements of struggles that need to be politicized before they are legalized" (16). This is an aspect of cosmopolitan theory particularly suited for analyzing the extraordinary story of *quilombo* recognitions in Brazil. For

2. *Quilombolas* are residents of *quilombos* who have been recognized as being descended from fugitive slaves, although often being "black" is sufficient.

these reasons, I believe it is useful to focus on scholars centered in the global South so we are able to conceptualize a more processual and less polarized meaning of "cosmopolitan anthropology" (Werbner) often viewed as a practice principally tethered to travel (Clifford).

I will not rehearse the political philosophical discussions of the Kantian foundations of cosmopolitanism as world citizenship which entails subjecting all relations to the test of uncoerced interaction and impartial reason. Rather, in what follows I will point out insights from that field which might serve as a gateway to the application of cosmopolitan theory to anthropology and move us toward a reinterpretation of the practices and political commitments of Brazilian anthropologists (cf. Hemming; Pacheco de Oliveira; Peirano 1985, 1998; Ramos 1990, 2000, 2008; Velho). David Held (18-20), for example, has developed a "layered cosmopolitan perspective" that "lays down the universal or regulative principles which delimit and govern the range of diversity and difference that ought to be found in public life." In a Habermasian move, Held builds on principles that all can "reasonably" assent to, "while recognizing the irreducible plurality of forms of life." Disagreeing with a "strong" form of cosmopolitanism he associates with Martha Nussbaum, in which special relationships (or loyalties) to family, kin, nation can never be justified, Held's layered perspective draws instead on a "weak" form, drawing on the work of Michael Walzer, asserting that while each person stands in "an ethically significant relation" to all other people, this is only one source of responsibility (17). In fact, Held asserts, cosmopolitan principles are compatible with recognition of different "spheres" or "layers" of moral reasoning.

Adopting Held's "layered" perspective allows us to consider how national laws might advance cosmopolitan values (and vice versa) in practice. Catriona McKinnon's explication of "cosmopolitan hope" provides a theoretical bridge to understanding the role of many Brazilian anthropologists in advancing a cosmopolitan project together with their interlocutors who live in villages in the backlands of the Northeast. McKinnon (236) tells us that cosmopolitans hope for "the extension of commitments to justice at the domestic level...to the global level." However, they do not hope in the colloquial sense of the word, but rather theirs is a "specific hope" or perhaps more accurately, a practical hope, by which is generated "a disposition to act so as to make the realization of hope's objective more probable whenever possible," which also involves a belief that an objective is "physically possible" (237, 238). In a similar vein, Catherine Lu (264) explains that a cosmopolitan ethic requires not only an acknowledgment of the humanity of others, but also intervention "against active and passive injustice," thus making "difficult but possible demands" on those dedicated to its ethic.

It is my contention that a requirement of "authenticity" for government recognition is an impediment to a collaborative production of cosmopolitanism, as envisioned by Santos and Rodríguez Garavito, Held, McKinnon, and Lu. To that end, a key point that emerges from my research is that recognition proceedings in Brazil no longer require proof of cultural or historical "authenticity." In the cases of the over forty indigenous tribal recognitions in northeastern Brazil since the early 1970s, anthropological expert reports that explicitly reflect the constructed nature of ethnic and cultural identities have not impeded recognition. With respect to *quilombos*, although the media and public have often associated the *quilombo* movement with 'African' cultural practices, proof of connections to 'Africa' have not been required for recognition (French "Buried Alive"). Perhaps even more important, historical proof of descent from runaway slaves, after an initial set of objections by some scholars (e.g. Price), has not been required since the mid-1990s, and in fact has been eschewed (French "Dancing"). In my view, adherence to the necessity for authenticity is the primary impediment to developing a fruitful, alternative cosmopolitan project (French "Legalizing"). I assert this in spite of the attraction that Gayatri Spivak's "strategic essentialism" holds as a workaround for advancing subaltern political and economic causes while holding in abeyance the fundamental problem that requiring "authenticity," a notion that continues to haunt the social sciences, creates for cosmopolitanism. By wrapping undesirable segments of the population in a cloak of "authenticity," it is hoped that tolerance will be advanced. However, we must ask, after Wendy Brown, is "tolerance" what we are in the market for? For this reason, the Brazilian case is ideal for investigating the relationship between authenticity and cosmopolitanism.[3]

3. In other settings, such as eco- and ethno-tourism, similar issues arise (see e.g. Bruner).

ANTHROPOLOGISTS AND THE QUILOMBO CLAUSE

The case of the Quilombo Clause of the 1988 Brazilian Constitution is useful for illuminating this relationship. The enactment of that clause expressed a desire for justice as a legal requirement on a domestic level: poor rural black communities who could show (in some form) that they were descended from *quilombos* were to be recognized as such and given title to the land they were living on, even if it meant divesting other landowners (large or small) of their title to the same land. But the requirement of proving descent from actual runaway slaves did not last long. As will be shown in this section, anthropologists were instrumental in loosening the requirements for recognition – a move that created vast opportunities for previously-designated rural black communities who often lived in shame of being "black" to connect to larger transcontinental movements for recognition and rights by national governments. As an expression of a "cosmopolitan hope," in addition to extending domestic efforts to global commitments to justice, the expansion of what it meant to be a "*quilombo*" also extended global hope for justice to the domestic arena.[4]

During the first half decade of its existence, the Quilombo Clause was interpreted to require for any community claiming to be a *quilombo* (anachronistic, but colloquial term for *remanescente de quilombo*) historical evidence of descent from an actual runaway slave community. By virtue of a process I call "post-legislative negotiation," activists and particularly anthropologists (with their history of political commitment) were instrumental in broadening the definition so that by the beginning of the new century the proof required for recognition had opened up such that the expression of a desire to be considered a *quilombo* (self-identification) was sufficient to meet the requirement (French *Legalizing*). It must be noted that recognition is only the first step to receiving title to land, a complex process that has been moved between government agencies more than once and which, unsurprisingly, has been controversial. As of April 2008, only eighty-two communities had received title out of 1,200 that had been certified as *quilombos*. However, recognition itself has brought important

4. An example of this is the 2001 Durban World Conference against Racism, in which Brazil was an important participant.

resources and aid from the Brazilian government and international attention that has also attracted concrete assistance, raised consciousness of the history of African slavery in Latin America, and has been instrumental in the revision of identities and cultural practices (French *Legalizing*).

In October 1994, the Association of Brazilian Anthropologists (ABA) constituted a "working group on rural black communities."[5] This was done under the presidency of João Pacheco de Oliveira, the anthropologist who coined the expression "ethnogenesis" in Brazil to indicate the process by which peasants were able to reassert an indigenous identity ("Povos," "A Viagem"). In 1987 Pacheco engineered an exclusive contract between ABA and the federal government requiring the government to engage only ABA anthropologists (rather than engineers or agronomists) as experts to produce the reports required by law for indigenous tribal recognition. The ABA working group issued a statement that defined *"remanescentes de quilombo"* through a series of negatives: "the term does not refer to residual or archaeological relics of occupation in time or of biological proof ... not as isolated groups or of a population strictly homogeneous ... not necessarily formed by insurrectionary or rebellious past." Rather, in the ABA's 1994 "Documento do Grupo de Trabalho sobre Comunidades Negras Rurais," they were defined as

> groups that developed practices of resistance in the maintenance and reproduction of their ways of life characterized in a determined place. The identity of these groups is not defined by size and number of members but by the lived experience and the shared values of its common trajectory and of its continuity as a group. They constitute ethnic groups conceptually defined by anthropology as an organizational type that confers belonging through norms and methods employed by indicating affiliation and exclusion (Barth). As to territoriality, the occupation of land is not by individual lots, with common use predominating. The utilization of these areas obeys seasonality of activities...characterizing different

5. The working group was composed of Ilka Boaventura Leite (UFSC), Neusa Gusmão (UNESP), Lúcia Andrade (Comissão Pro-Índio), Dimas Salustiano da Silva (Lawyer, Maranhão human rights organization), João Batista Borges Pereira (USP), Eliane Cantarino O'Dwyer (UFF-Treasurer), João Pacheco de Oliveira (UFRJ-President).

forms of use and occupation of space that take for their base, kinship and neighbor ties based on relations of solidarity and reciprocity.[6]

In 1996 a member of the group and strong proponent of a broadened view of *quilombo*, Eliane Cantarino O'Dwyer, visited Mocambo, which would later become my research site in Sergipe. There she arranged for an anthropologist and student of João Pacheco, José Maurício Arruti, to research its possible *quilombo* status.[7] Within a bit over a year, Arruti's report was published in the federal register and Mocambo, by this point officially designated a *quilombo*, was visited by national and international figures. It also began sending leaders of the community to regional, national and international meetings, just as their neighbors, the Xocó Indians, have done since their 1979 recognition.

The role of the anthropologist, Arruti, cannot be overstated. He worked with the elder members of the community to bring family stories into the open and to assist in resignifying them as slave narratives. This led to, among other things, a play produced by the Mocambo teenagers intended as a celebration of *quilombo* identity that is still performed today (French "Buried Alive"). In each visit since his first, Arruti has aided in writing letters and discussing strategies for dealing with internal factionalism and slowness in federal responses to needs.[8]

Another case of the embodiment of "subaltern cosmopolitan legality," was that of a nun and lawyer turned legal anthropologist, Mariza Rios. In the first days of the land struggle that would become a bid for *quilombo* recognition, Rios not only introduced the possibility of "becoming" a *quilombo*, but created mnemonics for the rural workers to remember which legal category they needed to use when testifying in the local court against the injunction actions instituted by powerful

6. My translation.

7. O'Dwyer was quoted in the *Chronicle of Higher Education* a few years later as being "worried that a narrow interpretation could defeat the spirit of the law, excluding other rural groups that need land. But at the same time Article 68 has opened a space for negotiation that didn't exist for rural people before. The government is looking at other issues, such as a group's autonomy, and not just its link to slavery'" (Mooney).

8. Although not Brazilian, I was also involved in the production of cosmopolitanism through my presence at meetings with the federal attorney during the year Mocambo received its title.

landowners (French *Legalizing*). Notably, Mariza Rios herself was born to a poor family in 1958, the youngest of nine children. After returning from a stint as a nanny at the age of eleven (while she was also attending school), Mariza worked in a shoe factory and attended high school at night. In her teens, she became involved with a youth group run by a congregation of nuns, and by the time she was 21, she had taken her vows. After two years as a missionary working with onion farm laborers in the interior of Bahia, she went to Rio de Janeiro to study law. Most recently, she studied legal anthropology with Boaventura de Souza Santos as part of a masters degree received with the financial assistance of the Ford Foundation. The mutual production of cosmopolitanism can be seen in the relationships of both Arruti and Rios with the people living in Mocambo, four hours by rutted road from the capital of the smallest state of Brazil.

These brief examples shed light on the intellectual practices that should contribute to a further theorizing of cosmopolitan theory and anthropology. Similar processes are unfolding in relation to the case of the Xocó Indians, who also live in the region. However, there is one crucial lesson to be drawn from this initial discussion, which is that requirements of authenticity are inimical to the production of cosmopolitanism. There is widespread agreement among sociocultural anthropologists worldwide that identities – even ethnic and racial ones – are socially constructed. Less understood are the processes by which social identities are conceived and developed. Theories such as "subaltern cosmopolitan legality" help us see how domestic law can successfully serve as the impetus for the transformation of collective identity and provide critical connection to global justice. Recognition and land title were won by the village of Mocambo and their neighbors, the Xocó, over the last couple of decades even though, and perhaps because, anthropologists called upon to assess the validity of their claims recognized that their identities were "constructed." The positive outcome of their claims demonstrates that authenticity is not a prerequisite for identity. Nor is authenticity a prerequisite for membership in a cosmopolitan community. In fact, authenticity is a barrier to cosmopolitanism. For these reasons, I suggest that through the prism of Brazilian anthropological practice, it is possible to theorize a production of cosmopolitanism that obliterates the false dichotomy between cultural specificity and universal human rights.

WORKS CITED

BARTH, Fredrik. "Introduction." *Ethnic Groups and Boundaries: The Social Organization of Culture Difference.* Ed. Fredrik Barth. Boston: Little, Brown and Company, 1969. 9-38.

BRIGGS, Charles L. "Genealogies of Race and Culture and the Failure of Vernacular Cosmopolitanisms: Rereading Franz Boas and W.E.B. Dubois." *Public Culture* 17.1 (2005): 75-100.

BROWN, Wendy. *Regulating Aversion: Tolerance in the Age of Identity and Empire.* Princeton, N.J.: Princeton UP, 2006.

BRUNER, Edward. "The Maasai and the Lion King: Authenticity, Nationalism, and Globalization in African Tourism." *American Ethnologist* 28.4 (2001): 881-908.

BUNZL, Matti. "Boas, Foucault, and The "Native Anthropologist": Notes toward a Neo-Boasian Anthropology." *American Anthropologist* 106.3 (2004): 435-42.

CLIFFORD, James. *Routes: Travel and Translation in the Late Twentieth Century.* Cambridge: Harvard UP, 1997.

ENGLE, Karen. "From Skepticism to Embrace: Human Rights and the American Anthropological Association from 1947-1999." *Human Rights Quarterly* 23 (2001): 536-59.

FRENCH, Jan Hoffman. "Dancing for Land: Law Making and Cultural Performance in Northeastern Brazil." *Political and Legal Anthropology Review (PoLAR)* 25.1 (2002): 19-36.

—. "Buried Alive: Imagining Africa in the Brazilian Northeast." *American Ethnologist* 33.3 (2006): 340-60.

—. *Legalizing Identities: Becoming Black or Indian in Brazil's Northeast.* Chapel Hill: U of North Carolina P, 2009.

FRIEDMAN, Jonathan. "Indigenous Struggles and the Discreet Charm of the Bourgeoisie." *Places and Politics in an Age of Globalization.* Eds. Roxann Prazniak and Arif Dirlik. Lanham: Rowman and Littlefield, 2001. 53-69.

HALE, Charles R. "What Is Activist Research?" *Items and Issues* 2.1-2 (2001): 13-15.

HELD, David. "Principles of Cosmopolitan Order." *The Political Philosophy of Cosmopolitanism.* Eds. Gillian Brock and Harry Brighouse. Cambridge: Cambridge UP, 2005. 10-27.

HEMMING, John. *Die If You Must: Brazilian Indians in the Twentieth Century.* London: Macmillan, 2003.

HODGSON, Dorothy L. "Cosmopolitics, Neoliberalism, and the State: The Indigenous Rights Movement in Africa." *Anthropology and the New*

Cosmopolitanism: Rooted, Feminist and Vernacular Perspectives. Ed. Pnina Werbner. Oxford ; New York: Berg, 2008. 215-30.

KAHN, Joel S. "Anthropology as Cosmopolitan Practice?" *Anthropology Theory* 3.4 (2003): 403-15.

KUPER, Adam. "Culture, Identity and the Project of Cosmopolitan Anthropology." *Man (NS)* 29 (1994): 537-54.

LU, Catherine. "The One and Many Faces of Cosmopolitanism." *Journal of Political Philosophy* 8.2 (2000): 244-67.

McKINNON, Catriona. "Cosmopolitan Hope." *The Political Philosophy of Cosmopolitanism.* Eds. Gillian Brock and Harry Brighouse. Cambridge: Cambridge UP, 2005. 234-49.

MARSDEN, Magnus. "Muslim Cosmopolitans? Transnational Life in Northern Pakistan." *Journal of Asian Studies* 67.1 (2008): 213-47.

MOONEY, Carolyn J. "Anthropologists Shed Light on Jungle Communities Founded by Fugitive Slaves." *Chronicle of Higher Education* 1998, B2.

NOTAR, Beth E. "Producing Cosmopolitanism at the Borderlands: Lonely Planeteers and 'Local' Cosmopolitans in Southwest China." *Anthropology Quarterly* 81.3 (2008): 615-50.

ORTA, Andrew. "The Promise of Particularism and the Theology of Culture: Limits and Lessons of 'Neo-Boasianism'." *American Anthropologist* 106.3 (2004): 473-87.

PACHECO DE OLIVEIRA, João. "The Anthropologist as Expert: Brazilian Ethnology between Indianism and Indigenism." *Empires, Nations, and Natives: Anthropology and State-Making.* Eds. Benoit de L'Estoile, Federico G. Neiburg and Lygia Sigaud. Durham: Duke UP, 2005. 223-47.

—. "Povos Indígenas No Nordeste: Fronteiras Étnicas E Identidades Emergentes." *Tempo e Presença* 15.270 (1993): 31-34.

—, ed. *A Viagem Da Volta: Etnicidade, Política E Reelaboração Cultural No Nordeste Indígena.* Ed. João Pacheco de Oliveira. Rio de Janeiro: Contra Capa Livraria, 1999.

PEIRANO, Mariza G.S. "O Antropólogo Como Cidadão." *Dados - Revista de Ciências Sociais* 28.1 (1985): 227-43.

—. "When Anthropology Is at Home: The Different Contexts of a Single Discipline." *Annual Review of Anthropology* 27 (1998): 105-28.

PRICE, Richard. "Reinventando a História Dos Quilombos. Rasuras E Confabulações." *Afro-Ásia* 23 (1999): 239-65.

RAMOS, Alcida Rita. "Disengaging Anthropology." *A Companion to Latin American Anthropology.* Ed. Deborah Poole. Malden, MA: Blackwell, 2008. 466-84

—. "Anthropologist as Political Actor." *Journal of Latin American Anthropology* 4.2 (2000): 172-89.

—. *O Antropólogo: Ator Político, Figura Jurídica*. Vol. 92, Série Antropologia. Brasília: Universidade de Brasília, Instituto de Ciências Humanas, 1990.

SANTOS, Boaventura de Sousa. *Toward a New Legal Common Sense: Law, Globalization and Emancipation*. 2nd ed. Law in Context. London: Butterworths LexisNexis, 2002.

SANTOS, Boaventura de Sousa and Caesar A. RODRIGUEZ GARAVITO. *Law and Globalization from Below: Towards a Cosmopolitan Legality*. Cambridge Studies in Law and Society. Cambridge, UK ; New York: Cambridge UP, 2005.

SPEED, Shannon. *Rights in Rebellion: Indigenous St ?ggle and Human Rights in Chiapas*. Stanford: Stanford UP, 2008.

SPIVAK, Gayatri Chakravorty. "Can the Subaltern Speak?" *Marxism and the Interpretation of Culture*. Eds. Cary Nelson and Lawrence Grossberg. Urbana: U of Illinois P, 1988. 271-316.

TSING, Anna Lowenhaupt. *Friction: An Ethnography of Global Connection*. Princeton and Oxford: Princeton UP, 2005.

VELHO, Otávio Guilherme. "Through Althusserian Spectacles: Recent Social Anthropology in Brazil." *Ethnos* 47, no. I-II (1982): 133-49.

WERBNER, Pnina. *Anthropology and the New Cosmopolitanism: Rooted, Feminist and Vernacular Perspectives*, A.S.A. Monographs. Oxford ; New York: Berg, 2008.

Poststructuralism in the Periphery: Nelly Richard's Intellectual Transpositions

Ana del Sarto

> Structures do not walk on the streets
> (May '68 slogan)
> Be realistic, demand the impossible
> (Graffiti in Paris 1968)

> The kind of activity encouraged and privileged by (capitalist) society represses the process pervading the body and the subject, [...therefore we must] break out of our interpersonal and intersocial experience if we are to gain access to what is repressed in the social mechanism:
> the generating of significance (Kristeva RPL 13).

Itineraries, Passages, Transpositions

In 1966, Julia Kristeva (Bulgaria, 1941) arrives in Paris as a graduate student. While she attends Roland Barthes' seminars, she begins publishing her works on semiotics in prestigious scholarly journals, such as *Critique*, *Langage*, and *Tel Quel*. The political and militant labor of the *Tel Quel* group is very well-known, not only in relation to the uprisings of May '68, but also in the enunciation of several radical theoretical and critical discourses disseminated later by the American Academia as Post-structuralism.[1] Only a few years later, in 1970, Nelly Richard (France, 1951) arrives in Santiago de Chile, after having graduated from the Comparative Literature program of La Sorbonne, University of Paris. Richard worked as an art curator in private

---

1. For a great analysis of Kristeva's participation in *Tel Quel* (1960-83), see Joan Brandt, "Julia Kristeva and the Revolutionary Politics of Tel Quel."

galleries, such as *Cromo* and *Cal*,[2] and as cultural critic and ideologue of the *avanzada movement*,[3] a neo- and post-avant-garde group very active in the Chilean plastic arts field during the late '70s and early '80s. In the same way that Kristeva introduced Mikhail Bakhtin's thought to Western culture – mainly his concepts of dialogism, polyphony, heteroglossia and intertextuality, although elaborating them in different contexts – Richard brought French poststructuralist theories into the Chilean and Latin American contexts, which were hegemonic during her school years. Perhaps their experience of diaspora was the necessary condition to stimulate the displacements performed by both Kristeva's and Richard's creative radicalization of critical theories. In fact, both have created heterogeneous and multi-layered discourses, in which inter- and transdisciplinary strategies perform cuts, breaks, and transpositions, which decontextualize the signifying practices they analyzed in order to insert them in different contexts to bear new meanings.

Paris in the '60s and Santiago in the '70s posed two strangely similar contexts. Even though it is extremely difficult to make comparisons between them, in both historical junctures, specific ideological and political struggles brought about critical revisions of the Structural paradigm then prevalent in the Humanities and the Social Sciences. The failure of the student insurrections and workers' strikes of May 1968 corroborated the rigidity of the orthodox Left, in this case represented by the French Communist Party, and supported intellectual uneasiness and political disenchantment among radicals and liberals. Similarly, though Chile constituted an exemplar model of the access to socialism via liberal democracy, the subsequent violence unleashed in the country fed anti-Marxist discourses which accused the Popular

---

2. See Richard's biographic entry in *Memoria chilena: Portal de la cultura de Chile.* "Nelly Richard." http://www.memoriachilena.cl/temas/dest.asp?id=cal(1979)richard.

3. Name of the group integrated by Lotty Rosenfeld, Juan Dávila, Virginia Errázuriz, Carlos Leppe, Eugenio Dittborn, Francisco Brugnoli, Juan Castillo, Gonzalo Díaz, Carlos Altamirano, Arturo Duclós, Claudia Donoso, Carlos Gallardo, Víctor Hugo Codocedo (plastic and visual artists), Diamela Eltit, Raúl Zurita, Enrique Lihn, Diego Maquieira, Gonzálo Muñoz, Juan Luis Martínez, Carmen Berenguer (poets and novelists), Osvaldo Aguiló, Adriana Valdés, Eugenia Brito, Nelly Richard (cultural and literary critics) Ronald Kay, Patricio Marchant, Pablo Oyarzún (philosophers), and Fernando Balcells (sociologist).

Unity (*Unidad Popular* or UP) authoritarianism of the advent of Pinochet's fascism. If the historical circumstances and socio-cultural contexts of May '68 and Chilean Socialism differed in many regards, both processes produced a critical examination of the limits of Structuralism, nourishing poststructuralists' theoretical transpositions in order to allow more flexible – though less effective – interpretations of the political and social realms.

The purpose of this essay is to trace the intellectual creative appropriations and transpositions that Richard's cultural criticism elaborates from the transgressive program Kristeva designed in *Revolution in Poetic Language* (1974).[4] Although the main topics of the texts I will analyze here are different, the constitution of subjectivity from the standpoint of sexuality in Richard's *Cuerpo correcional* (1980) and the crisis of the subject-in-process from the standpoint of poetic language in *Revolution in Poetic Language*, it is evident that the latter is the programmatic subtext of the former. In other words, in *Cuerpo correccional*, Richard emphasizes poetic language – the transposition of signifiers which expose the subject in crisis – as a primordial critical strategy. Insofar as poetic language liberates repressed energies and produces *jouissance* during the constitution of the present-subject (the enunciating subject) in / of the signifying practices (for instance, the artistic practices of *avanzada*), it revolutionizes the pre-supposed arbitrary logic while transgressing and subverting the ideological principles of the dominant system. Thus, the decentered, fragmented, heterogeneous subject – a subject-in-process, in its double and ambiguous denomination: subject in the making and on trial, Kristeva *dixit* – is the product and effect of a double articulation: the enunciation of critical discourse in poetic language, which allows for "the introduction of *jouissance* in and through the language" (RPL 80), and the ejection of fractions of the repressed in its own content. Consequently, this same process questions the reader as subject-in-process interpellated by the reading of these texts.[5]

---

4. Quotes from this book will be introduced by the acronym RPL.

5. Kelly Oliver affirms that "While Saussure may be correct to point out that the relationship between the signifier and the signified is arbitrary, it is the speaking subject who makes the connection between them," therefore, "for Kristeva, the subject is not only the transcendental ego," because "the subject that posits meaning is

Kristeva's poststructuralist premises, in which the *avanzada*'s practices are theoretically based, presupposed a high sensibility towards
modern nihilism (not only as a modern rationality and legitimacy crisis, but also as a crisis of values and meanings that support them),
detecting a "remnant of freedom [in subjectivities'] unacknowledged
suffering" (the central thesis of Sara Beardsworth's excellent analysis in
Julia Kristeva: Psychoanalysis and Modernity 8-12). Without these
premises, the pledge to the inherent negativity of marginal subjectivities, who through their singularity (in order to deconstruct both the
universals and the particulars) are the agencies questioning the social
order, could not be understood. Nevertheless, Beardsworth criticizes
Kristeva for leaving the issue of mediations between the subjective and
social transformations unattended (52). The social changes are presupposed as always already present through and in the mediation that language performs. Thus, any revolt of meanings would mark the onset
of a crisis not only to the agents involved, but to the social order itself.

Before going forward with my analysis, I will pursue a brief digres-
sion to clarify what is understood in this essay by Post-structuralism. It
is the ambiguous and many times contradictory set of critical theories
that reflect on the limits of classical Structuralism (Ferdinand de Saussure, Claude Levi-Strauss, Lucien Goldmann and Louis Althusser).
The totalizing rigidity of the concept of structure posed by a unitary
and rational subject is the focus of the critique. According to Tilottama Rajan, in "Trans-Positions of Difference: Kristeva and Post-structuralism," the concept of post-structuralism has been erroneously used
as a synonym of deconstruction, meaning that both negate all phenomena outside of language or through its discursive construction.
However, Rajan argues that Post-structuralism "is part of a greater
philosophical movement, which is generally conceived as post-organi-
cism or post-phenomenology." Hence, Kristeva's position "would be
within and against the theories of classic poststructuralism" (215),
characterized by her known ambiguity; because if the search for a

---

the result of a process that is prior to meaning." Hence, "Any language theory that presupposes a unitary subject cannot account for this pre-meaning element in the subject.
There is part of the language that cannot be accounted for, that part that does not
mean: nonsense, tones, rhythms. Kristeva suggests that ultimately these theories cannot account for transgression and pleasure" (*Reading Kristeva* 92).

"materiality preceding the sign" sets her at odds with many poststructuralists, such as Jacques Derrida, Michel Foucault and Jean Baudrillard, the founding of "significance without representation" draws her to others, such as Gilles Deleuze, Felix Guattari, and Francois Lyotard of the *Libidinal Economy*. In order to go beyond the problem of representation and significance through the system of signs, Kristeva's materialism searches to describe how the real, even when it does not have meaning in language, could be understood obliquely through the subject's expression. In other words, if the symbolic is equivalent to logos as the law of the same (identity), the semiotic attempts to enunciate the confused body's voice as trace of difference. For Kristeva, according to Rajan, "the linguistic sign is the source of identity and the material (body) is the site of difference" (222).

During the late '70s and early '80s, Richard begins a project of poetic-criticism which shook, even until the late '90s, the traditional parameters of the way cultural criticism was practiced in Santiago and reorganized the dissident discourses in the fragile Chilean intellectual field. It is completely arbitrary, and even fallacious, to establish the emergence of contemporary Chilean cultural criticism with the publication of *Cuerpo correccional* in 1980, and hold Richard personally accountable behind this thrust. However, it would be unfair not to recognize the shuddering and theoretical revisions provoked by the discourses which Richard put into circulation. From the incorporation of Post-structuralism, deconstructivism, and feminist theories to the critical interlocution of many postmodernist discourses, Richard's cultural critique tirelessly redesigns the conceptual, discursive, and thematic issues debated in the Chilean intellectual field.

"REVERBERATION CHAMBER," "REFERENCES MONTAGE"

In *Revolution of Poetic Language*, Kristeva characterizes poetic language's modes of articulation – the semiotic and the symbolic – always in the process of signification, as the most suitable means of disruption and transgression, "as a signifying practice, that is, as a semiotic system generated by a speaking subject within a social, historical field" (1). For these signifying practices to be transgressive, they must assume "the privilege of communicating regression [to the lost paradise, to the mother's body, to primary narcissism] and *jouissance*" (RPL 3) or the inexpressible and ineffable pleasure. In other words, they must allow the expression of the semiotic through the symbolic. Hence, their purpose is to communicate contents – remnants, residues, traces, marks – not only from the unconscious (the other within the self, the repressed), but also from the sources of *jouissance*, which will very soon acquire meanings retroactively through consciousness.[6] According to this, Kristeva interprets several linguistic theories about language's process of signification (primarily formalist and structural theories) and articulates or transposes them to new readings of psychoanalysis (mainly the role of the unconscious and drives in the process of constitution of the subject: Sigmund Freud, Melanie Klein, and Jacques Lacan). Having these transpositions as her standpoint and postulating one of the most popular French poststructural trends in the American academia, Kristeva establishes a project of destabilization of both natural language as well as the Cartesian transcendental subject, because only through the first one the second is constituted / constructed. Thus, Kristeva proposes a specific arrangement of the process of signification: on the one hand, she substitutes the Lacanian psychoanalytic categories – the imaginary, the real, and the symbolic – with new dimensions, such as the semiotic (the authority of the mother) and the symbolic (the law of the father), which constitute the subject; on the other hand, she deconstructs the fixed boundary between the signifier/signified binary through the constant production of signifiers from the invasions of the semiotic flows, which thus acquire a plurality of heterogeneous meanings always overdetermined by the repressive and homogeneous immobility of the symbolic.

Nonetheless, how could we understand the process of signification and the constitution of the present-subjects, so central for Post-structuralism in general, according to these assumptions? For Kristeva, signification always involves a *thetic* phase, that is, a specific position. The subject produces a break in the signifying process in order to assume that position, "establishing the *identification* of the subject and

6. Villalobos Alpízar defines a signifying practice, in Kristeva's terms, as "the constitution and crossings of signs within a sign system," which in their plurality would be tantamount to a "field of transpositions," that is, "passages from one system of signs to another" (10-14, my translation)

its object as preconditions of propositionality. [...] This image and these objects must first be posited in a space that becomes symbolic because it connects the two separated positions, recording them or redistributing them in an open combinatorial system" (RPL 43; original emphasis). This gap that founds the symbolic, this break which Kristeva denominates "*the thetic*," is what makes signification possible.[7] Paradoxically, this same break is the one that erases or veils the subject from the process, because in order to found itself it requires an identification, "the subject must separate from and through his image, from and through his objects" (RPL 43). In other words, the *thetic qua* limit or border opens the possibility of enunciation, even though it does not account for the source (the subjectivity) from which this latter emerges, because it excludes the same subject, the enunciating subject, who produces it.

With the help of Freudian and Kleinian theories of drives, Kristeva has questioned the process of producing this break. The introduction of the semiotic as the productive dimension in the construction of signifiers, and thus in the constitution of the subject, allows her to include in the signifiers the repressed traces (either from the unconscious or from *jouissance*) during the subject's own constitution. In this development, "we found the *thetic* phase of the signifying process, around which signification is organized, at two points: the mirror stage and the 'discovery' of castration" (RPL 46). The interrelation of these two psychoanalytic coordinates – the mirror phase (rejection of and separation from the mother's body) and castration (entrance in the symbolic) – is instituted as the original moment in which signification is produced and, as a result of the same process, subjectivity is configured. However, it is worth mentioning that, if in principle, signification is produced in the realm of the symbolic, according to Kristeva, the semiotic fragments play a fundamental role in the constitution of the signifiers, founding the constitutive ambiguity of the signified. In that sense, signification is perceived as a process of double articulation: on the one hand, the discharge of the drives produces a gap in the symbolic; on the other, the newly created signifier will facilitate other signifieds, which will be later reconciled through consciousness (the repressive symbolic).

7. See Section 5, Part I of RPL.

Kristeva's fundamental contribution focuses on the introduction of the semiotic as a category which names a dimension (space or receptacle) and/or a distinctive, although theoretically preexistent, phase to the symbolic. Therefore, the semiotic will never appear detached from the symbolic, because the semiotic "exists in practice only within the symbolic and requires the symbolic break to obtain [its] complex articulation" (RPL 68). For Kristeva, these two concepts, the semiotic and the symbolic, are materialized in a totality which characterizes both dispositions while involving them in a dialectical process: "the second [the symbolic] includes part of the first [the semiotic] and their scission is thereafter marked by the break between the signifier and the signified" (RPL 48). Kristeva's strategy consists in localizing the moment of dialectical negativity precisely in the semiotic (the *chora* or the mother's body), displacing it in this way from the socio-historical dimension to psychic and biological categories. It is true that Kristeva's theory makes possible certain articulations between the semiotic – the individual repressed unconscious – and the symbolic – the social as repressive machine. That is, the energies and flows repressed by the symbolic are liberated through the return of the semiotic, in such a way that provides the necessary negativity to destabilize the symbolic. Thus, "we shall have to represent the semiotic (which is produced recursively on the basis of that break) as a 'second' return of instinctual functioning within the symbolic, *as a negativity introduced into the symbolic order*, and *as a transgression of that order*" (RPL 69; my emphasis). Consequently, the introduction of the semiotic negativity into the symbolic does not restore the immediacy of the pre-symbolic. On the contrary, it is a transgression of positions, a reactivation of the inverted contradiction instituted by these same positions: the core of subjectivation and its possibility of emancipation, although temporarily, of each individual confronted with the constrictions of the symbolic.

PARADOXES OF RICHARD'S CULTURAL CRITIQUE

Ever since *Cuerpo correccional*, Richard's intellectual program of cultural transgression and political dissidence has focused on the reformulation of the articulations of the aesthetics, the cultural and the political spheres with the explicit purpose of transforming the real.

The material implementation of that project, put forth by the *avanza-da*'s movement during the late '70s and early '80s, was doubly risky: on the one hand, because of the danger involved in the mere enuncia-tion of any critical discourse under dictatorship; on the other, because of their own internal logics. Considering the social, the political, and the cultural as exclusively discursive repressive apparatuses – analyti-cally discernible dimensions of the symbolic – mired the possibilities of exploring and articulating the socio-political conflicts, contradic-tions, and antagonisms, or rather allowed them to elude the social mediations produced by intellectuals.

To the outside, instead of directly confronting the cultural and socio-political system to be transgressed, the *avanzada* adopted a posi-tion at the margins. In their project, marginality was much more than a simple strategic position in favor of or against the regime. The mar-gin allowed them to construe a destabilizing subject who adopted a "position of non-belongingness," an in-between position, "outside of the ideological conflict" between the Right and the Left, but not with-out its own ideological and political underpinning. The *avanzada* was always situated outside or at the margins of the socio-political conflicts between the regime and the opposition, between the establishment and the "militant cultural organizations" (*Margins and Institution* 121). For instance, in *Cuerpo correccional*, while Richard acknowledges the need to situate Carlos Leppe's works in "the productive national context" (8), she paradoxically postpones this undertaking. In its place, she produces a discursive contextualization, with which she aims to deconstruct diverse traditional parameters of Chilean culture as Western Culture. Chilean culture, as an object which produces peripheral differences, would be subsumed, and hence negated or con-firmed, within a supposedly universal framework. Richard is aware of the historical contexts in which the discursive formations she uses are inscribed. However while referring to them, she eludes them. This is one of the recurrent strategies of Richard's cultural critique, very simi-lar to Kristeva's transpositions.

In its internal logics, Richard's project involves much more than a set of "*bewildered* postulates," as Justo Pastor Mellado has argued in reference to her texts (*Dos textos* 45; original emphasis). In her decon-structive analysis of the *avanzada*'s art actions, Richard confronts not only the fundamentals of the canonical art criticism quoting Kristeva's semiotic dimension of poetic language as a meta-discursive tool, but she also transgresses the traditional voices of cultural and literary criticism. By enunciating her own discourse through a first person poetic voice (I/woman), Richard identifies herself while reconstructing the artist's process of subject constitution (separation of the mother's body and recognition of his own body) as the specular interlocutor, who is constructed through her interpellating call of the second-person subject (you/man).[8]

As it will be demonstrated in the following section, *Cuerpo correccional*'s delusions have an internal logic: Kristeva's psychoanalytic-semiotics. With this specific framework, Richard resignifies and transgresses not only the modern authoritarian culture of dictatorial Chile, but vindicates also an eclectic and heterodox aesthetic praxis, due to its original postmodernist and poststructuralist appropriations. However, both Richard's cultural critique and Kristeva's psychoanalytic-semiotics lack a thorough analysis of the articulations and mediations between the aesthetic project and the social, political, and cultural contexts to which they belong. In their double-edged purpose of letting the unconscious be present in the process of signification and, at the same time, of avoiding an ideological closure of the enunciation, Richard and Kristeva adopt strategies with ambiguous effects. In other words, they try to subvert and transgress the status quo, but the results are politically meager: only contingent subjective transformations are achieved.[9] In *Kristeva and the Political*, Cecilia Sjoholm argues that:

> The political dimension [of the unconscious] is its undermining of given categories of social identity and goal oriented projects, through a radical negativity at the core of the subject, resisting adaptation to linguistic and symbolic norms. The subject of negativity is irreducible to social and culturally determined identities. Its corporeal aspect allows for

8. In "Entre neo-vanguardia y post-vanguardia, la escena de avanzada," second part of *Sospecha y goce*, I analyze not only the implementation of this transgressive project and its consequent legitimation of the *avanzada*'s art actions, but also from its posterior decadence and dissolution, according to the transformations within and among these avant-garde groups and in the Chilean cultural context.

9. In effect, Kelly Oliver in *Reading Kristeva* intelligently and carefully analyzes the dangerous socio-political ambiguity of the oscillation strategies proposed by Kristeva.

a notion of universality based on fragility and vulnerability rather than laws and rights. [...Kristeva's] ambition is to formulate a politics conveying dimensions that tend to be overlooked in political philosophy and theory. The political domain must be displaced from the public to the intimate, and radicality is a negativity of movement and change, a heterogeneity of drive, body, language, and meaning. *Such a form of negativity is produced not between subjects but in each and every subject.* It gains its meaning through a metaphorical principle of love replacing the recognition of a traditional emancipatory politics (2; my emphasis).

This radical negativity is precisely what Richard is recovering and producing in *Cuerpo correccional,* establishing a political reading of the intimate as proposed by Carlos Leppe through his body art under dictatorship. To criticize the repression which emerges from the symbolic (dictatorship-state-father-Pinochet-culture-politics, that is, the symbolic as institution), Richard restores all those original drives, genetic traces or marks inherited through the mother's body (the semiotic-the repressed content), which will later burst into the signs and closures performed by the *thectic* or, in other words, by the institutionalization of the symbolic in the process of signification. Henceforth, in this case it is also appropriate to apply this criticism to Kristeva for the neglect of the nature of the social and of the necessary mediations in order that individual as well as collective actions generate social transformations. Both intellectuals, Richard and Kristeva, although with dissimilar goals and socio-historical urgencies, try to politicize the internalized signs, by transgressing and subverting the imaginary-symbolic, making them burst through their most tenuous thread.

CUERPO CORRECCIONAL

The insistently inhibiting and coercive function of cultural institution subdues the subject, who is in a state of renunciation and bodily sacrifice, which corroborates in Leppe the eminently traumatic dimension of the cultural convention (the shock) which victimizes the bodily and gestural nature (CC 11).

A title, two names, two nouns: the body and the correctional. Two chained signifiers, the correctional and the body, postulate a series of meanings in the incessant labor of signification; they are joined to avoid the closure of meanings. Two instruments, the correctional and the body, manipulated from the ambiguity of heterogeneous contradictions to transgress orders and to alter orderings. Two spaces, the body and the correctional, combined in multiple interrelations: while the body corrects and is corrected, the correctional molds it while being resisted and transgressed. Paradoxical intersections and tensions. If the correctional – language, institution, culture, the symbolic – works upon the body, the receptacle of drives and instincts, the semiotic, the body finally becomes correctional. The correctional represents what the bodies' lived experiences deny: poetics of ambiguity, politics of tension. How can we become liberated from the Other while promoting ourselves as the others? How do we cross the limits of the Other within our own bodies? How does the Other of the I express her/himself, or, how does the liberated body express itself? According to Kristeva, the semiotic constantly subverts and corrects the abuses and the improper representations posed by the symbolic. In other words, if the semiotic always festers the symbolic, it can only be manifested in the latter and is always arranged precisely by the *thetic* (the symbolic break) which makes signification possible. What this analysis demonstrates is not only the contingency of the process of signification but also its contextuality. How do we read, then, the concatenation of signifiers to boost diverse series of signification? How do we signify the unrepresentable? How do we put in tension those unsolvable conflicts in practices that disorganize univocal meanings? Is it possible that the signifier can be enunciated separately from the signified? How do we read only the series of signifiers without alluding to the different contexts in which they work? Or better yet, how do we enunciate signifiers that disarticulate the constituted networks of signifieds to establish transversal meanings?

The catalog-book *Cuerpo correccional*,[10] product of the collective work between Carlos Leppe, Nelly Richard and Carlos Altami-

10. Juan Pastor Mellado, in "Arte chileno: políticas de un significante gráfico," analyzes the nature of this text "not as a catalog, but as a book that tries to localize its own status between the artist's book and the book about the artist. In the first, the book is a support of the production of the artist's work; that is, it is not reduced to be a means of reproduction of a preexistent work. In the second, the writing of the text debates two possibilities: either it fulfills the norms of the book's definition on the function of the page in a regular text, in which – we can thus call it – the content is

rano,[11] was part of Carlos Leppe's retrospective artistic exhibition in Galería Sur, Santiago de Chile, in November 1980. The written text has four parts: Richard wrote the first two; the third part is a printed text of the script read by Leppe's mother, Aurelia Arroyo, over the projection of a video of the performance "Waiting Room"; and, the fourth is a future epitaph to the death of Aurelia Arroyo written by her son, Carlos Leppe, in poetic language. Richard's texts are the theoretical introduction, where she establishes the parameters of analysis, and the main body of the text, where she examines six of Leppe's performances: "Happening of the Hens" (1974), "The Coat Rack" (1975), "Gertrude Stein" (1976), "Reconstitution of a Scene" (1977), "Star Action" (1979), and "Waiting Room" (1980).

In this section, I will not analyze the visual and material support, or the editorial proceedings of *Cuerpo correccional.* Neither will I examine Leppe's performances, because that was done by Richard herself. I am more interested in Richard's theoretical and critical discourses, in the emergence of her specific writing practice in the formal disposition of the text. In other words, I will analyze the processes of signification materialized by Richard's writing on Leppe's performances, formalizing a specific way of practicing cultural critique through poetic language. Therefore, in this section, I will try to unravel the theoretical and critical premises from the concatenation of signifiers proposed by Richard. In order to do so, I will highlight the organizing

referred to as a specific object susceptible of being conveniently illustrated, or it attempts to acquire the "same importance" as the visual discourse, or better yet, it contemplates a return of the visual over the legible, establishing a space of graphic tension which will overdetermine its reading. The book I will comment on, then, is localized between both situations. On the one hand, the object of the text is Carlos Leppe's work and, on the other, the concept of writing as performance entitles the graphic issue to become the epistemological support of a specific scripto-visual analytic that is attempting to affect the recomposition of the Chilean plastic arts field during the late 70s."

11. Paula Honorato and Luz Muñoz assert that *Cuerpo correccional* was conceived by Leppe, sketched by Altamirano and written by Richard, in approximately four months. They worked intensely and full time on the text and its visualization in Richard's house in La Florida. At that moment, Leppe and Altamirano were funded by a fellowship from Amigos del Arte, which both of them had won for the second time, and also both of them were working in Francisco Zegers' advertisement agency, where they kept on discussing the editorial aspects of the book ("Del espacio de acá").

nubs of her textuality, so when compared to Kristeva's theoretical premises, I can prove not only the philosophical sedimentation which underlines *Cuerpo correccional*, but also the decisive influence of post-structuralist theories, or the "post-horizon" as I prefer to call it, in the later cultural critique proposed by Richard from *Revista de Crítica Cultural* (1990-2008) in Chile.

Richard constructs her object of reflection from the corpus of Leppe's performances from 1973 to 1980. If her analysis includes a chronological development, Richard privileges specific axes and aspects of Leppe's works (rejection of the mother's function, castration, and incest), "arranged according to a theoretical option: Kristeva's psychoanalytic-semiotic" (CC 8). Through an experimental use of poetic language, Richard decenters the concept of the traditional Cartesian subject in order to displace and expand the coordinates of representation in the processes of subject constitution and identity formation. Particularly in *Cuerpo correccional*, her poetic criticism focuses on the questioning of a certain psychoanalytic tradition (Sigmund Freud, Melanie Klein and Jacques Lacan) through a semiotic reading (Kristeva). The central fulcrum is the human body, Leppe's body, in relation to three different contexts: the collective, the biographical, and the cultural. As it was mentioned above, if Richard delays the urgent task of situating Leppe's work in the artistic "productive national context" (CC8), she never ceases to allude to other social contexts from which this work triggers new meanings.

Before starting with my analysis, it is necessary to highlight a specific formal element of this catalog-book, *Cuerpo correccional*, because it will influence the processes of signification and affect the construction of signifiers which break with conventionally normativized meanings. "The interlocution or dialogic proceeding [that] here justify the systematized use of the grammatical category 'you' (understanding that an 'I' is the referent)," that is, "I" the critic, Nelly Richard, situate "my" gaze in your actions and while I recognize you as a productive other, I explore my own subjectivity rehearsing myself, or recognizing myself as your equal, vulnerable in your refractions, disseminated in your own alterity. This proceeding has a double function: on the one hand, a communicative function, because "the correlation between your personality I/you structure the area of communication;" and, on the other hand, an interpellating function of sexual identity, "insofar as the correlation between gender feminine/masculine structure the area of sexuality" (CC14).

> *your subjugated interior in the printed version of your "Waiting Room"*
> *in your performing folds of two sexually consonant models:*
> *in your mother who recites you in your biographical antecedent/*
> *in me who recites you in your productive trance*
> *your dialogic interior spoken by the feminine cadence of two interlocutions/*
> *your rhymed masculine scission by two lenient styles/*
> *By a female scansion / (CC 99)*

How do we liberate the repressed? How do we express our *jouissance*? What mechanisms and strategies could be use to channel the expression of all the repressions that overload our bodies? How do we articulate our bodily demands? How do we name the unnamable drives? Several discourses and images crisscross *Cuerpo correccional*, so in their comparison, one could obliquely channel, through the other side of the enunciated, the subjectivity behind the mere enunciation, that is, the explicitly inexpressible. The text attempts to expose the trembling bodies to agitate the culturally constructed symbolizations. Hence, *Cuerpo correccional* is a multidimensional and polysemic text.

As I mentioned in the preceding section, the text is organized in four parts enunciated in three interlaced voices that embody different tones, so that in the cacophony of its echoes they liberate remnants of the bodily repressed materiality, without specifically naming it, although expressing *jouissance* at its limits: the paradoxical interweaving of enjoyment and pain. These three voices enunciate three different discourses. The discourse of the mother as well as that of Leppe himself, are love discourses, which express the unnamable facing the fatality of decomposition or the death of the loved one. Physically, death constitutes an unsurpassable and definitive limit; but psychically, the aggressive discharges of the death drive transgress the effects produced by the symbolic repression or coercion. That is why through repetition, from the transposition of the signifiers' multiple metonymic displacements or metaphoric condensations, these drives create new forms.

Besides these two discourses, Richard's discourse is split, embodying two contradictory tones. On the one hand, the academic and institutional register whose purpose is to justify theoretically the reasons behind the breaks in the processes of signification. This discourse is enunciated from a theoretical-critical position, which establishes its own authoritative conditions not only to break down, explain, and legitimize the text, but also to construct its own conceptual and analytical apparatus. On the other hand, this same voice plays with poetic language, offering a subjective register of the way Leppe's performances interpellate Nelly Richard as cultural critic and allowing her to posit her own subjectivity as an anti-Oedipal affective figure (pole of identification and recognition).[12]

Written from and with the body of Richard's own interpellated subjectivity, this discourse triggers several series of chained signifiers which metonymically displace and metaphorically condense contradictory meanings about the acquisition of any fixed and stereotyped sexuated identity. Between the ellipses and ruptures, this affective voice displaces the maternal pole of identification in Leppe's subjectivity in order to constitute an anti-maternal, although still feminine, pole: "*your dialogic interior spoken by the feminine cadence of two interlocutions/ your rhymed masculine scission by two lenient styles/ By a female scansion/*" (CC 99). These four parts, enunciated by four discourses, suggest divergent though complementary logics.

> *Your mother reciting you in your historiographic fragment/*
> *Your mother warrantor of your subjective entity because of your main biography:*
> *-your mother as the first (unified) corporal continent in your primary geography of the subject/*
> *As the trace of the organic union of your undifferentiated sexual and corporeal continuum* (CC97)

---

12. Paula Honorato and Luz Muñoz state that "Richard develops two writing tones in the book; one in the introduction which is close to the academic formalism and its function is to delimit the focus and the field of theoretical references in order to approach Leppe's work; and the other, in the main text, which assumes the first person to develop a theoretical and poetic reflection about each of the performances during 1974 and 1980" ("Del espacio de acá").

The mother (Aurelia Arroyo), her body and her affects, one of the constitutive identification poles, is a fundamental and decisive source in the genetic and biographical heritage of the artist (Carlos Leppe). The father, "absent from the sixth month of the pregnancy," according to her mother's narration, had never had any relation with his son. The unnamable pain of the mother, Aurelia, during the childbirth. Even though this text is one of the latest to formally appear in the catalog-book and is transcribed on transparent pages to allow the transposition of the images with the letters (a procedure which simulates the semi-otic transposition on/about the symbolic), its affective weight dissolves any story we have tried to construct until then. Since this voice pin-points decisive moments during childbirth and Leppe's childhood, it incorporates affective traces which retroactively make us, as readers, go back and revisit the processes of signification triggered by the dis-courses of the critic and the artist's performances. Because his mother tells us: "he could have not been born. [Because I don't] know how he was born...I suffered the unnamable. I was losing so much blood and he was not out of my body...It was horrible, he was born with forceps: an immensely big little-body. What a beautiful baby, I said. [...] If I die he will suffer, and if he had died I would have suffered the unnamable. I believe my life would not have any reason to keep on living and the only thing I will ask God is that both of us had died the same day, thus, no one would suffer" (CC 106-112). The only motive of concern for the mother is to avoid her son's suffering ... however, we know that we cannot feel immeasurable pleasure without pain.

When Aurelia Arroyo's body, Leppe's mother, is overcome by death, when her body will not vibrate any longer, will not speak to her son: "I [Carlos Leppe] will cover the four walls with tiles, the ceiling and the floor of my mother's room, and I will light white neon bars in all the edges. I will arrange sixteen urinal murals where people would urinate, offering their backs to my mother's naked and deceased body, sheltered in medical gauze and laid in a central stretcher. I will tune the video projector in each angle of the room, *exhibiting her as a diva, as what I am, as 'The Doll of the Continent'*. I will throw my cinemato-graphic kiss recorded in the unfinished tape, over her Sleeping Beauty mouth" (CC without pagination; my emphasis). Tiles, white neon bars, urinals, medical gauzes, cold, transparent, and liquid TV screens, all of them presenting Leppe with the image of his own desire, the body of his mother, as what he corporeally feels he is but physically he is not. This is the voice that closes *Cuerpo correccional* over an image of the Andean Mountains. An epitaph, a lapidary inscription floating in space, which accounts for a suffering voice because of the future mourning over the loss of the mother's body (referent of the speaking body in process of desidentification). Nevertheless, this is a celebratory voice, not only because it recognizes the process of separation in the rejected excess (reverse of negation), but also because it is precisely this same process which offers to the artist, and the critic, new possibilities for signification.

Richard's critical discourses, poetically enunciated, analyze these performances as body art practices. These are conceptualized as "signifying practices (producing and transforming socially communicable signifieds) whose materiality is somatic (the human body as subject and object of the process of materialization of the artistic meanings)" (CC 12). The use of the body – conceptualized as the genetic base ("biologically inherited") of the signifiers' production and, thus, of sexual differences – materializes, as interrupting instrument, the multiple possibilities of subversion of the cultural or socially imposed signifieds. In another text, "Bodies: parodic identities," I analyze the production of social signifieds from the body considering it as a sign contingently constructed for each specific moment. However, I would like to point out that if Richard conceptualizes these "signifying practices as a tool which produces and transforms socially communicable signifieds," she also emphasizes the transgressive capacity of such practices through the liberation of their repressed contents, while denying "the socially communicable signifieds" because they arguably constitute symbolic impositions.

Several of Richard's rhetorical strategies, such as the use of the poetic language through the construction of signifiers in order to propagate the liberation of the repressed and/or the expression of *jouissance* while disturbing the symbolic order, served to open spaces of dissent, resistance and opposition to the Chilean totalitarian military system. Evidently, *Cuerpo correccional* was the first challenge from the margins of culture to the politics of the authoritarian regime. In effect, transgressing the established artistic traditions in the field of the plastic arts, the *avanzada*'s practices politicized spaces of intimacy (body, sexuality, gender roles) destabilizing the borders between the public and the private. However, this politicization, which displaced the traditional intellectual parameters through which the body, sexuality, and gender were conceived, was not sufficient to transform the social relations which overdetermine the marginal subjectivities involved in these revolts of meanings. In other words, the political status of the subversions proposed by Richard was paradoxical, because if her original intention was to repoliticize spaces depoliticized by repression (bodies, cities, cultures), her theoretical premises would leave her at midway.

WORKS CITED

BEARDSWORTH, Sara. *Julia Kristeva: Psychoanalysis and Modernity*. New York: State U New York P, 2004.

BRANDT, Joan. "Julia Kristeva and the Revolutionary Politics of *Tel Quel*." *Revolt, Affect, Collectivity. The Unstable Boundaries of Kristeva's Polis*. Eds. Chanter, Tina y Ewa Ziarek. New York: State U of New York P, 2005. 21-36.

DIARIO MURAL DEL MAYOR FRANCÉS. *Los graffiti del 68*. Buenos Aires: Editorial Perfil, 1997.

HONORATO, Paula and Luz MUÑOZ. "Recomposición de escena 1975-1981. 8 publicaciones de artes visuales en Chile." Web. <http://www.textos dearte.cl/recomposicion>

—. *"Del espacio de acá / Cuerpo correccional."* Web. <http://www.textos dearte.cl/recomposicion/cuerpo2.html>

KRISTEVA, Julia. *Revolution in Poetic Language*. Trans. Leon Roudiez. New York: Columbia UP, 1984.

—. *Powers of Horror. An Essay on Abjection*. Trans. Leon Roudiez. New York: Columbia UP, 1982.

—. *Tales of Love*. Trans. Leon Roudiez. New York: Columbia UP, 1987.

—. *Black Sun. Depression and Melancholia*. Trans. Leon Roudiez. New York: Columbia UP, 1989.

MELLADO, Justo Pastor. *Dos textos tácticos*. Santiago: Ediciones Jemmy Button Ink, 1998.

—. "Arte chileno: política de un significante gráfico." May 2004. Web. <http://www.justopastormellado.cl/edicion/index.php?option=content &task=view&id=225&Itemid=28>

MEMORIA CHILENA: PORTAL DE LA CULTURA DE CHILE. "Nelly Richard." Web. 1979. <http://www.memoriachilena.cl/temas/dest.asp?id=cal(1979) richard>

OLIVER, Kelly. *Reading Kristeva. Unraveling the Double-Bind.* Bloomington: Indiana UP, 1993.

—, ed. *Ethics, Politics, and Difference in Julia Kristeva's Writing.* New York: Routledge, 1993.

RAJAN, Tilottama. "Trans-Postions of Difference: Kristeva and Post-structuralism." Olivier, *Ethics* 215-237.

RICHARD, Nelly. *Cuerpo correccional.* Santiago: VISUAL, 1980.

SJOHOLM, Cecilia. *Kristeva and the Political.* London: Routledge, 2005.

VILLALOBOS ALPÍZAR, Ivan. "La intertextualidad en Kristeva y Barthes." *Revista de filosofía de la Universidad de Costa Rica.* January 2003. Web. <http://www.articlearchives.com/955182-1.html>

PLATA QUEMADA: BANDITRY, NEOLIBERALISM AND THE DILEMMA OF LITERATURE AT THE END OF THE TWENTIETH CENTURY[1]

Juan Pablo Dabove

In comparison to the other chapters in this volume, I see this one as somewhat elegiac in tone. And, since I am from Argentina, I am afraid that this tone seems to be proper. After all, the *lamento* (lamentation) is, as Josefina Ludmer writes in *The Gaucho Genre,* one of the intonations of the fatherland. But there are some other reasons as well. In many of these chapters the collective dominant question – if never explicitly stated as such – appears to be "How to think a politics of the possible?" On the other hand, I am afraid that the reflections below on contemporary Argentine literature will be dominated by a *politics of the impossible.* Whereas other chapters may be dominated by "the fierce urgency of now," following Barack Obama, quoting Martin Luther King, with a sense that there is an anxiety or a desire to inhabit the present in a relevant fashion, in what follows I am concerned with literature, a practice whose value is defined precisely by its disjunction with the present.

1. I would like to thank Gustavo Escalante, Analía Ruscica, Mercedes Giménez, Fabricio Bazán and María Inés Giménez for their friendship, and for sharing with me their wealth of knowledge. This article would not have been possible without them. I would also like to thank Susan Hallstead and Bret Gustafson for their insightful reading.

THE VANISHING CREATURES OF THE TWENTIETH CENTURY

In July, 2008, I travelled with Gustavo Escalante and Analía Ruszica to Mercedes, a remote town in Corrientes province, in northeastern Argentina. On the outskirts of Mercedes, alongside state highway 123, the traveler finds the main sanctuary of the Gauchito Gil, a legendary nineteenth century bandit. After his capture and execution, Gil became a popular saint in the vein of the Mexican Jesús Malverde. For more than a century, the cult was a regional affair, mostly confined to the northeastern provinces of Argentina and the region of the Triple Frontier. Those who belong to the demographic and economic core of the country, the *Pampa Húmeda*, would only know about the Gauchito through immigrant construction workers or those employed in the domestic service, since these professions usually entail emigration from the northern provinces. However, in the last ten or fifteen years, the Gauchito Gil became a mass phenomenon. Every eighth of January, the alleged anniversary of the slaughter of the Gauchito, more and more people (now in the hundreds of thousands) from all over the country, from all walks of life, endure the brutal summer of Corrientes in order to give offerings to and ask favors from the saint. Since my research deals with depictions of banditry, I deemed a visit to this region important and later planned on incorporating the experience into my writing. Nonetheless, something I experienced in Corrientes merits attention. I would like to refer an anecdote, lateral to that research trip, but central to the purposes of this essay. Silvia, the kind and sociable owner of the bed and breakfast where we were staying, and a conspicuous and engaged member of the rather modest local intelligentsia, asked us to sign a petition opposing the project to dam the *Arroyo Ayuí* (a plan that for now seems to have died in the Federal Congress). This was a multi-million dollar project financed among others by the Hungarian-American billionaire George Soros, who planned to flood tens of thousands of hectares of the Iberá in order cultivate rice. The project would severely disrupt the local middle class since it would take over the economy of the region and disturb the rich ecosystem of the wetlands. Of course, we did sign the petition. But I also had a modest revelation: between the local bandit of the nineteenth century, who comes back to life as a postmodern cult (informed by both crude craftsmanship and Chinese manufacturing), and the global tycoon of the twenty-first century, who accumulates land in the savage fashion of the landowners of the nineteenth century, the twentieth century, the promise of Argentine modernity, was vanishing, or had already vanished. Silvia was the emblem of that embattled modernity, of its promises and its contradictions. Silvia despised, with equal intensity, Soros and the 'negros' who each January used the public fountain in the bucolic central square to freshen up (and, for an Argentine, the echoes of that image are unmistakable). Silvia was – like most of us – a survivor of another era, that of the educated and activist (and also classist and racist) middle class that occupied an (imagined) coherent public sphere, and that propitiated a project of development that wanted to be independent and integral. Taking into account the differences between a local intellectual and a novelist of international fame, this is the same problem that Ricardo Piglia faces and reflects upon in *Plata Quemada* (*Money to Burn*, 1997). To this topic, the dilemmas of the modern intellectual at the end of the century, as embodied in the character of Emilio Renzi (one of the main characters of the novel), I will devote the following pages.

PLATA QUEMADA

Plata Quemada was one of the most anticipated, controversial and successful Argentine novels of the 1990s.[2] It is the account of the short (from September 26th to November 6th, 1965) and brutal saga of a gang of Argentine urban bandits, comprised of Marcos Dorda (a.k.a. "*El Gaucho Rubio*"), Brignone (a.k.a. "*El nene*"), Mereles (a.k.a. "*El cuervo*"), and Mario Malito, the brain of the group. With the support of a vast (and never completely elucidated) network of politicians, policemen and army personnel, the gang holds up an armored truck transporting cash belonging to the municipality of San Fernando, in

2. The controversy had less to do with the novel itself, than with the Premio Planeta 1997 which, it was claimed, was improperly awarded to Piglia. The outcome of the protracted judicial battle that ensued tarnished Piglia's reputation in Argentina (see "Condenan a Ricardo Piglia"). But it certainly did not hinder the overall success of the novel. The 2003 Seix-Barral edition notes that between 1997 and 2003, Planeta reprinted the novel 12 times. It was also made into an award-winning, star-studded movie directed by Marcelo Piñeyro and released in 2000.

the Buenos Aires metro area. The bounty amounted to at least seven million pesos, or half a million dollars. Disregarding the implicit code of conduct between criminals (*la pesada*) and the police (*la taquería*) that calls for no unnecessary killings, the robbers recklessly murder two guards, the treasurer of San Fernando municipality and a bystander, while also wounding or maiming others. This puts the police in hot pursuit of the gang, which decides to betray its unnamed associates, to not divide the bounty, and to escape to Montevideo on its way to Brazil. This decision breaks yet another code of outlaw conduct: to never betray a loyal – or useful – accomplice. While hiding in Montevideo, the outlaws act in a careless and fatalistic fashion, jeopardizing their situation by exposing themselves too much. They further compromise their situation when they abandon and try to kill one of their Uruguayan associates. The gang ends up cornered in the apartment where it futilely sought refuge, besieged by a police force several hundred strong. The criminals, unwilling to surrender, resist in a desperate, defiant, and awe-inspiring way. The long siege is transmitted live by Uruguayan Radio Carve and Montecarlo TV. After hours of bloody gunfight the gang, fully aware of the impossibility of any escape, decides – I will come back to the topic of who, if anybody, 'decides,' – to burn, bill by bill, what remained of the half million dollars of the bounty. They send the flaming money floating down to the street, to the astonishment and anger of the crowd and the police. When the police launch their final assault, Mereles and Brignone perish, while Dorda, badly wounded, survives. Emilio Renzi, a reporter commissioned by the Argentine journal *El mundo*, writes the uncertain chronicle of the event. His chronicles are one of the main narrative voices.[3]

Even though it is set in the 1960s, this is a novel that works with (and reflects upon) the raw materials of its own present. *Plata Quemada* is, indirectly, a novel about the 1990s, the demise of modern Argentina, the triumph of neoliberalism, the wholesale commodification

3. Emilio Renzi's narrative voice is joined by a third person narrator, media accounts, and the direct and / or indirect speech (or thoughts) of many of the characters, such as Police Chief Silva, Malito, Nene, Dorda, Blanca, Martínez Tovar, etc. For an analysis of the very complex interplay of narrative voices in the novel, see Gutiérrez González

of social life and as a consequence, the enthronement of the market as regulator of said social life.[4] The novel provides an emblem for this whole process. Money: its possession, its acquisition by legal or illegal, dignified or undignified means, its contemplation, its imagining, its counterfeiting and its destruction is the central element around which the novel revolves. I thus consider *Plata Quemada* a social novel, in the same problematic sense that Piglia regards novels by Roberto Arlt, or the American crime novel, as social literature. According to Piglia, both move beyond the standard terms that define social literature (i.e. the Sartrean theory of engagement, the aesthetic of socialist realism or Lukács's theory of reflection) and address the social realm as complot, narrative web, and enigma whose core is the relationship between power (and the law) and fiction (as narrative) (*Crítica y Ficción* 22, 62, 176). Money, Piglia argues, is oftentimes the defining medium in that relationship.[5] Just like in Piglia's masterpiece *Respiración Artificial* (*Artificial Respiration*, 1980), in *Plata Quemada* the 'historical' issue is entangled with that of writing.[6] Like its predecessor, the political and aesthetic dilemma of literature (now at the end of the twentieth century) is embodied in the character of Emilio Renzi. Renzi is present in Piglia's fiction since *La invasión* (*The Invasion*, 1967). Laden with autobiographical features, Renzi is a dramatization (sometimes serious, sometimes ironic) of a certain totalizing way of relating to literature.

---

4. My reading of the novel dialogues with Joanna Page's excellent article. There is, however, a crucial difference (but not necessarily incompatible) between the two: if I read her article correctly, Page reads *Plata Quemada* as a reflection on state violence, and links that reflection to Argentina's dictatorial past. I read the novel as a reflection on more contemporary issues, and the demise of the nation-state.

5. According to Piglia, "The only mystery that American detective novels propose – and never solve – is that of capitalist relationships: money that acts as the legislator of social ethics and thus sustains the law is the only 'logic' in these narratives where everything is for sale" (Crítica y ficción 62). Arlt on his part, "does not construct his works using elements belonging to the immediate present, rather he addresses the laws that regulate society [....] he takes as his point of departure certain core elements, such as the relations between power and fiction, between money and madness, between truth and conspiracy, and he transforms them in form and in narrative strategy, he transforms them into the foundation for his fiction" (Crítica y ficción 22). All translations in this chapter are mine.

6. Idelver Avelar (*Untimely Present*) proposes that this dual focus is a defining feature of all postdictatorship Latin American (or at least Southern Cone) narrative.

More than once, Piglia has laid claim to his own convictions regarding the ethical and political preeminence of literature in the world. In Arltian fashion, Piglia dubs this preeminence "intensity."[7] But unlike *Respiración artificial*, in *Plata Quemada* the certainties that support this totalizing way of relating to literature are profoundly questioned (although, by necessity, never discarded). It is possible, therefore, to put forward the hypothesis that in *Plata Quemada*, through Renzi, Piglia revisits the assumptions that defined his practice as a 'modern' writer, one of the eminent writers of the second half of the twentieth century. Not by accident, the events narrated in the novel happen in 1965, and in the Borgesian *Epílogo* to the novel, Piglia explains that "the first contact with the story narrated in this book" happened in April, 1966 (249). Piglia published his first book of short stories in 1967. Therefore, we can think of *Plata Quemada* as a sort of fictional return to the original scene of Piglia's literature, a reflection on his entire literary production from the standpoint of the nineties, where Renzi, as the embodiment of the modern intellectual, is trapped between two logics that exceed him, two universes alien to him: that of triumphant capitalism and that of rhizomatic violence (rhizomatic since, as we will see later, there is an inextricable fluidity or lack of distinction between outlaw and lawful violence in the novel, and therefore, an impossibility to really map it).[8] It is in this inhabitable in-between that Renzi finds

7. "At heart, he is only interested in literature, he experiences everything and he sees everything from the point of view of literature and in this sense, I use Renzi to poke irony at myself. Everything that is not literature bores me, as a Czech would say. But I think that it would be better to say that Emilio Renzi is a sort of wandering Stephen Dedalus, a Quentin Compson who lives in Almagro, I mean, he is the young artist, the aesthetic character who considers the world with disdain" (*Crítica y ficción* 93). "For me literature is much more interesting than life. First, because literature has a much more elegant form, and second because it is a much more intense experience" (*Crítica y ficción* 172).

8. It is not an accident that *Plata Quemada* appeared between two major works written by members of Piglia's generation: *Escenas de la vida postmoderna* (*Scenes of Postmodern Life*, 1994), in which Beatriz Sarlo provides an analysis of the transformations of cultural life in Argentina in the 1990s, and *El cuerpo del delito: un manual* (*The Corpus Delicti: A Manual of Argentine Fictions*, 1999), by Josefina Ludmer, that traces a cultural / literary history of Argentina and that convincingly argues on the nature of crime in fiction as a cultural limit (*frontera cultural*), a tool to "differentiate and exclude." Ludmer's analysis is more than relevant for *Plata Quemada*. To a certain extent her approach informs my entire article.

the conditions of possibility – that are identical to the conditions of impossibility – for his now uncertain practice.

BANDITS AND MEN OF LETTERS

It should not be surprising that the problem of modern literature (and of the modern nation) is linked to that of outlaw violence. Modern Argentine literature was, in many ways, born of the impure alliance between bandits and men of letters. Domingo Faustino Sarmiento began *Facundo* (1845) by conjuring up the bloodied ghost of Quiroga (who Sarmiento considered the most representative in a 'lineage of bandits' that began with Artigas and ended with Chacho Peñaloza), so that Quiroga could explain the Argentine predicament (civilization vs. barbarism). José Hernández wrote his celebrated account of the life of the outlaw Martín Fierro (later exalted as the cornerstone of Argentine nationhood) when he himself was a fugitive due to his participation in the López Jordán uprising. Eduardo Gutiérrez wrote his many lengthy novels on rural bandits to make intelligible (and to indict) what he considered the ominous fate of Argentina under the aegis of Nicolás Avellaneda and Julio Argentino Roca, traitors to the Buenos Aires liberal project. In the process, he founded the Argentine popular novel.

From then on, the rural bandit became a privileged signifier articulated to changing scenarios in Argentine cultural wars. The violence of the avenger and the *haiduk* (*montonero*, in Argentina) was either derided as an emblem for the impossibilities of the national project (José Ingenieros, Ramos Mejía, Florencio Sánchez), or exalted as a heroic icon of just violence, by both the far Left and the far Right, by anarchists and authoritarian corporatists, by nativists as well as immigrants, by guerrilla fighters as well as dictatorship ideologues (see Prieto, *El criollismo*; Ludmer, "Los Moreira" in *El cuerpo del delito*, and *El género gauchesco*; Dabove *Nightmares* and "Borges y Moreira").

Plata Quemada is another link in this series and is in close dialogue with the *novelas populares con gauchos* (popular novels with gauchos) (Laera, *Tiempo*) written by Eduardo Gutiérrez in the 1880s. In *Respiración Artificial,* written and published during the military dictatorship called *Proceso de Reorganización Nacional (the Process of National*

Reorganization), Piglia explores a powerful parallelism: that between his own generation and the liberals who were exiled, marginalized or murdered by the Rosas regime ("Who among us will write *Facundo?*" famously asks one of the characters of the novel). In *Plata Quemada* Piglia positions himself as continuing the work of the heterodox writers of the 1880s. The story of the gang of bank robbers rewrites the stories of *gauchos malos* of the *gauchesco / criollista* cycle, since the novel explores another powerful parallelism: that between the modernizing leap of the last quarter of the nineteenth century, and the neoliberal, postmodern transformation of the last quarter of the twentieth century.

Indeed, for progressive intellectuals, the 1990s were a decade ushered in and seared by a double defeat: the defeat of the revolutionary project of the 1960s and 1970s and the defeat of the center-left democratic project of the 1980s. The hyperinflation that ravaged Argentina from 1989 to 1990 paved the way for the final imposition of the model of neoliberal reconversion in Argentina. Carlos Saúl Menem, president from 1989 to 1999, dismantled the welfare state and liberalized the economy, thus making the market the decisive agent in the social scene. In addition, he aligned Argentina with U.S. foreign policy, imposed the politics of 'forgetting and reconciliation' in relation to the immediate past (the Dirty War and the dictatorship) and of the rifts that had tore apart society since 1945, and he canonized a peripheral version of postmodern cultural populism (from Xuxa to Ricky Maravilla and Marcelo Tinelli) that was enthusiastically embraced by an exhausted middle class. In spite of the recent comeback of populist rhetoric during the current 'K era' (of the Kirchners) and in spite of the partial recuperation of the role of the state and the revisiting of the past through the reopening of the trials for the 1970s genocides, it is safe to say that the neoliberal project has triumphed in Argentina. Once again the model of export led-growth has been embraced. However, this time, it is an even more radical version of the nineteenth century one, since, twenty-first century Argentina is well on its way to becoming an economy based on the monoculture of soy. This is accompanied by a fast and in many cases violent concentration of land and an increasing dependence on the cycles of commodity prices in the international market. It is easy to imagine a twenty-first century Argentina as a simpler and at the same time more complex version of the nineteenth century one.

Plata Quemada runs counter to the two dominant narratives of its time: that of the end of history, and that of the end of the nation-state as the primary locus for identity affiliations. In these narratives, both history and the nation-state were to be replaced by global markets, since conflict as the engine of history and citizenship as the main subject position were to wane in the face of consumption as the all-powerful identity-making system. Piglia's novel, far from embracing this post-utopian utopia, returns to the 1960s. Against the postmodern commodification of the historical memory of the 1960s (and even of its most conflictive figures, such as Che Guevara),[9] Piglia sees the decade through the prism of one of its most confusing and refractory aspects, the politics of the outlawed '*Peronismo de la Resistencia*' (the resistance movement of a certain period of Peronism), exploring but deliberately not explaining its links with the extreme Right and the extreme Left as well as with organized crime. Also, unlike the narrative of the demise of the nation-state (sponsored not only by neoliberal ideologues, but also by other Latin American novels of the time dealing with criminal violence)[10] Piglia deliberately works within the nationalist imaginary and more specifically, within the tradition of national literature, thus tapping into the powerful Argentine tradition of the rural bandit.

Like Eduardo Gutiérrez, Piglia finds the criminal stories in police archives that help him think critically about contemporary reality.[11] Like Gutiérrez, Piglia tries to lay the foundations for a new kind of

9. The 1990s witnessed a deluge of works dealing with the most conflictive figures of the century: Eva Perón, Juan Perón, Jorge Luis Borges and Che Guevara, the foremost icon of the 1960s. But in most cases the narrative surrounding these characters is no longer articulated to any given conflict, as in the past, rather it is reterritorialized as Argentine (or Latin American) memory, thus erasing the dimension of conflict as an actual conflict from the historical or biographical narrative, even as the conflict itself is depicted.

10. In *La virgen de los sicarios* (1993) by Fernando Vallejo, *Rosario Tijeras* (1999) by Jorge Franco, or *Cidade de Deus* (1997) by Paulo Lins – some of the successful novels made into internationally celebrated films – the figures of the *sicario* (assassin), the drug dealer, and the *malandro* (con artist or roguish petty criminal) are convoked to better attest to the demise of the nation state as a social and cultural synthesis.

11. See Laera "Piglia - Eloy Martínez" for an excellent assessment of the relationships between nonfiction and fiction as a distinct series in Argentine literature, from the nineteenth century (including Gutiérrez) to the present (including Piglia).

popular novel. (In Piglia's case, we can refer to what Rama dubbed, talking about Vargas Llosa's *La guerra del fin del mundo*, the *novela culta popular* [highbrow-popular novel]). Like Gutiérrez, Piglia contrasts the legal (state-centered) perspective on outlaw violence to the oral law of the male challenge (a defining feature, as Josefina Ludmer reminds us, of the gaucho genre). Like Gutiérrez, Piglia positions his outlaws in an uncertain intersection between crime and politics, between horizontal alliances and vertical ones.

Dorda, the main character in *Plata Quemada*, is a '*Gaucho rubio*,' a 'blond' gaucho, like the real Juan Moreira, even though Gutiérrez invented a character whose main attribute was his pitch black hair and beard. (Also, like the real Juan Moreira, Dorda was not a "real" gaucho, but rather more of a rural-urban character, the "*orillero*" [hoodlum] of Borgesian fame.) But the similarities go well beyond mere nickname or physical appearance. He is described in the same fashion as Gutiérrez's *gauchos malos*. Dorda, as far as the narrator is concerned, is "*a matrero, un retobao, un asesino, hombre de agallas y de temer en la provincia de Santa Fe, en los almacenes de la frontera* (an outlaw, a rebel, a murderer, a gutsy and feared man in the Province of Santa Fe, in the frontier general stores" (224). There are two important points to note here. The first is the use of the form "*retobao*" by the third person narrator (and not by one of the characters who also narrates), a usage typical of "gaucho" pronunciation distinct from the standard form *retobado*, as has been handed down from the gaucho genre. The word "retobao" is a staple in the gaucho genre as well as in Gutiérrez's novels, as uttered by the rural police officials (*los justicias*) or the rural Justices of the Peace, both of whom were the primary evildoers in the genre. Second, the reference to the "frontier general stores" in Santa Fe is significant. Towards the middle of the twentieth century in Santa Fe province (at least, in the area where Dorda lived), there was no longer any frontier proper in the classic sense of an area of weak, sporadic or nonexistent sovereignty of the nation-state.[12] So, on the one

12. The same was not true of other areas of the country, such as the dry pampa (*pampa seca*, as opposed to the *pampa húmeda*), the Chaco region, Misiones, or Patagonia, where classic social banditry lasted well into the twentieth century and where social bandits of mythical status, such as Vairoletto, Mate Cosido, or the Velázquez brothers, were active.

hand, the voice of the narrator is intersected by the voice of the gaucho genre. On the other, a realist novel changes to a sort of crossroads of temporalities where Dorda is simultaneously a modern criminal (he sports a machine gun, not a dagger), living in a modern society (Santa Fe was the success story in agrarian Argentina, where a class of white farmers to which the Dordas belonged established and achieved a degree of prosperity), and sometimes a nineteenth century *matrero*, living in frontiers beyond the reach of the law, carrying on the "traditional" forms of sociability (the *pulpería* [bar] fight). This is also evident in the following quote:

> This lasted until the afternoon in which they were playing *sapo* at the general store, all of them quite drunk, and they began to make fun of him [Dorda] and they laughed and they kept making jokes at his expense. The Gaucho could not speak and defend himself. He only smiled, with empty eyes. Old man Soto made him the butt of all his jokes that evening: they provoked and provoked him until the Gaucho murdered him treacherously. He did him in when Soto was drunkenly trying to climb onto his horse, trying to reach the stirrup with his leg and the Gaucho, as if he were trying to stop that ridiculous dance, produced a weapon and killed him. He was the first one in a series that had no end (according to Bunge, quoting the Gaucho). All his misfortunes (*desgracias*) started that day (224).

This was a drunken fight with fatal results motivated only by the prescriptions of male honor, like the ones in *Martín Fierro* or *Juan Moreira*. Also, just like in the gaucho genre (read through Borges), the killing is not a murder but a *desgracia* (an unfortunate event).[13] And just like in Borges's *orillero* fights, or Gutiérrez *folletines*, this *desgracia* opens up an "infinite series"[14] in which the gaucho / Gaucho becomes

13. Borges notes in "La poesía gauchesca": "The true ethics of the *criollo* [. ..] maintains that to shed somebody else's blood is not that important, and that to kill is something that just happens to men. [...] 'Who did not owe a death in my time?' I heard one afternoon the mellow complaint of an elderly man. I will not forget, either, an *orillero* who once told me with utmost seriousness 'Mister Borges, it is true that I have been in jail many times, but always for murder.'"

14. For an examination of the "infinite series" of challenges that make up the *gaucho malo* biography, see Laera, Tiempo, and Dabove "Sobre algunas ficciones de violencia."

at the same time a fierce, cool and supremely elegant fighter[15] (possessed of a martial elegance that contrasts with a cheap and showy sense of personal elegance) intent on the humiliation and suppression of the hated police (40).[16] This uphill battle, this infinite fight, pervades Guitérrez's *gauchos malos* with a distinct sense of fatalism, to the point that Moreira's death is, to an extent, "suicide by police." Malito's gang is pervaded by the same fatalism (98) that prompts them to take unnecessary risks, such as Nene's sexual escapades to Plaza Zavala (reminiscent of Moreira's to the brothel "*La Estrella*") where he meets Margarita Taibo (a.k.a. Giselle, a.k.a. *la morochita del norte de Río Negro* [99]), and the whole gang's orgies that bring them into contact with a taxi boy who would later inform on them to the police (134).

Just like in classic bandit narratives, Dorda's identity oscillates between monstrosity, abjection and epic. And he appears, like the Rob Roy of Samuel Taylor Coleridge, in open disjunction with his own time.[17] As Brignone puts it "Let's assume that there is a war, or that he would have been born in the era of General San Martín, the Gaucho, Nene used to say; he would have a statue erected in his honor. He would be, I don't know, a hero. But he was born at the wrong time" (79). This affirmation echoes some classic statements by Sarmiento on the two 'bandits' that together with Rosas epitomize the River Plate predicament: José Gervasio Artigas and Facundo Quiroga.[18]

15. "The bravest and coolest guy that you have ever seen (according to Brignone). Once, with a 9mm gun, he made a stand against the pigs in Lanús and kept them at bay until Nene was able to break through, driving backwards, and rescue him. It was awesome. He was just standing there, shooting, holding his gun with both hands, completely cool, boom, boom, with an elegance worth seeing, and all the cops shitting themselves" (79).

16. "Dorda killed him for no reason at all. And certainly, not because the policeman represented a threat. He had killed him because he hated the police more than anything in the world, and he thought, in an utterly irrational fashion, that each policeman that he killed was not going to be replaced. 'One less' was Gaucho's motto, as if he were diminishing the ranks of an enemy army that could not be renovated."

17. "He came an age too late; / Or shall we say an age too soon?" ponders Wordsworth in the superb poem "Rob Roy's Grave" (1803-1807).

18. On Artigas, Sarmiento says: "Had the Spaniards entered Argentina in 1811, it is possible to think that our Bolívar would have been Artigas" (17). On Quiroga: "The first ray of the May sun illuminated for him the glorious career of military service to the fatherland. And there is no doubt that, with his strong temperament

Much like in classic bandit narratives, in *Plata Quemada* the demise of the bandit is brought about by female treason. Indeed, females are twice traitors. Mereles's lover (Blanca Galeano) reveals under duress what she knows about the gang's escape to Uruguay (89). Margarita Taibo, on the other hand, disowns her relationship with Nene, accuses him of rape, and most likely provides information that leads police to the gang's hideout (201).

Dorda and Nene are a couple. But the homosexual topic in the novel has less to do with gay culture than with the archetypal gaucho couples of the gaucho genre (perhaps with a passing nod to Osvaldo Lamborghini).[19] Such is the case of Fierro and Cruz (Cruz dies sweetly in the arms of Fierro, who is devastated by this death), Moreira and Andrade (who kiss each other on the mouth, and who embrace each other like two tender lovers), or Santos Vega and Carmona (who profess each other a love beyond death such that when Carmona dies, Vega is unable to survive him much longer). This has less to do with gay culture than with a circulation of desire among men in certain social spaces such as jail, bars, boxing, and certain professions - including, notably, literature (*Crítica y ficción* 206).

And finally, the drawn out siege of the gang could be understood as a rewriting of Moreira's last fight. Completely surrounded in confined spaces (an apartment, a room), Moreira (and Malito's gang) put up a fight where bravery, martial skills and manly bravado, in the face of vastly superior police forces, amount to "the most formidable siege ever recorded by the River Plate police" (133).

But this analogy has a limit, since *Plata Quemada* has, vis-à-vis its precedents, both a deficit and an excess. On the one hand, *Plata Quemada* does not harbor populist or leftist illusions about the idea of the

---

and his instincts bent towards destruction and butchery, moralized by disciplines and ennobled by the sublimity of the pursuit, Facundo would have returned one day from Perú, Chile or Bolivia as one of the generals of the Republic" (83).

19. The episode in *Plata Quemada* in which Malito sodomizes and kills a policeman who had tortured him is, I would argue, a direct rewriting of one of the best known texts by Lamborghini, "El niño proletario" (included in *Sebregondi Retrocede*, 1973). "Malito looked for [the cop] and kidnapped him one night when the guy was getting out of a bus in Varela. He drowned him in a ditch. He forced him on his knees and he submerged his face in the mud, and they say that he pulled the guy's pants down and he raped him while the cop shook with his head under water (20).

gang as a metaphor for 'the people.' Piglia deliberately departs from the well-established tradition that presents criminality as pre-political popular (or class) rebellion. (This tradition can be traced as far as back as Friedrich Engels, and has its foremost representatives in Eric Hobsbawm and Fernand Braudel. In Latin American literature, perhaps the best literary examples of this tradition are *Seara Vermelha*, by Jorge Amado and *Redoble por Rancas*, by Manuel Scorza).[20] In the tradition of the gaucho as an icon of resistance, the constitution of a popular subject is decisive. A foremost example is the scene that opens the film *Juan Moreira*, by Leonardo Favio, when Moreira's corpse is the axis of a spontaneous revolt against the state, under the cry of "*Viva Juan Moreira, mierda!*" It is crucial that in this revolt, the *paisanos* (poor inhabitants of the countryside) have nothing to gain but the vindication of the memory of one of their own. In *Plata Quemada*, to the contrary, the popular is entirely absent. This absence can be doubly specified: in the novel there are no proletarians nor real activists, only criminals, policemen and the elements that revolve around them (such as male and female prostitutes, psychiatrists, etc.), a journalist (to whom I will return), and the derided middle class (the bank treasurer, the shop owner whose vehicle is stolen during the getaway, the bakery owner who calls the police, the owner of the deli, Blanca's parents, the witnesses of the siege), all of whom lack a story and for whom money is the principle of reality. The urban bandits are institutionalized subjects who become hardened criminals in jail, in the reformatory, or in the psychiatric ward. Therefore, in their criminal careers they do not resort to a previous cultural or human capital – in terms of knowledge or social reciprocity – as an asset. The criminals have no allies, real or virtual, only accomplices or paid associates. Nor do they have a community that they could rejoin. That is why their only option is exile, and why they constantly betray everybody, yet do so, not even, in fact, through betrayal (of a prior social trust), but through dishonoring a contract.

However, connected to this deficit, there is an excess, an event, in the sense that Baudrillard gave to the word in his essay on terrorism; one that is completely absent from bandit narratives and that makes

---

20. For a discussion of banditry as pre-political rebellion, see Dabove, Nightmares, Introduction.

the gang's isolation and incomprehensibility even more radical: the burning of the money. This is a purely performative, completely public act since the entire country can watch it. But at the same time, it is a completely secret act. It just happens, unexplained, inexplicable. The novel dwells extensively on the perspective of the characters inside the apartment, and the apartment is under constant audio surveillance. (The operator of the listening device, Roque Pérez, is one of the significant 'voices' that narrates the events [179, 188]). But, in spite of this, the novel never represents the process of decision making that led to the act. Suddenly, from a viewpoint outside the apartment, we see (along with everybody else) a column of white smoke. And then, when the viewpoint shifts indoors, we realize that even those who are burning the money seem to be horrified by their actions ("To burn money is a sin," states Dorda, who is in charge of burning it). This is crucial and is not a simple oversight: the burning of the money is an act without a subject (that is what makes it an event), or to be more precise, an act for which the Western imagination cannot imagine a subject: "Money was the only thing that could possibly justify the deaths; if they did this, they did it for money. But if now they are burning it, that means that they have no morals, nor motives, and that they act and kill gratuitously only because of their taste for evil, pure evil" (190). The burning of the money is a 'gratuitous act' (the reference to Roberto Arlt, as read by Masotta, is unavoidable), an occurrence of 'pure evil.'[21] Dorda indeed reflects on the nature of evil. Significantly, he does not make it a personal attribute or a personal failure: "Evil – said Dorda, very high because of the mixture of speed and cocaine – is not something that you do voluntarily. It is a light that comes and carries you away" (73). There is no 'evil will,' since evil will is, for Western thought at least since Plato, an epistemological impossibility. (The will, the argument goes, may want things that society regards as evil, but the will, the very act of volition, considers them good, since they satisfy the will. Hence, the will only wills good. Hence, evil does not exist as the object of volition, or it exists only negatively). The gang is close to this paradox of pure evil, of the evil will, when they burn the money without a purpose (not even a purpose

21. Laera ("Piglia-Eloy") mentions the gratuitous act not in relation to the burning of the money, but in relation to Nene's "treason" to his own class.

of defiance), and they do it without manifesting a will: "*una luz que viene y te lleva*" (a light that comes and carries you away).

The burning of the money breaks all social pacts, even those that include criminals.[22] But it does this not with the goal (stated or unstated, conscious or unconscious) of founding a new social one, nor of returning to a previous one (Nene, Cuervo and Dorda are not Luddites or peasant rebels). They do not seek a 'world upside down;' "*Todos comprendieron que ese acto era una declaración de guerra total, una guerra directa y en regla contra toda la sociedad* (All of them understood that the act was a total declaration of war, a direct and methodical war against all society)." In essence, it was a war not only against the entire society (*toda la sociedad*) but against all society (*toda sociedad*), including their own "criminal society."

In society money is not only the means of exchange of goods. Exchange has become the rationale for all human interactions. The burning of the money is, on the one hand, a repudiation of that logic, but it is also, as the novel expresses, an act for which there is no possible exchange in the form of punishment or retribution. Killed, maimed, or tortured, the criminals ultimately won, because they put themselves beyond winning or losing. The mob that abuses Dorda, already half-dead, is certainly letting loose a 'primal instinct' of revenge (242). But revenge is a form of exchange and communication destined by definition to fail to exorcise an act that does not belong to the orbit of exchange or communication.

BURNT MONEY

"Somebody does something that nobody understands, an act that exceeds everybody's experience. That act does not last, it has the fleeting quality of life itself, it is not narrative, but it is the only act that is

22. "The people, indignant, immediately remembered the destitute, the poor people, the inhabitants of the countryside who live in very precarious conditions, and the orphaned children whose future would have been guaranteed with that money [...] Just by saving one of those orphans, those cretins would have justified their lives, said a lady. But the witnesses added: they are evil, they are bad to the bone, they are just beasts. The television cameras filmed and then broadcasted all day long the repetition of that ritual" (192).

worth narrating" (*Prisión Perpetua* 35). The burning of the money is such an event. It has a foundational character, since it makes Renzi's evolution from a journalist to a writer possible. The burning of the money has indeed an aesthetic dimension that the novel emphasizes:

> The way in which they burnt the money is proof of their genius as well as of their evil, because they burnt the money making the hundred peso bills that they were incinerating very visible, one after another, the hundreds burnt like butterflies whose wings are touched by a candle's flame and they flutter for a second still, already on fire and they fly through the air for an infinite instant before burning down to the ground, consumed by the flame.
> And after all those unending minutes in which they saw the bills burn like birds of fire, there remained only a pile of ashes, a funerary tribute to society's values (as one of the witnesses declared on TV), a most beautiful column of blue ashes that glided down from the window, like the drizzle of the burnt remains of the dead that are spread on the ocean or the meadows or the forests, but never over the filth of the city streets; never should the ashes float over the stones of the concrete jungle (193).

But this is not what is decisive here, quite to the contrary. This aesthetic translation (burning bills as butterflies or firebirds) is really a way of reterritorializing the event (and by doing this, it suppresses its power to produce commotion) making the burning of the money a kind of *memento mori* or perhaps, an illustration of the *Vanitas vanitatum omnia vanitas*. In fact, there is a powerful collective impulse to provide a narrative that incorporates what just happened into the order of things. The novel affirms that the act "paralyzed the city and the entire country with horror," but the reterritorialization occurs simultaneously with the event itself, under the form of the TV and radio broadcasts. They amplify the horror by giving it maximum exposure. At the same time, it distances as a spectacle (and horrifying spectacles are a privileged mass media commodity, in particular in the 1990s mass media). In this way, a "Medieval Sabbath" or an 'act of cannibalism,' as the TV host Jorge Foister puts it, inevitably become a 'reality show' where horror is edited and suppressed, while exposed, because of its exposure, for mass consumption. (This transformation of a horrifying reality in mass media spectacle appears in the novel, for the first time, when Lucía Passero, the bakery owner, witnesses – and causes – a death. But for her, watching from behind the window, "was like watching a movie that was played for her alone" [124])

There is another attempt in the novel at understanding (or taming) the event, this time from an 'empathetic' point of view, by incorporating it into the flow of academic discourse:

> In an interview with the journal *Marcha*, the Uruguayan philosopher Washington Andrada pointed out that he considered the terrible act a kind of innocent *potlatch* carried out in the context of a society that had forgotten that ritual, an absolutely and completely gratuitous act, a gesture of sheer expense and sheer waste that in other societies has been considered a sacrifice offered to the gods, because only the most valuable deserves to be sacrificed, and there is nothing more valuable among us than money (192-193).

However, the philosopher fails in two respects. A potlatch is never a gratuitous act. It is an act of destruction, of course, that has no discernible economic motivation or rationale. But it is still an act of exchange, since it earns the performer the act of prestige and preeminence, and it is above all, an act of community building , quite the opposite of the event discussed here.

Renzi is the only character who tries to understand the act on its own terms even though he is not free from assigning a transcendental (sacrificial or tragic) meaning to the event. This occurs when he calls Dorda "a Christ [...] a scapegoat, the idiot who suffers everybody's pain" (240). But for the most part, Renzi is acutely aware of his lack of epistemological or ethical privilege, as assigned to the modern intellectual. One should recall that Renzi, in *Respiración Artificial* appears comfortably installed in all the intellectual, political and ethical guarantees that defined the modern writer. Renzi is on the good side of History, on the good side of the cultural wars of his time. And he knows it. The novel is firmly (and subtly) installed in the horror of the dictatorship, but that horror is not intensified by self-doubt. In *Plata Quemada*, Renzi is dispossessed of all those assurances. First and foremost, his knowledge of the fact that he is narrating is entirely imperfect.[23] Many

---

23. In addition to this, Renzi's position in structural as well as ethical terms is rather precarious. The novel is a critique of the role of money in society. But Renzi,

facts, crucial to the complete or even sufficient understanding of the story remain in the dark. For example: the degree of involvement (if any) of the gang with the *Peronismo de la resistencia* is never clear. Sometimes it seems that this involvement is just a claim by the police, made out of paranoia or to legitimize extreme measures taken against the gang. Sometimes, it seems that it is a claim by the bandits themselves, made either out of delusional fantasies or sarcastic attempts at legitimation (132, 162). Similarly the degree of involvement of the police and / or the army with the gang is never clear (140). These uncertainties, in turn, make the main scene of the novel (the siege and the burning of the money) completely obscure (in spite of their enormous visibility). Something is happening, criminals are fighting the police. But: is this a law enforcement operation? Is this a monumental cover up? Is this a bloody revenge that a criminal faction (in police uniform) is exacting from former allies, on a spectacular scale? "We had the experience but missed the meaning; an approach to the meaning restores the experience." T.S. Eliot's quote serves as an epigraph to *Prisión Perpetua*. In *Plata Quemada* we have (we think we have) some of the facts (the experience), but we do not have the meaning. Therefore, we have nothing. (Renzi, the one supposedly in charge of providing that meaning, leaves us completely in the dark, because he is in the dark.) Or, to put it another way: Renzi inhabits, in a conscious fashion, that lack of meaning that defines the space of literature.

In *Respiración Artificial* Renzi is a rather overbearing and pedantic *porteño*. But he is the undeniable main character of the novel. *Plata Quemada*'s Renzi is a secondary character, full of doubts and misgivings. He is full of doubts, except one: he understands that the one who is closest to the meaning of the event that defines the novel (and his future career as writer) is the one who is incapable (and unwilling) to explain it to him: Dorda, the true artist of the novel.

Dorda is the artist of the novel in two ways. First, he possesses all the mythic features of the avant-garde or 1960s artist: he is deranged, he is a multiple addict, he is suicidal and nurtures his own demise, he

its chronicler, writes for money, and not even for a lot of money. And unlike the great nonfiction writer of the 1960s, Rodolfo Walsh, who engaged in arduous and problematic investigations in which crime and politics intersected, Renzi writes with fear, and he writes what he is allowed to write, as he himself confesses to police chief Silva.

has mystical tendencies, he is misunderstood (243), he does not care about money (69), he does not have an oeuvre (his 'art' is pure performance), he is unaware of the fact that he is an artist, he is, in effect, in touch with evil.

But he is an artist in a more decisive, 'profound' way. Renzi, much like a dedicated student, looks for words in a dictionary, and asks for his supervisor's permission to use big words (such as *hybris*, or *muthos*) in his chronicles (91, 106). Dorda, on the other hand, has a tortured relationship with language. He is aphasic (79) and he does not know how to express himself (and therefore goes weeks and months without talking). But, precisely because of this "he knows how to transform words into living things, needles that poke your flesh and destroy your soul like an egg broken by the edge of the frying pan" (186). For Dorda, words have personal resonances, such as in the case of '*pusilánime*' (pusillanimous) (160) or '*pupilo*' (pupil) (221). For Dorda, language does not translate reality; language is coeval with reality: "Dorda watched the serial movies and he always translated the movie as if he were inside it, as if he lived all the events in the movie: 'Once he was expelled from the movie theater run by the local parish because he put his dick out and he started to pee: he was watching a kid in the movie who was urinating, his back to the camera, in the middle of the night, in the middle of the countryside...' verbatim from the sacristan to Dr. Bunge in the psychiatric report" (81). This is why he is also the one who is constantly reading the world as a system or as prose made up of obscure signs, with an invariable ominous meaning of which he is the interpreter (12).

But above all, Dorda is an artist, and radically so, because the burning of the money is a radical experience with signs (that is what money is, after all: a sign) that goes far beyond mere experimentation or mere scandal (or mere intention). The burning is a performance that is, by definition, intransitive, immanent, incommunicable (although emphatically communicated), that escapes all translation, all foundation, all sharing, with a power to produce commotion that can only be imperfectly exorcised: a truly artistic act. It is artistic as well as political, since it intervenes in the symbolic economy of the polis, but it intervenes only as an irrecoverable interruption.

Renzi moves towards that ideal of art and is forever excluded from it. He is condemned to move in between this ideal and the mundane realities of twentieth century Argentina. But in his failure to reach it, he finds his condition of possibility as a writer. Borges famously stated in "La supersticiosa ética del lector": "I do not know whether music can despair of music or marble of marble. I do know that literature is an art that can foresee the time when it will be silenced, an art that can become inflamed with its own virtue, fall in love with its own decline, and court its own demise" (217). *Plata Quemada* narrates the experience of the beginning of writing, and in that beginning, it narrates the clear consciousness of the end.

As I said, modern Argentine literature is born in the nineteenth century of the impure alliance of bandits and men of letters. At the other end of the historical cycle, in *Plata Quemada* Piglia adds another impure alliance: that between Renzi and the *Gaucho Rubio*. The bandit allows Renzi to imperfectly access the experience from which he will become a man of letters, and at the same time divests him of all the certainties about that condition.

WORKS CITED

AVELAR, Idelber. *The Untimely Present. Postdictatorial Latin American Fiction and the Task of Mourning*. Durham and London: Duke UP, 1999.

BAUDRILLARD, Jean. *The Spirit of Terrorism and Other Essays*. London: Verso, 2003.

BORGES, Jorge Luis. *Obras Completas*. Vol. 1. Buenos Aires: Emecé, 2005.

"Condenan a Ricardo Piglia y a la editorial por el Premio Planeta." *Clarín*. 1 March 2005. Web. 15 March 2009. <http://www.clarin.com/diario/2005/03/01/sociedad/s-03015.htm>

DABOVE, Juan Pablo. *Nightmares of the Lettered City: Banditry and Literature in Latin America, 1816-1929*. Pittsburgh: Pittsburgh UP, 2007.

—. "Borges y Moreira: las pasiones del gaucho malo." *In Memoriam JLB*. Ed. Rafael Olea Franco. México: El Colegio de México, 2009. 350-375.

—. "Eduardo Gutiérrez: narrativa de bandidos y novela popular argentina." *Historia crítica de la literatura argentina. El brote de los géneros*. Ed. Noé Jitrik. Vol. 3. Volumen Director Alejandra Laera. Buenos Aires: Emecé, 2009.

—. "Sobre algunas ficciones de violencia en la obra de J. L. Borges: bandidaje, melancolía, ley." *Variaciones Borges* 22 (2006): 167-89.

GARABANO, Sandra. "Homenaje a Roberto Arlt: Crimen, falsificación y violencia en Plata quemada." *Hispamérica* 32.96 (2003): 85-90.

GUTIÉRREZ, Eduardo. *Juan Moreira*. Buenos Aires: Perfil, 1999.

—. *Hormiga Negra*. Buenos Aires: Perfil, 1999.

—. *Santos Vega*. Buenos Aires: Imprenta La Patria Argentina, 1880.

—. *Una amistad hasta la muerte. Continuación de Santos Vega*. Buenos Aires: N. Tommasi y Cia, 1886.

—. *La muerte de Buenos Aires*. Buenos Aires: N. Tommasi y Cia, 1888.

GUTIÉRREZ GONZÁLEZ, Josué. "Notas para un mapa de voces en *Plata quemada*." *Palabra y el Hombre* 125 (2003): 115-26.

HERNÁNDEZ, José. *Martín Fierro*. 1872-1879. Eds. Elida Lois and Ángel Núñez. Madrid: ALLCA XX, 2001.

Hijos de Fierro, Los. Dir. Fernando E. Solanas. Perf. Julio Troxler, Martíniano Martínez, Tito Almerjeiras. Original Music by Roberto Lar, and Alfredo Zitarrosa. Buenos Aires: Colección Solanas, 1990. Film.

HOBSBAWM, Eric. *Bandits*. New York: Pantheon Books, 2000.

Juan Moreira. Screenplay by Leonardo Favio and Zuhair Jury. Dir. Leonardo Favio. Perf. Rodolfo Bebán, Edgardo Suárez, Jorge Villalba, et al. Clásicos del cine argentino. International DVD Group S.A, 2001. Film.

LAERA, Alejandra. "Piglia - Eloy Martínez. Contribuciones a la relación entre realidad y ficción en la literatura argentina." *Milpalabras* 3 (2002), n/a.

—. *El tiempo vacío de la ficción: las novelas argentinas de Eduardo Gutiérez y Eugenio Cambaceres*. Buenos Aires: FCE, 2004.

LAMBORGHINI, Osvaldo. "El niño proletario." *Sebregondi Retrocede. Novelas y Cuentos*. Barcelona: Ediciones del Serbal, 1988. 63-69.

LUDMER, Josefina. *El género gauchesco: un tratado sobre la patria*. Buenos Aires: Sudamericana, 1988.

—. *El cuerpo del delito: un manual*. Buenos Aires: Perfil Libros, 1999.

PAGE, Joanna. "Crime, Capitalism, and Storytelling in Ricardo Piglia's *Plata quemada*." *Hispanic Research Journal* 5.1 (2004): 27-42.

PIGLIA, Ricardo. *Respiración Artificial*. Buenos Aires: Seix Barral, 2002.

—. *Crítica y ficción*. Buenos Aires: Anagrama, 2006.

—. *Plata quemada*. Buenos Aires: Planeta, 1997.

—. "Teoría del complot." *Ramona* 23 (2002): 4-14.

Plata quemada. Screenplay by Marcelo Piñeiro and Marcelo Figueras. Dir. Marcelo Piñeiro. Perf. Eduardo Noriega, Leonardo Sharaglia, Leticia Bredice. Santa Monica, CA: Strand Releasing Home Video, 2002. Film.

PRIETO, Adolfo. *El discurso criollista en la formación de la Argentina moderna*. Buenos Aires: Sudamericana, 1988.

SARLO, Beatriz. *Scenes from Postmodern Life*. Minneapolis, MN: U of Minnesota P, 2001.

SARMIENTO, Domingo Faustino. *Facundo o Civilización y Barbarie*. Caracas: Biblioteca Ayacucho 1977.

Intellectuals in Cuba: Facing a Future That Is Already Present[1]

Arturo Arango

With respect to Cuba, time seems to become disrupted, dislocated. For the past several years, perhaps from the moment that the capitalist restoration began in the territories that once comprised the former Soviet Union and in the countries which under similar doctrinary principles called themselves 'Socialist,' there has been a sense that Cuba is a country on the verge of change, reform or collapse, in transition towards another system or towards a different model of socialism. That delayed expectation, as well as the tension that has accumulated within and outside the Island about the political future of the country and the changes that the new living conditions and the different international contexts have inexorably provoked in common citizens, make the past, the present and the future appear as temporal dimensions that intermingle, without precise limits, as capsules that expand or contract and even overlap, depending on the circumstances.

In the already distant year of 2001, Iván de la Nuez titled his collection of texts authored by twelve Cuban writers *Almanaque: Cuba y el día después* (*Almanac: Cuba and the Day After*). These authors had been called upon to give their impressions about "the future of the

1. Translated by Rosalía Bermúdez.

country." In his prologue to the anthology, de la Nuez explains: "If there is one thing that these writers know is that it is not enough to merely think about the future. It is necessary to situate oneself in it" (9). With this, he set into motion the time machine in which we have been existing to this day. He reveals an obvious paradox:

> The Future, in capital letters, has already been inhabited by them. Were they not born and raised hearing that the 'future belongs entirely to socialism?' [...] Only now, upon awakening from the futurist dream, they are forced to imagine and live in a world that differs from the one that was promised – as if they were precariously balanced on a tightrope between a future that has been lost and a future that is possible (de la Nuez, "El hombre" 9-10).

In spite of having been conceived a decade after the dissolution of the Soviet Union and the beginning of the Cuban crisis euphemistically called the 'Special Period,' *Cuba y el día después* is situated in a context that already, as of now, belongs to the past. That context expressed the disenchantment, the failed values and the vanished promises, as well as the confusion of uncertain and unknown prospects that supposedly awaited us. It also represented the new tensions and hopes reawakened by the transformations that dissolved the commercial and political configurations progressively implanted in Cuba since 1960 and, more concretely, since 1973. In 2001, the evidence of the 'lost future' was even greater than the visibility of the 'possible future', although the alternatives defined by Iván de la Nuez have not varied substantially from that time to the present:

> Children of the Revolution and at once children of the culture of books, these writers will live in a future in which the Revolution, and the culture of books are perceived as a *limit zone*; a frontier where the most radical proposals include a hint of their respective disappearances, whereas those that are most balanced can only attain their continuity through the radical transformation of the meaning those terms have had until now (de la Nuez, "El hombre" 9; original emphasis).

Six years later, at the beginning of the series of conferences titled "Cultural Politics during the Revolutionary Period: Memory and Reflection," during the inaugural debate of the series, Desiderio Navarro made clear what the final significance was of the action that gathered 600 people in the Che Guevara conference room at the *Casa de las Américas*: "This is not about Pavón and his mishaps, but rather about the vision of socialism and democracy that inspired him and that lives on today, even unconsciously, in the minds of many. In a final analysis, this is not about the withered color of an old quinquennium but about the *color of our future*" (Navarro 24; original emphasis).

In January of 2007, when Cuban television presented to the audience the specter of Luis Pavón,[2] aged and with an amended political and cultural biography, Cuba's possible future seemed to be much closer; and not only as a result of the passing of time, but rather because a new event, this time of a natural order, had incremented the perspective for change on the Island since July of 2006. I am referring to Fidel Castro's illness, and to the formal proclamation, signed by Fidel himself, of a provisional government to be headed by Raúl Castro. The tremendous mobilization provoked by a televised program lasting a mere five minutes was the result more of the tensions that propelled the country towards the future than of the festering wounds of the past, the pending debates and the traumas that still needed to be exorcized. The vast majority of intellectuals, artists and writers that participated, in one way or another, in that mobilization, which took the form of a web of exchanges about the political culture of the Revolution, were aware of the fact that an unseen and unusual option of participating in the design of the future could be opening for Cuba. The wheels of time, previously overshadowed by inertia, seemed to gain momentum and speed, while the present, the past and the future once again intermingled in an almost physical and corporeal way. On the night of January 30th, while the public who listened to the texts read by Desiderio Navarro and Ambrosio Fornet was fundamentally composed of individuals who had been direct victims of the repression that occurred in the cultural spheres during the '70s, several dozen young people remained outside of the building for hours, anxious to participate in a debate, which for them signified not the absolution of past debts, but rather the renewal of those conflicts. The televised specter of Pavón, like an aged and mistaken King Hamlet, also

2. Luis Pavón Tamayo was president of the *Consejo Nacional de Cultura de Cuba* from 1971 to 1976. See Navarro, *La política cultural del período revolucionario*.

provoked young writers, artists and students in the Humanities, particularly those of Journalism and Social Communication, to take an interest in researching that past, which had been cloaked in silence.[3]

In his introductory text for the series of lectures, Navarro defined four positions about society and culture "that struggled not only at a macro social scale, but often within one's own mind." What is interesting, in terms of these irregularities in the flowing of time which I am attempting to identify, is that in presenting them as 'models,' they are implicitly projected to the future. The struggle – in whatever scale you want to consider it, but primarily amongst persons, groups or ideological tendencies – is not to sustain some of those positions, but rather to implement them and make them hegemonic or, instead, to allow two or three of these models to survive in a more or less enduring or precarious harmony.

According to Desiderio Navarro, those conflicting models are:

1) What Marx called "military communism" (*comunismo de cuartel*) (artistic monism: a demand for an apologetic and acritical art, the artist only as an entertainer or an illustrator of a specific thesis)
2) Democratic socialism (artistic dialogue which includes and fosters a socio-critical art)
3) State capitalism or "market socialism" (artistic pluralism with the exclusion of socio-critical art, open towards America-centric globalization and the fostering of a culture destined for national and transnational markets)
4) Neoliberal Capitalism (the surrendering of art to national and transnational markets; neutralization and eventual recuperation of socio-critical art by the market)

The projection of these models toward the future is most obvious in the second model: Democratic Socialism, which amongst all of them is the one that has not yet been carried out, the one that has

---

3. Among many other actions, we could consider, for instance, unpublished dissertations such as those by Daniel Salas González, Anneris Ivette Leyva García y Abel Samohano Fernández, and Jennifer Enríquez Romero, all of them presented for the degree of "*licenciatura*" in 2008 at the *Facultad de Comunicación*, Universidad de La Habana. Also, *Sobre un vacío periodístico*, audio-visual by Jesús Hernández, was produced following his strategy to simulate interviews about events not reported by local newspapers.

remained a mere aspiration, perhaps a utopia, and which has up until this time only achieved minor and limited spaces of its implementation within Cuba's cultural field.

In his recent book, *El estante vacío* (*The Empty Shelf*), Rafael Rojas also identifies the group that ascribes to the second model and recognizes, from a different perspective, what I previously described as a propulsion toward the future. [4] According to Rojas, our dilemma lies in that "[in spite of] the desire to imprint an anti-Stalinist or Post-Soviet content" to Cuban Socialism, "institutionally [this ideology] has not ceased from being totalitarian." So, we aspire to "an impossible *organicity*, one only attainable after a change of regime, in a leftist democratic government" (Rojas 144). I take the opportunity now to comment upon what I perceive to be two fundamental errors in Rojas' perception, errors that are related to the ways in which we establish our respective positions regarding the future of Cuba. The first of these is to assume "that the adjective [socialist] is understood by the government as a sign of unconditional loyalty" (145). Over the past fifty years, in the political history of Cuba, there abound examples that belie this univocity. It would be more than enough to cite the closing of the journal *Pensamiento Crítico* (*Critical Thought*) and the disintegration of the Philosophy Department at the University of Havana in 1971, both defenders of a more heterogeneous socialism, in ideological terms, a Marxism that did not ascribe to Soviet doctrines.

In my opinion Rojas' error lies upon three mistaken suppositions: the first of which is the consideration of the word socialist in a single dimension and the idea that what he calls 'the power structure' does not perceive the different ways in which the term is used; which, as happens with the word 'revolutionary,' can acquire a similar significance. The ambiguity of both of these terms is evidence, in the final analysis, of that very spectrum which Navarro groups into his four

4. In his book Rojas mentions: "Desiderio Navarro, Víctor Fowler, Julio César Guanche, Arturo Arango, Rafael Hernández, Celia Hart…" (144). In fact, the list is much longer and it should start with the essayists and historians that belonged to the ex-Department of Philosophy at the University of Havana and the journal *Pensamiento Crítico*. I am referring, among others, to Fernando Martínez Heredia, Aurelio Alonso, Juan Valdés Paz, Eduardo Torres Cuevas, Oscar Zanetti, Pedro Pablo Rodríguez, Germán Sánchez, etc. In this respect, see Fernando Martínez Heredia, "Pensamiento social y política de la Revolución."

models, three of which could be qualified as socialist or even revolutionary. The other erroneous supposition is to consider the 'power structure' as a fixed and homogenous tendency. Even the centralism that has characterized the Cuban state has experienced periods of contraction and expansion. The diversity of tendencies that coexist under the umbrella-concept of unity became more visible especially during the early stages of the Revolution, when the state had to retreat (as occurred especially at the beginning of the '90s). The third mistake is to assume that the majority of the intellectuals living in Cuba believe that "any trace of Stalinism has been abandoned" and that we are satisfied with "the 'self-criticism' of the grey quinquennium and the recognition of the victims on the part of the state" (Rojas 145).

On the contrary, it seems obvious to me that in recent years, in various forms, that notion of intellectual engagement (the so-called *compromiso del intelectual*, commitment of the intellectual) prevalent in the 1960s – which I now prefer to place under the perspective of what Edward Said called "the public role of writers and intellectuals" – has been renewed. In this sense, in the words of Said: "part of what we do as intellectuals is not only to define a situation, but also to discern amongst the possibilities for active intervention, whether we implement them ourselves or recognize them in others that have preceded us or are already been working on them: the intellectual as sentinel" (174). Such reactivation of political activity in a prominent zone in the Cuban intellectual field has obviously implied the positioning of individuals and also the occupation of spaces from which to undertake what Said calls 'active intervention,' and this has been happening as much within and outside of the Island.

I will reflect upon some voices that seem to illustrate these positions, some of which have also held a prominent protagonism in these debates. From Miami, in a recent article, Emilio Ichikawa addresses Barack Obama's declarations regarding the necessity for a new policy to rule the United States' relations with Cuba, turning to a new reading of the Platt Amendment, the appendix that the United States Government imposed upon the first Cuban Constitution of 1902. For Ichikawa, the text presented by Senator Platt was "simple and sufficient" and constituted "a ruling for the contention of the excesses and deviations of a people that, precisely because it was initiating itself in the art of self-government at the beginning of the 20th century, had not shown yet its capacity to accomplish that task." In a tie that binds together the beginnings of the Republic with a post-revolutionary future, Ichikawa places the country in a new neocolonial position: one which, according to him, Cuba will sooner or later have to accept.

In *The Empty Shelf*, Rafael Rojas also focuses intensely on these temporal dislocations which I have been detecting thus far. Rojas writes:

> Not recognizing that the kingdom of the Messiah, with the duality pointed out by Agamben, has come to an end, past, present and future are not constituted as such, and the subjects lose their historical orientation. Cuba's temporality starts to function in a synchronic and not in a diachronic way, in a kind of carnival of simultaneity that makes it difficult to set the foundations for a new sovereignty (137).

Therefore, the future, in order to fulfill itself, would require a historic break that would fix without ambiguity the limitations of a past in which the historic time of the Cuban Revolution would remain as a period that has been definitively surpassed.

On February 23, 2009, on the eve of the elections for a new Cuban president by the *Asamblea Nacional del Poder Popular* (National Assembly of Popular Power), Iván de la Nuez published an article titled "Cuba Returns to the Present." At last, for de la Nuez, the speculations about the future of Cuba were over. The persistent, unsettling and inevitable questions ended the speculations about the future of Cuba and seemed to have finally found an answer. In his opinion, specialists on Cuban issues "have frequently ignored the common citizens of the country, the younger generation, and any single individual who had a solution to propose." In this manner, the new agents of change would not be "in the Army, in the dissident sectors, in exile or in the Church" but instead they would be "unpredictable citizens that have been outside of the regular focus of attention and now demand their time for action" (de la Nuez, "Cuba"). The prediction that de la Nuez made has not come to pass, or at least in any obvious way, but this does not diminish the sharpness of his observation. But what matters now is contrasting his prediction with Rojas' vision. For him, Cuba needs a historic break. For de la Nuez, the necessary changes will be dictated by the needs of ordinary citizens and by their present demands. What this article celebrates is the possibility that these tensions, which have always referred us to the future, to the unknown, and to the improbable, are about to come to an end and the lives of the citizens will finally be fulfilled, here and now.

Victor Fowler's position in an interview titled "*Necesitamos fabricar escenarios de encuentro*" ("We need to create scenarios for encounters") is also riddled with doubts similar to those expressed by Iván de la Nuez. If we were to refer to characterizations of a certain conventional style, both of them could be categorized as reformist: their proposals for change, their predictions, although perhaps not identical, depart in both cases from transformations that neither ignore nor cancel out the past or even the present of socialist Cuba. Fowler states:

> We should try to think without resentment in order to make the pre-sent more livable and to give more space to the future. I don't have an answer that could convince everyone that surrounds me that, indeed, socialism as a system merits rescue, and in our current context we should all be concerned about. Socialism proposes beautiful things and achieves beautiful things and also creates terrible things, terrible situations... I cannot tell people "this is the way," but in each situation with which I am presented, I can demand of myself to think without resentment, to try to make the present more livable and to impede as much as I can the des-truction of those values in which I believe. Not long ago someone told me that they no longer had any of the hopes they had before but that they still believed that this system was trying to do something for the disadvantaged. It is a nice way to look at it, to reduce the ideological dis-putes to a normal level (Veiga González) (36).

In Fowler's response I also perceive the same sort of exhaustion that is present in the article by de la Nuez: prior to "making more space for the future," it is necessary to "make the present a bit more livable."

I will move forward now in this ideological arc that I have been rendering towards two attitudes much more deliberately committed to the Cuban Revolution and the notion of socialism: that of Desiderio Navarro, about which I have already outlined some ideas, and that represented by Fernando Martínez Heredia.

In the text I have been citing, Navarro gives his point of view about the role of intellectuals as part of his adherence to the idea of demo-cratic socialism. For Navarro, "*all* of the nation's problems, not only the cultural ones, are *our* problems, for two reasons: because we are *intellectuals* and because we are *citizens*; three reasons if we add our role as *revolutionaries*" (20). His conception of democratic socialism, seen from the perspective of the critical insertion of intellectuals, is not presented as an option, but rather as the necessary way for the system to survive, and includes among its assumptions, the capacity on the part of the revolutionaries "to be tolerant and respond publicly to social criticism from other ideological viewpoints;" "not only tolerate but facilitate social criticism about their actions emergent from the perspective of the same principles, ideals and values that are proclaimed as their own" and "to ensure that the intellectual, in order to publish what is truthful, does not need to resort to [...] diasporic public spheres as well as to other cultural spaces and sources of foreign patronage" (20). Navarro recognizes that this capacity is negatively affected by "the actions of local political forces that are hostile to social criticism," for which the intellectual "will be in the position to exercise the five Brechtian virtues: the courage to express the truth, the acumen to recognize it, the art to make it as manageable as a weapon, the criteria to choose those individuals that can efficiently use it, and the astuteness to disseminate it widely" (23).

For Fernando Martínez Heredia, "only those that learn to execute liberty and justice can change themselves and their society. Without thoughts and feelings that are superior to the conditions of existence there will be no socialism." This is an essential principle in the notion of socialism that he has coherently defended since the foundation of the journal *Pensamiento Crítico* (*Critical Thought*). According to this notion, socialism needs "to accumulate in its favor sufficient cultural forces that are effective and attractive in the struggle against capitalism, and above all in the struggle for the transformation of the people as well as of interpersonal and social relations, of nature, and of the functioning of its own institutions." Martínez Heredia, like Navarro and Rojas, recognizes that in Cuba "there is a silent struggle between the values of socialism and those who will only find satisfaction in the return to capitalism," a struggle that in his opinion originated in the regressions that occurred as a result of the crisis of the '90s, also called by Cubans the 'Special Period' (Orta Rivera). What Martínez Heredia brings to this ideological scenario is the idea that, in order to face such regressions, in other words, in order to make socialism viable, above all "the mobilization of human resources and materials for systematic actions directed against existing inequalities and in favor of increasing the opportunities for the most disadvantaged social groups" (159) is essential.

In such circumstances, the social sciences are obligated to be superior to the existing conditions; "it does not do much good if they only 'correspond' with them." Martínez Heredia associates the idea of democracy with that of inadmissibility in socialism of "repeating the division between the elite and the majority of the population in the production and consumption of valuable intellectual and cultural products," because "the consumption of the goods that a very cultured society produces can be neither administered nor concealed, as if the masses were unable to make good use of them" (161). What Martínez Heredia finds contradictory is that "neither the conditions in which the social sciences develop today nor the social sciences themselves have enough development considering our present and future challenges." On this point the author of *The Exercise of Thinking* (*El ejercicio de pensar*) coincides with some of the principal themes in *The Empty Shelf*: "there is a notorious deficit of theoretical formation, it is urgent to overcome our current theoretical level and, nevertheless, we lack updated information for interested people [...] and in many institutions adolescents and young students are still being taught unacceptable versions of Marxism" (Martínez Heredia 160).

Born in 1974, Julio César Guanche defends a socialism very similar to that of Martínez Heredia: "socialism in not only a mode of distribution but rather a cultural shift towards the understanding of life: a morality of liberty, of justice and human fraternity" (Guanche 55).

It is not surprising then, that all of these authors, in referencing the same theme, share numerous points of contact, of tangency, and intersection about the incongruities, the criticisms and perceptions they analyze. In a very schematic way the topics of these intense debates that are taking place regarding Cuba are gathered around a small series of themes that, for some, are: democracy, civil liberties, freedom of expression, an abandonment of socialist economic forms and of economic control on the part of the government; for others, reforms within the socialist system, a fulfillment of the basic necessities for the most impoverished, a democratization of the system and an expansion or reformulation of the spaces for civil participation. Naturally, the fact that a word like 'democracy' appears in some works but not others does not necessarily guarantee a complete concurrence of criteria. On the contrary for Rojas, for example, "a leftist democratic government" refers unequivocally to a socio-democratic government, since his idea of democracy is related to electoral and representative structures, the diversity of parties, periodic elections and total plurality in the political debate, etc. For Navarro, Martínez Heredia and Guanche, on the other hand, democratic socialism signifies an equality of economic and cultural opportunities for all social sectors, favoring those that have been historically most disadvantaged, and the adoption of forms of public participation in governmental decision-making and the creation of an open heterogeneous cultural magma that would acknowledge social criticism. Along this line, for Rafael Rojas the absence of contemporary theoretical thought within Cuban culture is a result of censorship imposed by a totalitarian regime, while, for Navarro, Martínez Heredia y Guanche, this is a result of the dogmatic impositions of a certain kind of socialism arising from Stalinism which has created a significant limitation towards the development of another kind of socialism, which, like Navarro, I have been referring to as democratic.

This is not only about opposing positions, but rather, in some cases, about an interesting and decisive inversion of values regarding the polarities of center-periphery, dominator-dominated, as if each of these parts were reversing Rosa Luxemburg's famous idea: "Freedom has always been and still is freedom for those who think differently." For some, the complaints point to the foundations of the Cuban state (the dominator) and the discourse of the opposing sectors (the dominated) that extend even beyond, including the representatives of any form of thought that does not fall into the ideological molds set forth by the state. For others, the relations that would encompass the 'fundamental contradiction' would be those of socialist Cuba, threatened and pressured by the United States and even by many other so-called 'First World' countries, particularly those that today comprise the European Union (the dominant). At the core, both stem from the same demands for diversity, freedom of thought, and right to elections, but the hierarchies are diametrically opposed. What in some circles of the Cuban social sciences is called the 'Cuba-U.S. dispute' occupies a crucial place in these positions. As we saw earlier, for Emilio Ichikawa, Cuba should recognize and accept the United States' role of supremacy and yield to it. Rojas, on his part, tends to minimize or be unaware of the pressure that this has exerted upon the positions taken by the Cuban government over the past five decades. For the majority of us that defend, even among our contradictions, the idea of socialism, that dispute has marked and shifted the frontiers between what is ideal and what is possible. In the words of troubadour Silvio Rodríguez, "Cuba is not only what it has chosen to be, but also what it could be, given the opposition of a huge and close exterior power" (Bimbi).

This inversion of values to which I am referring could be an approximation of what Said cited to Pierre Bourdieu and his collaborators. According to them, "Clinton and Blair's neoliberalism, that was built upon the conservative dismantling of great social accomplishments of the welfare State (such as healthcare, education, employment and social security) during the Thatcher and Reagan administrations, has created a paradoxical, symbolic counter-revolution" (Said 175). This is a conservative doxa, but it presents itself as progressive; it attempts to recover the order of the past in some of its more archaic aspects (particularly in matters related to economic relations) but it translates regressions, inversions, renditions, into reforms or revolutions leading to a new era of abundance and freedom (as it happens with the language of the so-called new economy and the celebratory discourse about electronic webs and the Internet) (Bourdieu, quoted by Said 175).

According to Rojas, some of us (Navarro, Martinez Heredia, Guanche, Rafael Hernandez, Fowler and myself) aspire to an impossible organicity. So, in his opinion, our work, our efforts will be, in the end, useless. We consider, though, from an opposite position, that although those who work towards a capitalist restoration of Cuba present themselves as libertarian, the forms of capitalism that they propose, even in their less aggressive forms, would end up deepening the condition of the economically and culturally disadvantaged sectors of society, whose defense and dignity legitimize a model like the one proposed by Martínez Heredia.

Following that same line of thought, in the current conditions of hegemonic globalization, to ignore or to underestimate the tensions of domination-emancipation which for centuries have dominated U.S and Cuban relations, is at the very least, naive. It is worthwhile to recognize that this conservative doxa which presents itself as progressive, is favored by authoritarian factors that have been established within the Cuban Revolution and have reduced or even subtracted liberties that are essential to the models of socialism proposed by Navarro, Martínez Heredia and Guanche. It is, once again, the oscillation between the past and the future, the compression of historic time: the future promised in the '60s and vanished in the '90s that is now substituted by the capitalist and neocolonialist past of the '50s. At the same time, the democratic socialism sustained by the essential ideas of the '60s proposes a future that has once again been hindered by the present.

The essential themes I had previously outlined, and perhaps simplified, take shape as a group of issues that acquire an intense symbolic value and that are systematically discussed in the spaces where the intellectual and political Cuban debate takes place most of the time. A brief listing of these spaces (which, for the most part, could be considered themselves actors in the debate) would offer evidence of the importance that journals continue to have within Cuban culture. Among the forums that facilitate this debate are *Encuentro de la Cultura Cubana* and its corresponding digital version, *La Gaceta de Cuba*, *Temas*, *La Jiribilla*, and numerous other blogs with diverse cultural and political affiliations.[5]

Among the most notable changes within the Cuban cultural space and that of the media, one of the most important in recent years has been, without a doubt, the use of email.

In a country suffering from a strict control of information and of the press and where the domestic use of the Internet by ordinary citizens is virtually non-existent (in spite of the fact that the service is widely available in professional settings, though with bothersome slowness and inefficiency), the email access that certain individuals do have available, often in their own homes, has allowed artists, writers,

---

5. I am making reference only to those who operate primarily from the field of artistic and literary culture, leaving aside those who work exclusively from the fields of political science, or in general from the social sciences, such as *Rebelión* or *Kaos en la Red*, to cite just two very active sites from the Left. Also the journal *Espacio Laical*, publication from the *Consejo Arquidiocesano de Laicos*, that in its latest issues has inserted on the cover sentences like: "Dialogue is the way towards consensus" and the exhortation from the Pope John Paul II "Let's open Cuba up to the world....and let the world open up to Cuba!" and has published texts that refer to very sensitive aspects of the political and social situation in Cuba, such as the dossier titled "Cuba and its International Relations."

journalists and professionals from diverse fields, as well as students and bureaucrats, to weave a dense and almost impenetrable web of information. As we know, in January of 2007 this web demonstrated its efficacy with the so-called 'battle of emails' motivated by the already mentioned presence of Luis Pavón on Cuban television. In reference to this specific situation, Desiderio Navarro affirmed that this event confronted the people with two evident facts: "the inactivity or lack of operational capacity of the spaces supposedly destined to public expression and debate (both institutional and public), and the unseen possibility to constitute a substitute, *ad hoc*, and immediate public sphere" (Navarro 17). In the article I have previously quoted, Iván de la Nuez states:

> The new technologies, restricted [in Cuba], have shown original indicators. Fidel Castro himself, who initially employed television as a medium for didactic ideology (there has not been any other socialist regime so televised) has most recently become a blogger. In a state whose mechanisms for control are pre-digital, YouTube shows students severely criticizing the president of the Cuban parliament. In a culture whose press is precarious and has served all sides as a weapon for combat, there are hundreds of Internet blogs that air and discuss a variety of issues. In a country with such a monopoly on opinion and official communication, there is no longer impunity for hiding the truth.

This web also has recourses of solidarity that I cannot call anything but 'socialist.' Some Cuban intellectuals that reside outside of Cuba, and others that still live there and have easy access to the Internet, dedicate their time to posting online bulletins conceived to provide for the informational necessities of their compatriots on the Island, and those bulletins are at the same time disseminated *ad infinitum* along with the inevitable spam. In fact, the majority of the material I have cited in this work has been drawn from such sources.

The issues that characterize these debates, which I have already mentioned succinctly, take place on different spatial-temporal levels. Perhaps the two that are most sensitive are the assessments about the history of the Republic (1902-1959) and the city of Havana, its past and its future.

In terms of the first, for many years the historiography generated by the Cuban Revolution and the history divulged in educational pro-

grams and other promotional activities had the tendency to simplify
this history, to disregard it or demonize it. As I wrote in the (anonymous) editorial in the monographic issue that the *La Gaceta de Cuba*
dedicated to the commemoration of the centenary of the Republic:

> This is a theme that has become, in recent years, a polemical topic we
> cannot avoid, and although it is imperative that we look at this issue, that
> we pay attention to it, that we study it in order to better understand it
> (and better understand ourselves), this must be done from the perspective
> of a country that grew and transformed itself, and of a revolution that was
> born from those past five decades as well as from the preceding centuries,
> a revolution which put an end to the neocolonial status of the island and
> to the bourgeois powers that had frustrated the realization of the emer-
> gent Republic ("Intelectuales" 2).

With regard to this period, it is revealing to observe the sort of
process or figure that is recovered, reread, replaced from one site to
another on the political spectrum and the contradictory reappropria-
tions of some remarkable individuals such as José Lezama Lima, Jorge
Mañach, Virgilio Piñera or Lino Novás Calvo, among others. Mañach, in particular, has been an emblematic figure for those that aspire
towards a return to republican democracy, while Julio Antonio Mella,
Pablo de la Torriente Brau and Antonio Guiteras serve the same role
for those who seek a democratic revamping of socialism. The point of
ultimate idealization of the Republic has been established, in recent
months, around the figure of Fulgencio Batista, whose biography is
being whitewashed and ennobled by some writers and journalists, fundamentally those settled outside of Cuba.[6]

The vision opposed to the approach taken by *La Gaceta de Cuba*
tends to idealize that period, especially the cultural and social life of
Havana, its extraordinary vitality, and its constructive boom. According to that perspective, the Revolution could be considered an interruption of that cultural and economic momentum, and the future of
Cuba could be thought of, from this perspective, as a continuation
of an era frustrated by the arrival of the Rebel Army in the city that
Guillermo Cabrera Infante recreated so well in *Tres tristes tigres*.

6. In this respect, see Prieto: "Bleaching Batista," 50-53.

One of the strategies used for this idealization of the Republican history precisely involves Havana. The vision of Havana as a heterogeneous city with an intense nightlife, with buildings emulating those of New York, is presented as an enormous wall that obscures the true face of the nation that lies beyond: the impoverished, miserable, and unknown interior. In the book I have been referencing by Rafael Rojas, Havana is frequently used as a synecdoche which supplants the rest of the country.[7] It is not a rhetorical turn stripped of ideological and even political meaning. Upon focusing on the destruction and neglect of the Havana of today, it is often not recognized that, during the first decades of the Revolution, that abandonment resulted from the necessity to tend to the immediate needs of other areas which were impoverished for centuries.[8] When we think about Cuba merely in terms of today's Havana, what has been erased is the complex and intense web of positions that are integrally related to diversity, a lacuna that in large part depends on the geographical position of the interpreting subject.

This Havana, which has served as an intellectual battleground, is also an *Aleph* of sorts, in which not only Cuba but also other past, present, and possible countries are summarized or concentrated. Havana expands its territory, substituting the totality of the Island, lingering in time and containing at once the past, the present and the future. Aside from Rojas' synecdoche of Havana, there is another one that various authors have identified as the one that expresses the nostalgia of its republican past, relived in the '90s in the music of *Buena Vista Social Club*. Along with this vision, we have the city of the present, "more and more dystopic, with its damaged, uncomfortable and dysfunctional topos, that keeps losing its sense of place," as described by

7. See, for instance: "Su lectura puede resultar útil a la hora de pensar La Habana…" (119). And: "La Habana postsoviética es una ciudad donde se organizan prácticas y discursos que se saben posteriores al tiempo mesiánico del socialismo" (150).

8. Antonio José Ponte recognizes this fact in the editorial that opens the dossier "La Habana por hacer." It is remarkable that when Ponte asks himself how livable these new cities have been, he responds with a characterization: "dormitory city" (*"ciudad dormitorio"*) that would not correspond to Bayamo, Santa Clara or Las Tunas, but to the Havana neighborhood of Alamar. Also, when he gives a positive example he chooses Villa Panamericana, which also belongs to Havana.

Mario Coyula, for whom "cities ought to know how to age gracefully, without recreating the useless nostalgia for the youth that was lost" (Coyula 67). Coyula is conscious of these temporal unhingings in which we are entrapped, and opts for the present, similar to the way in which de la Nuez and Fowler do: "To make a city function and to maintain control over it requires anticipating change," he writes, "but the act of imagining the future is always an exercise that can easily go from being entertaining to horrifying. Perhaps it would be better to concentrate on the present moment and respond to this question: Are we laying the sort of groundwork that this nation deserves?" (Coyula 68).

For those who think about the journal *Encuentro* from exile, the future acquires a different value. From spaces outside the country, it is only possible to envision the future, and the dossier in which this journal (number 50 of the 2008 edition) examines the city must disregard Coyula's proposal and focus on the "Havana in the Making" ("*La Habana por hacer*").

Although there are other themes and other subjects that I could include in the debate, what I also want to bring to the forefront is the fact that being immersed in timelessness and simultaneity, we Cubans take part in a dialogue that feels like a conversation among deaf people. It is as if everyone were speaking in a time of their own which others cannot access. The visions of democracy and individual liberties, the disputes between Cuba and the United States, are organized into two irreconcilable groups; those that conceive of the future of the country in terms of post-revolutionary time and those that opt for a continuity of a socialism that must be renovated and rethought.

The four models defined by Navarro obviously do not exhaust the ways in which the future of Cuba can be conceived, but I would like, for now, to add just one more possibility, which I will call 'friendly nationalism' (*nacionalismo amable*). I am referring to the sort that promotes the reconciliation of all Cubans, that calls for the abandonment of political hostilities, that is founded upon a sort of national messianism. In the editorial of the first issue of 2009, *Espacio Laical* proposes the construction of something that it calls 'Casa Cuba,' which is defined in two ways: "The first, *Cuba as a single and grand family,* where its members may have differences but also recognize the bond between them: the love for the things they have in common that emerges from a shared history. The second, *Cuba as a home,* a place where all can find welcoming and understanding; a space where everyone feels the comfort that their dreams and accomplishments, their joys and sadness are truly *shared*" (5; original emphasis). The Panglossian tone of this call and of others similar to it conflicts with that irreconcilable dialogue we alluded to before in which it seems impossible to reach an agreement. From my point of view, all of them would be willing to accept the formation of that *Casa Cuba* that they, the common Cubans, demand, amongst others, as long as each one feels that they are in a position of power, in control of a game in which we must not forget the role of foreign interference. Thinking again with Rosa Luxemburg: under whose orders would this consensus be constructed?

Meanwhile, for Cubans, it is inevitable that one must live in the present. We are, whether we like it or not, in that 'here and now' described by Iván de la Nuez. And along with those that have lived through the totality or the majority of the years of the Revolution, there are those that will necessarily live, govern and decide how the future will look, those whose visions it might be worthwhile to venture a look, albeit briefly.

A few years ago, in reading two anthologies by poets born between 1970 and 1985, I wrote:

> The abandonment of anecdotes in favor or other forms of writing in which contemplation, description or introspection prevail, has brought with it the positioning of contexts in a much more personal and intimate space, which is more difficult to identify in terms of a concrete history or even a precise geography. This poetry establishes, with some exceptions, a dialogue with a "here and now," where essentiality prevails over circumstantialities ("Existir" 23)

And further:

> In this discourse that seems not to be able to find space, to be asphyxiated between the past and God, family and future, present and potential prospects, there is, nevertheless, a faith in life that seems to negate and oppose the somber visions I have been referring to so far. Or, more than oppose them, to affirm and feed itself from those same visions and those pains.

Because

> This is not a poetry to be used, or maybe its main use and utility could be the exorcism it creates with the recognition of bitterness and pain, or the consolation if offers through self-awareness. Every glance over specific circumstances, over history or the future, emerges from an individual perspective" ("Existir" 23)

I return now to Edward Said and the role of intellectuals and writers. According to this author:

> In the dawn of the 21st century the writer has assumed more and more the attributes of an adversary which are characteristic of intellectuals in activities such as speaking the truth to power, giving testimony about prosecution and suffering, and providing a discrepant voice in the conflicts with authority [...] and particularly in the symbolic role of writers as intellectuals who testify the experience of a country or a region, giving this experience a public identity forever inscribed in the global discursive agenda (167-168).

To give testimony, to testify, are actions pertaining to the present. And I have the impression that the young Cuban artists and writers, from a more existential and introspective perspective, explore their present with pain and acuity, and experience it with the same intensity, without defining, at least in any explicit way, those idealized or possible futures that unsettle another sector of Cuban intellectuals.

Following Said, in prefacing the compilation of texts published between 1993 and 2005 and awarded a prize in a competition sponsored by *La Gaceta de Cuba*, Haydee Arango pointed out that the "overwhelming specificity of our daily life since the '90s and the deficient critical evaluation of Cuban society in the mass media could explain why current narratives predominantly take on the issues, situations, figures and conflicts that relate to their most immediate reality," following a procedure that Arango refers to as a "testimonial necessity." And she further emphasizes: "For the most part, these stories are differentiated by their quotidian contingencies and the conflicts that are generated by social spaces" (Arango 7, 13). This past year *Teatro cubano actual: Novísimos dramaturgos cubanos* published a selection of texts by authors whom (eight out of ten) were born in the 1980s. In the prologue the young theater critic Yohayna Hernández affirms that "the newest authors centralize the human being as a biological, sexual and moral subject with the will to have an impact on aesthetic rather than on political or social issues." It is a tendency that I find common amongst these young artists and writers, whose action predominantly unfolds through representation rather than through discourse. Hernández continues, emphasizing a characteristic that is contemporaneous with these playwrights: "There is an emphasis on auto-thematization, the texts register personal searches and disorientations, in which reality intervenes through the visions of the individual upon the social" (Hernández 8).

"The role of writers and intellectuals" that Said refers to, in which the old boundaries between those who make explicit social interventions and those who act primarily through fictional mechanisms, would be erased, at least in the case of Cuba, and could be expanded to other artistic expressions, primarily in audio-visual mediums. This process was initiated in the '80s around the famous exhibit titled *Volume 1*, and had a particularly vital and renewing moment at the end of that decade. In the past few months the *10th Havana Biennial* served once again as a space where these actions revealed themselves with particular force, as is demonstrated in the political conflicts that emerged around the works by Tania Bruguera in the series "Tatlin's Whisper" (*El susurro de Tatlin*) and, to a lesser degree, from the exhibition "The Amendment in Me" (*La Enmienda que hay en mí*), by Carlos Garaicoa.[9]

For six years Tania Bruguera also organized the *Cátedra Arte de Conducta* (Course on the Art of Conduct), at the *Instituto Superior de Arte de La Habana* (Superior Art Institute of Havana). Among the activities in this unique teaching space, along with the 10th Biennial, they also presented the exhibition *Estado de excepción* (State of Exception), with works by young graduate artists of the department. Mailyn Machado, critic, essayist and curator for this exhibit along with Bruguera explains the actions promoted by these shows:

> What people start to consume are not objects but social behaviors. This was the theoretical premise of the *Cátedra*, based on relational

9. In this respect, see *Declaración del Comité Organizador de la Décima Bienal de La Habana* and Nirma Acosta: "Disidencias y coincidencias en la Bienal de La Habana"

aesthetics. From there, the consumption of social roles derived, almost in an instinctive and natural way. The artist became a creative substitute who either reactivated weakened or inefficient functions, or generated others that were totally new. A service art with a double form of efficiency: symbolic and functional.

If there remains doubt regarding the new role of artists, writers and intellectuals, Machado assures us that, "the artists go beyond the consumption of roles, now to reproduce those that are assigned to power: to make things visible and, more importantly, to shorten the abyss between representation and reality."

It is an abyss that is centered on the visibility of reality and specific subjects, which have been emphasized, almost redundantly, in recent Cuban documentaries. I am not speaking necessarily, or even predominantly, of those produced within an institutional framework, although after arduous negotiation they may be accepted by them. They are almost always works produced either independently or by the International School of Film and Television San Antonio de los Baños. I am thinking of documentaries such as *De buzos, leones y tanqueros* (Divers, Lions, and Tankers) by Daniel Vera, *Buscándote Havana* (Searching for You, Havana) by Alina Rodríguez, *Tacones cercanos* ('High Heel Blues') by Jessica Rodríguez, or *Reconstruyendo al héroe* (Reconstructing the Hero) by Javier Castro, whose protagonists exist in those disadvantaged sectors to which Martínez Heredia refers: outcasts of a rare and perhaps inexplicable dignity, that search for their precarious riches in the garbage bins throughout the city; immigrants that come to Havana from the poorest regions of the country and who continue their marginalized condition, now illegally, in the city that certain demagogical discourse calls "the capital of all Cubans:" a transvestite who practices prostitution and as a result of homophobic aggression is left with a deformed face; twenty-six mothers of delinquents whose bodies, riddled with scars, reference the twenty-six wounds that the Cuban hero of the Independence, Antonio Maceo, received in combat.

The protagonists of these documentaries can also be identified in other works produced by young Cubans. *Almacén* (2001) and the series *Sucedió en La Habana*, (It Happened in Habana) (2001-2005) by Henric Eric Hernández, show the experiences of people living within a collective community and the declarations of prostitutes and pimps, respectively. The characters in the theatrical production *Aneste-sia* (Anesthesia) by Agnieska Hernández live on the edges of a Havana threatened by a strange epidemic: where the people suffering from the disease are unable to experience pain. The protagonist of *La hijastra* (The Stepdaughter) by Rogelio Orizondo is a disabled woman that has just lost her mother and is living with an alcoholic father. Armando Capó, for his documentary *Nos quedamos* (We Stayed), selected a group of people living in a home partially destroyed by a hurricane, which moreover, had been invaded by bees. Along with the inhabitants of this unique place, Capó also interviews two blind men, asking them: "How do you see the future?" The most significant in this instance is that it relates to the series titled *Venimos o nos vamos* (We Come or We Go), which under the motto "Cuba changes" was proposed as an educational exercise for third year students in 2008-2009 at the International School for Film and Television San Antonio de los Baños.

The catalogue could extend much further to include examples found in poems, stories and recent films. In my opinion what matters is that in all of these instances is that we encounter persons or characters firmly planted in their present, whose individual memories hardly matter except to themselves or to those that gather their testimonies or recreate their existence: they live in a present state where the only possible word would seem to be survival.

For Mailyn Machado, "that search for knowledge, for research," that implies among others, the sorts of subjects I have described:

> [...] is the response of art to the empty spaces left not only by social representation but by the concrete functions that the context does not manage to generate. But it is also the design of a new map of national identity. A reformulation of *Cubanía*. But of a *Cubanía* that manifests itself not in the reproduction of the image of a uniform national identity, but through the multiple visions of a culture that now comes back to us in all its complexity (Machado).

In the field of culture, the majority of young Cuban writers and artists today maintain a tense and permanent negotiation with institutional spaces and find themselves perpetually on the borders of per-

missibility. Contrary to what occurred several years ago, new technologies allow for producers that once required the patronage and
support of state-run agencies to disseminate their work in precarious,
albeit independent, forms, which in turn has affected the ways in
which these sorts of negotiations take place. In the face of these institutions, artists no longer occupy a subaltern position and often the
institutions are the ones placed on the defensive.

Within the political realm, official spaces for participation that
the Revolution established decades ago have become exhausted, subject to a vexatious and asphyxiating paternalism on the part of the
state. It is not surprising that this generation has abandoned the future
for which they are being called upon always as objects, but never as
the subjects that participate in their own definition. For this reason,
in their works, the future always appears as something suggested,
almost in hiding. Perhaps now, what is most recognizable are the
strategies from which they have been attempting to operate within
the political sphere and that include the redesign of a more inclusive
and complex Cuba, presented as a country with strong and visible
contradictions.

I would like to conclude with a description of a work: "Sequence of
One" ("*Secuencia de uno*") by Nancy Martínez, which was part of *State
of Exception*. The piece is based on one of these machines – a kind of
arcade game – that for one dollar (or a Cuban peso) allow the lucky
user to catch a stuffed animal with the use of mechanical claws. But
on this occasion, within this transparent box under the mechanical
hands, the figures are substituted by rag dolls in the likeness of Fidel
Castro. There is not just one Fidel, but four, each one of them representative of a specific era. The time they reference is revealed by the
relative size or slenderness of the images, by the grey hairs that begin
to invade his beard. The last of these figures sports the Adidas outfit
which has been Fidel's trademark since 2006. They are all friendly
figures that express a certain tenderness and affection. But at the same
time there is an indubitable reversal of roles comparable to this moment in our lives in which we begin to be the parents of our own parents, or the children of our children. In this work there is a violent
manipulation of historic time: past and present are confined, subdued,
within a small transparent box.

WORKS CITED

ABREU ARCIA, Alberto. *Los juegos de la escritura o la (re)escritura de la Historia*. La Habana: Casa de las Américas, 2007.

ACOSTA, Nirma. "Disidencias y coincidencias en la Bienal de La Habana." *La Jiribilla* 412. 31 March 2009. Web. <http://www.lajiribilla.co.cu/2009/n412_03/412_49.html>.

ARANGO, Arturo. "Existir por más que no te lo permitan. Lectura de una poesía dispersa." *La Gaceta de Cuba* 6 (2003): 23.

—. "Intelectuales en los cien de la República." *La Gaceta de Cuba* 3 (2002): 2-47.

ARANGO, Haydee. Antologar un premio. *Maneras de narrar. Cuentos del Premio La Gaceta de Cuba* (1993-2005). La Habana: Unión, 2006. 7-13.

BIMBI, Bruno. "Cuba no sólo es lo que ha elegido, también lo que ha podido." *Crítica*. 17 May 2009. Web. <http://www.criticadigital.com.ar/impresa/index.php?secc=nota&nid=24502>.

BOURDIEU, Pierre et al. *La misère du monde*. Paris: Editions du Seuil, 1993.

COYULA, Mario. "El trinquenio amargo y la ciudad distópica." Navarro 47-68.

"Declaración del Comité Organizador de la Décima Bienal de La Habana." *La Jiribilla*. 31 March 2009. Web. <http://www.lajiribilla.co.cu/2009/n41203/41250.html>.

DE LA NUEZ, Iván, ed. "El hombre nuevo ante el otro futuro." *Almanaque. Cuba y el día después. Doce ensayistas nacidos con la Revolución imaginan el futuro*. Barcelona, Mondadori: 2001. 9-20.

—. "Cuba regresa al presente." *El Periódico de Catalunya* 1 (2009): 4.

ENRÍQUEZ ROMERO, Jennifer. "El Quinquenio Gris... ¿La Gaceta Gris? (Un acercamiento a la revista cultural *La Gaceta de Cuba* durante en el período comprendido entre 1971 y 1976)." Diss. Universidad de La Habana, 2008. Unpublished.

GUANCHE, Julio César: "Debatir es participar, participar es intervenir." *La Gaceta de Cuba* 4 (2008): 54.

HERNÁNDEZ, Agnieska. *Anestesia. Tablas* 1 (2007): Addendum 70.

ICHIKAWA, Emilio: "Obama y Cuba." *El Nuevo Herald*. 27 April 2009. Web. <http://www.cuba.com/local_news.php?id=727&news_from=&title=EMILIO%20ICHIKAWA:%20Obama%20y%20Cuba%20(El%20Nuevo%20Herald)>.

LEYVA GARCÍA, Anneris Ivette, and Abel SAMOHANO FERNÁNDEZ. "In medias red: deb@te intelectual entre política y cultura. Acerca de los rasgos distintivos, en el espacio público cubano, del intercambio sobre política cultural

promovido por intelectuales desde el 5 de enero de 2007." Diss. Universidad de La Habana, 2008. Unpublished.

MACHADO, Mailyn: "El arte cubano: una isla en la red." Unpublished.

MARTÍNEZ HEREDIA, Fernando. "Pensamiento social y política de la Revolución." Navarro 139-162.

NAVARRO, Desiderio, ed. "¿Cuántos años, de qué color? Para una introduc-
ción al Ciclo." *La política cultural del período revolucionario. Memoria y
reflexión*. La Habana: Centro Teórico-Cultural Criterios, 2008. 15-24.

ORIZONDO, Rogelio. *La hijastra. Teatro cubano actual*. La Habana: Alarcos,
2008. 277-316. Web. <http://www.tablasalarcos.cult.cu/alarcos.htm>.

ORTA RIVERA, Yailín: "Fernando Martínez Heredia: No hay dueños de las
ideas." *Juventud Rebelde*. 29 de marzo de 2009. Web. <http://www.juven
tudrebelde.cu/cuba/2009-03-29/fernando-martinez-heredia-no-hay-
duenos-de-las-ideas/>.

PONTE, Antonio José. "La Habana por hacer." *Encuentro de la Cultura
Cubana* 50 (2008): 86.

PRIETO, Alfredo. "Bleaching Batista." *La Gaceta de Cuba* 1 (2009): 50-53.

ROJAS, Rafael. *El estante vacío*. Barcelona: Anagrama, 2009.

SAID, Edward. "El papel público de los escritores y los intelectuales." *Criterios* 34 (2003): 167-181.

SALAS GONZÁLEZ, Daniel. "A la cultura, ida y vuelta. Una revista cultural en
el sistema de comunicación institucional cubano del periodo especial."
Diss. Universidad de La Habana, 2007. Unpublished.

VEIGA GONZÁLEZ, Roberto. "'Necesitamos fabricar escenarios de encuentro.' Entrevista a Víctor Fowler." *Espacio Laical* 4.3 (2008): 30-36.

III. Alternative Epistemologies
and Political Agendas

POLITICAL-EPISTEMIC INSURGENCY, SOCIAL MOVEMENTS AND THE REFOUNDING OF THE STATE

Catherine Walsh

> *Hay veces, muchas, tantas que la sonrisa nos arrancan, que las rabias buscan sus propios caminos, nuevos, otros. Y el "no" que levantan ya no sólo resiste, también empieza a proponer, a proponerse.*
>
> [Sometimes, many times, it is the smile that gets us started, that the anger looks for its own paths, new, other paths. And the "no" that now rises up does not just resist, but also begins to propose, to determine.]
>
> Subcomandante Insurgente Marcos, 2008

Who are the intellectuals shaking ground and opening new routes of thought and action today in Latin America, or in what those in the region increasingly refer to as "the America of the South" (an intentional shedding of the imposed weight of "Latinity")?[1] What are their projects and how do these projects – and the thinkers themselves – resignify and reconstruct the very idea of "intellectual"? What do these projects promise and afford not just for the rethinking of intellectuals but for the rethinking of Latin America in general, and for the refounding of society and State in particular? That is to say, how do they open and enable imaginaries, visions, and courses of action "otherwise" that work towards an ethical coexistence for all, imaginaries, visions, and ventures that go way beyond the achievements and horizons of white-*criollo*-mestizo thinkers? Such questions seem to get at the essence of this seminar and volume; they also underline and frame, in a broad sense, my intervention.

---

1. For a thorough analysis of the imperial and colonial weight present in the idea and naming of "Latin" America, see Mignolo.

In the last two decades, and at the very least in Ecuador and Bolivia, it is social movements – particularly the social-political-ancestral movements of Indian and African descendent peoples – that are leading and orienting the most significant intellectual projects. These intellectual projects find their roots in (1) indigenous and Afro-ancestral principles, cosmogonies, and philosophies of life; (2) histori-cal struggles against the persistence of colonial-imperial matrices of power imposed from without and within (including *mestizaje*), and conceived and signified with relation to capitalism and its recent neoliberal project; and (3) the desire and urgency to rethink and reconstruct society and State through the guiding principles and polit-ical projects of interculturality and plurinationalism, principles and projects for society in its totality.

Such projects and the political-epistemic insurgency that drive them are, without a doubt, indicative of what Subcomandante Mar-cos refers to above as the conversion of a historic and emphatic "no" to concrete proposals, proposals that engage a thinking and praxis of and toward a present and future that walk with the past; what in the *kichwa* language is understood as *ñaupa*. Such thinking, praxis, and path not only challenge past intellectual projects (white-*criollo*-mestizo and oligarchic) of 'nation,' but more importantly afford con-crete alternatives to the hegemony of the present day neoliberal project and model.

This paper purports to analyze and explore the political-epistemic insurgency of indigenous and African-descendent social movements and the intervention this insurgency is making in the refounding of Ecuadorian and Bolivian society and State, most particularly as reflect-ed in the new Constitutions. Concretely, it takes into account three central questions:

- What does it mean to go beyond notions that conceive indigenous and Afro-movements from the lens of social opposition, giving attention instead to their political-epistemic insurgency and inte-llectual agency, an agency that goes beyond the participants them-selves?
- How is this insurgency and agency enabling a rethinking and refounding of national society and State, and what are the contribu-tions of indigenous and Afro-thought to this reconceptualization and refoundation?

- What is the decolonial significance of this social, political, and epistemological transformation, and what are implications it affords for "rethinking intellectuals in Latin America", the theme of this volume, but also for rethinking Latin America (or rather the America of the South) in/through/with these intellectuals?

This last question leads to another issue or concern: that is, the response of the "academy" towards these intellectuals, their intellectual project, and those allied with it.

FROM SOCIAL-CULTURAL RESISTANCE TO POLITICAL-EPISTEMIC INSURGENCY

We are here to say enough with resistance. Of the resistance of 500 years to the taking of power for 500 years, Indians, workers, all the sectors to end with this injustice, to end with this inequality, to end above all with this discrimination, oppression to which we have been subjected... Today begins a new life of justice and equality for the Bolivian people, a new millennium for all the people of the world (Evo Morales, Inaugural Speech, January 2006).[2]

Until recently, "resistance" was the defining term used both by social movements themselves and by those who purport to study these formations; the "no" referred to above by Subcomandante "Insurgente" Marcos. Yet as both Evo Morales and Subcomandante Marcos make clear, resistance – the emphatic "No" understood as defensive opposition – a social, cultural and political stance "against" – is giving way to (and transcending into) an offensive that purports to intervene in and transgress, not just the social, cultural and political terrains but also, and most importantly, the intellectual arena. I refer to this increasingly visible and potent offensive action and intervention as political-epistemic insurgency.

The concept of insurgency is certainly not new. It has been used to refer to insurrections and rebellions, to contestatory actions and historical initiatives that endeavor to transgress, disrupt, displace, and invert structures, politics, and practices of power and domination.

2. www.probolivia.net/posesion.html

Yet seldom are such references conceived with regard to knowledge and epistemology. In contrast to resistance and defensive opposition, insurgency – in the way that I understand and employ it here – marks and suggests a proactive protagonism of creation, construction, and intervention that today – and possibly more than in any other time in history – is assuming force. It is evidenced in the resurgence of collective action and in the new political and epistemic paths that this action – most particularly that of indigenous and Afro-movements – are opening, paths that lead to and enable new arrangements of thought, knowledge, and of thinking within and towards the political, and to new constructions of life, living, and societal articulation.

To speak of political-epistemic insurgency (or insurgencies) then is to move away from perspectives that only see, study, observe, and describe social movements from the lens of oppositional social action. Such lens, of course, responds, in part, to the theoretical-conceptual constructions of social movements as objects of study, constructions grounded in Euro-United States-centric perspectives and frames, which are, most often, uncritically assumed and legitimated by Latin American social scientists and by the Latin American academy. It is such perspectives and frames that universalize the notion of social movements, defined first with regard to class struggle, and more recently – the "new" social movements – with relation to concerns of identity and culture; some authors, such as Touraine, even go so far as to associate these "new" movements with liberal democratic reform.

The emergence in the decade of the '90s of the indigenous movement in Ecuador, the Zapatistas in Mexico, and the MST or landless movement in Brazil, among others, have triggered other theoretical, considerations, including those that pose political subjectivities. Yet, the lens of oppositional social action still remains as the dominant and stable referent and frame; that is, the perspective that social movements resist and oppose. The idea and realization that they are making thought and intervening with and through this thought in the social, political, and ideological realms are ones that have had much less consideration. Of course of even less consideration is how this intervention moves beyond that traditionally considered as "ethnic struggle", and comes to permeate and effect the "national", including its colonial-imperial constructions and legacies, and its institutionalized structures of power.

The lens of resistance and opposition is also one that has been assumed by these movements themselves. The now famous watchword or phrase that organized activities and posited a critical consciousness in 1992: "500 years of resistance", is reflective. The struggles and mobilizations then were most often conceived as "working against." And although the social / ideological actions, most particularly of indigenous movements, put in play a thinking grounded not only in cultural reaffirmation but also in the problem of what the Ecuadorian indigenous leader-intellectual Luis Macas called the "colonial tare", such thinking was then perceived as part and parcel of social resistance (Torrez; Walsh). The shift today made evident in the words of Evo Morales and Subcomandante Marcos but also in the recent pronouncements of Ecuadorian indigenous intellectuals that the movement is "political and epistemic" marks a new historical phase that portends to move beyond reactive resistance and towards the construction of a new social project, not just for indigenous peoples but for all.

To speak then of political-epistemic insurgencies is to reveal the political and epistemic "actionings" that find their ground in and assemble social, collective, and ancestral knowledge, action, and thought, and that work to affect – through this knowledge and thought – the constellations that organize and signify social institutions and structures, including, and most of all, those of the State. It is in this shift from social opposition to political-epistemic actions of intervention, a shift clearly being evidenced in Bolivia and Ecuador, that we can understand and witness a project or projects of decolonial orientation.

My use of the "decolonial" here recalls Emma Pérez's reference to the "decolonial imaginary", understood as a political project and an alternative model of (re)conceptualization (for Pérez: of histories, historiography, and oppositional conscience). But I am also thinking of the decolonial as a critical, political, epistemological posture of intervention that, in addition to encouraging another model of reconceptualization, puts at the center of debate both the lived experience of coloniality as a constitutive component of modernity, and the initiatives, strategies, and contestatory forms that, as Nelson Maldonado-Torres argues, "pose a radical change in the present day hegemonic forms of power, being, and knowledge" (70). What in the contexts of Bolivia and Ecuador today denote formations, positionings, political practices, rationalities and modes of thought that go beyond, surpass, and radically differ from concerns, agency and the capacity of the Left. As García Linera (2006, 2) notes, "Evoism in Bolivia modifies the debate by putting forth the possibility that social movements themselves can access levels of State decision-making." But as the new Constitutions make evident, the radical shifts are not just in terms of access to State, but more importantly, with regard to the very re-thinking and re-founding of State and society.

THE RETHINKING AND REFOUNDING OF THE STATE: SOCIOPOLITICAL AND EPISTEMIC RUPTURES, INNOVATIONS, AND INTERVENTIONS

As the discussion up to now intimates, the ways of doing politics, (re)articulating political subjectivities, and acting, thinking, and intervening politically are clearly shifting. Some years ago, Fernando Coronil described these then emergent changes as tied to *el devenir histórico* – the historical process or transformation – that because of its temporal character makes it possible to think in continuities and legacies as well as in ruptures and innovations (Coronil 117). Yet as the current contexts suggest it is not always (or only) temporal frames that structure and construct *el devenir*. It seems rather – and at the very least in the cases of Ecuador and Bolivia – that there are also other logics, rationalities, and modes of thought at play that make spiral (not lineal) the relation. In this sense, the paradigms used to analyze the historical transformations of the past fall short; similarly limited and lacking are the agency and capacity – of analysis, action, and intervention – of the traditional Left.

The emergent ruptures, innovations and *devenir* that are of interest here are those which are entwined with the continuities and legacies of ancestral struggle, and of the movement of this struggle towards an insurgent intervention, one that is evolving less in the streets and more in the mind frames of the populace. Such intervention calls forth "other" strategies of action and of social, political, economic, cultural, and epistemic struggle that take as their base colonial continuities and legacies, including those entangled in what Silvia Rivera Cusicanqui refers to as the matrix or colonial horizon of *mestizaje* and what Javier Sanjinés calls *mestizaje* as a discourse of power.

This intervention also marks, as Bolivian Vice President Álvaro García Linera explains, a clear distinction with what has typically been understood as Latin American social movements (2):

> Before, the strategies of the subalterns were constructed by way of a cohesionary political vanguard that was able to build movements that were this vanguard's social base. This was the case in many countries of Central America, in Chile, and, in part, in Brazil. In other cases, it had to do with a democratic legal or an armed political vanguard that was able to win over or connect with social movements, giving this vanguard legitimacy and projection, as occurred in distinct moments, in Peru and Colombia.

As was mentioned before, the processes today in Bolivia alter the notion that social movements are necessarily outside the realm of the State. In fact, the election of Evo Morales in Bolivia is a consequence of the decisive role that social movements in this country have played since 2000, deploying "political, ideological, and epistemic actions that intend to revert the constitutive features of a cultural exclusionary, politically elitist and economically inequitable State, deepened in the last 15 years by the implementation of the neoliberal model" (Torrez 3). It was the wars of water and of gas along with the emergence of the "indigenous question" – tied to articulations of Andean ancestrality and an Aymara Nation – that, in Bolivia, reveal a new politics of collective action aimed at not just contesting hegemonic models but generating alternative proposals. This politics can best be understood with regard to the crisis of the Nation-State, internal colonialism, and the inefficacy of both the *mestizo* project and revolutionary nationalism in constructing and consolidating the Nation and "the national". Its focus has been to rupture and deconstruct the homogenous, monocultural, and uninational conceptions and epistemological constructs that organize and define State and Nation, interpolate the hegemonic regimes of colonial and (neo)liberal confection, and put forth a political and epistemic actioning focused on decolonization.

Similarly, in Ecuador it has been the indigenous movement that since the early '90s has consistently challenged both the exclusionary character of the Nation-State and imperial-neoliberal impositions like privatization and free trade. Their varied strategies and interventions including massive uprisings, legal demands, electoral involvement, local government transformation, the insertion of collective rights, and State participation, have made them political actors that the State can no longer ignore. These interventions have also helped raise awareness in society of the indigenous difference and presence, and enable alliances with other critical sectors.

The new Constitutions in Ecuador and Bolivia – both approved in public referendums, the first on September 28, 2008, and the second January 25, 2009 – are reflections and results of the social, political, and epistemic agency and intervention of these movements.[3] It is this agency and intervention that has moved beyond the particularity of "ethnic" demands, enabling and orienting a radical re-thinking and re-founding of society and State for all, and a re-founding based on three key transformations.

The first transformation finds its ground in the destabilization of the hegemony and dominion of Western logics and rationalities. The second transformation is marked by the going beyond or overcoming of the multicultural constitutional reform of the 1990s that recognized cultural diversity and collective rights while strengthening the uninational and monocultural structure. And, the third is a thinking "with" other logics, rationalities, and sociocultural-ontological-existence-based modes of life and living. Together these transformations disturb and disorder the uninational and monocultural foundations of State and society, and the neoliberal capitalist frame and model. In a refounding and not simply a reforming of State, the Constitutions work to reconfigure the political map, institutional structures and the relation State-society, and confront injustices and inequalities not just of peoples but also of their logics and rationalities, knowledge systems and systems of life/living. They also work to recognize and build the plurality within the Nation and the plurality and distinctiveness of nations within the Nation, that is, the plurinational State.

While space does not permit a broad analysis of the Constitutions, three key examples from the Ecuadorian Constitution serve as a clear

---

3. While it is not the purpose of this article to analyze the Constituent Assemblies that crafted the constitutions, it is important to note that in contrast to past Assemblies aimed at constitutional reform, these recent Assemblies were made up of representatives of social movements and civil society rather than of political parties.

illustration of the sociopolitical and epistemic turns. The first is the ancestral principle of *sumak kawsay* in Kichwa, *buen vivir* in Spanish or what we might translate as "living well", a principle present in the Bolivian Constitution as well, there named as *vivir bien* in Spanish or *suma qamaña* in Aymara. This principle is the transversal axis of the Ecuadorian Constitution, and, without a doubt, its momentous milestone. As the preamble states, "we have decided to construct a new form of citizen coexistence, in diversity and harmony with nature to reach *el buen vivir, el sumak kawsay.*"[4]

By assuming this principle, the Constitution questions and transgresses the foundational models and practices of the State, and its more recent neoliberal policies, including that of neoliberal welfare with its focus on the individual and an alienating individualism of consumption and "having". The principle of "living well" understood as the harmonious interrelation of and among human beings with other beings and their surroundings, is assumed in relation to key elements such as water and food, culture and science, education, housing and habitat, health, work, community, the legal rights of peoples, nature, and to territory and land, economy, social participation and control, and Latin American integration, among others. By linking human beings with their environment and seeking to build a new form of citizen coexistence based in diversity, interrelation, and harmony, the Constitution moves and sustains an "interculturalization" by enabling a conception and negotiation of life thought from and with ancestral difference and its principles. As such, it works to weave a new social, political and cultural identification for the country which takes distance from capitalism and its modern-Western archetype of society.[5]

The second example concerns nature. Typically considered little more than environment or a natural resource to be protected and controlled by humans (part of the Cartesian logic), nature in the Ecuadorian Constitution, in contrast, is the subject of its own rights:

---

4. Available at http://www.asambleaconstituyente.gov.ec/.

5. In the Bolivian Constitution, "living well" is developed principally in relation to the economic organization of the State, serving as the basis for the decolonization and reestablishment of the existing system rooted in capitalism and the neoliberal project.

Nature or *Pacha Mama*, where life is materialized and reproduced, has the right to an integral respect of its existence and the right to the maintenance and regeneration of its life cycles, structure, functions, and evolutionary processes (*Constitución de la República del Ecuador*, 2008, Art. 71).

Nature also has the right to its reparation and restoration (Art. 72). This understanding of nature as Mother Nature finds its foundations in the thinking, principles and practices of ancestral peoples. From the point of view of indigenous philosophy or worldview, *Pacha Mama* or Mother Nature is a living being with intelligence, feelings, spirituality; human beings are elements of her. Nature, both in the concept of "living well" and in the "collective well-being" that Afro-descendents identify as their life-philosophy base (principles that while similar, differ in their historical base), forms part of ancestral visions rooted in an integral harmony, a harmony that westernized society and the capitalist neoliberalized system has not only let go to waste, but destroyed (Walsh).

The third example pertains to science and knowledge, areas not typically of constitutional concern. By highlighting science and knowledge as integral to the philosophy of "living well," pluralizing their meaning to include ancestral knowledge – defined as also scientific and technological – and requiring that these knowledges and sciences be part of the educative system from elementary school to higher education, the new Ecuadorian Constitution turns on its head the dominant geopolitics of knowledge. Moreover, by linking ancestral knowledges with *sumak kawsay* or "living well" and giving the State the responsibility of potentializing these knowledges (Art. 387), the Constitution takes on and considers a logic radically distinct from that of the modern, Western, individual, instrumental, and rational means-end. Here knowledge is interwoven with life.

In these three areas – knowledge, nature, and principles of life – the Ecuadorian Constitution portends to "think with" indigenous and Afro-descendent conceptualizations, cosmogonies, and philosophies. And while the Bolivian Constitution also demonstrates the operation of logics otherwise, I underline the Ecuadorian Charter here because of the political epistemic change it affords in a country that self-identifies not as majority indigenous – as Bolivia does – but as majority mestizo.

Of course this is not to suggest that all sectors identify with the Charter or that, for some, it is not seen as a threat to development, progress, and modernity. Still, and now as law, this Constitution along with that of Bolivia marks a new age enabled by the political-epistemic insurgence and intervention of indigenous movements, one that establishes, builds, and articulates logics, practices, ethics, philosophies, and ways of life and living that interrupt the Western modern, capitalist, colonial design, encourages a "thinking with", and ushers in a new decolonial project.

IN CLOSURE: POLITICAL-EPISTEMIC INSURGENCE AND IMPLICATIONS

Without a doubt, in Bolivia and Ecuador today, the primary and most significant intellectual projects are those of re-thinking and re-founding the State. The fact that these projects find their base in the ancestral principles of Indian and African-descendent communities, are constitutive of these movements' political-epistemic insurgency and intellectual agency, and of their ability and capacity to put forth a social project for all – something that the white-mestizo intellectual project has never done – is demonstrative of the significance of the change underway and its decolonial character.

While the implications are many, for the purposes of this seminar and volume, and as a way of closure, I can mention three. The first has to do with the displacement of the white racialized intellectual paradigm – of who intellectuals are and who are intellectuals – and the intellectual authority of the academy and its ties to State. The struggle to maintain this "authority" was clearly witnessed throughout the Constituent Assembly processes in both countries, most particularly in the allegations of white-mestizo intellectuals – including of the so-called Left – of indigenous fundamentalisms and essentialisms, and of the omission of class struggle and analysis.

The second is with regard to the changing understanding of what have been referred to as social movements, their function, nature, and goal. Here the shift is from their conception as organized resistance and opposition to a more proactive stance entailed in political-epistemic insurgency. Challenged as well is the idea of cosmology as little more than folklore; in the Constitutions, cosmology or *cosmovisión* is the transversal principle and tool that disputes modernist neoliberal thinking and lineal conceptions of time, progress, and modernity. The third implication is the disruption of universalizing frames. Here I refer most specifically to the frames that ground and underscore what we understand – in Latin America and the world – as State, knowledge, and life. Turned upside down is the notion that the non-Western is particularistic, traditional (read: non-modern and non-developed), and local, unable to achieve universality or to be universalized. What is rather at work is a radically distinct process of "pluriversalization", that portends to plurinationalize and interculturalize by creating new decolonial conditions of power, knowledge, being, and life that, while emerging in these two countries, are not limited by borders.

Taken together, the processes being lived in Ecuador and Bolivia today open ground not just for the "rethinking of intellectuals" – the focus of this volume – but even more importantly for the re-thinking and re-founding of Latin America itself, that is, for the emergent constituting of a reconceptualized America of the South from its own pluralities and realities. Such constitution challenges the Euro-United States-centric archetype and the neoliberal model that indigenous communities have referred to as death, and endeavors towards a very different design based on relationality and an ethical coexistence centered on life. Herein lays the insurgence and the new project at hand.

WORKS CITED

CORONIL, Fernando. "¿Globalización liberal o imperialismo global? Cinco piezas para armar el rompecabezas del presente." *Comentario Internacional* 5. Quito: U Andina Simón Bolívar, 2004. 103-132.

GARCÍA LINERA, Álvaro. "El evismo: lo nacional popular en acción." *OSAL Observatorio Social de América Latina* 19. Buenos Aires: CLACSO, 2006. http://bibliotecavirtual.clacso.org.ar/ar/libros/osal/osal19/linera.pdf

MALDONADO-TORRES, Nelson. "La descolonización y el giro des-colonial." *Comentario Internacional* 7. Quito: U Andina Simón Bolívar, 2007. 64-78.

MIGNOLO, Walter. *The Idea of Latin America*. Malden, MA: Blackwell, 2005.

MORALES, Evo. "Discurso de Posesión." La Paz, January 2006. www.proboli via.net/posesion.html

PÉREZ, Emma. *The Decolonial Imaginary. Writing Chicanas into History.* Bloomington: Indiana UP, 1999.

RIVERA CUSICANQUI, Silvia. "La raíz: colonizadores y colonizados." *Violencias encubiertas en Bolivia.* Comps. Xavier Albó y Raúl Barrios. La Paz: CIPCA: Aruwiyiri, 1993.

SANJINÉS, Javier. *El espejismo del mestizaje.* La Paz: PIEB, 2005.

SUBCOMANDANTE MARCOS. "Comunicado del CCRI-CG del EZLN. Comisión sexta- comisión intergaláctica del EZLN." Web. 15 Sept. 2008. <http://www.ezln.org>

TÓRREZ, Yuri. "Vuelta de tuerca. Insurgencia política y epistémica de los movimientos sociales en Bolivia (2000-2005)." *Fenómeno Evo. Reflexiones sobre colonialidad del poder, política, movimientos sociales y etnicidad.* Ed. Yuri Tórrez and Esteban Ticona. Cochabamba, Bolivia: Verbo Divino, 2006. 3-40.

WALSH, Catherine. *Interculturalidad, Estado, Sociedad. Luchas (de)coloniales de nuestra época.* Quito: U Andina Simón Bolívar/Abya Yala, 2009.

MAYA DAYKEEPERS AND THE
POLITICS OF SACRED SPACE

Ixq'anil, Judith M. Maxwell

Maya daykeepers or *ajq'ija'* are known by various epithets, both in academic literature and in daily usage. They have been called *chimanes* "shamans," *zajorines* "diviners," or simply *brujos* "witches." Since Spanish priests first came to Mesoamerica, Maya religious practices have been labeled heretical, even satanic. Spiritual leaders in the New World have been persecuted as witches and heretics; in the early colonial period, their divinatory texts were confiscated and burned; altars were smashed; ritual practice was driven underground. Part of the revindication of Maya cultural practices has been returning Maya spiritual ritual to the public domain.

Despite centuries of repression, spiritual leaders within the Maya community kept alive the traditions of worship, dedication and thanksgiving; they ministered to the sick, provided council for families, mediated disputes, inaugurated agricultural cycles and blessed the harvests. They maintained lines of communication with ancestral spirits and the guardians for the sacred landscape that surrounds and sustains the communities. With the 1995 signing of the fascicle of the Peace Accords dealing with indigenous rights and identity, daykeepers began to publicly celebrate important festivals. In 2000, the Waqxaqi' B'atz' celebration at Iximche', the ruins of the pre-invasion Kaqchikel capital, drew over a thousand spectators.

As people began to reaffirm their rights to practice traditional Maya spirituality, they explored ways to refer to the *ajq'ija'* when speaking Spanish, which would not reflect the pejoration of *zajorín* or *brujo*. An early suggestion was to equate them with the community leaders of the Catholic Church, the priests. Formal letters and official petitions during the late '90s referred to *sacerdotes mayas* (Maya priests). However, this practice never caught on at the local level. Townspeople understood *sacerdote maya* as a Catholic priest who was of Maya descent. The dimensions of this dilemma of naming are illustrated by the difficulties of finding an *ajq'ij* experienced by Guatemalan Maya in a small Honduran town.

In 1992, I went with a group of Kaqchikel Maya and U.S. scholars to visit Copán, Honduras. We arrived in the late afternoon. Ma B'eleje' Ey, the oldest man among the Kaqchikel in the group, came up to me after we had settled into our hotel rooms and asked that I, as the senior woman, go with him to find an *ajq'ij* to do a blessing and thanksgiving ceremony for us before we entered the archaeological precinct. Knowing that the Copanec Ch'orti' population was heavily assimilated, I didn't hold any great hopes of finding a local *ajq'ij*, but I agreed to accompany Ma B'eleje' Ey. We started by visiting the Fashes. William and Barbara Fash were leading archaeologists at the site, and I thought they would know the local specialists. William did not know of any *ajq'ija'* and said that traditional practice was mostly limited to household nostrums and private prayers. He referred us to some of the Ch'orti' workers, however. We visited several workers in turn. In addressing our inquiry to the Ch'orti', Ma B'eleje' Ey had to use Spanish, as Ch'orti' and Kaqchikel are not mutually intelligible. So Ma B'eleje' Ey asked if they knew of a *sacerdote maya*, Maya priest. The workers uniformly responded that the local priest was not Maya, but Spanish. Understanding that the question was being interpreted in the Catholic framework, Ma B'eleje' Ey rephrased to say that we were looking for someone who knew of the old ways, the old practices. For some this rephrasing drew a blank, for others it elicited a nod and a smile. We were referred to the artisans who carved miniature stelae for sale in the tourist market. Hoping that this contact with Maya cultural representation might lend itself to spiritual practice as well, we sought out the carvers. They were bemused by our query, but finally one worker who had been involved in the excavations and restorations at Copán for years smiled broadly and said, "Oh, you mean *brujos* (witches)." Ma B'eleje' Ey reluctantly agreed to that characterization. We both felt a moment of hope, that having agreed on a referent, we might be directed to someone who could do the ceremony for us. However, the man remarked that when National Geographic had done their spread on the ballcourt at Copán, they had wanted to do an inaugural ceremony before the game reenactment. The National Geographic team had gone into Guatemala, to the Ch'orti' town of Jocotán, hired an *ajq'ij*, and brought him to Copán for the ceremony. Given that we had no means of zipping over to Jocotán and back, Ma B'eleje' Ey and I revised our plans for commemorating the visit to this important site of ancestral achievement. We bought some candles and incense and celebrated in a more domestic way, with Ma B'eleje' Ey leading the prayer and making the offerings.

In contrast, in Guatemala, the resurgence of *ajq'ija'* has taken on national dimensions. In 1993 indigenous peoples of the Americas held a summit in Chimaltenango, Guatemala. One of the many issues they discussed was traditional spiritual practice. The manifesto produced as the memoriam of this meeting included the affirmation of the right of religious freedom.

In 2005, 200 *ajq'ija'* gathered in Chimaltenango. Again one of the declarations dealt with semantics. The *ajq'ija'* affirmed that traditional Maya practice was not a religion, since religion sponsors dogmas and dogmatic beliefs divide families and have caused rifts within communities. Rather Maya beliefs and practices were defined as "spirituality." The *ajq'ija'* stressed that one could be Christian, either evangelical or Catholic, and still participate in Maya spirituality. Daykeepers with whom I spoke after the summit were hopeful that their ecumenical stance would be reflected by the organized churches in their communities. Some Catholic priests have made accommodations to include Maya spirituality in the life of their communities, even co-celebrating some masses. However, others remain adamantly opposed to the Maya traditional practices. Just two years ago, the priest in Tecpán Guatemala refused to baptize children with Maya names. Evangelical ministers and their flocks have been less accepting of Maya ceremonial practices, while exempting curing from their opprobrium. Some staunch evangelicals even serve their communities as "callers," specialists who cure soul loss. They characterize their service as medicinal rather than spiritual.

Amid this clash of definitions and expectations, Maya ritual specialists have re-emerged as community leaders. Settling on the Spanish phrase, *guías espirituales*, they actively seek to guide their clients and their communities into full participation in Guatemalan society. Even during the days of repression and the early period of re-emergence post-conflict, government and military leaders tacitly recognized the central role the *ajq'ija'* play in their communities, providing spiritual guidelines for communal and personal action, mediating disputes, as well as curing and performing necessary rites. During the 90s, *ajq'ija'* were targeted for assassination. The *Prensa Libre*, a leading national paper, published running totals of *ajq'ija'* who had been killed. Nonetheless, the ranks of daykeepers have increased.

Traditionally, one is called to the vocation, often through dreams. If one ignores the dreams or other manifestations of the calling, illness ensues. Some daykeepers recount having suffered multiple illnesses, which they cured by visits to pharmacists and physicians, until finally consulting an *ajq'ij*, who was able to tell them that their illnesses indicated a spiritual burden or responsibility that they needed to assume. Today many young people have answered the call. In Tecpán, site of the pre-contact Kaqchikel capital and the first Spanish capital of Guatemala, as many as thirty young people, between the ages of 18 and 25 are daykeepers. One veteran *ajq'ij* remarked that these young daykeepers have raised the bar for prayer-making, since their ritual utterances, *choloj*, do not include Spanish borrowings. While older daykeepers continue to invoke *dios mundo* and a panoply of Catholic saints, middle-aged and young daykeepers concentrate on ancestors and famous Maya leaders whose names are immortalized in colonial documents such as the *Popol Wuj* and *Kiwujil Xajila'*.

In re-emerging into the public sphere, the *ajq'ija'* have reassumed many of their leadership roles, both within and beyond their communities. Before further addressing the pan-national organizations and intellectual projects of the *ajq'ija'*, it is useful to describe briefly their function as keepers of the days, linking the sacred calendar of 260-days to places of worship on the landscape.

The pre-contact Maya manipulated a series of calendars including the *cholq'ij*, the solar year, the vague year, the long count, the lunar calendar, and the 819-day count, among others. The *cholq'ij*, 260-day ritual calendar, has continued to be actively used through to the present.

This calendar is used divinatorily, and in determining propitious days for beginning enterprises, for undertaking journeys, for planting, for curing, and for offering thanks.

The Maya inhabit an animate universe, although some elements are more animate than others. The landscape is invested with animacy and energies, both positive and negative. *Ajq'ija'* through the ages have identified areas with high concentrations of energy, which can provide portals for communication with the ancestors and the inherent spirits. These areas are identified as altars, *tem ch'atal* or *mesas.* Each *tem ch'atal* is associated with a day in the 260-day calendar.

Each day has a patron and a *nawal* or spirit pair. Table 1 provides a brief overview of the twenty day names, each with its patron, primary domains of responsibility, and *nawal.*

Table 1. Maya day names, patrons, and *nawals.*

Day	Gloss	Patron	Domain	*Nawal*
Imox	lizard	alligator	intelligence, mental agility	alligator
Iq'	wind	lightning, breath	mental health, change	wind
Aq'ab'al	night	light	beginnings of undertakings, clarity, planning	night/dawn
K'at	net, burn	weaver	interrelationships	spider/iguana
Kan	serpent	rattlesnake	curing, justice	rattlesnake, serpent
Kamey	death	death	ancestral wisdom/contact, curing	death
Kej	deer	cardinal points	nature, harmony, vitality	deer
Q'anil	seed	Venus	fertility, corn	rabbit
Toj	payment, lightning	rain	just recompense	rain
Tz'i'	dog	dog	loyalty, protection, justice	dog

Day	Gloss	Patron	Domain	*Nawal*
B'atz'	howler monkey[1]	scribe, howler monkey	literacy, record-keeping, art, playfulness	howler monkey
Ey	tooth[2]	elders, principals	wisdom	an elder
Aj	cane	abundance, resurgence	home, agriculture	cane
I'x	jaguar[3]	jaguar	leadership, physical prowess	jaguar
Tz'ikin	bird	bird	economic success, providence	bird
Ajmaq	owl[4]	owl	communication with the deceased, respect for traditional knowledge	owl
No'j	thought	councilor	reason, creativity	earthquake
Tijax	obsidian	warrior	curing, justice	obsidian
Kawoq	storm	storm	women's issues, safeguard home, provide security	storm
Ajpub'	blowgunner	leader, hunter	planning, renewal especially of the home and community	lord, ruler

1. Dialectal homophony with /b'ätz'/ or thread, has lead to reinterpretation as thread, with a corresponding domain shift to linkage, especially in marriage.

2. Recutting from preceding numerals in counting the days has led to reanalysis of *Ey* as *B'ey* "road" (cf. *ka'ib' ey> ka'i(b') b'ey* "two Ey > two B'ey"). Auguries have accordingly shifted to include travel, journeys, commuting for work, study, or marketing.

3. Near homophony with *ix,* the feminine noun classifier, also leads to identification with women and traditional female enterprises.

4. Near homophony with *ajmak,* "sinner," has drawn new interpretations, as "sin, sinner, blame, fault." The day is often now interpreted as one on which to atone.

Each of the twenty days occurs thirteen times in the 260 day cycle. The days run consecutively in time. That is One *Imox* is followed by Two *Iq'*, then Three *Aq'ab'al*, etc. However, within ceremonies, all thirteen iterations of the day are counted at once: one *Imox*, two *Imox*, etc.

Each altar on the landscape is associated not only with a day, but with its numeral coefficient. A ceremony should be performed at the altar on the corresponding day in the 260-day count. Active altars have caretakers, *warinela' chajinela'*, ritual specialists whose responsibility is to keep the site clean and to offer prayers corresponding to the site. However, other *ajq'ija'* may visit the site to perform ceremonies for clients. Altars appropriate to the type of petition being made will be chosen for such dedicated prayers and offerings.

Each ritual performed at a site contributes to the energy of the altar. Heavily-frequented altars can build up vast reserves of power, which contribute to their efficacy. Such powerful altars may become pilgrimage sites, so that petitioners may travel long distances to make offerings, seek guidance, and ask for boons.

In the central highlands of Guatemala, each town has five altars which set the spiritual bounds of the town, protecting the community. Four altars are roughly aligned with the cardinal points, east, west, north and south. These altars are typically found on physical prominences, mountaintops, or exposed rock faces near the mountain crest, though other natural features, caves, rock overhangs, streambeds and springs may also serve. The fifth altar, typically, was located in the center of the town. As a general rule, the oldest Catholic church in the community overlies this altar. In most towns, traditional worship at this central site has been interdicted or supplanted by Catholic ritual, though some communities have working accommodations of form and practice. Perhaps most famous is the Church of Santo Tomás in Chichicastenango, where the front steps of the church are covered with supplicants, burning incense, and strewing flower petals, while inside the church raised cement pallets on the floor provide fire-safe bounded areas for the offerings of candles, incense, *agua florida* ("a mild cologne") and flowers that accompany traditional ritual. In San Mateo Ixtatán, the interior of the church limits the offerings to more traditional votive candles, to be placed individually on tables or racks, but the cross in front of the church and one placed with a niche carved into the hillside before it – a niche which extends back to the pre-contact Chuj buildings beneath the city – are active sites for prayer-making and more traditional offerings. Still in most towns, the central altar has been redefined as that of the Catholic Church, often with a concomitant loss of knowledge of the day patron, or an identification with a patron whose properties align with that of the town saint. In Comalapa, the patron saint is San Juan. His saint's day is June 24th. Though falling early in the rainy season, San Juan is known as *llorón*, a crybaby. It is expected that it will rain without fail on his feast day. *Toj*, whose patron is rain, is thus associated with this central altar. Events in the history of the town, including being razed by fire in the early 1900s and scarified by the military encampment established just beyond the western guardian, further point to *Toj*, the avatar of retribution, as the central patron.

Most of the patron altars of a town do not lie on municipal property, and those that do are not, by virtue of being within this public domain, necessarily freely accessible.

The northern altar of Tecpán Guatemala, *Oxlajuj Kej*, 13 Deer, sits just above the spring which provides most of the town's water. While the spring and the altar are on public land, access must be obtained from the owner of the farm whose lands surround the spring. The current owners, who are trying to develop a tourist center, with swimming pools and a spa, are willing to allow daykeepers and their clients to cross their fields and climb to the rock face *q'alpul* through their coffee plantings; the previous owner had prohibited trespassing.

A slightly different case can be seen in the neighboring community of Sta. Apolonia. Its southern altar also lies just in front of the town's principal water supply. When a water tank was built and the spring encased in concrete, the surrounding area was cordoned off and barbed wire was strung. The altar rests now within the fenced-off area. The town government and the altar's caretaker grant access to those who come with respect to make offerings, though fifteen years ago they drove off would-be looters who were attempting to saw through the base of the carved stela at the site. The townspeople subsequently set the stela in cement to firmly affix it in place. The jaguar-headed *tenon* (a keystone fitted into a carved niche) that accompanied the stela was secured by rebar rings set into the cement. Here the townspeople have defended the area and, though limiting access, give permission to those who wish to make offerings at the site.

At *El Cementerio*, a similar defense of the local patrimony played out. In the early '90s a man digging a well in his courtyard found a post-classical carved tufa altar, roughly 1.5 meters square. He shifted his well excavation, but dug out an area around the altar, though leaving it *in situ*, about 2 meters below current ground level. Word of his discovery rapidly spread. People began to arrive to offer prayers at the site, paying a modest fee of two quetzales, which went toward maintenance of the area. The national Museum of Anthropology and Ethnography learned of the find and dispatched a team of archaeologists with a flatbed truck to bring the altar back to the storage/research unit of the museum in the capital. Local *ajq'ija'* met to counter this expropriation and they report that the research team from the capital became lost and never located the community, returning to the capital with an empty truck. Subsequent conversations with the *ajq'ija'* led to an agreement to leave the altar in place.

Some landowners view themselves as custodians, even assuming responsibilities of *warinela' chajinela'*, with regard to site maintenance. The owners of the coffee plantation on which the powerful cave *Oxlajuj Kan*, thirteen Snakes, lies only charge two quetzales, twenty cents per person for admittance. Over the past fifteen years, they have paved the winding path up the mountainside to the cave, provided benches after steep stretches, bordered the cave mouth in concrete blocks, and set up waste receptacles.

The man whose land houses the pilgrimage altar at *Ch'ajyu'* (Sacred Mountain) charges twenty quetzales ($2.70) for access. He has constructed outlying buildings for his household, all around the "cave" mouth, so that visitors must come through his central patio, where he will explain his rules for keeping the site clean.

However, not all sites are so well-tended. The traditional western altar of Tecpán has been forcibly deactivated. The hilltop altar had been marked by a large cement Christian cross for over fifty years, and indeed the area was known as *Cerro de la Cruz*. However, five years ago the land was bought by a devout Evangelical. He first blocked access to the site by road, planting pine trees in the roadway. He then began to run cattle over the area. Nonetheless the site continued to be heavily used by *ajq'ija'* and their clients. The owner then fenced off the area. Pilgrims continued to cross the barriers. Finally, last year, the owner toppled the cross, broke it into chunks, and buried the chunks. He then plowed the area in front of the cross on which the offering fires had been laid. He continues to run cattle and horses on the land and has threatened to fire on anyone trespassing. Few people now dare to go to the hill to perform rituals.

In other places, public works have dislodged altars. South of Sololá on the Pan-American highway, a scenic overlook was constructed so that tourists could pull off of the highway and admire the view of Lake Atitlán. A small market for the sale of goods to tourists was built next to the parking area. The earthmoving required in order to level this area for parking and commerce threatened the altar, *Pujujil*, an altar mentioned in the 16ᵗʰ century Xajil Chronicle. Unable to negotiate design of an overlook further up the road, the *ajq'ija'* relocated the central stones of the altar to a site lower on the hillside.

In other communities such as Sta. Cruz la Laguna, radical shifts in the religious climate of the town have led to wholesale abandonment of the local altars. Townspeople who felt the need to offer prayers for their ancestors, their families, crops or business needs report going to pilgrimage altars on the other side of the lake rather than risking local opprobrium by frequenting the local altars.

In San Juan la Laguna, Catholic Action erected a statue of the Virgin Mary and a pillar commemorating the Papal Jubilee and 500 years of Evangelization in the New World over the altar site to the north of town, covering the whole votive area with a floor of cement.

In San Pedro la Laguna, Catholic Action built a chapel in front of one of the major guardian sites to the northwest of town. A few years later they sought an injunction against the *ajq'ija'* who continued to use the altar, lighting their offering fires there regularly. Catholic Action leaders complained that the smoke from these votive fires was blackening the back wall of the chapel. They ordered the *ajq'ija'* to move the altar stones. The *ajq'ija'* refused, but said that the Catholic Action leaders could move the stones if they dared. So far they have not dared, and the case is being adjudicated in courts.

Also in this community, an archaeological site consisting of four small "temple" mounds sat on private property, in a coffee field. Gradually the owner shifted enough stones from three of these structures to level planting ground, incorporating the stone blocks in terraces. The eastern mound, site of most ritual activity here, was not leveled, but the townspeople feared that it would be and brought suit to protect the hillock. The courts made this mound a national patrimonial site, expropriating it from the owner. Nonetheless, access is still through the owner's coffee plantings. Now token offerings are left at the site, but major ritual activity has shifted further to the west, to an altar in a cornfield, whose owner allows ready access.

Many other examples of contested spaces may be cited. But let these suffice as indicative of the ongoing struggle for the right to define space as sacred and to maintain access to such sites. It is the duty of the *ajq'ija'* to take spiritual and physical care of their communities. Those who serve as *warinela' chajinela'* must maintain the vigor of the spiritual energies inherent in these sites and keep the area clean. As leaders of their communities, the *ajq'ija'* have sought redress in the national congress, asking that their right of access to these areas not be abrogated. In 2006, a *punto resolutivo* (a resolution) was passed by the congress which said that community leaders were charged with guaranteeing the safekeeping and open access to sacred sites. This resolution was followed in 2007 by a draft of a law of sacred sites. This initiative did not receive the three readings required to be enacted. Again on June 17, 2008, a law of sacred sites was proposed to the congress. This law gives *ajq'ija'* a central role not only in the preservation of active altars, but in defining sacred space. The law stipulates that when pre-Hispanic artifacts are uncovered a panel of *ajq'ija'* must be called in to determine if they or the area in which they are found is sacred. Should it be designated as a sacred site, it must be left intact and *in situ* and given over to use as a place of devotion. This would hold even in the face of eminent domain projects, such as road building or municipal construction. The law, having received its first reading(s), has not been[5] read into the record the third and final time needed to ratify and enact it. This law would provide official recognition of the leadership position of the *ajq'ija'.*

Ajq'ija' have formed their own coalitions. The group *Oxlajuj Ajpop* unites *ajq'ija'* from around the country. On their webpage (www.oxla jujajpop.org) they define their spheres of activity as religion, the Maya

---

5. At the time this chapter was originally written, there was still hope that it would clear the 2008 assembly. It did not. As of July 2009, a revised version of the bill had not been reported out of committee, opponents claiming sharply that the law is unnecessary since it either replicates responsibilities ascribed to the Department (*Ministerio*) of Culture and Sports or violates principles of private property.

judicial system, Maya medicine, agriculture and biodiversity, internal economic development strategies, cultural creativity, Maya epigraphy, education and dissemination. They consult with lawmakers and others in working to implement Maya consuetudinal law in local and regional arenas. They are seeking means to have herbal medicines, midwifery, and bonesetting integrated into the national health care system. They are advising cooperatives on non-chemical pesticides and agricultural practices that can allow intensive use of soils without depleting them. *Ajq'ija'* are also active in debates over formal education reform, and serve on the board of directors for CNEM, the *Consejo Nacional de Educación Maya*. They are pioneering an initiative to use *awas*, proverbs, as the central axes in curricular development. Another group of *ajq'ija'* are central figures in *La Coordinadora y Convergencia Maya Waqib' Kej*. This group was created during the indigenous summit held in Peru in June of 2006. Their platform is one of political action, seeking to recenter Guatemalan political structures around Maya concepts, ideals and necessities.

Active in every sphere of the life of their communities and their nation, the *ajq'ija'* today are a diverse group. Among them are elders, residents of their home communities, who have dreamed, studied with others, and practiced their craft for over half a century. They are joined by middle-aged practitioners, many of whom have studied abroad, including journeying to India, China and Nepal. They, in turn, are joined by many bright young people, some of whom are among the 5% of Maya people who have a university degree. Far from seeing an apocalyptic end of creation in 2012, the *ajq'ija'* are planning for and working toward the *nuevo amanecer*, the new dawn, proclaimed in the *Popol Wuj*. The current president of Guatemala, Álvaro Colom, has even trained as an *ajq'ij*. Though some saw this concern with Maya spirituality as instrumental, others acknowledge that the *ajq'ija'* have re-emerged after centuries of repression and are actors behind and on the political stage of Guatemala.

In the early '80s, during the re-emergence of Maya intellectuals amid the chaos of the genocidal war, Fortunato Pablo, a leader from *Todos los Santos*, noted that the Maya needed to study their history, one obscured by the Hispano-centric texts of the national schools, because without a past, they could not build a future. Modern *ajq'ija'* respect the past and offer explicit ties to and communication with ancestors and past leaders. But they are also actively involved with building their communities, forging ties with other indigenous groups in the Americas and in Europe, and connecting with development agencies. Their traditional role as mediators, healers, and spokesmen has prepared them as culture brokers. As diverse as the populace they serve, the *ajq'ija'* are not quaint practitioners of an outmoded, outdated belief system, but the intellectual architects of a Maya future for their communities and for Guatemala.

Maya Knowledges[1]

Ajpub' Pablo García Ixmatá

Maya knowledges are the foundation for the construction of a society that is inclusive and egalitarian, and for a more humane – and human – process of development in the countries where Mayas live today. More than ever, the Mayas of today live amid a myriad of social and political abuses in every country where they are present. For example, one of the phenomena that is seen in Maya communities in Guatemala, Chiapas and Yucatán is the influence that imported religions or religious sects and the Western educational system have had. These seek to do away with the customs, values, and knowledges of Maya grandmothers and grandfathers, and argue for an assimilationist paradigm and a Spanish-speaking, Christian matrix. This has caused many to think, act and practice in different ways within Maya communities. Because of this and due to the urgent necessities and demands of communities immersed in poverty, the commonsensical discourse of most people argues that if one does not become a professional or study for a degree, he or she remains behind and loses, or stays in poverty. This idea has a powerful influence that is currently manifest in the argument that if a Maya practices Maya customs, he or she does not

1. Translated by Nicole Solawetz and Bret Gustafson. We thank Ajpub' and Judith M. Maxwell for their assistance with K'iche' translations and their exegesis of complex terms and phrases.

earn anything. Many Maya brothers and sisters thus opt against freely practicing Maya knowledges for the simple reason that it is seen as not being profitable within the political and economic life of the country.

In this context, the knowledges of the Maya people have been relegated to the historic past. Maya knowledges, philosophy and epistemology have been subordinated, bottled up into containers, or reduced to folklorics. Centuries of suppression of anything Maya have resulted in a lack of systemization and dissemination of fundamental Maya knowledges. For these reasons, the Rafael Landivar University, through the work of the Institute of Linguistics and Education, and with the support of PROEIMCA (Central American Intercultural Multilingual Education Program) and DIGEBI (General Directorate of Bilingual Intercultural Education), has undertaken research and investigation of Maya knowledges. This research, which I describe below, will provide a foundation for Maya education, and will be the first research study to invest resources into Maya higher education.

This project has served as a motivation for students and teachers and has brought happiness to the grandmothers and grandfathers, who will be sharing their knowledge through an experiential dialogue with researchers. One of the worries of the grandmothers and grandfathers is that they are not taken into account in decision- making processes, since today's youth is undergoing changes in mentality, attitudes, and values – increasingly seeking to understand reality from a Western kind of education and point of view. This Western training asserts that the correct way to understand being *(el ser)* and nature *(naturaleza)* is pure science, in which study is rooted within the human subject *(el ser)*, the only privileged subject of research which imagines that all other elements of nature are inert objects.

On the other hand, this research adopts the position of the Maya knowledges, in and for which all things have life and exist in interdependence, one needing the other. A single element cannot act alone, and for this reason in the work of Maya Science one must understand trilogies, and quaternities, in order to conform dualities. For Maya knowledges there are no objects of investigation, only subjects. For instance, in this research, we use the concepts of subject and subject-community actor. The subjects are persons with knowledge about his or her own community who are involved in a learning process with their family, the community itself, and of course, with the grandfathers and grandmothers. Meanwhile, the subject- community actors are the Maya grandmothers and grandfathers themselves. They are the people who have guided the community, the lives of beings *(la vida del ser)*, and the care of nature, and they are the ones who manage the calendars, principally the spiritual and material calendars.

There are many good studies that have been carried out about Maya culture and people, but the problem that they have had is that they fall short. They do not reach the necessary depth and they have been focused through Western rules or methodologies. In contrast, with the above grounding in community subjects, and in components like the Maya spiritual and material calendar, one is necessarily immersed in Maya spirituality and in the active practice of the philosophy of Maya values as part of the process to recognize, learn and develop knowledges – the task of Maya Science. The subject, thus grounded, must be sure of what they have to do and this part is essential as a methodological base. If this is not done, the knowledge and results achieved by research are relegated to the superficial.

In what follows, I would like to describe some of this ongoing work, providing some ideas for reflection about research and knowledge production from the point of view of Maya knowledges.

MAYA PHILOSOPHICAL AND SPIRITUAL ORIENTATION

This orientation is based in our own internalization into the meaning and sense *(sentido)* of Maya spirituality. This process of questioning implied engaging the Western philosophical conception of Being *(el Ser)* in juxtaposition with the conception of Maya life *(la vida Maya)*. The subject of "being" in Western philosophy is centered on the person as the only living being in nature, with all else being inert and therefore without life. In the Maya conception, the "being" is everything that there is in the universe, because everything has life and all things complement each other. Water, the stone, the tree – all have life and are indispensable for the ongoing existence of the universe. It is this concept which shaped our orientation to Maya knowledge as directed at understanding that everything is a subject in a process of investigation or knowledge production. In this way the student-researcher is possessed of knowledge of his or her own culture, and the knowledge bearing subjects of the communities are the actor-subjects of knowledge as well, yielding a dialogue and exchange to enrich the knowledge of all involved.

ORIENTATION TO MAYA PRINCIPLES AND VALUES

According to Salazar, the concept of value identified in Maya philosophy is *Ruk'u'x Na'oj* which means Heart and Energy of Thought and Knowledge (*Corazón y Energía del Pensamiento y Sabiduría*) (40). *Ruk'u'x Na'oj* is the set of values that provide the foundation for the identity of a person and his or her social coexistence and relationships with nature, sustain the life of the family and the community, motivate attitudes to create, construct and resolve, and manifest spirituality. *Ruk'u'x Na'oj* is what gives strength and clarity to the fundamental concepts of ideas and knowledge. *Ruk'u'x Na'oj* manifests itself in all things, actions, and attitudes, and in writing, symbols and song among others. These values are passed down from one generation to the next in a natural way through social relationships, through family activities and life, through spirituality and through established educational practices of the community.

There is also in this concept the implication of a kind of cleansing and the establishment of a base from which to develop a healthy and strong profile of human beings. The student researchers participating in the project experienced this during their orientation and training, acquiring concepts such as order, discipline, and the maintenance of constant communication with the grandfathers and grandmothers. This lived experience of values is seen as central to developing a Maya Science. The Maya grandmothers and grandfathers know very well how they develop, become stronger and find an intellectual balance through spirituality. They also know well the times and the spaces to realize this balance of knowledge. In this perspective, this indicates that beginning from spirituality, one can construct respect, obedience and reflection in order to obtain and transfer knowledges, a basis for the development of Maya Science. In this context, all things have an origin point, a beginning *(un principio), jun ruk'u'x,* and all things are ordered in accordance with the energies of each being. Just as nature has an order, and has balance, and harmony, all beings have a synchrony and exist through interconnections between one element with another. These interconnections are essential in the orientation and formation of being.

With this backdrop, the research project was named *Mäy Na'oj, Mäy Soloj Mäy Choloj*, a phrase which says and expresses everything.

Mäy means sublime, profound, clarity.
Na'oj refers to knowledge, idea, experience, wisdom.
Soloj means to untie, untangle, clarify, liberate.
Choloj means to orient, order, guide, speak, present, preach, publish.

Maya knowledge is taught in different ways and from different sources from and for the community as a whole where Maya knowledges are alive and fortified. It is there that knowledge is sowed, cultivated, and developed in practice – through dialogue, council, speeches and guidance, and through the personal experience of being, in this case of the Maya grandfathers and grandmothers. It is cultivated and developed through language and the practice of collective coexistence in [and with] other beings and with nature itself, knowledges developed through practice and familial and communitarian coexistence.

What is the Maya Being? Through a sense of knowing and feeling, the emerging response of the student researchers entails some of the following discoveries:

Maya Values	Who transmits them
Respect	Grandfathers and grandmothers
Solidarity	Father – Mother
Responsibility	Brothers and Sisters
Mutual Aid	Spiritual Guides
Trust	Uncles and Aunts
Mission	
Spirituality	
Equality	
Value of the word	
Humility	

Some of the testimonies of student-researchers reveal other aspects of this process of knowledge production and discovery:

From a young age, my grandparents, my parents and my aunts and uncles always instilled in me the term *awas*, something like 'prohibited because it is sacred,' a form of education that remains with me today and is shown in my actions such as:

Avoid eating a fruit that is *cuache* (double, like an attached twin), because it is *awas*, and other actions that I avoid doing for the same reason. I offer thanks for my food in which I begin with the oldest and move to the youngest [of my family], one by one. I greet adults with reverence and refer to them as *lal*, the formal "you" (singular) or *alaq* the formal "you" (plural).

I have in my K'iche' vocabulary terms such as *loq'alaj* (holy), *awas* (proverb, something sacred), *nan* (title of respect for older woman, madam), *tat* (title of respect for older man, sir), *chawila awib'* (take care), *maltyox* (thanks, thank god); *utzilal* (goodness), *k'ixb'al* (shame), *tz'aqat* (exact, complement), *wajil nutz'aqat* (my complement).

I try to share and to help others.

I share and try to inspire others with what I know about sacred Maya knowledges.

I always share conversation with elders.

I know my *nawal* (spirit guide), and that of my spouse and children. I always keep in mind the fact that my actions have consequences. I always use the K'iche' language in any setting. I like and live Maya music.

Another student shared the following:

In my youth, I did not believe in what was said in my house because of the influence of my studies. Nonetheless when I turned thirty, I began to understand my roots and together with other Mam companions to organize educational talks about cultural values. I also began to participate in ceremonies in the Mam language, especially the celebration of the ritual date *9 Father B'e*.[2]

2. This refers to a year bearer ceremony celebrating the new year, in this case 2008, when *9 Father B'e* was the year bearer.

HOW ARE KNOWLEDGES SOWN THROUGH AND FROM CULTURE?

Knowledges are sown through dialogue, advice, speeches, orientations and the very example of life between two or more members of a family and within a community. In the family setting, the wise teachings and life experiences of grandmothers and grandfathers are transmitted around the hearth, during mealtimes, at work, on the daily stroll and at the family's or community's ceremonial festivities. In this way the life experiences of the grandmothers and grandfathers that have left their tracks and traces from their passage through the community, especially if they have assumed responsibilities within the community, also serve to instill wise teachings in its members.

The dialogue among elder men and women is another source of knowledge. Through such dialogue, decisions are made about what elements or necessities must be discussed and which teachings they need and which ones they don't. In this way, elders use the wise words *Pajon tzij, tz'aqat tzij, cholon tzij, no'jin tzij* (Measured words; exact, accurate, perfectly apt words; ordered words; well-considered words). When the elders dialogue in order to orient and educate the family or community, they never fail to mention these beautiful phrases: *Kichin o kixin qiiy qamam,* meaning, 'it is for our sprouts, for our grandchildren, for our children.' With that they emphasize saying that this is for *ri kik'aslemal, k'aslemal rixin qatinamit qamokaj,* for 'their life, that of our community and that of our family.' They are always in search of a space where knowledge can be sown and cultivated so that all are in tune with the realization and execution of this knowledge and how to take them into practice.

In taking these teachings into practice, responsibilities emerge for each being, such as *Ijqalem* (responsibility), *Saamaaj* (work), *Ajob'en-em* (harmony or love of others), *Poponal wachil* (to have perseverance and to fulfill one's obligations in actions that one realizes for another). The fundamental part of the person or the being is the *K'aslemaal,* where reason is born and where resides the reason for caring for and having balance in life and reason itself. With this fundamental aspect of the person, knowledges are already being sown within, but one must still prepare and experience life in order to support and sow the teachings of the grandmothers and grandfathers. It is necessary to clearly understand *Ruuk'u'x k'aslemaal,* which means that all things have *Ruuk'u'x,* heart, essence, spirit, life. One must also have knowledge about the life of nature which is transmitted through spirituality and communication with the *Ajaw* and with *Rajawal k'aslemal* the guardians of life.[3]

In order to understand the steps that need to be followed in the sowing of knowledge within culture, it is necessary to have *Yuqb'al k'u'x,* trust in what is taught and sown for the formation and guidance of others. If one does not trust and have confidence in what is being done, the result will be negative. In this way it is important to listen to the grandmothers and the grandfathers so that they are the ones to show the way and to be the source of wisdom, that they are the green fields free of pollution who might unify knowledges for the development of families and communities.

KNOWLEDGE IS SOWN WITH A CLEAR OBJECTIVE IN THE LIFE OF COMMUNITIES OF THE MAYA PEOPLE

All knowledge is: Action and the effect of KNOWING.

TO LIVE in HARMONY, meaning, to know and respect all things visible and invisible, the proximate and the distant.

TO LIVE in PEACE, and this should begin with oneself. It is important to know how to listen to and understand internal peace because this is the path that will lead to understanding others so that there is peaceful coexistence among us who live in community. Peace is the spiritual force that produces tranquility, through which the life of a person is formed from the family.

To have A HEALTHY LIFE: This means that the life of a person must be focused on internal and external cleanliness as this is fundamental to personal, family, and community life and life in the workplace. Around this, healthy knowledges about how one conducts oneself emerges. From this point one can perceive beauty, order, quality, and the doing of good things for and through life.

---

3. *Ajaw,* generally Lord (God); *rajawal k'aslemal,* the lord of life, existence, prime mover, creator spirit, giver of life.

In this way, the grandmothers and grandfathers understand the magnitude of understanding and the intelligence of being with Nature; just as they know about natural and balanced reason of BEING from the point of view of familiar and community organization.

KNOWLEDGE IS GENERATED COLLECTIVELY

Knowledge is generated in the first place within the family. These ideas reached in consensus from the home are taken to the community or organization, as ideas or contributions of the grandfather for the group. The groups may be made up of elders from the community, with community authorities, the *cofradías* (spiritual brotherhoods), the *Ajq'ija'* (the daykeepers, spiritual guides; see Maxwell, this volume), etc. According to the magnitude of the knowledge that they want to share, it may be necessary to come to a consensus and carry out a consultation with the *Ajq'ija'*, who will say if it must be done or not, or whether to practice or approve a certain knowledge by and for the community. It is necessary to come to a *K'o chi nitikirisax ri na'oj* (one/we must plant [the seed] of this idea, understanding; we must engender this idea), in which after the consultation, it is necessary to respect the last word and to continue constructing or consolidating the principal idea. It is also necessary to evaluate the consensual ideas, or, *k'o chi nkisol wi man utz ta' rusamajixik ri na'oj* (we must reach a consensus to be able to work with, to develop the idea). Once this evaluation takes place, one must be careful with how these ideas must be corrected (*ruk'ojoxik*) for the guidance and practice of these knowledges. One person cannot do this alone, it is necessary that it be done among two or more people. Once the corrections are established comes what is called *K'iyik (K'a ri nipee k'iyik)*, meaning the growth and the production that is the nursery or planting bed of knowledges within the family and the community.

HOW TEACHINGS GROW FROM CULTURE

Knowledge and teachings grow through the healthy advice of the elders, of parents and of communities:

Ya'ik na'oj   Orientation
Tzijonik   Conversations
Tijonik   Educate
Nab'ey Pixab'   First advice
Nikusax ri na'oj pa qak'aslem, ruk'aslem ri qach'alal, ri qatinamit.
This idea is used / central to our lives, the life of our companions, our people.

Each one of these elements is used in the life of the person, the family and the community. In this way knowledge grows and is transmitted from childhood, through youth and even up to the council of elders and councils of *Ajq'ija'* (spiritual guides), *Iyomaa'* (midwives, grandmothers who receive grandchildren, wise grandmothers), *Cholonelaa'* (guides, organizers of events, seminars, workshops), and authorities such as the current *cofradías* and indigenous authorities.

How are knowledges harvested from culture?

Eqalen k'aslemal   Importance or value of the life of the
          being
Utz ch'ob'oj Utz b'anob'al   Good thinking, Good actions
Utz ch'ob'oj Utz b'eyal   Good thinking (logic) and Good
          methods (ethics)

The first step is the act of getting closer to the meaning of the term *Eqalen k'aslemal* or the importance or value of the life of being.[4] It is given importance by the being itself because it has a relation with its own nature and its existence. It also takes meaning in relation to death and what happens after death. It is based in the organization of the community or town. Knowledges come to be understood better through spiritual guides such as the *Iyomaa'*, *Cholonel*, *Solonel*,

---

4. See also above, on *eqalen k'aslemal* as guidance for how knowledges are harvested from culture. *Eqalen k'aslemal* refers approximately, in literal terms, to a 'responsibility in life.' This stresses the importance and value of life of/on an individual. This importance stems from being, from having a relationship with one's own nature, with Nature, and with lived existence. This importance obtains to, through, and beyond death.

nuk'unel (organizers), *ajkum* (curer, born healer, physician), *Ajq'ija'*, and *wiqol b'aq* (bonesetter), among others. Surely in other Maya communities there are the *Ajchun* (healer, from the Mam language) or even a *Chinamital* (community leaders). Each one of these principal members of Maya communities have *utz ch'oboj utz b'anob'al* and *utz ch'ob'oj utz b'eyal* (as above: ethics, logic) in each one of their functions in order to transmit the teachings to each new generation of the community. These dialogues unfold even among themselves in an effort to better understand and harvest the teachings for the families and the community itself. The order in which knowledges are harvested is very important.

One of the points that must not be separated within the life of the being is that all that surrounds me is my other I, because according to the teaching that I receive from the grandparents, from my family or my community, in some way everything comes around and has an impact on me and on the other person, be it in a negative or positive way. All of these knowledges are those that orient the life of a being or of a people.

In Maya culture there exist various elements that are woven together to harvest and project knowledge.

To'onik   to help

Helping is not only helping others, but first helping myself. I must revitalize my spirit or the spirit of being through positive energies and positive knowledges. It is because of this that one must be concerned with having the essential energy to be able to HELP. To help so that one does not become weakened in their knowledges and their life. If I am strengthened, I can help my other being, which might be my family, my children, or my community where the importance of working in *KAMON* with my other being arises. All of this promotes the development of the being, of the family and of the community in general. It is a way in which one is able to live in community, in harmony, to mutually care for life, the life of nature, the life of the animals, the life of all of the elements that surround us. Only in this way will there be life in harmony. Today it is my turn to help, and I give all that I have in hopes that tomorrow if I am in need the same will be done for me.

So that all is well, one must have a *Ch'ajch'oj K'aslem*, meaning a being must live an Honest Life. In other words, it can be said that the being must have a clean and healthy life. This is another way to harvest and share in a healthful way with family and community. This term implies honesty and cleanliness in spiritual and material work. In the material, the person must harvest and learn knowledges by doing community service, agricultural work, in the use of words through sending clear messages inside and out of his or her community. Just as one must manage spiritual messages clearly with oneself, with the family and with the community. If all of this is taken advantage of or harvested well for the being, it will have strength and the fortune to obtain whatever it needs.

Utz k'aslemal   equilibrium and harmony

The *Utz K'aslemal* is one more step toward understanding and harvesting knowledge in the life of a being. All of the elements in nature have their point of balance and harmony. In the Maya culture, it is necessary to know, learn about and have *Utz K'aslemal* with nature. If one has balance and harmony with oneself and with nature, then this person has achieved the education and formation necessary to be able to educate and further harvest knowledge for the family and the community. The use of the sacred calendar is extremely important in obtaining different types and levels of knowledges in order to reach this equilibrium in the formation and education of the being. The calendar is a medium for achieving and maintaining equilibrium of knowledges and for strengthening the practice of values and the way in which they can be used in the formation of being.

THE MAYA LANGUAGE IN THE PROCESS OF THE PRODUCTION OF KNOWLEDGE

The Maya language, like all languages of the world, is one of the fundamental bases for the transmission of knowledges and the formation of the culture of a people, in this case the culture of the Maya People which has been transmitted from generation to generation. This transmission is done through language, through the use of the

word, council, narrations of events and communication with the
Ajaw. The acquisition of knowledge is a long process that requires
effort and for which it is necessary to acquire certain levels of permission
from the grandparents in order to bring it into practice without
complications. Furthermore, it is necessary to reach a level of commitment,
with oneself and with nature, committing myself to not use the
teachings to carry out evil or seek superiority over others.

Language is an instrument in the development and understanding
of these knowledges. For example, take the living use of the concepts
of *Nana Tata*. If it were not for the power of language, we would not
know how to understand the message that each term gives, transcending
the singular meaning of any given word. NANA, implies
many things. It says to us: respectable woman, grand woman, elderly
woman, authority, wisdom, respect, female guide, life, and woman.
The same happens with the word TATA, for men.[5]

This is important because key elements for the development of
knowledge come from language. For example, consider the phrase
Uk'u'x Kaj Uk'u'x Ulew, in the K'iche' language. It says many things,
but the closest translation would be Heart of the Heavens, Heart of the
Earth. We cannot find an exact translation into Spanish. Yet as seen
through the teachings of the grandmothers and grandfathers, all things
have *Uk'u'x*, each element has an essence, movement, energy, power.

Another source is the use of metaphors. In Maya languages these
are a key part of the diffusion of knowledges. For example, in the system
of conceiving the world, we can see, that beginning with the family
all things share a sense of being. For example, THE HOUSE, the
house has a heart (the center of the house); a head (the roof); ears
(the left and right walls); a face (the front of the house); a back (the
back wall); a mouth (the door) and so forth. Many such things like
the house also have a metaphorical relationship with being and with the
world. These are not simply 'beliefs' or myths as some may argue.
The reality is that they are the basis for creating new kinds of learning,
or as others might call it, sciences. Each element has a shared meaning
and power with *Winaq* (person, people) or being.

5. The terms *nana* and *tata* are titles of respect for elders, referring to those people
who have served and serve their communities, their families, and to those who
come to them for advice or help.

Colors are also important in the context of speeches or guidance given by the grandparents. The colors green, *rax*, indicates first; *kaq*, red, symbolizes power or authority; *saq*, white, symbolizes help or support; and *q'aq*, black, symbolizes danger.

There are other elements of order and logic of the organization and life of the Maya people, such as the use of the lunar (material) and sacred (spiritual) calendars. These have a great importance in relation to the symbolic meanings that link the calendar and its various temporalities, the body, and the elements of nature (see also Maxwell, this volume). These include:

Calendrical Terms	Elements of the Human Body	Elements of Nature
b'aatz'	tact, hearing, sight, brain	monkey, thread
b'eey	taste, brain	tooth, path
aaj	heart, brain	cane, abundance
i'x / b'ajlam	feet, brain	jaguar, vitality
tz'ikin	brain	bird, liberty
ajmak	sight, brain, hand	blame, evil
no'j	brain, intelligence	sky, cloud.
tijax	strength, energy	flint, obsidian.
kawoq	blood, sight	storm, water, rain.
ajpub'	body, wisdom	blow-darter (*cerbatanero*), hunter
imoox	brain, nervous system	alligator
iiq'	gallbladder, brain, nose, lung	lightning
aq'ab'al	vision, brain	dawn
k'aat	eyes, brain	net, spider web, fire
kaan	genital organs, brain	snake
kame	all senses, brain	death and rebirth
keej	shoulders	deer, authority
q'aniil	the entire organism	Venus, germ, embryo, inception, life
tooj	brain	rain, offering
tz'i'	smell, brain	dog, justice

The calendar is the fundamental base for the transmission of all knowledges, *Etamanem Na'oj* (the fundamental base of knowledges). Another platform where the thought of the grandmothers and grandfathers exists in practice is in oral tradition. One example might be the story of the Lazy Man and the Vulture. This well known text is original to Mesoamerican indigenous peoples.[6] The story is embedded with key values, and stresses how we must know, respect and obey the norms of each one. The values are those narrated by the grandfathers when they recount the story, which include the value of work in our lives, respect, cleanliness, the use of the steam bath or sauna *(temascal)*, responsibility, the sacredness of the earth, the sacredness of corn, the value of council, respect for the word, and respect for everything that has life. Each person has to fulfill a mission, showing thankfulness and cooperation, among others. In the narration of the grandparents, these lead us to an infinity of teachings and wisdom. They carry us toward the realization of 'science' – of agriculture, health, spirituality, language, community and family organization.

Because of these various dimensions of knowledges, it is necessary to take council: *K'amon tzij k'amon na'oj, chi kechi' chi kewach qati't qamama'* (To receive words of clarity and light, to receive wisdom and guidance, from the mouth and words, from the eyes, face and presence, of our grandmothers, our grandfathers). These words and phrases, such as *qati't qamama'* (our grandmothers, our grandfathers), a very great title that grandparents carry, reveal complex meanings that are incredibly rich when they are broken down. Consider some of the following terms:

k'am	*-on*	*tzij*
obtain, receive, conclude, resume	perfect participle	word, truth, clarity, light
		na'oj knowledge, wisdom, idea, decisions, advice, feeling, clarity

6. In the story, a lazy man and a buzzard agree to change places. The buzzard is a good worker, but cannot take the heat of the sauna *(temascal)* to clean himself after a day in the field. The man cannot find food as a buzzard. The change works for neither of them. One should not desire the life of another; nor should one be lazy.

chi from	*ke-* their	*chi'* mouth, lips, speech, word, authority
		wach eyes, above, face, visage, presentation, agreement
	q(a)- our	*ati'it* elder woman, maturity, experience, guide, authority, security, dignity, respect, force, energy, councilor, woman, life
	qa-	*mama'* elder man, maturity, experience, guide, councilor, respect, force, energy

Language is a valuable instrument of communication, and one of the rich components in its structured use in Maya languages is the use of pairs (two terms that have one unique meaning, such as *qati't qamama'* or *tata nana*), trios (groups of three words), and quartets (groups of four words).

CONCLUSIONS

Researchers of today have made classifications of Maya knowledges from a personal point of view or based on the knowledge of another culture, categorizing our knowledges, for example, as myths, stories, or tales. In reality, this is now the task of Maya Science, from the Maya culture for Maya culture and for the life of the Maya people. Those who read this chapter may say that Mayas are pacifists or conservatives or positivists, but the reality is that our knowledges are integrated and holistic. In exploring some of the knowledges described above as compiled through our research project and the work of our student researchers, we are drawing conclusions about knowledge and Maya knowledges. I have argued for the importance of Mayas doing research from the point of view of their knowledges. It is clear that there is a central role for Maya and indigenous knowledges in strengthening communities in the face of the various crises that have been unleashed in various ways in our country. We also seek to understand whether the Maya are ready to confront the challenges of constant global change, from the perspective of the knowledges of Maya grandmothers and grandfathers.

I have argued that the knowledges and teachings of the grandmothers and grandfathers are transmitted through language, speeches, conversations, and formal and informal orientations according to the necessities of the BEING or *WINAQ*, of the family, of the group or of the community. The narrations or speeches that are given to the being are a multidisciplinary tool for acquiring them and managing them. They are a training, the construction of scaled steps for acquiring wisdom and the practice of knowledge. The council and guidance is the base that orients the development of being, strengthens knowledges and the organization of the life of an individual, family or community. Council unites a being with the community, so as not to promote a detachment from this mutual dependence.

The life of the being is sown in a particular place in order to be able to talk and to understand what surrounds them through the energies of elements in duality. This duality is the point of entry or the base for the realization of protocol with the community subject actor. Without this, the realization of any project is impossible. Through these knowledges comes the practice of science, learning, organization, and respect of the life of nature as my other self.

There is still much that many researchers formed in the West will take a long, long time to understand – the sacred secrets of the life of the being, the secrets of medicine, and the protection of food and the environment. I offer the following reflection to [non-indigenous] colleagues who have worked with indigenous peoples and still call the teachings of the elders "positivist."[7] Were you able to understand – in depth – the ways of protocol in indigenous communities and do so according to cultural norms? Were you immersed in the ways that

---

7. Here the term "positivist" (*positivista*) is not used in reference to the notion of Western positivism as a form of logic that refers essentially to the triumph of facts. Rather it refers to the use of the term *positivista*, in some Guatemalan intellectual circles, as a way of criticizing Maya intellectuals as overly emphasizing the positive (in a normative sense) aspects of their spirituality, while hiding or ignoring the negative. Maya intellectuals respond that this is an invalid criticism, since the ability to balance the positive and the negative is crucial to being able to maintain one's life path.

spirituality and materiality are lived in the indigenous culture? Did you analyze the ways that the Maya or indigenous woman is the one who carries and complements the practice and knowledge of science? With these questions, a new way is opened. It is narrow, but it teaches and guides us to understand how to find the duality in all things that confronts us in the life of the Maya people.

This project – and this chapter – marks the beginning of a process of unlearning and decolonizing knowledges that were produced in classrooms of four walls. The model of knowledge formation and learning of indigenous peoples has a distinct kind of logic, one different from that imposed by the educational systems of each country. Yet the [Maya] system does not seek to reject these knowledges completely, but rather acknowledge that it is in the interests of indigenous peoples to know their own systems of knowledge, and to know Western [knowledge's] strengths and weaknesses.

Nk'awumaaj chi eewe ewonojeel. Thank you to everyone.

Ajpub'

WORKS CITED

Salazar Tetzagüic, Manuel. *Cultura e interculturalidad en Guatemala.* Guatemala: Institute of Linguistics and Education, 2004.

THE COMMUNAL AND THE DECOLONIAL

Walter Mignolo

My original contribution to the conference on "Rethinking Intellectuals" was a talk entitled "The Advent of Indian and Afro-Intellectuals in the 20th Century." In hindsight, I feel that I was not effective in communicating what I intended. I ran a series of slides, in Power Point, describing about a dozen prominent indigenous and black intellectual figures from the Caribbean and South American. I added in the mix an Argentine philosopher of German descent, Rodolfo Kusch, since Kusch is the only white (a son of immigrants) whose philosophy is akin to and runs the same course as the thoughts and concerns of indigenous and Afro-intellectuals. That is, it delinks from hegemonic "Latin American" thoughts and literature (and we can add art), from the Right and from the Left that once stood for – with good and legitimate reason – Latin American ideas and literature. Although I concentrated on three figures (Rodolfo Kusch, Fausto Reynaga and Sylvia Wynter), I thought that the focus on these three prominent figures plus the gallery of other figures would be enough to convey the idea I wanted to convey. It did not. I noticed that the audience was a little bit disoriented. One of the questions attracting some attention, followed up after the lecture, was the question of value in Marx. One participant pursued it later by giving me a lecture on Max Weber! Now, remember that my talk was about the advent of indigenous and

Afro-intellectuals in the 20th century. Certainly, Marx and Weber are indigenous Europeans, and although Weber overlapped two centuries, perhaps he could count for the twentieth century. But advent? I thought they were rather established intellectuals. Still, I did receive advice on comparing Fausto Reynaga with Frantz Fanon. Nonetheless, it seems I dramatically failed in my lecture to orient the audience to think about the question of "what is at stake in the advent of indigenous and Afro-intellectuals in 'Latin America'?". Either I failed or the question did not want to be heard.

In the written version I present here I have changed tactics and I respond to my own questions in a different way. For lack of time, I will concentrate on the consequences of indigenous intellectual labor, which fits the themes of several other chapters in this volume (see Walsh, Maxwell, Ajpub' this volume).

1. IT IS HALF OF THE STORY BUT IT SEEMS LIKE THE WHOLE

When Evo Morales was elected president of Bolivia in December of 2005, Maurice Lemoine, an editorial chief of *Le Monde Diplomatique* wrote an enthusiastic article in which he celebrated that "*la Bolivie Indienne rejoint la gauche Latina.*"[1] The situation was indeed not only the contrary, but the claim was idly formulated: The "*gauche Latina*" (led by Creoles and mestizos, that is, by Bolivian whites) and the "Indian decolonial" were two totally different projects with a common enemy: the local pro-neoliberal elite that had been ruling the country since the mid 1980s when Gonzalo Sánchez de Lozada was Minister of Finance and Jeffrey Sachs was one of his advisors.

What Lemoine called the *gauche Latina,* which, by now is the most visible political force in Latin America, is grounded in a genealogy of thoughts of European provenance, roughly, Marxism-Leninism. Their 'recognition' of and alliances with the indigenous struggles goes in the same direction; although following different paths, coming from different experiences and genealogies of thoughts tied to societal visions of the common (not the communal). This is the common in the imperial sense of the British Commonwealth or in the liberal dilemma

---

1. See http://www.monde-diplomatique.fr/dossiers/bolivie/.

formulated by Garret Hardin in his influential article "The Tragedy of the Commons" (1968), or yet in the Marxist oriented version that was debated in a recent workshop at Birkbeck College on "The Idea of Communism" (March 2009);[2] all belong to the genealogy of European thoughts and experiences – which may not translate well into the Andes. Imagine Europeans trying to break through and propose that the Indian conception of the communal be inserted into the French Constitution and become part of France's everyday life. It may not work. Well, the reverse may be also true.

The communal being advocated today by Aymara and Quechua intellectuals is something else. It comes not only from social organizations before high civilizations in Tawantinsuyu and Anahuac (baptized the *Indias Occidentales* by the Spaniards and later *America* by non-Spanish Europeans), but from five hundred years of experience coexisting under Spanish colonial rule and under nation-states after independence, during the nineteenth century.

2. THE OTHER HALF OF THE STORY

The communal refers to a type of social organization that was disrupted by European invasion but subsisted for five hundred years. The Zapatistas are reactivating it in the organization of the *Caracoles*, or *Juntas de Buen Gobierno* (Casanova). *Los Caracoles* adopted and adapted indigenous ways of life and social organization, putting into practice one of the basic principles of Zapatista political theory: "to govern while obeying." That means that there is no supreme position in such a governing structure and a "state of exception" would not emerge as a political problem because simply, it is preempted by the very structure of governance. Now, the immediate question asked is: can this be extended to all of Mexico or even to be a formality of global governance? To ask the question in this form is to fall into the trap of thinking that the political theory behind *Los Caracoles* is a "new" theory that would replace the liberal based constitutional platform of the Mexican State. We have to start thinking in terms of pluriversality rather than in universality, a challenge not yet accepted

2. See "The Idea of Communism."

by many thinkers from the Left. I will come back soon to this point. The very existence of *Los Caracoles* contributes to understanding what the Zapatistas mean when they pronounced the second fundamental political principle: "a world in which many worlds would coexist."

Thus, *Los Caracoles* shall not be interpreted as a new abstract universal to replace the already existing ones proposed by the Right and by the Left, but as something else – neither Right nor Left. That something else is the communal, and the way to get to it is through decolonial thinking and doing. For if *Los Caracoles* would follow the rhetoric of neoliberal globalization and pretend that the rest of the world be organized as such, it will not be a decolonial but an imperial project. *Los Caracoles* should be thought out indeed as global but not as universal. Global means that it is possible to think of similar organizations, based on local histories, all over the globe. But it cannot be thought out as universal, in the sense that the entire globe shall be organized as such. However, the 'global communal' is not a happy cosmopolitanism but rather pluriversal and global localism, if we can put it in this way (see the last section for this argument). In such a structure there would be no need for a G8 or a G20. Instead of a new benevolent socialist *mission*, a decolonial horizon presents itself as an *option* (a pluriversal and global option).

Certainly, to move in such directions is not easy. But neither can one do it by rethinking communism or revamping – from the Left – the idea of the common. When noted French philosopher Alain Badiou talks about "the common" he refers to Jean Jacques Rousseau, the Jacobins, and the Chinese Cultural Revolution spirited by Mao Zedong (see "The Idea of Communism"). He doesn't mention what is behind Mao's Cultural Revolution that is alive, and transformed, in China today. De-westernization is a current expression in East and South East Asia today. For example, the 'surprising' sea change in Japan's recent elections, with the ascent of the Democratic Party after 54 years of ruling by the pro-USA Liberal Democratic Party, is not alien to the increasing force of discourse on de-westernization. Yet de-westernization is neither Right nor Left. It is akin to decoloniality in that it questions Occidentalism, racism, totalitarian and unilateral global decisions, imperialist principles of knowledge. But it differs from decoloniality in that de-westernization does not question capitalist economy. It questions who controls it, the West or the Rest of economically 'emergent' countries.

China is not only an economic powerhouse. It has given ample evidence already (as with the seventh Doha Round and the positions adopted by China in the meeting of the G20 in London in July 2009 to deal with problems of the global financial crisis) that it has been taking decisive positions questioning the monopoly of Western authority in global decisions and positioning itself by distancing from both Western capitalism and Western versions of socialist futures. The struggle for the control of knowledge and authority informs and grounds decisions. And behind the struggle for the control of knowledge and authority there is a growing Chinese nationalism (questioned by Western media) that is neither Left nor Right but something else: this something else is being articulated as "de-westernization."

Thus, when Alain Badiou places the Chinese Cultural Revolution next to Rousseau and the Jacobins, he is advocating the reorientation of the European Left. The Cultural Revolution is meaningful to Badiou, but one can imagine that Rousseau and the Jacobins will have less or no meaning in their own local histories. One can surmise that the same conclusion could be applied to Maurice Lemoine's dictum: most likely the Bolivian Left appreciated Lemoine's endorsement while most likely Indian intellectuals and leaders did not care much about it, if they even cared at all. One might imagine that if you belong to the population of European descent in Bolivia, then the "the Latin Left" might apply to you. Yet this is not the same if you are Aymara or Quechua or Chiquitano – indigenous peoples of Bolivia – for whom the idea and experiences of the communal is meaningful while the commons or the French *comune* is something alien to your experience. Thus, if the idea of the commons is meaningful for the European Left and the *comuna* is meaningful for the Bolivian Left, while the idea of the *communal* is meaningful for decolonial Indian projects – what do we do?

I see two ways of starting to undo the logical puzzle:

One would be a Hegelian solution, a synthesis. Critical media theorist Douglas Kellner proposed a few years ago a synthesis between the Frankfurt legacy of critical theory and the philosophy of liberation. He noted first that they both provide complementary perspectives on liberation. For a Philosophy of Liberation, racial and patriarchal oppression is crucial, but was not among the main concerns of critical theorists. He noted that critical theory instead tends to be ethnocentric, focusing on liberation within Western capitalist society.

Second, and consequently, Kellner goes on to suggest that one obvious way to articulate the difference would be to indicate that critical theory projects a "First World" (FW) perspective while a Philosophy of Liberation projects a "Third World" (TW) perspective. But he is not happy with pursuing this avenue because such generalization occludes the fact, he says, that there are differences within the FW and within the TW, differences that may occlude "internal" forms of domination. Moreover, he states, since we all live in one world we do not want to just underline differences, but need to point out commonalities.

What are the problems with this argument and are they relevant to the issues I am raising here? Certainly, commonalities shall be kept in focus and the fact that there are internal forms of domination within the FW and within the TW is also clear. However, what shall be kept in mind also is that neither Critical Theory nor the Philosophy of Liberation 'represent,' or stand for, the FW and the TW respectively. What is crucial and undeniable is that each theory emerged as critical responses to particular forms of domination, local histories, sensibilities and genealogies of thought about the FW and TW respectively. Two forms of localism if you wish – one is European localism and operates as an internal critique to Eurocentrism; the other type of localism emerged from the margins of Europe – from its colonies and from locales in which Europe (and in the second half of the 21st century mainly, the U.S.) interfered. European universal localism impinged on non-European histories and engendered in them the sense of localism to prevent the imposition of a foreign localism. In that regard, both localisms have much in common but they are not subsumable into each other, nor they should be.

Why – after all – shall we aim for a synthesis and not for a world in which many worlds (in this case, theoretically worlds) would coexist and work together in their respective *lieu*? Is there a necessity to make one out of two? Secondly, given the historical power differential in the structure of knowledge, a synthesis will end up with Critical Theory on top and the Philosophy of Liberation as a runner up in the Third

World. If for the Philosophy of Liberation racism was of the essence, it is because philosophers of liberation realize that racism operates also in the domain of knowledge, not only 'down there' in society. Philosophy of Liberation, in other words, made an early statement about the fact that knowledge is geopolitical and knowledge has been ranked, hierarchically, in relation to regions of the world (developed-underdeveloped), imperial languages (Greek and Latin behind the six main modern and imperial European languages: Italian, Spanish and Portuguese during the renaissance; and after the Enlightenment German, English and French). Philosophy of Liberation was not only a TW philosophical intervention – it was at its inception written in Spanish. At the same time, Critical Theory was not only in the FW but was expressed in the German language. And we know the power differential between Spanish and German since the eighteenth century when the South of Europe was invented, by the North, and the imperial difference (internal to Europe) was created.

3. AND NOW WHAT?

Now we are in a better position to return to the communal. What is the communal? Let's start with a simple description offered by the Aymara sociologist Félix Patzi Paco.[3] By communal, Patzi Paco refers to collective management of resources and at the same time to the rights that families, for example, have to the uses and benefits of what is collectively produced and shared. He makes clear that the communal has its millenarian foundation in agrarian societies in the Andes and currently applies in urban centers as well – e.g. El Alto, in La Paz. Thus in contradistinction with 'modern' in which the fields of knowledge have been isolated from one another, in the communal system all forms of knowing and doing interact. Making this distinction means that the communal is not an object to be studied by sociologists, economists, political scientists or psychologists, but that the communal has embedded its own epistemology in its organization. In the same way

3. For a detailed description of *Ayllus* and *Markas*, where the communal system operates, see Yampara Huarachi; on the arrival of capitalism and "*haciendas*" coexisting but displacing the sovereignty of the *ayllu*, see Sebill.

that European societies had embedded an epistemology upon which the social sciences were founded and built.

For example, the notion of 'property' is meaningless in a vision of society in which the goal is working to live and not living to work. Therefore, economy as a discipline is being called into question by the sheer fact that there is not only one economy, capitalism, with the rest either traditional or irrelevant. It is in this context that Evo Morales has been promoting the concept of *buen vivir* (to live well) or, in Quechua and Aymara, *suma kamaña,* a concept also included in the Constitution of Ecuador (see Walsh 2009; this volume). There is a horizon of life behind the communal that cannot be subsumed under some abstract universal ideal of the commons. And once again, while the European Left could sympathize with the directions Bolivia and Ecuador are taking, it is also the case that what is going on in Ecuador and Bolivia has little to do with the reorientation of the European Left. So the "Indian Left" is not really joining the "Latin Left." There is no Indian Left in the first place but rather *decolonial thinking and doing.* This is the point that Maurice Lemoine misunderstood when he celebrated the election of Evo Morales. The election of Evo Morales was the culmination of a long process in which Indians were coming into their own, sometimes welcoming the Left, but subsuming it in their own decolonial projects.

What are the memories behind the idea of the communal and why is the communal linked to the decolonial? Well, we have to have some basic understanding of the organization of Tawantinsuyu, the organization of the Incanate, improperly and Eurocentrically called the "Inca Empire." Knowledge of Ancient Greece and Rome will not do. And I would say that it is here where the divide between the Left (and obviously the Right) and the decolonial begins.

"Tawantinsuyu" means the world divided in four *suyus,* or sections. Imagine the two diagonals of a square without the square. The spatial shape of Tawantinsuyu was derived from the constellation called the Southern Cross, which you obviously cannot see from the Northern Hemisphere and which was one of the constellations that made Americo Vespucci realize that he was somewhere else, not in the Indies imagined by Columbus. At the center, where the two diagonals cross each other, we find the city of Cuzco, , whose name meant 'the belly of the world,' similar to Jerusalem for Jews and Christians or Mecca and Medina for Islam. Each *suyu* was organized around a group of *ayl-lus* (somewhat similar to the organization that the Greeks called *oykos*) and each group of *ayllus* was organized respectively into a larger structure called *markas*. Each *ayllu* in each *suyu* belongs to a *marka*, and each *marka* is administered by a *Mallku* who in turn reports to the *Apu-Mallku*, who is the ruler in each *suyu*.

Now imagine the same structure in each of the four *suyus*. How are they interrelated? Each *ayllu* of a given *suyu* is defined by a territory that includes not just a piece of land, but also the ecosystem of which the land is one component. The territory is not private property. It is not property at all, but the *home* for all of those living in and from that territoriality. Remember, we are not here in a capitalist economic organization. Nor am I saying that this is ideal. I am saying that it was, and that it still is real and that you cannot just ignore it with whatever argument you can come up with; for instance, that you believe that it is romantic or that you believe that a socialist organization of common-based Marxist principles shall dispose of and do away with *ayllus, markas and suyus;* or that we should be serious if we want to defeat capitalism.

The fact is that from Indian perspectives, the problem is not only capitalism, but also Occidentalism, which includes capitalism and Marxism. An Indian leader like Fausto Reynaga (1906-1994), an admirer of Marx (whom he referred to as *el moro genial,* the genial Moor, though he despised the Bolivian Left of his time), made clear the distinction between what he called *La Revolución India* (the Indian Revolution) and the "Communist Manifesto." Marx – according to Reynaga – confronted the bourgeoisie from the perspectives and interests of the working class and proposed a class struggle within Occidental Civilization, while the Indian Revolution is a revolution against Western Civilization, including the Left, which originated in the West (Reynaga, 382).

In a nutshell: the Marxist option defines itself as an option in the struggle against capitalism. The decolonial option defines itself as an option in the struggle against Occidentalism and the economy is one dimension of the colonial matrix of power. It would have been difficult for Karl Marx, Antonio Labriola or Antonio Gramsci to fight against Occidentalism at that point. They did not see it. But for Mahatma Gandhi in India, Ali Shar'iati in Iran, Frantz Fanon in

Martinique-France-Algeria, or Fausto Reynaga in Bolivia, it was obvious that the proletarian revolution was a far cry, and that there were other urgent needs beyond the gaze of European Left's struggle against liberalism and capitalism. Marxism focuses on class struggle. Decolonialism focuses on racism that justified exploitation of labor outside of Europe and now inside of Europe because of immigration. Marxism and decoloniality are two different agendas that could work in collaboration if both understood their own limits and possibilities. But if the idea is that the "Bolivian Indian joined the Latin Left," the collaboration may not work. If the idea is that "The Latin Left joined the Bolivian Indians under Evo Morales," we may be closer to a significant shift in the geography of understanding of what decoloniality means.

Now suppose that on a given morning you pick up a newspaper in England, France, Italy or Spain, for example, and you read something like this headline: "The Process of Political Territorial Reconstitution in the Conjuncture of the Constitutional Assembly in Bolivia." Then you start reading the article which informs you that:

> in May and June of 2002, indigenous authorities from *ayllus* and *markas* organized a march that lasted more than 30 days in order to press Bolivian society for the need for a Bolivian Constitutional Assembly to rewrite the existing constitution...From the perspective of indigenous leaders and communities this was part of a long struggle that in its present form started in 1980, when a new form of politics, identity IN politics, make it possible for an indigenous organization to organize themselves, makes claims and to reinscribe the ayllu in the present and future organization of Bolivia. For Indian people, the *ayllu* forms life, experiences, political and territorial organization, and the hope of projecting a future of collective and communal organization.

This is a free translation of an article published by Aymara intellectual Carlos Mamani Condori (2008). Certainly, the probabilities of reading something like that in European newspapers are close to nil. That is why it was easy for Maurice Lemoine to say that the Indian Left joined the Latin Left. Not only was that not the case, as you may begin to understand, but it is not at all clear that Indians who are connecting the communal reconfiguration of the *ayllu* with the decolonial option will have any urgency to join the Latin Left at all (Ticona).

This is the moment when you can ask, yes, I see, it is a nice idea, but can it be implemented and how? Well, I do not have the answers for these complex questions but I have some ideas of how to start thinking about them. Let's start with three:

First, Patzi Paco made an important point in his proposal for a communal system as an alternative to the liberal system. First of all, this entails the reconstitution of *ayllus* and *markas*, a task that is also being pursued by a national organization called CONAMAQ, which means *Consejo Nacional de Ayllus y Markas del Qullasuyu*.[4] You now know what *ayllu* and *marka* are. We can add to that the meaning of *Qullasuyu*. As you remember, Tawantinsuyu was divided into four *suyus* (Chinchaysuyu, Qullasuyu, Kuntisuyu and Antisuyu). The area that is today Bolivia was built as a national-state on the territory of Qullasuyu and from the Spanish colonial organization of the Viceroyalty of Peru with its center in Cuzco. From a modern chronological perspective, Tawantinsuyu was relegated to the past, to a history that stopped with the arrival of the Spaniards. The advent of the Republic of Bolivia, in the nineteenth century, superseded colonialism and, of course, the organization of Tawantinsuyu. But from the Indian existence and perspective, that was never the case. The reconstitution of *ayllus and markas* of Qullasuyu is fundamental to understanding what a plurinational state might mean. And the idea of a plurinational state is already inscribed in the new constitutions of Bolivia and Ecuador (see Gustafson; Walsh, this volume). The idea is not coming from the Jacobins, Rousseau or Mao. It is coming from the simple existence and memories of millions of Indians who are not convinced that they can live the existence and memories of millions of Europeans and their descendants in the Andes, whether these come from the Left or from the Right. Shall we still think that these ideas belong to the past, and the Jacobins and Mao to the present? If you think so, you should explain why. Certainly, you can find Indians who join the Left or the Right. That does not negate the fact that the reorganization of Qullasuyu is an Indian project and not a leftist one. Therefore, the reconstitution of *ayllus* and *markas* is not just for Indians, but for Bolivians as well.

Second, does it mean that the proposal is to replace the Bolivian liberal-(neo)colonial state founded after the independence from Spain

4. See http://www.conamaq.org.bo/.

by the Qullasuyu? Such a route would not lead to a plurinational state. It would be an Indian national state instead of a Creole-Mestizo National state that forced Indian leaders and communities to rewrite the constitution. There are indeed other organizations claiming their right to intervene in the constitution of a plurinational state. The point I am trying to make is that the Indian communal system and the idea of decolonizing the actual state, education, and economy are not grounded in the genealogy of thought and memories of the European Left and its expansion or adoption within non-European regions.

Last but not least, the idea of a communal system as an alternative to the (neo) liberal system, one that emerged from the memories and lived experiences of Indian communities today, shall not be reduced to Bolivia only, but should have a global scope (global not universal, as I explained above). A global scope does not mean here that the *ayllu* system shall be exported like other previous models (Christian, liberal, Marxist), but that it is an invitation to organize and reinscribe communal systems all over the world that have been erased and dismantled by the increasing expansion of a capitalist economy which the European Left was unable to stop. If *ayllus and markas* are the singular memory and organization of communities in the Andes, there are memories of communal organization all around the globe that predate and survived the advent of capitalism, which is what makes possible the idea of a communal system that is not mapped in advance by a totalitarian ideology, of any kind or color. Once again, the Zapatista dictum – "a world in which many worlds" can coexist – may be a world of communal systems in a pluriversal and not universal world order.

4. PLURIVERSAL LOCALISM

In the introduction to his book *Iranian Intellectuals and the West: The Tormented Triumph of Nativism* (1996), Mehrzad Boroujerdi distinguished between 'Orientalism in reverse' (where subjects which became Oriental objects in Western knowledge, responded by making the West the other) and 'nativism.' By so doing, "Orientalism in reverse" accepts the rules of the game and attempts to change the content – not the terms – of the conversation. "Nativism," in Boroujerdi's conceptualization is something different. Frantz Fanon offers to him a paradigmatic example of nativism (14):

> Nativism stands in the same relation to Orientalism in reverse as Eurocentrism does to Orientalism proper. Both Nativism and Eurocentrism provide an ontological and epistemological umbrella under which it becomes possible to develop a theory of history and a political platform. Whereas Eurocentrism does advocate such ideas as the uniqueness and superiority of the West and its unequivocal manifest destiny, Nativism champions the cause of abandoning, subverting, and reversing these same meta-narratives and master codes. Nativism was born of the lamentable circumstance of colonialism and the agonizing milieu of the post-World War II period of decolonization. It represents a cultural reflex on the part of many Third World intellectuals from Southeast Asia to the Caribbean eager to assert their newly found identities.

The reader may suspect that we are here confronting another essentialist proposal. The interesting aspect of the proposal is that Frantz Fanon comes up, for an Iranian intellectual, as the paradigmatic example of nativism. Let's then translate nativism into localism and be clear that locals have been conformed by the formation and transformation of the colonial matrix of power. I suspect that Boroujerdi has something else in mind – something that is not just nativism, which is correlated with nationalism (cf., *natio*, place of birth). In fact, what he has in mind is the "nativistic" confrontation that emerged from Third World leaders after the Bandung Conference. He provides a list in which Amilcar Cabral and Fidel Castro, Mao Zedong and Frantz Fanon, Albert Memmi and Gamal Abdel Nasser, Jawarharhal Nerhu and Leopoldo Sedar Senghor, etc., each belong next to the other. At first sight, the list is confusing, but there is a logic to it: they are all males, certainly, with a decolonial or a Marxist agenda in the colonial world. The point is, then, that nativism emerges because of the advent of a powerful intellectual and political elite, some of them still linked to Europe through Marxism, but in the colonies, and some plainly already decolonial. Localism, crossed and conformed by historical forces (in this case, Persia, Islam, the Western creation of the Middle East as a region and the Middle East becoming part of the Third World) thus emerges as a pluriversal response and confrontation with universal Eurocentrism.

Eurocentrism, in the last analysis, is Western localism (or perhaps nativism is a good name for Eurocentrism) with a global design that became synonymous with universalism. And the Marxist Left, for better or worse, belongs to that world. One of the problems I see in the reorientation of the Left today is precisely how to detach itself from the imperial spirit where it was born. On the other hand, the proliferation of global political society makes Marxism dispensable for imagining and enacting global futures, although Marx continues to be indispensable for understanding industrial capitalism. The challenge for the Left today is how to disengage from that legacy, abandoning any pretense to a global design that will save the world. Non-Western localism is plural, since there are multiple memories and colonial wounds infringed by racism, ways of life, languages, beliefs, experiences connected to the West, but at the same time not subsumable to it. Localism (which shall not be confused with "national fundamentalisms" or "nativism from the Right") should be pluriversal and therefore decolonial. Since localism originated from the lamentable circumstance of colonialism, or better yet, from the logic of coloniality common to different Western imperial/colonial expansions (Spain, France, England) and its surrogates after the sixteenth century (imperial Russia, Soviet Union, Japan), a trade mark of localism is the decolonial thread that connects and makes pluriversality a global project. The communal, in the sense that it is being rethought and reenacted in Bolivia, is a significant contribution to global pluriversality (and, locally, plurinational state). Decolonial localism is global or if you wish cosmopolitics, which should also be distinguished from current versions of liberal cosmopolitanism.

5. CONCLUDING REMARKS

It was something along this line of argument I had in mind with the title "The Advent of Indigenous and Afro-Intellectuals in the 20th Century."[5] If "localism" has been cast as a response to Westernization from the Third World, then "Latin" America has to be counted as part

5. For access to this work, see the conference website at http://latinamerican studiesprogram.com/.

of the emergence of localism. However, regionally, there is still a conflict to be solved between Creole and mestizo intellectual elites and the
advent of Afro and indigenous leadership. The "Latin" aspect of South
and Central America and the Caribbean is called into question. Next
to *Latinidad* emerge the claims of *Africanidad* and *Indianidad*. Certainly, *Africanidad* and *Indianidad* are not homogeneous groupings.
Neither is *Latinidad*.[6] And unless we erase the differences and think in
terms of the people or the multitude, projects that emerge from (and
that do not necessarily represent the totality of an ethno-group), shall
be taken into serious consideration. Otherwise, how would a plurinational state be conceived and organized if there is only one "people" in
the nation? That idea was indeed in the foundation of the mono-
national state. The point is that there are epistemic and political
projects that emerge from each trajectory. There is no project that represents the totality, which does not mean that such projects shall not
be counted because they do not represent *all the* Indians, *all the* Afros
and *all the* "Latins" in South and Central America and the Caribbean.

That is one of the consequences of the advent of indigenous and
Afro-intellectuals and leaders in the 20th century. That is how political and decolonial localism is being articulated in Bolivia, Ecuador,
Brazil, Martinique, Haiti, Jamaica, and Trinidad and Tobago. In the
last analysis, and drawing a larger picture, we can see now that "cosmopolitan localism" (certainly an oxymoron) may be the emerging
community, since imperial cosmopolitanism (following the steps of
Kant) is no longer viable. However, this oxymoron should be taken
seriously, since "cosmopolitan localism" is an expression equivalent to
"A world in which many worlds will coexist" and of "pluriversality as

6. There is another aspect of the argument that shall be mentioned. When a
non-Indian defends the Indian cause or sometimes even when indigenous intellectuals defend their own cause, white intellectuals, generally liberals, Marxists or post-
modernists reply that "you are romanticizing the Indians or the ayllu" or whatever.
It may be. If it is, it runs parallel to the romanticization of Greece and Rome by
imperial European nativism. The point is that you cannot be exempt from the
charges you attribute to those who dissent with your views without putting yourself
in a position of imperial epistemic supremacy. That is what Sor Juana was saying in
the sphere of patriarchal domination when she said "*Hombres necios que acusais a la
mujer sin saber que sois la causa de lo mismo que juzgais*" (Brutish men you are that
accuse the woman without knowing that you are the cause of that which you judge).

a universal project." And I mean here universal: it means that the formula "a world in which many worlds will coexist" is only possible if the many worlds in coexistence agree that the world shall be pluriversal. That hegemonic belief would then be not only global, but universal. The advent of indigenous and Afro-intellectuals in South America and the Caribbean as well as the growing influence of intellectuals and activists around the world that delink from the genealogy of thoughts grounded in Greece and Rome and modern Europe (from Aristotle, to Saint Thomas and Saint Paul, to Spinoza and Marx, etc.), are debunking the idea of linear progress and development in the making of a horizontal plural world. Evo Morales' request that the UN no longer be the club of the selected few but should incorporate all existing nation-states in the world, in its deliberation, is one example of a growing force not only at the level of the state and the UN, but in the thinking and doing of the global political (not civil) society.

WORKS CITED

BOROUJERDI, Mehrzad. *Iranian Intellectuals and the West: The Tormented Triumph of Nativism,* Syracuse: Syracuse UP, 1996.

GONZÁLEZ CASANOVA, Pablo. "Las razones del Zapatismo y la otra Campaña." *OSAL* 6 (2006): 291-303.

HARDIN, Garrett. "The Tragedy of the Commons." *Science* 162: 1243-1248.

KELLNER, Douglas. "Critical Theory, Poststructuralism, and the Philosophy of Liberation." 2001. Web. <http://www.uta.edu/huma/illuminations/kell7.htm>.

LEMOINE, Maurice. "La Bolivie indienne rejoint la gauche latina." *Le Monde Diplomatique* 22 December 2005. Web. <http://www.monde-diplomatique.fr/dossiers/bolivie/>.

MAMANI CONDORI, Carlos. "El proceso de la reconstitución política-territorial en la coyuntura de la Asamblea Constituyente. 25 July 2008. Web. <http://www.scribd.com/doc/4093276/mamani>.

PATZI PACO, Felix. *Sistema Comunal. Una propuesta alternative al sistema liberal.* La Paz: CEA, 2004.

REYNAGA, Fausto. *La revolucion India.* La Paz: Partido Indio de Bolivia, 1970.

SEBILL, Nadie. *Ayllus y haciendas. Dos estudios de caso sobre la agricultura colonial de los Andes.* La Paz: Hisbol, 1989.

TICONA, Esteban. *Lecturas Para La Descolonizacion: Taqpachani Qhispiya-sipxanan Liberemonos Todos*. La Paz: Agruco, 2005
—. "The Idea of Communism." 15 March 2009. Web. <http://www.lacan.com/essays/?page_id=99>.
WALSH, Catherine. *Interculturalidad, estado, sociedad. Luchas (de)coloniales de nuestra 'epoca*. Quito: Universidad Andina-Abya Yala, 2009
YAMPARA HUARACHI, Simon. *El Ayllu y la territorialidad en los Andes*. La Paz: Universidad Publica del Alto, 2001

IV. Global Networks
and Transnational Flows

SOCIAL SCIENCES AND THE ENGLISH LANGUAGE[1]

Renato Ortiz

Globalization is preferentially declined in English. I say preferentially because despite the fact that the existence of other languages is constitutive of our contemporary reality, a single language, among many, holds a privileged status. There are objective reasons that things developed in this fashion, and those reasons have nothing to do with phonetic or grammatical groundings. It would be foolish to think about the existence of languages in such a substantialistic way, though many have done so. Linguists teach us that every language is able to conceptually express the human experience, so there is no such thing as a superior language. Furthermore, we know that only humans have a language coherently articulated in a complex system of signs, and that the diversification of languages is something that occurred quite early in societies of the past. Regardless of the available (and unconfirmed) hypotheses about the origins of language – monogenesis or polygenesis – the truth is that, as soon as they were put into action, they evolved in separate communities, spreading across several regions

1. This paper was published as "As ciências sociais e o inglês" in *Revista Brasileira de Ciências Sociais* 19.54 (2004): 5-22 and in English translation by Arlete Dialetachi in the *Revista Brasileira de Ciências Sociais* [online] 2.no se. (2006). The present version was translated by Bret Gustafson with the assistance of Gonzalo Aguiar.

of the planet (currently there are some 6,500 languages spoken in the world). Taking into consideration such diversity and the impossibility of the existence of a universal language – for that all human experiences would have to converge on a single source of meaning – it would be unwise to delimit our discussion around the premise of a univocal world. The process of globalization is not a synonym of homogenization, nor of Americanization; it is a condition in which the hierarchies and relations of force surely exist and are unequal, but they do not necessarily imply the elimination of diversities. In this sense, the disappearance of the national languages, idealized by some as equivalent to universal brotherhood (that was the belief of Kautsky and many scholars of the II International) and by others as a nightmare, is a false problem. Nonetheless, this introductory note of caution does not elucidate much about the topic in question, because it is not the uniformity of languages that is at stake, but rather the fact that they participate in a situation of globalization marked by relations of power.

The diligent, patient, reader notices that much of the literature regarding the scattering of English across the world is relatively recent. It developed particularly in the late seventies and through the eighties, when a series of books was published about this scattering on an international scale.[2] These authors wished to document empirically the presence of English in several countries and spheres of activity – from science to advertising – as well as to understand the reasons that English came to occupy such a situation of preponderance. Two factors stand out in this kind of study. The first one concerns the standard. Given the existence of established references – the British and North American standards – the diffusion of English raised a problem: how to understand, in countries whose official language was English, the idiomatic variations which did not fit in the model. Would it be more appropriate to use the expression "English" or "English(es)," singular or plural?[3] Kachru, an Indian linguist, considers that the nativization of English would result in the creation of an autonomous model, original, different from the British legacy, but equally valid. Others extrapolate their research methodology, applying it to different regions of Asia, which implied equating the legitimacy of regionally developed

2. Fishman, Cooper, and Conrad, Baily and Görlach; Cooper; Greenbaum.
3. I cite, among others, McArthur.

varieties to the level of the exporting matrices, England and United States (Kachru; Parakram). Therefore, there is a dispute among the English speaking countries about the existence or inexistence of a sole standard (or two, at the most) which might order a hierarchy of these languages. The debate about the standard, predominant among foreign language teachers (who seek "the best" for their pedagogical activities, always reaffirming North American and British excellence), is based on a misconception whose concealment generates political and cultural dividends. It is the ratification of a hegemony redressed as a linguistic truth.

This is an ancient debate. Since the formation of the nation-state, in which the monopoly of language was one of the definitive features of the process of national integration, the exigency of a generalized reference for everybody has the intention of opposing other existing ways of speaking. Bourdieu reminds us that the French Revolution had as a goal the imposition of a legitimate language against regional idioms and dialects. "The conflict between the French of the revolutionary *intelligentsia* and the dialects or *patois* was a struggle for symbolic power in which what was at stake was the *formation* and *re-formation* of mental structures. In short, it was not only a question of communicating but of gaining recognition for a new language of authority" (*Language*, 48). Those tensions are not situated only in the past; they are recurrent and actualized in the context of the proliferation of conflicting languages within the same geographic area today. This is what occurs in the United States, where the English Only movement, an ardent advocate of monolingualism, has the goal of discrediting and limiting immigrants' demand for a bilingual education (Wiley and Lukes). In the case of English as an international language, the dispute over authority is not confined to the boundaries of a nation, but now involves countries with differentiated histories and cultures. However, the terms of the discussion are similar. For, after all, the postulated standard has no empirical reality; it is simply a concept imagined by those holding a position of power who believe that such standard confers them a certain capacity, the capacity to "correct" others. The existence of such a standard is invoked as a justification for the control and safeguard of the language of origin. The polemic over the existence or inexistence of a standard occurs especially when the speakers are involved in some field of contestation. For this reason, even today, in moments of tension (the situation of globalization), the controversy reappears in full force, and often with switched signals. For example, we have the dispute surrounding the Toulon Law, which officially regulated the utilization of foreign terms in the French language. Here, the notion of a standard is recovered as an anterior stage of "purity" being threatened and corrupted by the excessive use of English (Durand).

A second aspect concerns the Anglocentric dimension of these studies, and, quite often, an ideological mantle in which they are cloaked. They are marked by a profound optimism and an unmasked sense of superiority, as if the expansion of a language were really a synonym of civilization and progress. In light of the undeniable appearance of the empirical evidence, it is repeated with pride that "no other language has undergone similar expansion since Greek and Roman times." These analyses lack even the minimum of a critical spirit, leading us to believe that the grandeur of a language is exclusively due to the diglossic strategies of its speakers. The major argument underlying this theoretical current can be summarized as follows: a second language is learned only when the speaker expects to obtain advantages by using another language whose range of action is broader. I quote one of these studies conducted during this period. The authors, after describing a series of factors that could eventually influence the diffusion of English – political attitudes, religion, urbanization, economic development, linguistic diversity, military presence – conclude:

> To say that English is spreading around the world as a function of the combination of particular variables is a summarizing statement, based on the effects of innumerable human interactions and motivations. Individuals, not countries, learn English as an additional language. An individual learns English, moreover, not because of abstractions such as linguistic diversity or international trade balances but because the knowledge of English helps him to communicate in contexts for which, for economic or educational or emotional reasons, he wants to communicate and because the opportunity to learn English is available to him. That the summarizing statistics employed here revealed pleasing symmetries and sensible regularities should not allow us to forget the human behavior underlying them. The study of language spread, then, must proceed not only from the manipulation and analysis of summary data at very great levels of abstraction but also from the observation of human behavior

at first hand. [...] Primary data of great contextual specificity must be sought, as well as secondary data far removed from the everyday arenas in which languages are learned and used and abandoned [...] (Fishman, Cooper, Rosenbaum 106).

Thus, the use of English would thus arise from the advantages that it offers to those who use it. Its status is, therefore, one of neutrality, and it functions above all as the most comprehensive means of communication. At this point, linguists with different theoretical inclinations converge on a similar diagnosis. This is the case of Kachru, an unyielding opponent of the idea of the existence of a British or North American standard. When it comes to understanding English's presence in India, in contraposition to other existing languages, he tells us: "English does have one clear advantage, attitudinally and linguistically: it has acquired a neutrality in a linguistic context where native languages, dialects, and styles sometimes have acquired undesirable connotations..." (Kachru, cited in Pennycook 9-10). This is obviously illusory, for its use in India is marked by political contradictions and ideological controversies (Sonntag). However, it is important to emphasize that the previous argument, that of functional neutrality, is reaffirmed. From this perspective, the expansion of English would not simply be something to be demonstrated analytically, but a benefit for everyone. The linguists appear to reason like the cultural anthropologists of the 1940s, who assumed that the acculturation process derived exclusively from the contact between two different cultures, regardless of the context in which such interaction occurred. Thus, the explanations regarding religious syncretism or African messianism had nothing to do with the colonial situation of the actors involved; facts of that nature were seen as external, alien to what was happening.[4] That is why among culturalist anthropologists, as well as linguists, colonialism and imperialism were taboo themes; after all, in the last instance these were seen to have a relationship of exteriority to what one sought to understand.

But these reflections about English become even more problematic when texts of a specifically ideological nature are considered. Among

---

4. I refer the reader to the classic text of Ballandier, in which the author, in criticizing the culturalist perspective, creates the concept of the "colonial situation."

others, I recall the book by Jeremy Tunstall, *The Media are American* (1977). With ample factual documentation – regarding television, cinema, advertising, and the press – he sought to understand North American predominance in the world. His arguments are exemplary:

> English is probably the major language most shaped by and most attuned to media use. [...] The English language is relatively free of separate scholarly 'high' and vulgar 'low' forms – compared for example even with German. [...] English also has an unusually small gap between its written and spoken forms. [...] English has evolved as a language with and through the media, especially the press. [...] English contains a greater variety of pithy phrases and simple words from which to choose [compared with French for example] and the English-language version is usually shorter than the version in any other language. And English has simpler grammar than possible rival languages such as Russian. English is the language best suited to comic strips, headlines, riveting first sentences, photo captions, dubbing, subtitling, pop songs, hoardings, disc-jockey banter, news flashes, sung commercials (127-128).

Thus it is not only about communicative neutrality or diglossic advantages; but that in its "essence," English was intrinsically superior to other languages. As the language of rationality and modernity, English would be the primary cause, not the manifestation, of North American supremacy (much of which ideology is still displayed in the realm of common sense in times of globalization). The strong reaction to this apparently naive approach, which at its core is a deeply interested analysis, should be taken into account; and, in my view, has had important, positive implications for the understanding of the current problematic. In this sense, the book by Robert Phillipson, *Linguistic Imperialism* (1992), has the merit of introducing new parameters into the debate, particularly the role played by colonialism and imperialism in the configuration of the present world. From this point of view, the colonial legacy, associated with the expansion of capitalism, would not be limited to purely economic questions. Its implications would extend to a domain that, until then, had been excluded, by the linguists, from its area of influence. Phillipson's text opens the door to others wishing to write about English "as an ideology," so that the reasons for its expansion cease to be sought in its internal properties or in the mere fact of interaction between speech participants. It is precisely this dimension, seen before as an exteriority – the political, economical and military organization of interests considered as irrelevant or secondary for analytical understanding – that becomes decisive for explanation. David Crystal, interested in the English dispersion around the world for some time, writing later and, revising somewhat his previous point of view, could then say:

> A language does not become a global language because of its intrinsic structural properties, or because of the size of its vocabulary, or because it has been a vehicle of a great literature in the past, or because it was once associated with a great culture or religion. [....] A language has traditionally become an international language for one chief reason: the power of its people – especially their political and military power [....] But international language dominance is not solely the result of military might. It may take a militarily powerful nation to establish a language, but it takes an economically powerful one to maintain and expand it. [...] The growth of competitive industry and business brought an explosion of international marketing and advertising. [...] Technology, chiefly in the form of movies and records, fuelled new mass entertainment industries which had a worldwide impact. The drive to make progress in science and technology fostered an international intellectual and research environment which gave scholarship and further education a high profile.
>
> Any language at the center of such an explosion of international activity would suddenly have found itself with a global status (9-10).

The reading of this literature allows us to formulate a question: to what extent is it distinguished – or not – from the debate about globalization? Is there any conceptual discrepancy between the affirmations "English as an international language" and "English as a global language," or is this simply a question of outcome of terminological imprecisions with little significance? I believe there are substantial differences, and it is important to emphasize them. First, there is an explicit disconnection between these studies and the texts about globalization, though many are contemporaneous.[5] We must keep in mind that, through the eighties and the early nineties, reflections about globalization were limited to some specific domains – advertising and

5. There are exceptions that confirm the rule, such as the article by Swaan ("Notes").

business management (I refer to the literature about global marketing). The social sciences paid it little or no attention, for the field of
ideas was polarized between moderns and postmoderns – Habermas
versus Lyotard. Even Phillipson's book, published in 1992, is not free
of this critique, since it was based on a traditional definition of imperialism (Hobson, Lenin) open to some incorporation of theoreticians of
dependence. Globalization is excluded from the discussion. On the
other hand, it is worth noting in the studies conducted by the linguists
the constant presence of two terms: diffusion and dispersion – symp-
tomatically one of the key texts on the matter bears the title *The
Spread of English*. I believe that, at this point, the comparison with the
anthropologists can be taken up again, but now in association with
diffusionism.[6] Kroeber said that

> [w]hen an invention passes from the inventor to other individuals, we
> call that its successful cultural acceptance. Diffusion may be viewed as an
> extension of the process, on a much larger scale, by which an invention or
> innovation – or sometimes even an older cultural trait – spreads from the
> society in which it originated to new societies and becomes established in
> their cultures.
>   This is much like the passing on of culture to the younger generation
> within the evolving society, except for being foreign-directed instead of
> domestic. In other words, new culture is transmitted geographically as
> well as chronologically, in space as well as in time, by contagion as well
> as repetition. The spread in area is generally called diffusion, as the inter-
> nal handing on through time is called tradition (410).

Therefore, the definition presupposes the existence of an irradiat-
ing center and of a common space shared by distinct cultures. That is
why diffusionism is so interested in the comparison between areas of
civilization and the migration of cultural traits from a given area to
another (acculturation and syncretism). The argument postulates as
well a clear distinction between internal and external, elements pertaining to a "system of departure," the source of the irradiation, and
those situated at the "point of arrival." Diffusion expresses the moment
of contact between two cultures, two civilizations. Linguists reason in

---

6. I take up here the argument of my book *Mundializacão e cultura* (1994).

an analogous way. English is a language that possesses its own history and centrality, which, through different mechanisms (schools, institutions, religious missions, etc.), is diffused around the world. At the point of contact, when it encounters other languages, diglossia or assimilations occur. This means, from the point of view of the speaker, that one is dealing with a language distinct from their own. The criticism from an anti-imperialist viewpoint is based on the same premises (Ortiz, "Revisitando"). The concept of imperialism presupposes the existence of a center, a nation. It is the nucleus of a domain that encompasses the planet, apportioning it in accordance with the unscrupulous appetite of a few industrialized countries. Therefore, imperialism has an identity: it is English, North American, German, French, Japanese. Each focus of diffusion seeks to propagate and impose its ideas and its way of life on peripheral nations. What is external to the national reality of the peripheral countries can thus be seen as alienation, as something extraneous, separated from its own "authenticity" (remember that the concept of alienation was crucial in Third World thought, both in Latin America and in Africa – as in the case of Frantz Fanon).

However, the globalization phenomenon is different from the internationalization one. With globalization, nations cease to be autonomous, independent entities, which interact with each other, and become territories traversed by the flow of world modernity. In such a context, it makes little sense to talk about a diffusing centrality or about a clear opposition between external and internal, foreign and autochthonous. To say that English is an international language means considering it in relation to its internal integrity, circulating between nations. Another thing is calling it a global language, that is, a language that traverses distinct places of the planet. It is significant that the studies of its diffusion consider it an "additional" element, that is, something added to a pre-existing base.[7] Hence the insistence on the teaching of a second language. For example, when an author such as Claude Truchot analyzes the penetration of English among the French scientists in the 1980s, he treats the theme in the classic terms of diglossia. There is a contact between two distinct codes, one high, the

---

7 As in the title of Fishman's text.

other low (obviously, the low one corresponds to French), in which the speaker uses, as a communicative strategy, one of those available. The predominance of English occurs because it is the language of scientific exchanges, that is, it acts as an international language with greater amplitude. Therefore, from the perspective of the scientist using it, English is a "foreign" language. This is not to criticize this kind of explanation; but it is important to emphasize that it only partially solves the problem. With the advent of globalization, it would be interesting to know if only English possesses this attribute or if it should be construed otherwise, for its position is entirely redefined. I would say that, in the context of globalization, English is no longer a foreign language, something imposed from the outside, but has become an internal language, autochthonous to the condition of world modernity. This is, in my opinion, the meaning of David Crystal's statement in the introduction of his book *English as a Global Language* (1997). This radically changes things.

Linguists often utilize the metaphor of ecology, dealing with languages as ecological systems. A first sense raises the idea of threatened nature; in this case, with the intention of developing mechanisms of protection for the species, ensuring the condition of existence of certain languages in adverse situations – for example, the decrease in the number of speakers would lead to language extinction. This interest in biodiversity has even led some authors to suggest the development of a linguistic-ecologic policy, focused on multilingualism, the preservation of cultures and respect for human rights (Phillipson and Skutnabb-Kangas). I am aware that this approach is important, and that the affirmation of the equality of rights is fundamental in the struggle for the ideal of a fair and equitable "worldly civil society." However, what interests me about the ecological metaphor, within the scope of this article, is the fact that this metaphor refers us to the spatiality of things. Ecology, as an environment, defines a context, a specific territoriality. Well, we know that the process of globalization implies a radical transformation of the notion of space, in which categories such as diffusion or imperialism become inoperative (cf. Ortiz, "Another Territory"). How should we consider then the ecological configuration of languages with regard to their environments and to other languages? I think that the contribution of Abram de Swaan (*Words of the World*) is relevant, since it provides us with the possibili-

ty of understanding the subject in close correlation with the movement of globalization.[8]

Individuals do not always have the possibility of choosing their languages; this attribution is shaped in the topographic context in which
they live. But what is the cartography of the globalized world? Swaan
abandons the two-dimensional idea of planes – the localization of languages in the space of each country or each culture – by suggesting a
three-dimensional design inspired by the model of astronomy. The
linguistic map may thus be imagined as a galaxy, comprised of suns,
planets, and satellites articulated to the same gravitational system. It is
thus possible to distinguish constellations internal to this universe, the
world. The bilingualism of individuals (but not necessarily of the totality of the planet's beings) would have the task of organizing communication between the different parts that make up this universe. Most
languages, 98%, would be situated at the lower portion of this universe; they are the languages of memory, unwritten, but which would
be made up of a restricted number of speakers, 10% of the Earth's
inhabitants. Peripheral languages would gather around a central one,
as if they were moons gravitating around a planet. The central languages, some one hundred of them – among them Quechua, Bam-
bara, Czech, Romanian, etc. – in their majority, but not exclusively,
are national languages used in the press, radio, television, courts, and
the state bureaucracy. Above those would be the super-central languages, whose range of action is broader, no longer restricted to the
boundaries of a sole country. These would be the suns around which
the planets (central languages) and the satellites (peripheral languages)
would revolve. Twelve languages would belong to this group: Arabic,
Chinese, English, French, German, Hindi, Portuguese, Japanese,
Malay, Russian, Spanish, and Swahili.[9] Each one of them would constitute a constellation, and English would occupy the hyper-central
position, that is, it would be the nuclear node of this linguistic galaxy.
Such a model illustrates how linguistic exchanges happen in the interior

8. A similar perspective was developed by Calvet.

9. There is a controversy in relation to the number of these languages. Calvet
questions Swaan's inclusion of Japanese and German, which for him would be languages with a large number of speakers, yet concentrated in the same geographic
space.

of a single ensemble. In this sense, English, as an expression of globality, becomes transformed into a structuring component of something that transcends it. Its North American or British origin becomes secondary. The roots of its previous territoriality are no longer important; but rather its existence as a deterritorialized, appropriated, and resignified language in the various contexts in which it is used. It is a generalized phenomenon in the sphere of culture, in which many national and local traditions are redefined in terms of globalization. It is the case of the Donald Duck character, the Hollywood stars, and the Western genre, which have lost their Americanism; the same occurs with Doreamon, Pokemon and Yamamoto's *haute couture* in relation to Japan; or, pop music in relation to England. The same way in which they become expressions of a global collective imaginary, the English language, by being reterritorialized in the space of world modernity acquires another meaning. By becoming global, it is free from its prior rootedness, becoming an artifact to be legitimately 'deformed' or 'distorted' by the speakers of a single galaxy.

Swaan considers every language to be a "hyper-collective good." They are objectively available to individuals (who, for using them, must go through a learning process) just like how rivers and lakes are part of our environment. Such objectivity allows them to be compared to economic goods. Languages may then be construed as standards and networks of communication. The standards are conventions, protocols for the operation of a machine, procedures to coordinate certain actions; the networks are systems of connections, just like the electrical grid with its cables or the telephone network with its signals, which are able to articulate a point in space to an interconnected totality. There are, in the market, different technical standards for several kinds of competing networks – PAL and Secam for television (hence the importance of the choice of digital standard for the television system of a country); or the programs provided by Microsoft, which run only on some computers. For the individual it is important to know what benefit can be provided by a given standard, and they may, at any time, change their newspaper subscription, choose another cable television package, and so on. Linguistic loyalty is an extreme case of consumer loyalty, since the individual cannot easily change their language. It is an interesting argument, but we must consider its implications. Swaan states (*Words*, 28):

Whenever people opt for appliances with a specific standard, subscribe to a particular supply network or learn a given language, by doing so they increase the utility of that standard, network, or language for all other consumers, subscribers, or speakers who are already using it.

This means that the practice of English, whether as a means of communication, affirmation of prestige, or literary expression, implies the strengthening of the English language's standard in the market of linguistic goods. Its authority is reinforced when people employ it in their daily affairs – from the post-colonialist who publishes their critical work in English, to the Brazilian businessman who uses it during trips abroad. A revealing example of that legitimacy occurs in the field of pop music, in which English is widely utilized, regardless of whether or not it is understood by young consumers. As a matter of fact, the diffusion of this musical genre on a planetary scale does not depend on the difficulty of its decodification. But what does a language that is not understood mean? Bourdieu, in his critique of linguistic structuralism, used to say that "listening is believing" (*The Field*). The symbolic forces determine those that speak and those that listen, and the principle of authority is reinforced at the moment in which the communication is completed. Paradoxically, we have got to the point in which people enjoy what they do not understand. They listen because they believe. The language's legitimacy is such that it does fine without the understanding of those who do not know it.

English is the language of science. The reasons for this, in addition to those discussed above, are tied to profound post-war transformations. Science and technology, which until then were evolving in relatively separate spheres of knowledge, integrated into a single system. Historians teach us that the Industrial Revolution resulted more from the pragmatic inventions of certain individuals than from a wide and systematic scientific knowledge. Yet the scenario of the late nineteenth century is transformed by a second industrial revolution. The electric industry is a direct consequence of scientific investigations, as well as the invention of the telegraph, the generator, the electric motor, and the radio. But it is not yet possible to observe the inverse, that is, a clear and persistent influence of technological investigations on the functioning of the scientific universe. This tendency takes over throughout the twentieth century, and the expression "technoscience" clearly reveals its new dimension. Technologies presuppose a continuous investment of capital, the formation of specialized teams, and the creation of research laboratories. In the beginning, this is concentrated in the United States, for, when World War II was over, that was the only industrialized country where the educational and technological infrastructure remained intact. With the expansion of higher education and the development of research institutes, an unprecedented scientific resurgence occurs, associated with technological policies through which scientific creations are linked to the discovery and perfection of research techniques. The history of the computer is a good example of the interweaving of economic, military and scientific dimensions within a single project. As a data and information processor, the computer will stimulate a whole field of activities, from laboratory experiments to business administration (whose range of action is often transnational). Science, technology and management – differentiated spheres of practice and knowledge – become more proximate as units that feed on and are reproduced by the manipulation, control and processing of information. I do not believe it exaggerated to say that the key-elements of what we understand as the society of information were primarily elaborated in English (concepts, models, formulas, and procedures).

It is not difficult to follow the advance and the itinerary of this supremacy. To understand it, we may, for instance, observe changes in high school curriculums related to the teaching of foreign languages. Yun-Kyung Cha, using a series of statistical data from all countries of the world, presents some interesting elements for reflection (29). (The data should be taken with caution, particularly in the case of comprehensive analyses like this one; but I believe that they are eloquent.) In the middle of the nineteenth century (1850-1870), the French and German languages, together, were taught in 91% of existing high schools (45.5% respectively) and English in 8.3%. Between 1900 and 1944 those figures changed: English (39.6%); French (47.9%); and German (16.3%), showing a reasonable balance between the languages. Between 1972 and 1986 this picture underwent a definitive alteration: English (72%); French (17.6%); and German (0.8%). Considering that high school is an important factor in the learning of a foreign language, a decisive condition in the world of sciences, we can infer the extent of the transformation in the teaching standard. Another way of approaching the matter is observing the exponential growth of the articles published in English in some scientific areas (Tsunoda). In mathematics, the *Bulletin Signalétique* shows that, between 1940 and 1980, the number of texts in English increased from 49.5% to 71%, while those in French decreased from 31.2% to 6.1%, and in German from 13.2% to 1.6%. The *Berichte Über die Gesamte Biologie* indicates that the publications in English increased between 1926 and 1980, from 26.7% to 55.9%, while those in French decreased from 16.4% to 1%, and in German from 50% to 42.1%. In journals with North American origins the disproportion is more evident: *Physics Abstracts* shows that between 1950 and 1980, the texts in English increased from 70.3% to 88.6%, with publications in other languages almost insignificant. Some linguists, among them Richard Baldauf, have formulated historical series that allow us to get a clearer view of the different areas of knowledge. Between 1965 and 1988, the articles published in English in the area of biology increased from 50% to 75%; in engineering, from 82% to 86%; in medicine, from 51% to 75%; and in mathematics, from 54% to 82%. It is a trend that becomes stronger and stronger as years go by, in all specialties. However, it is not only the articles that confirm this movement; the citations, in other words, the works referenced, reinforce the trend. A study conducted on the most significant geology magazines of the area illustrates this aspect quite clearly (Reguant and Casadellà). In periodicals such as the *American Association of Petroleum Geologists Bulletin* (United States) and the *Journal of the Geological Society* (United Kingdom), the references to texts written in English are practically exclusive (95.5% and 91.6%, respectively). These are predominant as well in the publications of other countries: *Geologische Rundschau*, 64.4%; *Estudios Geologicos*, 40.3%; *Rivista Italiana di Paleontologia e Stratigrafia*, 48.3%; *Engineering Geology* (the Netherlands), 90.2%. So a circuit is being closed: articles are preferentially written and cited in English.

Based on these statistics, we should not infer that all scientific production, nor even a majority of it, is carried out in English. Although there are no available data on a global scale, we can argue that the scientific literature in non-English languages has increased. It suffices to observe the proliferation of journals in the most diverse countries and the scientists' participation in specialized meetings and conferences. However, as Baldauf emphasizes, the representation of these languages (and journals) in the literature surveyed in the major databases has declined. In spite of being regarded by many as representative of scientific production, the databases, as a matter of fact, form a distorted projection of what is really happening. A great portion of what is produced is simply ignored due to the fact that it is not formalized and formatted as easily available information, that is, as information understandable by a broad group of people. There is also a self-selection process among publications, hence the dispute among scientists about the reliability or non-reliability of the *Science Citation Index*. However, it is important to understand that a literary corpus, operating as a standard of reference, is globally legitimated only when made available in English. Hence the strategy of many groups, particularly in the 'Third World,' of separating their activities into 'local' and 'universal.' The local ones are written in the national language, and their vehicle is the journals of the country; the universal ones concentrate the 'elite' scientists, whose ambition is to make themselves more visible in the global scenario and whose interest is to publish their works in renowned international magazines. In such a case, the elaboration of articles and papers tends to maintain English as an international language (Russell). Another strategy is to produce journals entirely in English or to publish, in domestic journals, a significant number of texts in this language. That is what occurs in several specialized publications: *Anales de la Asociación Química Argentina* (53% of texts in English), *Biocell* (Argentina, 100%); *Brazilian Journal of Genetics* (100%), *Computation and Applied Mathematics* (Brazil, 100%); *Arquivos de Neuro-Psiquiatria* (35%); *Archives of Medical Research* (Mexico, 100%); *Revista de Biología Tropical* (Costa Rica, 41%).[10]

The expression *lingua franca* is recurrent. It is usually associated with Latin, a language that was once regarded as the language of knowledge. Such an image may be accurate, but it disguises other truths. First, there is an incongruence, that is, the application of a concept extraneous to the categories of a given period of time. In the Middle Ages, for example, *scientia* was equivalent to "a true or certain knowledge," and applied only to theology, logic, physics, and mathe-

10. See data in Gómes, Sancho, Moreno and Fernández.

matics (Blair). Astronomy and optics, for their part, were called middle or half-sciences, since they lent their principles to other disciplines. Navigation, accounting, surgery, pharmacy, and building construction were practical specialties, or, in other words, arts. Latin was the language of *scientia*, while the other forms of knowledge were expressed in the vernacular. Secondly, in the prevailing hierarchy, using the vernacular language was equivalent to a disqualification or lowering in rank. That is, Latin was not only an international language, but also a prestigious means of communication. In strict terms, we should say that no *lingua* is *franca*; it just exercises in given domains, the "function of being" *franca*. In this sense, English, within the universe of natural sciences, acts predominantly as a *lingua franca*; its role is concentrated on transmitted information, minimizing other dimensions of the life in society (prestige, aesthetics, feelings, etc.). But if this is possible, and this is the element valued by scientists – the use of a language emptied of other connotations with the intention of maximizing instrumental communication – what can be said about the social sciences? I take from Barthes a remark that he made when comparing literature and science:

For science, language is merely an instrument, which it chooses to make as transparent, as neutral as possible, subjugated to scientific matters (operations, hypotheses, results) which are said to exist outside it and precede it: on one side and *first of all*, the contents of the scientific message, which are everything; and on the other and *afterwards*, the verbal form entrusted with expressing these contents, which is nothing. [...] For literature [...] language is the *being* of literature, its very world: all literature is contained in the act of writing [...]. [T]hough science needs language, it is not, like literature, *within* language[.] (4-5, emphasis in original).

We must keep in mind that the quality of being instrumental should not be seen as something negative, in the Frankfurtian meaning of instrumental reason, or, when referring to literature, as an impoverishment of the language (although sometimes Barthes has this intention). It is a deliberate choice to utilize language as a tool, whose result is highly rewarding – the scientific discourse. The consequence is the wide consensus (although not unanimous) existing among scientists in relation to the use of English, that is, the fact of it being instrumental and efficient.[11] But what is the reason for this instrumentality? Richard Harris and Paul Mattick, working with language properties and their relationship with information, present an interesting argument. They consider that each scientific domain uses language in a delimited fashion, which is why it is easier to translate scientific rather than literary texts. This means that the information provided in the message is given not only by the individual meaning of the words, but also by the relationship between them, their co-occurrence and combination. For example, we may enunciate the phrases "for me it is preferable to be the last to leave" and "I would rather be the last to leave." There is a variation in the form but not in the transmitted information. Things are different when it comes to scientific discourse, in which there is a strong restriction on the co-occurrence of words. In biochemistry we can say "the polypeptides were washed in hydrochloric acid," but "the hydrochloric acid was washed in polypeptides," although grammatically accurate, would be an implausible statement. With the analysis of the co-occurrence of the words in scientific discourse, it becomes possible to define fields of sublanguage separated from the utilized language. According to the authors:

> If we examine the structure of, for instance, the biochemistry sublanguage of French and the biochemistry sublanguage of English – that is, the subsets of nouns, verbs, and other elements and the various sentence types made of them – we find that they are in all essentials identical. If we mark the various word subsets in the English biochemistry sublanguage by letters – for example, by using P for 'polypeptides' and for other molecules that might be treated by washing, W for certain laboratory operations, and S for certain solutions – we could represent the sentence types by sequences of these word-class symbols. Such a sequence would be 'PWS' here. We can show that the same symbol classes and sentential symbol-sequences suffice to characterize the word classes and sentence types of the French biochemistry sublanguage. This means that articles in whatever language in the given biochemical field could be represented by sequences of the same types of formulas (76).

From the perspective of logic and linguistics, they are searching for a possible grammar of science, which is certainly complex. What is

11. See among others, Alberch.

important for our discussion is that the reasoning presented to justify the existence of sublanguages in the sciences reveals much about its discursive nature. By fixing the sentences in determined positions, information can be represented and liberated from non-informational aspects of the language. This process of reduction, which Barthes regards as "transparent" and "neutral," is only possible when information is the central interest in the transmission. The discourse must be as denuded as possible from its external characteristics to express information as faithfully as possible.

The social sciences are much too tied to contexts; which is why the universalization of their discourses is so difficult. The criticism of Jean Claude Passeron (1995) of Popperian scientific idealism is suggestive and helps guide the discussion. The author points out that sociological research proceeds along theoretical pathways that must always begin anew, since they are never definitively separated from the "literality" of the enunciations that give them meaning. Therefore, it is not possible to start from a general theory, an abstract series of concepts, and be capable of deducing what might be found in reality. That is why the comparative method – the capacity to establish relationships – is fundamental. The social scientist does not have a laboratory for experiments. The very notion of experiment, as carried out in the natural sciences, is unfamiliar. The pathway of abstraction demands, therefore, a constant comparative or relational effort. Furthermore, the subject of the social sciences is in permanent mutation; it is historical. In this sense, sociological practice is always stenography or tachygraphy, as Octávio Ianni (1997) calls it. This is a suggestive picture. Tachygraphy and stenography are abbreviated languages; from the richness of the language they retain only a few traits. Tachygraphic notations contain a degree of abstraction that is not contained in the breadth of language; by being simpler, they gain in universalization. However, such universalization is never complete, emancipated; since the notations are tied to the "literality of the enunciations." Sociological thought is always a translation, something intermediary between the ideal of universality (which is necessary) and the rootedness of social phenomena. Obviously, context and language are mutually inflected. The discourse of the natural sciences is justifiable because it is able to reduce language, distill it from its sociocultural web, something that is unthinkable when we wish to understand society. In this case, English cannot operate as a *lingua franca*, not on questions of principle, or of national pride, but due to the nature of the constructed knowledge.

Several obstacles can be highlighted, such as, for instance, the issue of translation.[12] The passage from one language to another, far from being immediate, as if both of them belonged to a same sublanguage, is necessary – the thought and the work must circulate, this is imperative for all sorts of knowledge – but difficult. An additional effort of interpretation is always required, since there is no such thing as a literal translation. Terms, concepts and abstractions must search for equivalents when they pass from one code to another. The language reinforces the discursive bond to the grounded location where the social sciences are carried out. But it is not just about a direct translation; there are different traditions, and, often, translating them from one language to another does not mean merely finding the adequate word, but considering an entire expressive constellation. When we say, for example, '*questão nacional*' or 'national question,' the phrase could hardly be reduced to "nationalism." *Questão nacional* implies a backdrop against which an entire intellectual discussion is in progress in Latin America, from the late nineteenth to the late twentieth century, involving thinkers, artists and politicians. It regards the issue of national identity, the construction of the nation and modernity, the critique of the importation of ideas, the inferiority complex of the colonized countries, and the quandaries of peripheral modernity. 'Nationalism' is only one facet of a much wider set of problems. *Questão nacional*, or 'national question' also concerns an entire bibliographic tradition, from Vasconcelos in Mexico to Gilberto Freyre in Brazil, from the developmentalism of CEPAL (*Comisión Económica para América Latina*, Economic Commission for Latin America, ECLA) to the theory of dependence. Even the equivalence of the French expression – *question nationale* – is questionable, for we are talking about constellations of distinct meanings. As a matter of fact, even in the literature written in Portugal (the term refers to decolonization in Africa) or in Spain (concerning the discussion about Iberianism), the meaning is totally different. *Questão nacional* is a tachygraphic expression tied to the history of the Latin American and peripheral countries, in search of their identities.

12. Swaan ("English") calls attention to this point.

Barthes said that language was for literature its very being, and that it consisted of, and was concentrated in, the act of writing. We could not, certainly, say that language is the 'being' of the social sciences. There are techniques of research, methodologies, theories, or, in one word, obligations, that keep it away from literature. But writing is a common element to these two traditions. The social scientists are right when they insist on the importance of methodological rules for understanding society. But they sometimes forget to acknowledge the fact of those rules being materialized in a text. Writing is the support and concretization of the conceptual aspect. The same information, the same data, can be stitched together in different ways by different authors. There is no object outside of the text; its content, in order to exist, must be formalized. A large part of the argumentative exposition is a matter of composition. Primary information is evaluated and filtered before appearing on the blank page or on the computer screen. Composition is crucial for intellectual work. In this sense, the construction of a sociological object occurs through the medium of language; as such, the utilization of a given language is not casual, a mere subtlety of style, but a decisive question of the final formulation. I will take an example from my own research, when some time ago I suggested a conceptual distinction between "mondialization" *(mundializacão)* and "globalization" *(globalizacão)*.[13] When talking about economy and technology, we make reference to processes that are reproduced in the same fashion in the whole world. There is a single global economy, capitalism, and a single technical system (computers, Internet, satellites, etc.). Thus 'global' brings to our mind the idea of uniformity or unity. However, it would be inadequate to maintain the same concept when it comes to the sphere of culture. There is no global culture; only a process of *mondialization* of culture *(mundializacão da cultura)*, which is expressed on two levels: a) articulated to the economic and technological changes of globalization, its material base is

13. Translators' note (BG): According to the *Oxford English Dictionary*, "mundial" in early English (1450s-1620s) meant "mundane or worldly," now obsolete, referring to profane, secular, or economically interested motives rather than spiritual concerns. In the OED mundial, mundialization, and more commonly "mondialization" reappear as English neologisms for the French *mondialisation* in the late 20th century, referring, generally, to "globalization." We thus use "mondialization" here.

world modernity; b) a space for different conceptions of the world, in which diverse and conflicting forms of understanding coexist. That is why I would rather say that English is a *mondial* and not a global language because I preserve in this affirmation the difference between the diversities of the cultural sphere and the uniformity *(unicidade)* of the economic and technological domains. The mondiality of English occurs in the interior of a transglossic universe inhabited by other languages. The reader may accept my proposition or not, regarding it as useful or insufficient, but I can elaborate it only because the Portuguese language possesses two distinct terms – *mundializacão* and *globalizacão* – which could be filled with different contents. If I had originally written in English, I would have had to be content with *globalization, global culture,* and *global language.*

We can also consider other dimensions of the contrast between the social and natural sciences. Several studies show that, in the natural sciences, journals are regarded as "primary" documents, vehicles of "first hand information."[14] The journal is the medium, *par excellence,* of ongoing science. It is situated on the border, in the gap established between what is already known and what is about to be known. Researchers and laboratory teams privilege it in contraposition to the book, which is regarded as an informative manual, a secondary support for the generation of new theories and discoveries. Thus, publications tend to value the recent results, which provide dividends to the whole area of research; hence the insistence of many journals, especially those with a better status in the worldly ranking, in demanding articles whose results have not been published yet. The pressure of time is such that many groups of scientists, especially the physicists, resort to another strategy: the pre-edition. As soon as an article is finished, the investigator, or the group of investigators, submits it to the approval of some journal and simultaneously publishes it at their institution, distributing it by e-mail. Information and time are therefore crucial elements that favor the use of English. People need to express themselves in a more comprehensive way, in the shortest time possible.

On the other hand, the book is the support privileged by the social sciences. Even the articles are longer, as opposed to the short (sometimes *very* short) texts of the natural sciences. It is not simply a matter

14. See, among others, Josette de la Vega, *La communication.*

of prestige (which exists both in the 'human' and 'exact' sciences). Here the concept of information possesses a different relevance. It belongs to a theoretical and explanatory ensemble, and, often, this interpretative framework is more important than the data that are being transmitted (which does not mean that the information is irrelevant). The social sciences are more interpretative than informative; they require a period of time for maturation and analysis. In consequence, there is no urgency to publish the research results right away, and if, by chance they circulate in another language, it is necessary to wait for their translation. The rhythm of this process is marked even in the kind of material used and valued by the social scientist. In the natural sciences, the race to expand the boundaries of knowledge causes certainties of the past to be made rapidly obsolete by new discoveries. Thus, recent, up-to-date information possesses an irreplaceable value. In the social sciences, the validity of materials utilized in research sometimes extends to centuries ago, when it comes, for instance, to the reading of the classics. Some studies of the practice of social scientists with regard to utilization of bibliographic data show that everywhere both the materials of reference and the citations cover quite extended periods; in other words, in this sphere of knowledge texts and information age slowly.[15]

Nevertheless, in spite of these notable differences, the presence and supremacy of English cannot be denied. A study of the relationship between the languages and disciplinary areas, performed between 1981 and 1985 with the *International Bibliography of the Social Sciences* database, compiled by the International Committee for Social Science Information and Documentation, presented the following results: in anthropology: English, 55.5%; French, 14.4%; Spanish, 7.7%; Russian, 7.2%; German, 6.3% ; in political science: English, 50.1%; French, 16.5%; German, 7.9%; Russian, 7%; Spanish, 6.3%; in sociology: English, 49.7%; French, 17.6%; German, 7.5%; Russian, 6.1%; Spanish, 5%; and in economics: English, 55%; French, 13%; German, 7.5%; Russian, 6.1%; Spanish 5% (Kishida and Matsui). Certainly, the predominance of a language strongly depends on how the databases are put together. Another work, from 1991, comparing two databases, one of UNESCO (*World List of Social Science*

15. See, among others, Stone and Romanos de Tiratel.

Periodicals) and the other the *Social Sciences Citation Index* (SSCI), provides interesting information. In the UNESCO database, 64% of the compiled journals belong to the group of countries with a high income; 22% to the group with a median income (including the majority of the Latin American countries); and 14% to the group with a low income. In the SSCI, the low income countries are represented with only 0.7% of their journals, the median income ones with 2.3%, and the high income ones with 97%. With the exception of the United States, there is a significant decrease in the number of journals of the other countries: Brazil (from 81 in the UNESCO database to 3 in the SSCI); France (from 295 to 23); Germany (from 217 to 51); Mexico (from 47 to 2). The presence of the English language in the UNESCO database, counting only the United States and Great Britain, represents 32% of the total sample. In the SSCI, this figure is increased to 79% (Narvaez-Berthelemot and Russell). The problem is that the databases do not only store information; they are also artifacts of prestige. Some of them have more legitimacy than others. This is the central point. English, in its quantitative presence, creeps in, little by little, as a qualitative hegemony. This becomes clearer when one analyzes the difference between the frequency of the texts published in English and the citations of the works written in English. Based on the SSCI source, between 1990 and 1992, Glänzel categorized publications according to their country of origin, distinguishing, as well, the national and the international articles (collaboration of at least two investigators from different countries). The result is revealing. France, underrepresented in the initial sampling, appears with 2.9% in national articles and 9.4% in international ones, but its rate of citations is a mere 0.8%. Therefore, a dramatic decrease occurs in the total of published articles. The United States, with 56.9% of texts in national journals and 6% in international ones (a figure lower than that of France), sees their representation validated, for their citation rate increases to 76%. On the other hand, Great Britain, Australia and Canada, countries whose majoritarian language is English, maintain a balance between published texts and citations. Those same results are confirmed when some North American and British magazines are analyzed: *American Sociological Review* (98.6%), *Sociology* (98.8%), *The Sociological Review* (99.3%), *British Journal of Sociology* (99.5%) and *Theory Culture and Society* (89.6%) (cf. Yitzhaki).

If English does not act as *lingua franca* in the social sciences, what would the meaning and implication of its dominant presence be? My feeling is that, due to its comprehensiveness, this language has acquired the ability of regulating and ordering the discussion on a global scale. In journalism, to order *(pautar)* means to select among many existing problems, making them relevant and visible. This kind of procedure favors the existence of a hegemonic set of mondial-ized representations, which start to be accepted as valid, naturalizing methodological procedures and diverse problematics. 'Cultural stud-ies' or 'multiculturalism,' for instance, cease to be analyzed in relation to the context in which they were conceived, and in which they make sense, impose themselves as 'universal.' Bourdieu and Wacquant, in the text "On the Cunning of Imperialist Reason," critique this phe-nomenon.[16] Although their central argument is, in my view, mistaken – since the authors synthesize acritically the concept of imperialism and demonstrate a narrow understanding of globalization (for them a synonym of Americanization) – what is at stake is precisely the issue of "false universalization," the issue of how certain ideas and worldviews are disseminated and legitimated among different societies without previous critical reflection about them. This is only possible because in the globalization debate there is a tendency to see it as equivalent to universalization. What makes this equivalence believable is the con-cept of territoriality. By expanding their boundaries, by deterritorializ-ing themselves, the universal and the global would participate in the same movement, transcending local differences. Thus, when some sociologists discuss the relationship between universalism and particu-larism – I am thinking of Robert Robertson – the term global appears as an intrinsic attribute of universalism, and what is left to particular-ism is a territorially localized and reduced expression.

There is no doubt that the social sciences are being transformed with the process of globalization. The shifts in social relations require a new vision and the definition of new categories of thought. Certain-ly, when focusing on the world as a topic for reflection, the scholar is released from the space circumscribed by the territoriality of the regions or of the nation-state. But it would be a mistake to imagine that sociological analyses have become "more universal" than in the

16. For an interesting critique of these authors, see Friedman.

past. The status of the sociological explanation, as Passeron qualified
it, remains unchanged. The economists also insist on saying that global capitalism contributes to the universalization of the spirit. The literature which occupies itself with marketing and business does not
hesitate in affirming that individuals consume global products because
they are fulfilling universal desires. Such undue approximations
between global and universal derive from the recurrent utilization of
the spatial metaphor. That is, all of this is nothing more than an
expansion of spatial limits. However, "universal" is a philosophical category and "global" is a sociological one. The first one means transcendence, an abstract relationship that does not necessarily materialize in
an immediate form – that is what allows the illuminists to speak of
"humankind" *(gênero humano)*. By saying global market, global sociology, global economics, we identify things and processes that develop
on the plane of the real history of mankind. Thus, by assimilating very
different concepts, we would be suggesting that the universal materializes in the global, which is obviously false. The English language par-
ticipates in this collective illusion, and, once more, the comparison
with natural sciences is revealing. The possibility of English becoming
an international language derives, as well, from the fact that the natural sciences are paradigmatic, in the sense provided by Kuhn. They
presuppose a sole system of reference, in relation to which scientific
practices are organized. Characteristics like these – commonality and
comprehensiveness – allow us to associate scientific practices with the
idea of universality. Their laws, findings and explanations are equally
valid. However, the social sciences are not paradigmatic in this sense.
As a last resource, if focusing on the context, we should say that the
ideal would be the knowledge of all languages in which the social sciences are represented, in order to obtain, not a universalization of the
spirit, but a library of languages at the service of a greater richness of
thought. Although this is an unachievable feat, it is important to keep
it in mind, for the cosmopolitanism of ideas can only exist when we
take into consideration the diversity of the concepts and the "accents"
(sotaques) of sociological traditions.

Nevertheless, what we are seeing is movement in the opposite
direction away from any kind of diversity of interpretations. The
worldwide translation market provides us with a good image of this.
In the United States and the United Kingdom, less than 5% of the

published works are translations (including literary works). In France and Germany, this figure is approximately 12%, while in Spain and Italy it goes as far as 20% (cf. Heilbron). This means that, the more central a language in the world market of linguistic goods, the lower the rate of translated texts in the corresponding countries. The corollary of this axiom is that translations between peripheral languages become rarer and rarer, for they should necessarily pass through the mondial vernacular. As a matter of fact, when observing the expansion of databases, the creation of information systems, the publishing of books and articles, the increase in the citation of works written in English, and the coming of online magazines – all of which is preferentially conjugated in the English language – we get the false impression that such comprehensiveness is a synonym of universality. Being published and quoted in English would not be, therefore, the result of the expansion of a circuit, of its territorial amplification, but the primary condition of thought (hence Anglo-American authors adapt so well to monolingualism; after all, outside of it little scientific relevance exists). Writing in another language would also cease to have meaning, [since] to be circumscribed by a determinate form of expression is a condition perceived as a limitation. This becomes even clearer when certain value judgments are extrapolated from the area of the natural to the social sciences. The strategy of elite groups in the areas of physics, chemistry, and biology, in countries with non-English languages, of writing and publishing in English, implies that there is a hierarchical unevenness between the local and the universal. Hence the tendency to say that magazines published in a national language are focused on local aspects, with less importance for the development of scientific knowledge. One can debate the validity of such a hierarchy, but it is based on the existence of paradigms accepted by the international scientific community. In the case of the social sciences this does not occur, but, even so, the parallelism is implicitly accepted. *Global English* becomes *universal English*. We thus have not only a hierarchy among languages, marking the inequality between them, but also the establishment of a subtle element of intellectual segregation. The homology postulated between local-global / particular-universal closes the circle, reducing other interpretations to the subaltern status of localism. It is conveniently forgotten that cosmopolitanism is not a necessary attribute of globality and that particularism of thought can be formulated equally in a dialect and in a global language, for in the condition of world modernity it is plausible, and commonplace, to be globally provincial.

WORKS CITED

ALBERCH, Pere. "Language in Contemporary Science: the Tool and the Cultural Icon." *Sciences et langues en Europe.* Chartier and Corsi 257-264.

AMMON, Ulrich, ed. *The Dominance of English as a Language of Science.* Berlin/New York: Mouton de Gruyter, 2001.

BAILEY, Richard and GORLACH, Manfred, eds. *English as a World-Language.* Ann Arbor: The U of Michigan P, 1982.

BALDAUF, JR., Richard. "Speaking of Science: The Use by Australian University Staff of Language Skills." *The Dominance of English as Language of Science.* Ammon 139-165.

BALLANDIER, Georges. "La situation coloniale: approche théorique". *Cahiers Internationaux de Sociologie* XI (1951): 9-29.

BARTHES, Roland. *The Rustle of Language.* Trans. Richard Howard. Berkeley: U California Press, 1989.

BLAIR, Ann. "La persistence du latin comme langue de science à la fin de la Renaissance." *Sciences et langues en Europe.* Chartier and Corsi 21-42.

BOLTON, W. F. and CRYSTAL, David, eds. *The English Language.* New York: Peter Bedrick Books, 1987.

BOURDIEU, Pierre. *Language and Symbolic Power.* Translated by Gino Raymond and Matthew Adamson. Cambridge: Harvard UP, 1994.

—. *The Field of Cultural Production: Essays on Art and Literature.* New York: Columbia UP, 1984.

BOURDIEU, Pierre and WACQUANT, Loic. "On the Cunning of Imperialist Reason." *Theory Culture and Society* 16.1 (1999): 41-58.

BRETON, Pierre. *História da informática.* São Paulo: UNESP, 1991.

CALVET, Louis Jean. *Pour une écologie des langues du monde.* Paris: Plon, 1999.

—. *Le marché aux langues: les effets linguistiques de la mondialisation.* Paris: Plon, 2002.

CHA, Yun-Kyung. "Effect of the Global System on Language Instruction, 1850-1986." *Sociology of Education* 64.1 (1991): 19-32.

CHARTIER, Roger and CORSI, Pietro, eds. *Sciences et langues en Europe.* Paris: EHESS, 1996.

CRYSTAL, David. *English as a Global Language*. Cambridge: Cambridge UP, 1997.

COOPER, Robert, ed. *Language Spread*. Bloomington: Indiana UP, 1982.

DURAND, Jacques. "Linguistic purification, the French Nation-State and the Linguist." *Language, Culture and Communication in Contemporary Europe*. Hoffmann 75-92.

FERREIRA, Leila, ed. *A sociología no século XXI*. São Paulo: Boitempo, 1997.

FISHMAN, Joshua. "Sociology of English as an Additional Language." *The Other Tongue*. Kachru 19-26.

FISHMAN, Joshua, Robert COOPER and Andrew CONRAD, eds. *The Spread of English*. Rowley (MA): Newbury House, 1977.

FISHMAN, Joshua, Robert COOPER and Y. ROSENBAUM. "English around the world." *The Spread of English*. Eds. Joshua Fishman, Robert Cooper and Andrew Conrad. Rowley MA: Newbury House. 1977, 77-107.

FLAITZ, Jeffra. *The Ideology of English: French Perceptions of English as a World Language*. Berlin/New York/Amsterdam: Mouton de Gruyter, 1988.

FRIEDMAN, Jonathan. "Americans Again, or the New Age of Imperial Reason?" *Theory Culture and Society* 17.1 (2000): 139-146.

GLÄNZEL, Wolfgang. "A Bibliometric Approach to Social Sciences: National Research Performances in 6 Selected Social Sciences Areas, 1990-1992." *Scientometrics* 35.3 (1976): 291-307.

GOMES, Isabel, Rosa SANCHO, Luz MORENO and María Teresa FERNÁNDEZ. "Influence of Latin American Journals Coverage by International Databases." *Scientometrics* 46.3 (1999): 443-456.

GREENBAUM, Sidney, ed. *The English Language Today*. Oxford: Pergamon Press, 1985.

HARRIS, Zellig and Paul MATTICK. "Science, Sublanguages and the Prospects for a Global Language of Science." *The Annals of The American Academy of Political and Social Sciences* 495 (1988): 73-83.

HEILBRON, Johan. "Toward a Sociology of Translation: Book Translation as a Cultural World-System." *European Journal of Social Theory* 2.4 (1999): 429-444.

HOFFMANN, Charlotte, ed. *Language, Culture and Communication in Contemporary Europe*. Clevedon: Multilingual Matters, 1996.

IANNI, Octávio. "A sociologia numa era de globalismo." *A sociologia no século XXI*. São Paulo: Boitempo, 1997.

JABLONSKI, Nina and AIELLO, Leslie, eds. *The Origin and Diversification of Language*. Berkeley: U of California P, 1998.

KACHRU, Braj. "Models for Non-Native Englishes." *The Other Tongue*. Kachru 48-74.

KISHIDA, Kazuaki and MATSUI, Sachiko. "International Publication Patterns in Social Sciences: A Quantitative Analysis of the IBSS file." *Scientometrics* 40.2 (1997): 277-298.

KROEBER, Alfred. *Anthropology: Race, Language, Culture, Psychology, Prehistory.* New York: Harcourt, Brace & World, 1948.

LEVITT, Theodore. "The Globalization of Markets." *Harvard Business Review*, May-June (1983).

MCARTHUR, Tom. "The English Language or the English Languages?" *The English Language*. Bolton and Crystal 1987.

NARVAEZ-BERTHELEMOT, Nora and Jane RUSSELL. "World Distribution of Social Science Journals: A View from the Periphery." *Scientometrics* 51.1 (2001): 223-239.

ORTIZ, Renato, ed. *Pierre Bourdieu*. São Paulo: Ática, 1983.

—. *Mundialização e cultura*. São Paulo: Brasiliense, 1994.

—. *Um outro território: ensaios sobre a mundialização*. São Paulo: Olho d'Água, 1996.

—. "Revistando a noção de imperialismo cultural." *Crítica contemporânea: cultura, trabalho, política, racismo*. Ed. Josué Pereira da Silva. São Paulo: Annablume, 2002.

PARAKRAM, Arujna. *De-Hegemonizing Language Standards*. London: Macmillan, 1995.

PASSERON, Jean Claude. *Raciocínio Sociológico*. Petrópolis: Vozes. 1995.

PENNYCOOK, Alastair. *The Cultural Politics of English as an International Language*. London: Longman, 1994.

PHILLIPSON, Robert. *Linguistic Imperialism*. Oxford: Oxford UP, 1992.

—. "Voice in Global English: Unheard Chords in Crystal, Loud and Clear." *Applied Linguistics* 20.2 (1999): 265-276.

PHILLIPSON, Robert and SKUTTNAB-KANGAS, Tove. "English Only Worldwide or Language Ecology?" *TESOL Quarterly* 30.3 (1996): 429-452.

REGUANT, Salvador and CASADELLÀ, Jordi. "English as *lingua franca* in Geological Scientific Publications: A Bibliometric Analysis." *Scientometrics* 29.3 (1994): 335-351.

RICENTO, Thomas, ed. *Ideology, Politics and Language Policies*. Amsterdam/Philadelphia: John Benjamins, 2000.

ROBERTSON, Robert. *Globalization: Social Theory and Global Culture*. London: Sage, 1992.

ROMANOS DE TIRATEL, Susana. "Conducta informativa de los investigadores argentinos en humanidades y ciencias sociales." *Revista Española de Documentación Científica* 23.3 (2000): 267-285.

RUSSELL, Jane. "Publishing patterns of Mexican Scientists: Difference Between National and International Papers." *Scientometrics* 41.1-2 (1998): 113-124.

SINHA, S. and A.K. DHIMAN. "Science Citation Index: A Failure Under Indian Scientific Environment." *Annals of Library Science and Documentation* 47.2 (2000): 63-66.

SONNTAG, Selma. "Ideology and Policy in the Politics of the English Language in North India." *Ideology, Politics and Language Policies*. Ricento 133-149.

STONE, Sue. "Humanities Scholars: Information Needs and Uses." *Journal of Documentation* 38.4 (1982): 292-313.

SWAAN, Abram de. *Words of the World*. Cambridge: Polity Press, 2001.

—. "English in the social sciences." *The Dominance of English as a Language of Science*. Ammon 2001 71-83.

—. "Notes on the Emerging Global Language System: Regional, National and Supranational." *Media Culture and Society* 13.2 (1991): 309-323.

TRUCHOT, Claude. *L'anglais dans le monde contémporain*. Paris: Robert, 1990.

TUNSTALL, Jeremy. *The Media are American*. New York: Columbia UP, 1977.

TSUNODA, Minoru. "Les langues internationales dans les publications scientifiques et techniques." *Sophia Linguistica* 13 (1983): 70-79.

VEGA, Josette de la. *La communication scientifique à l'épreuve de l'internet*. Paris: Presses de l'École Nationale Supérieure des Sciences de l'Information et des Bibliothèques, 2000.

VESSURI, Hebe. "Recent strategies for adding value to scientific journals in Latin America." *Scientometrics* 34.1 (1995): 139-61.

WILEY, Terence G. and LUKES, Marguerite. "English-only and standard English ideologies in the U.S." *TESOL Quarterly* 30.3 (1996): 511-35.

YITZHAKI, Moshe. "The 'Language Preference' in Sociology: Measures of 'Language Self-Citation,' 'Relative Own-Language Preference Indicator,' and 'Mutual Use of Languages.'" *Scientometrics* 41.1-2 (1998): 243-254.

ACTIVIST INTELLECTUALS IN A WIRED WORLD

George Yúdice

> Cyberspace . . . is based on a model that is very dif-
> ferent from that of modern media, [which unders-
> tands] information as 'data,' a world of active emitters
> and passive receivers, unidirectionality of flows, tight
> ideological control, and the production of news media
> that reflect the world as seen by those who rule it. . .
> [In contrast, cyberspace] is based on interactivity [and
> relationality], . . . where all receivers are also poten-
> tially emitters, . . . a decentralized archipelago of relati-
> vely autonomous zones, in which communities produce
> their own media [and information], ... [and where]
> network cultures without the fixed and homogeni-
> zed identities assumed by the mass media [...] and
> [...] intercultural exchange [are created] (Escobar).

I chose this epigraph, from a recent article by Arturo Escobar,
because it portrays the ideal scenario of a public sphere in which
everyone is an intellectual, understood as someone who can project
his or her opinions, values, and sensibilities and engage in exchanges
with others in a range of networks whose density of intersections
constitute public space. Cyberspace refers to a society consisting of
myriad groups and whose communicative potential and political
agency are commensurate with the new interactive media. On this
view, the multiplicity and interactivity of the new media are consistent with the rise of social movements of all kinds that obviate the
need for traditional intellectuals as spokesmen and mediators. Moreover, in a world in which formal politics loses legitimacy, a wide-
ranging array of individuals, from workers and indigenous people to
housewives, have assumed the power to give their opinions and seek
to sway others, in myriad forms of discourse and performance, from

street corners to community radio stations to local community centers to blogs and social networking sites. In other words, an increasing number of people, from an increasing number of social situations, speak in their own names, without the need for socially sanctioned intellectuals to do it for them. Not even *testimonialistas* or *cronistas* like Poniatowska or Monsiváis. Which is not to say that such intellectuals disappear. Many continue to be critics, even of movements which they support, as in the case of Monsiváis' critiques of the EZLN. And many others become organic to what Castells (2000) has called the "network society." Indeed, traditional intellectuals increasingly serve collaborative, supportive or other functions for social movements that emerged in circumstances different from their own experiences and backgrounds.

This reconversion of traditional intellectuals, as well as the formation of intellectuals organic to social movements and other forms of association, such as youth groups, of which I will speak later, is in part shaped by the communicative ecology in which they emerge. I am not speaking here about a technological, communicational or infrastructural determinism, nor of a celebratory voluntarism that one finds in some autonomists, but rather of a more holistic analysis, "that balances structure and agency and studies how social shaping processes are accomplished in the more or less conflictual, competitive, or cooperative interplay of social actors who are understood as being embedded in institutional and structural contexts, which in turn provide both limits and resources for creative action" (Schulz 296). [1]

---

1. For example, Negri and Hardt's enthusiastic encomium of the Internet as democratic collaboration, evident in parts of Empire: "The democratic network is a completely horizontal and deterritorialized model. The Internet, which began as a project of DARPA (the U.S. Defense Department Advanced Research Projects Agency), but has now expanded to points throughout the world, is the prime example of this democratic network structure.... This democratic model is what Deleuze and Guattari call a rhizome, a nonhierarchical and noncentered network structure" (298-99). Negri waxes so sanguine that he sees the Internet as the instrument of communism. He writes of "levels of cooperation and sharing . . . everywhere, even writing an article on a computer means having to rely on a common knowledge, which is to say the Internet . . . . contrary to what is believed, people have become more communist than before" (27).

This is what I mean by the field of force in which the media play a part, a field of force constituted by cultural traditions, educational systems, governmental policies, economy, geography, civil society, social movements and so forth that both existed before the Internet was introduced and which were altered by other events, for example, economic crises or political upheavals, just when cyberspace made its appearance. This is the case of the social movements of the 1980s, which exploited the bulletin boards and email lists made available by Association for Progressive Communications (APC) in 18 nationally based networks, among them Alternex in Brazil and LaNeta in Mexico (Ribeiro, "Cybercultural"). Much of the communication in those networks had to do with the organizational and outreach activities of NGOs, which gained the ability to operate simultaneously in local, national and global circuits. Since then, the development of the world wide web, blogs, and other Internet and mobile telephony formats have been accompanied by an enormous multiplicity of networks, from more or less stable activist organizations to the swarm activities of the so-called anti-globalization movement, even terrorist activities and governmental surveillance strategies to counteract them.

As will be quite evident as I make my way through this essay, I am not describing a situation in which intellectual work and activism have passed willy-nilly into cyberspace. Cyberspace is a crucial medium and shaper of action, including assisting in face-to-face local encounters, political rallies, and so on. To give an example from the U.S., the political triumph of Barack Obama did not take place in the cybersphere, but in a range of spheres, from appearances at school auditoriums and churches to television and radio interviews and ads, to volunteers going from door to door. Yet the Internet counted, in a big way. As one analyst observed, the fact that the social media were in place, especially list servers, blogs, and above all social networking sites, made it logical for the Obama campaign to do what had never been done before: campaign in every state that is to have local significance at a national scale. "Given the power of social media, everyone who has the interest has the ability to influence and mobilize networks of friends. A blue dot in a sea of red could now make a real impact . . ." (Snyder).

One first impact of the Internet and mobile telephony is that they extend and augment the plural activities that take place in associations,

NGOs, movements and networks. As such, this extension has an impact on the notion of the public sphere, which has become not only more plural but also multi-scaled across local, regional, national and international dimensions. Indeed, one could say that even the notion of scale has been affected. But this does not mean that local action disappears; on the contrary, there are many kinds of media assisted forms of local action, such as local assemblies convoked by community radios, networked with other actors and institutions to provide information, or videoconferencing that enables participation of actors at a distance. This is also a way for local actors to participate in important discussions when travel is not a viable option. Is such participation any less *in situ* than if the person where there in the flesh?

Of course, cyberspace does not result exclusively in "a decentralized archipelago of relatively autonomous zones, in which communities produce their own media [and information]," as in Escobar's somewhat romantic encomium. Escobar's utopianism is counterbalanced by Gustavo Lins Ribeiro, his coeditor, who in *World Anthropologies*, writes: "Every technological innovation is ambiguous, with the potential for both utopia and dystopia" (1996). This ambiguity is foregrounded when we recognize that the cybersphere is open to surveillance of all kinds, and new consumer-media capitalist enterprises which actually promote the pluralization of spheres of speech and performance, which they *monetize* (the word that is used in the business) in social networking sites or on reality shows. Moreover, the proliferation of 15-minute fame celebrities, whether on MTV's weight-losing *Model Maker* and its Latin American versions or in the political campaigns that have produced Joe the Plumber, or the myriad musicians or everyday performers on YouTube, each with his or her own expression and viewpoint, should encourage us to take caution when we think we've discovered the utopian archipelago in cyberspace. And, of course, there are other problems with the idealization of the Internet, not the least which is still the digital gap, which although it is closing, is not doing so fast enough. The growth in Internet access in Latin America jumped by 813.1% from 2000 to 2008 but penetration was still a low 28.8% of the population, as we can see in table 1 (Internet World Stats 2008):

LATIN AMERICAN INTERNET USAGE					
LATIN AMERICA COUNTRIES/ REGIONS	Population (Est. 2008)	Internet Users, Latest Data	% Population (Penetration)	User Growth (2000-2008)	% Users in Table
Argentina	40,481,998	20,000,000	49.4%	700.0%	12.3%
Bolivia	9,601,257	1,000,000	10.4%	733.3%	0.6%
Brazil	196,342,587	67,510,400	34.4%	1,250.2%	37%
Chile	16,454,143	8,368,719	50.9%	376.2%	5.2%
Colombia	45,013,674	13,745,600	30.5%	1,465.6%	8.5%
Costa Rica	4,195,914	1,500,000	35.5%	500.0%	0.9%
Cuba	11,423,952	1,310,000	11.5%	2,083.3%	0.8%
Dominican Republic	9,507,133	3,000,000	31.6%	5,354.5%	1.8%
Ecuador	14,354,569	1,759,500	12.3%	877.5%	1.1%
El Salvador	7,066,403	763,000	10.8%	1,807.5%	0.5%
Guatemala	13,002,206	1,320,000	10.2%	1,930.8%	0.8%
Honduras	7,639,327	424,200	5.6%	960.5%	0.3%
Mexico	109,955,400	23,874,500	21.7%	780.2%	14.7%
Nicaragua	5,785,846	155,000	2.7%	210.0%	0.1%
Panama	3,309,679	745,300	22.7%	1,556.2%	0.5%
Paraguay	6,831,306	530,300	7.8%	2,551.5%	0.3%
Peru	29,180,899	7,636,400	26.2%	205.5%	4.7%
Puerto Rico	3,957,098	1,000,000	25.3%	400.0%	0.6%
Uruguay	3,477,778	1,100,000	31.6%	197.3%	0.7%
Venezuela	26,414,815	6,723,616	25.5%	607.7%	4.1%
TOTAL	563,995,884	162,466,535	28.8%	813.1%	100%

Moreover, there is unevenness in the rapid progress in access: cities, and even shantytowns within cities, get access at a much faster rate than rural areas, some of which may not even have electricity. I will have more to say as I near my conclusion regarding what to do about these downsides of intellectual work and activism in and about the Internet and digital technologies. But for now, let me continue with the role of intellectuals.

The description of the *South by Midwest II* conference, for which
the earlier version of this essay was written, highlights the agency
– what the organizers call the "transformative role" – played by intellectuals, identified as "social actors within and beyond academia who
operate through movements, think tanks, NGOs, cultural, literary,
political and artistic fields, and the media." The purpose of this essay
is to foreground the terrain on which this agency is carried out and
how it shapes and informs that agency. In other words, we need to pay
attention to the material features and the structuring of the atmosphere
or space – the force field – through which the operation takes place,
and by that I do not mean only what the conference organizers emphasized as movements, think tanks, NGOs, and so on, but the space
available to those actors to communicate. My focus necessarily evokes
the concept and phenomenon of the public sphere or its corrective
plural form of public spheres. According to classical philosophical and
sociological theory, the public sphere is the space in which society,
self-organized into a number of associations, institutions and relationships opens up a dimension of discursive interaction between the family and the state.

Parenthetically, I need to state here that the evolution of public
sphere theory has moved beyond the private/public dichotomy, in particular to focus on the ways in which counter publics continually
question what goes on in the presumed general public sphere. I am
referring to the phenomenon captured in the slogan "the personal is
political" that became the common sense of social movements, beginning with the feminist movement in the late '60s (Hanisch). There has
been much debate on the gains and losses from this incursion into the
private, and it is important to consider that the virtualization no
longer of just public life but precisely of private life that we encounter
in TV, and even more so in cyberspace, is a major force to contend
with. This interrogation of the private, or what was deemed private,
such as identity matters – sexuality, ethnicity, religion, etc. – is in great
part what animates electronic and digital media. And it is a great source
of profit, as I will remark later. But I continue now with the relationship between intellectuals and the public sphere.

It is obvious that the concept of the intellectual requires its companion concept of the public sphere, his or her scenario of discursive
and performative action. Habermas develops both concepts simulta-

neously in his landmark *Structural Transformation of the Public Sphere*, although the concept of the intellectual is backgrounded in that book. There is a more generic discussion of opinion-forming debate than a showcasing of the intellectual as a figure. We see Habermas' deliberators acting in coffeehouses, journals, and public plazas, but these are secondary characters compared to what we see in other works that focus on salient figures, as we are accustomed to in conventional literary or historical studies. Intellectual activity in Habermas' conception is a public activity conducted by large numbers of people, and this is also the case in the entities mentioned by the conference organizers that have augmented and pluralized the public sphere: movements, NGOs, etc.

Habermas' argument is well-known, but it is worth summarizing: He developed his account of the public sphere to argue for the unrealized potential of deliberative communication, a space where a "multitude of wills or opinions guiding political action (are) formed on the basis of rational-critical discourse" (Calhoun 1899). In his idealized portrayal of an original public in the 18th century, personal differences relating to class and political-economic status were rooted in the private sphere, but debate in public, presumably open to all, did not encounter barriers. Of course, as numerous critics have argued over the years, cultural capital – or accumulated knowledge and skills sanctioned by the dominant classes – did in fact matter and inhibit equal access, as did femaleness and colonized status. Yet for Habermas, the decline of the public sphere begins with the development of mass society, and the emergence of professional opinion makers and measurers whose practices led to a loss in openness. Moreover, with the orientation of the media toward consumer capitalism, publicity became the sphere of the manufacturing of consensus. Intellectuals split into two categories: on the one hand, publicizers, marketers and cheerleaders of capitalism, and on the other the so-called public intellectuals who stand above the fray and criticize the deterioration of the public and, if possible, go against the grain of financialization and commodification to recuperate its undistorted potential.

In Latin America, the public sphere was even more restricted than in the Western European context, with enormous exclusion in terms of production and even representation. In other words, the opinions of the majority of poor and working classes, indigenous, Afro-descendant peoples did not circulate in what was taken to be the public space of print journalism, radio and TV, at least until the emergence of community radio stations. As a recent study on radio and the new media observes, Quechua, spoken by more than 10 million people in Bolivia, Ecuador and Peru is largely absent from television, although there are more than 180 radio stations in Peru alone that offer programming in Quechua (Girard 4). While radio is crucial for the circulation of information important to the community, it does not generally circulate nationally or on the largest, commercial networks that have the best frequencies because profit is made from publicity, and this in turn is pitched to consuming publics with disposable income. I will return to this point in a moment because publicity-driven profitability, tied to consumerism, is, like "cultural capital," a gatekeeping function. I will argue that the transformation of societies toward dignified treatment of all of its citizens and residents requires strong regulatory and proactive communications policies that go beyond the boundaries of the nation-state.

With radio and now the Internet, it is possible for most communities to circulate their programming and thus reproduce their social and political values and their cultural forms, although there is still the problem of publicity-driven profitability that fosters major investment in the quality of media packaging, and hence of larger audiences. This problem is particularly acute in Latin American countries, especially the smaller ones, where local music is virtually absent from the airwaves. Take, for example, the situation of radio in Costa Rica. The *Asociación de Compositores y Autores Musicales de Costa Rica* (ACAM) collects royalties from Costa Rican radio stations for the music they play and distributes them proportionally to the corresponding collection societies. While ACAM represents Costa Rican artists, it nevertheless ends up working on behalf of foreign interests, for it distributes 95% of royalties to U.S. (ASCAP), Mexican (SACM) and Spanish (SGAE) collection societies. Radio station directors play top 40 and top 100 hits, exclusively represented by these collection societies, because advertisers will purchase airtime only in connection to programming that they believe will attract the largest audiences. Hence, Costa Ricans get to listen to Britney Spears, Rihanna or Enrique Iglesias rather than any Costa Rican musicians. The only radio that plays them is the University of Costa Rica station.

Foreign content is privileged over local heritage. In this regard, as an intellectual who has also become an activist in educational and media policies, Jesús Martín Barbero promotes the application of international discourses that pry open the notion of heritage from their traditional emphasis on the built environment, privileging nation-defining monuments of a glorious indigenous or colonial past, to so-called intangible forms, like ritual, festival, oral narratives, designs, and so on, and which can take their place alongside the other forms to define a more inclusive, pluri-ethnic nation. Heritage, as many scholars, like Jesús Martín Barbero ("Entrevista"), Lisa C. Breglia (*Monumental*), Robert Albro ("The Challenges"), and indigenous communicators like Mario Bustos of Conaie, argue, becomes a political resource. Hence, intellectual activism in the field of heritage. Radio and the Internet, with their focus on the oral and the visual, help, in Martín Barbero's view, to expand the range of discourses through which politics are named and performed, beyond the exclusionary character of the discourses of the lettered city ("A Latin"; "Entrevista"). This expansion can lead to the recognition of the multiplicity of sensibilities of ethnic minorities and the myriad groups, especially media-oriented youth groups, found in all societies.

The work of Mario Bustos, former director of the Communications Department of the Confederation of Indigenous Nationalities of Ecuador, Conaie, is relevant. In an interview with Daniel Mato in 2001, he discusses this political and cultural view of communication, oriented toward generating a plural but unified discourse and image that defines the movement and that can be circulated in all media. As in Michael Warner's observation that counter public spheres "are embodied, given stylistic registers, that are not absorbable into official public space" (Warner), Bustos argues that Conaie's communications are aimed at developing consciousness, and do not respond to ideological or doctrinaire motives, nor to the national directorship, but are meant to circulate and take up the discourses of the grassroots communities (Bustos 8). An important part of that discourse has to do with revitalizing and legitimizing the heritage of the peoples that constitute Conaie, against the colonial legacy that deauthorized them. Moreover, this revitalization of ancestral heritage is not simply for the purposes of "remaining there," which I understand to mean that the revitalization of heritage is not for the purposes of fixing it in folklore.

Instead he says, the purpose is "to project it by developing it" (Bustos 10). By projecting it, he means circulating it, which he likens to the circulation of blood that nourishes the collective body. For Bustos, communication is not just technology, but a flow that circulates in subjectivity (Bustos 9).

Moreover, Bustos argues that for this flow to be effective, it has to carry contents that relate to the people's identities:

> I think that many of the people who begin to have an awareness of their being begin to look for instruments for identity formation . . . . It's like those little spiders who look like they're in danger . . . of disappearing or falling, and that someone is about to step on them, destroy them, eat them, and they hold onto their thread and disappear, and thus go on living. Hence, what's important is that Internet, television, radio and all [of those media] can transform – life is a global space – into spaces that are like those little threads for the spider, so long as the Internet, radio and television have elements that sustain those threads. If not, the threads will not have the same characteristics as those of the spider web, and then you fall, you grab onto the [feeble threads] and you fall. And to deal with that I think it's important to engage in the elaborate and rich work of recuperating identity, of speaking with identity, of conceptualizing and developing [one's] world view (14).[2]

How does one understand the phrase "life is a global space," which Bustos interpolates in the middle of this statement about identity? Elsewhere in the interview, Bustos explains that international solidarity provides some of the resources and information the movement needs to do its work. For example, the information regarding rights, heritage and other issues that is generated in the declarations of international and hemispheric meetings of social movements, such as the World Social Forum, or intergovernmental summits relating to hunger. "We download that information and circulate it," he says (Bustos 5). Such information is precisely the kind of resource that contributes to the revitalization of heritage. "For us, international cooperation consists of acts of solidarity, that is, they are neither paternalistic actions nor impositions, nor do we consider them as instruments. What is important, first, is that human relations begin to flow and secondly

---

2. This and all translations herein by the author.

that the knowledge that [those relations] have us socialize or share be a knowledge that contributes to our needs" (Bustos 7).

Bustos links international solidarity to interculturality, which is another dimension that he refers to when speaking of the pluriculturality of Ecuador. It seems to me that we can understand this interculturality in two ways. The first is that of the collaborators that Joanne Rappaport refers to in her book *Intercultural Utopias: Public Intellectuals, Cultural Experimentation, and Ethnic Pluralism*. She contrasts the intellectuals whom she calls *colaboradores* and *solidarios*, to the grand intellectuals of yesteryear who sought to articulate national imaginaries. Those national intellectuals articulated exclusive imaginaries even as they referred to indigenous or Afro-inflected *mestizajes*. In the aftermath of dictatorship, exile, economic crises, migration, and the emergence of social movements, those intellectuals no longer had a function to carry out as "keepers of truth" or national imaginaries. They either became experts, or went into NGOs and universities, but largely abdicated their public function. On the other hand, Rappaport observes that *colaboradores* did not suffer the same crisis as other intellectuals in Latin America. Instead, they reconverted by working together with initiatives led by indigenous peoples:

> Indeed, they have played a role in articulating new national imaginings in Colombia. But they have not served as mediators between the state and indigenous societies, a role that has been assumed, instead, by indigenous leaders themselves. *Colaboradores'* efforts have been more closely focused on fostering the organizing capacity of the grassroots . . . *Colaboradores* do not speak *for* a subordinated sector, but are speaking with them . . . They are not ventriloquists . . . they listen, and on the basis of their listening, they contribute to an intercultural dialogue at the heart of the indigenous movement (62).

Rappaport explores how the intercultural work of translation and appropriation of ideas across cultures "in the interests of building a pluralistic dialogue among equals . . . harnessed as a vehicle for connecting such domains as indigenous bilingual education to the political objectives of the native rights movement" (5), produces a situation in which outsider and insider intellectuals co-construct their practice. This is a phenomenon that Daniel Mato has also addressed in "Not 'Studying the Subaltern' but Studying *with* 'Subaltern' Social Groups . . ."

(Mato 479), shedding light on the transnational character of this practice. Robert Albro's research in Bolivia also highlights how the activist
Aymara intellectuals of the Andean Oral History Workshop (THOA)
have rearticulated the *ayllu* concept in collaboration with international cooperation agencies that "actively promote 'community self-man-
agement' and actively facilitates the goals of indigenous cultural
renaissance" (Albro, "The Culture" 399).[3] As in the case of Bustos, the
ayllu and other Andean concepts acquire the authority of cultural
heritage, which become a resource "available to popular protesters
for framing local associational life as a democratic alternative" (ibid).
Importantly, THOA's work on the *ayllu* as cultural heritage also
informs popular media, including videos and *radionovelas*, broad-
cast on Radio Pachamama in El Alto (ibid). Moreover, the mediated
work on the *ayllu* and other cultural heritage is the topic of blogs associated with Radio Pachamama.

The focus of Rappaport's or Mato's work is not to highlight the outsider who becomes an organic intellectual in indigenous movements,
but the intercultural work that indigenous intellectuals and their *colaboradores* and *solidarios* do. Some of this work is also transnational, a
point that Nancy Fraser raises with respect to the theory of the public
sphere, which in her view was conceived problematically as circumscribed to the nation state, which was also the scope of the media in
which publicity circulated. One could apply Edward Said's insights
in *Culture and Imperialism* to point out that not only national minorities and the colonized but also competing colonizer states were present
in the representations that circulated. We're not dealing here with
"ideas out of place," as Roberto Schwartz called the foreign ideas that
constituted the alienated but necessarily national scene of literary and
intellectual activity in colonial and postcolonial Brazil. Fraser raises two
important points regarding public spheres that circulate transnational-
ly, as in the case of the interaction of indigenous movements and international cooperation agencies, or TV and music radio, or networks of
activists and intellectuals, or migrant hometown association Internet activity: (1) how is public opinion legitimized in these transnational

---

3. *Ayllus* are self-sustaining political and social units characteristic of the pre-
Incan and Incan peoples. They consist of extended family groups that can include
non-related members bonded by relations of solidarity and responsibility.

spheres and "could public spheres today constrain the various powers that determine the conditions of the interlocutors' lives? (2) And if so, how does one carry out that constraint on power? What sorts of changes (institutional, economic, cultural and communicative) would be required even to imagine a genuinely *critical* and democratizing role for transnational public spheres under such conditions?" (Fraser 19).

Fraser does not have an answer for these questions, but I think the approach that Rappaport and Mato take to intercultural intellectual activism is a step in the direction of answering the legitimization question, which is to say, that the expansive reach of intercultural networks provides legitimacy. Regarding the second question, the political efficacy question, Fraser divides it into two functions: the translation condition and the capacity condition. Again, transcultural intellectual work does much of the translation necessary to render the communicative power of public spheres into law or administrative power. The major problem is what administrative agency will "implement the discursively formed will to which it is responsible" (Fraser 22). Her answer is another question: "if the modern territorial state no longer possesses the administrative ability to steer 'its' economy, ensure the integrity of 'its' national environment, and provide for the security and well-being of its citizens, then how should we understand the capacity component of efficacy today?" (Fraser 23). The obvious answer is for such transnational public spheres to gain something akin to state power, which, although it may not be able to control transnational phenomena, such as the media, corporate penetration and migration, at least it can attempt to regulate them to some degree.

There is one interesting case in which a few Latin American states are attempting to deal with the most urgent problem: migration. In many if not most cases, migrants continue being citizens of the Latin American country in question, but they live abroad, mostly in the U.S. In the case of Mexico, the Dominican Republic and El Salvador, remittances constitute the first or second contributor to the GNP, in El Salvador a whopping 18%, greater than any other sector of the economy (Pleitez). Should the U.S. send back the migrants, the national economies would shrink dramatically. Let me dwell briefly on the case of El Salvador, where much intellectual work has been done to reconfigure it as a transnation, that is, as a nation with one third of its population living and working abroad (Huezo Mixco). Intellectuals at

the UNDP, some of them ex-combatants in the FMLN-FDR, formulated a report in which they argue that it is crucial to open public
spheres and the very notion of cultural heritage to migrants, who in
any case have been contributing not only economic remittances but
also cultural ones, which are understood by some to undermine the
traditional national heritage (PNUD). The problem to be solved in
this case is not the equal footing of indigenous peoples in the definition of the new pluricultural nation, but that of migrants. The report
suggests that it is necessary to recognize that national identity is a co-
production among the diversity of social groups not only residing
within the national boundaries but also all other groups linked in some
way with that territory. And in order to recognize this, a new cultural
policy is needed that acknowledges the transnational co-production.

This proposal generated an intense debate with migrant groups in
the U.S. Some, including myself, felt that migrants were being called
on to save the Salvadoran nation that, to begin with, had expelled or
exported them as a kind of cash crop. Now, according to the view of
the Salvadoran government, if only they would continue to recognize
themselves as Salvadorans and feel kinship with the families they left
behind, they would continue to send remittances. After drafting the
report, the authors traveled around the United States to discuss it
with migrant groups in Los Angeles, New York, San Francisco, and
Washington, D.C., etc. They met with organizations that represent
migrants, like CARECEN, CISPES, NALACC, and with university
programs dedicated to Central American Studies, like the one at
Northridge, California. And they got an earful. In one particular
response, Beatriz Cortez, director of the Central American Studies Program at Northridge, criticized the report for its premise that before the
wave of migration set off by the civil war, there was such thing as an
imagined community of the Salvadoran nation. She objected particularly to the claim that the migrations had made that nation unknown
to itself. She also objected to the lack of knowledge that the residents
in El Salvador have of the migrants, the lack of interest in their cultural production. She criticized the programs that seek to rescue the Sal-
vadoranness that the migrants are presumably losing. There is a vast
diversity within El Salvador that multiplies as it becomes a set of
transnational flows, rather than a transnation as the UNDP drafters
proposed. Finally, what she proposes is that if Salvadoran policy makers

want to involve Salvadorans in their development projects, they will have to do so accepting many cultural changes that have taken place in the transnational space, and not try to rein in that transformation by rescuing a nation that never existed (Cortez).

This debate can be found throughout the blogosphere and migrant organizations. Some argue that there is no way to reconstitute either the nation or the transnation, for by the third generation, 94% of migrants will speak English exclusively and by the fourth generation, Salvadorans will be either English-speaking Latinos or through inter-marriage have become something else. There is one area in which the debate has made a transition to the transnational public at large: the renaming of the monument to the *hermanos lejanos* (distant siblings), or good migrants although the territorial population had taken to calling them *hermanos mojados* (wetback siblings), in part as an ironic pun on the monument – *El hermano lejano* – that the government built to honor migrants.[4]

The Monument to the Distant Siblings happens to be surrounded by a pool nourished by a fountain; hence one of the inspirations for the joke. San Salvador's Mayor's Office, the newspaper *La Prensa Grá-fica* and the Association of Salvadorans in Los Angeles (ASOSAL) organized a competition to rename the monument in order to rid it of its association with distance, and to emphasize brotherhood and solidarity. The responses were sent by email and included in the "*Departamento 15*" section of the *La Prensa Gráfica*.[5] Returning to Fraser's point about efficacy, it is obvious that the transnational debate has generated a set of recommendations to the Salvadoran state, which it is ill equipped to implement effectively.

SUBALTERN YOUTH ACTIVISM

Let me turn now to a different kind of postnational, subaltern intellectual activism: youth activism. I will begin with black youth in

4. See the image at http://www.sansalvador.gob.sv/?p=133.
5. El Salvador has 14 Departments. The 15th is not yet a legal state or district, as is the case with space reserved in Dominican electoral law for the senators and deputies elected by Dominican nationals who live abroad.

Brazil's *favelas*. The paradigmatic example are the young musicians of the Cultural Group AfroReggae, which was formed in 1993 after the police raided the *favela* of Vigário Geral and killed 21 innocent residents. Young black males in Rio's *favelas* are caught between the rock of the police and the hard place of narcotraffickers, and the police forces sent in to secure what is thought to be uncontrollable only increase the violence. The *favelas* are contexts in which, even if there are schools, the threat to school-age residents is many times higher than to middle-class youth. The violence further isolates *favela* residents, closing them off from the city's public spaces. They are relegated to often unpaved mountain-side communities while the middle classes live by the beach, which although characterized as public space is policed to keep these youth from occupying it. Security scholar Elizabeth Leeds argues "that the kinds of violence experienced by low-income urban populations in Rio de Janeiro within the context of larger globalization of urbanization trends mentioned, the absence of adequate social policies, and most importantly the state's mishandling of public safety policies create a dynamic whereby violence increases exclusion which, in turn, perpetuates the violence" (24).

Many *favela* youth make recourse to funk and rap music as a means to establish bonds among themselves in their neighborhoods clicks and gangs. Music is, indeed, one of the most potent, if not the most potent cohesive in group identity. As Rossana Reguillo explains, music provides a language that conveys the emergent feelings of social identity for youth, the possibility of breaking the straitjacket of their own skin. Of course, this does not mean the construction of a publicity or public sphere in the Habermasian sense, but something more akin to the subcultural practices studied by Dick Hebdige. Participation in those musical genres about which youth are passionate generates "places of practice" that permeate "body, home, street, city, the world and the information highway" and that distinguish them. Through these places of practice, embodied in music, there opens up a "first 'liberated territory' with respect to the authority of adults, a crucial space of autonomy for youth." These musics articulate an "us" and "shared certainties" comprised of tastes and perceptions that are political, affective, sexual and social.

I have written about this group many times, so I will be very brief here.[6] Suffice it to say that funk and rap are means for these youths to give public space their own accents and tonalities. Music is the cement, so to speak, that holds together the logics of collaboration, consultation, complex networking among heterogeneous actors, and valuing the cultural systems of the community that have been put into practice by the *Grupo Cultural AfroReggae* (GCAR), an ensemble of fusion bands, theater and circus acts, and mentors to *favela* youth. We might say that music is the form of expression that circulates in their public spheres, and they are taking them into a range of other areas, such as the state police and security departments, in an effort to reduce police brutality. AR Coordinator José Júnior expanded the work of GCAR to the reform and consciousness-raising of the police. As such, these youths conduct an unusual, almost inverse type of intellectual activism regarding violence and police brutality. They move from their local, organic situation to the general in order to reform the police for the sake of survival. Júnior and several AfroReggae band members took their practice of collaboration in music-making to the Belo Horizonte police department to bridge the gap between the police and poor youth through cultural activities involving theater, music, percussion, graffiti and circus. Teaching the police to play music was not simply about percussion but about getting into the body of the other, permeating the "body, home, street, city, the world," as I quoted from Rossana Reguillo above. Experiences like these generate a subaltern knowledge, which is used as a resource to raise the consciousness of others, including the police, as reported in the article by Sanches (2006).

Of course, if one asks what percentage of poor youth AfroReggae has been able to withdraw from narcotraffic, or what percentage of brutal cops they have converted, the answer would not be encouraging. Yet the impact of this kind of work is not simply quantitative. AfroReggae, like other groups I mention below, build networks that can amplify their effect across wide-ranging spaces. Within GCAR's network they already had ties with Secretary of Security of Rio de

6. Much of this history of AfroReggae is in my book *The Expediency of Culture*. See chapter four, "The Funkification of Rio," and chapter five, "Parlaying Culture into Social Justice" (Yúdice).

Janeiro, Luiz Eduardo Soares, and his research program on security at the Universidade Cândido Mendes, and together they devised a program – *Projeto Juventude e Polícia* – to work to reform the concept and practice of security. Elizabeth Leeds, director of a police and security initiative sponsored by the Ford Foundation, was another member of this network.[7]

As Secretary of Security at both state and national levels, Luiz Eduardo Soares advocated the elimination of narcotrafficking gangs and the larger forces that support them. However, he has also advocated policies that established links between the various sectors of society. His objective was to undo the divided city imaginary by mobilizing culture to promote the "symbolic relinking of everything that is split and separated" (Soares, MV Bill and Athayde 149).[8] He recognized that rap music in Brazil was one of the means by which the events of everyday life, often unconnected, are brought together in music, like putting a jigsaw puzzle together (148). This symbolic connection is a major piece of his idea of security, and is consistent with new international research and practice, in which "security means stable expectations, positively and widely shared . . . In other words, security is confidence. Confidence in others, in society, in State institutions. Shared expectations: here we are in the realm of intersubjectivity, where culture is woven" (185-6).

For Soares, as for AfroReggae, security had to be disarticulated from a discourse of surveillance and violence to a discourse of interculturality, and as such, it has been part of public discourse. Security inheres where there is a public sphere open to a diversity of languages and expressive modalities. Moreover, a secure society is one in which no one uses the cultural space of an individual, group or community without permission for the purposes of advertising or business or tourism. That is, security means not being stereotyped, for those stereotypes will be used against you. A secure society implies a public

---

7. For a detailed account of the Youth and Police Project, see Ramos.

8. The language used by Soares – *religação simbólica entre tudo o que está partido e separado* (a symbolic reconnection between all things that are torn apart and separated) – points out the relationship between community building and religion. *Religação* derives from the Latin *religare*, which is the etymological root of religion. In Portuguese, *ligação* is also the word for calling on the telephone, that is, for communication.

sphere permeable to all, one which includes everyone's heritage. What AfroReggae and other musicians like them do is court media celebrity in order to reconvert it into social action. As such, they work within the sphere of the mainstream culture industries. In fact, AfroReggae's coordinator, José Júnior, launched a new TV program in 2008 featuring questions about urban violence and what *favela* youth and their collaborators are doing about it.[9]

This need to establish security has led Luiz Eduardo Soares to collaborate with cultural activists in Rio's *favelas*, from AfroReggae, to MV Bill,[10] one of the best known rappers, and Celso Athayde, his producer and record label executive. Together they coauthored *Cabeça de porco*,[11] a book on narcotraffic violence that gathers together interviews with petty drug traffickers in nine Brazilian cities to get an understanding of why they got into the drug traffic.

One of the conclusions is that many of them would prefer to do something else, particularly because of the sense of insecurity in that way of life. This point is brought home poignantly in another book coauthored by MV Bill and Celso Athayde, *Falcão: Meninos do Tráfico*, which is also a documentary film in which they strove to show the human side of the youth who become cannon fodder for narcotraffickers.[12] Athayde, like the coordinator of AfroReggae, is the catalyst of an artistic project within Rio's *favelas*, *Central Unica das Favelas* (CUFA), which translates more or less as Coordinating Hub of the *Favelas*.[13] It has a recording label, which produces the popular rappers MV Bill and Nega Gizza.[14] CUFA also has eight video and filmmaking production

---

9. AfroReggae TV Program, http://www.youtube.com/watch?v=0ISLJ1zMy50

10. The MV in MV Bill's name stands for *mensageiro da verdade*, messenger of truth, in classic hip hop fashion.

11. In the language of Rio's *favelas*, *cabeça de porco* (a pig's head) means problems without solutions, confusion.

12. The first part of the film is available on YouTube: http://www.youtube.com/watch?v=yI4urSYqkog

13. *Central* is also the word that is used for a telephone switchboard, thus putting the stress on communication – in this case – media communication, as in Soares' *religação*.

14. You can hear Nega Gizza explain the work of CUFA in HIPNOTIK '05 Nega Gizza, http://www.youtube.com/ watch?v=NkPce-fYa48. And you can hear her rap with MV Bill and K-Milla in Mv Bill, K-Milla e Nega Gizza *Cantando Falcão!* http://www.youtube.com/watch?v=aHdKPoiPUzM. Accessed on March 7, 2009.

units and residents borrow the equipment to make films about their reality. CUFA has opened up audiovisual space and debate and has even placed its film in the largest commercial network in Brazil. When the film *Cidade de Deus* was released, MV Bill initiated a debate on the quality of the representations of the *favela*, in which he was born and raised and in which he still lives. For MV Bill and his fellow *cufarios*, the struggle over representations in the media is crucial.

The networks dealing with *favelas* must work on many fronts, from the police and the media and Internet to many other issues. And within those networks they seek to circulate their texts, their *tecidos* or weavings, throughout the media; TV, radio, and internet blogs. Their cultural work and the networks they have created may not eliminate the root causes of violence – such as the economic and political interests that enable the drug and arms traffic; indeed, this requires a sincere effort on the part of government to include politically-minded *favela* dwellers via institutions, jobs, and a self-generated presence in the media. So while the initiatives explored here may not succeed on their own, they nevertheless maintain hope and plant the seeds that may blossom into action as they are nourished by the multiple actions of the networks.

INTELLECTUAL ACTIVISM IN AND ABOUT INTERNET AND NEW MEDIA

There are other youth groups whose activism does not revolve around social justice issues but almost exclusively around their social networking, in which cultural practices like music are most salient. They are counterpublic spheres in the sense that Warner gives the term. They have generated discourses around which they identify, for example, funk in Rio's *favelas*, *tecnobrega* in Belem do Pará, *champeta* in Cartagena de Indias, *cumbia villera* in Buenos Aires, and so on. What makes them interesting, aside from their repudiation of mainstream norms, is their defiance of copyright laws and their adoption of what anthropologist and TV and Internet producer Hermano Vianna has called *música paralela*.

In his travels over 80,000 kilometers and 82 cities in Brazil to document the musical diversity of the country, Vianna came across *tecnobrega* in the northern city of Belem do Pará, a techno form of *brega* music. *Brega* in Portuguese means corny and the epithet was used years ago to refer to the sentimental pop music of Roberto Carlos and his followers. Vianna found that over 3,000 parties and 849 concerts were held each month, and that the music had a thriving business without the participation of major recording studios and without using copyright to protect the CDs. In fact, musicians used local pirates (hence the allusion to the parallel economy of the genre) to distribute their music because that is where most people go to buy their music. But even more important than that is the fact that most of the money to be made from music is in the concerts and not in the sales of CDs, which function more like a business card. Recordings were part of a social commons, to which people feel committed. That is, virtually no one believes in music as a form of property. It is either a community service, for which someone could be paid, or it is simply part of what everyone shares, the commons.

Vianna was inspired by this model of music production and dissemination to invent a new format, the Internet portal in which people from throughout the country could upload their music, or their literature, art, film and video, in networks around which specific publics were created. *Overmundo* was patterned after YouTube and Orkut, but as a national portal that would enable the vast diversity of cultural production to be exchanged and commented on. In other words, each different form generates its own publics and counterpublics that revolve around aesthetically or socially specific discourses. They also challenge any notion of expert gatekeeping. The critics are the participants in the networks. And finally, users became authors; it is mostly user-generated content that one finds in *Overmundo*.

From a juridical point of view, it is important to understand that these publics are experienced outside the intellectual property regime. Instead of copyright, participants used Creative Commons licenses to protect their work from becoming a source of profit for businesses that have nothing to do with the network. Now that digital TV will become the standard in many countries, copying will be a normal feature of viewing, unless the industry foolishly seeks to protect their images from reproduction. Overmundo, which like thousands of new initiatives seeks to capitalize on the opportunity that digital TV offers to small and locally produced content, opposes protection, on behalf of citizen rights, as we see in the site.[15]

15. See http://www.overmundo.com.br/.

As Ronaldo Lemos, Vianna's associate in *Overmundo* and director of Creative Commons Brazil observes, *música paralela* blurs the boundary between the legal and the illegal. Much of the music created draws on sequences from other recordings, but there is no sense that the pieces borrowed, as in any intertextual composition, require holding to an intellectual property regime. The genius is not in the small sampled sequences but in the way of putting them together. And that genius should not be copyrighted.

Brazil is probably the only country in which intellectual property law has become a matter of activism. In part, the issue stems from Fernando Henrique Cardoso's government's refusal to honor copyright law in the production of generic versions of patented AIDS drugs. It is beyond the scope of this essay to elaborate on the specifics of the case, but suffice it to say Brazil must produce generics by law whenever there is a pandemic, if generics enable the government to provide universal pharmaceutical coverage. The Swiss transnational pharmaceutical company, Roche, reduced the price of the drug even below the cost of producing the generic version in order to salvage the intellectual property regime. Nevertheless, the case mobilized many people, not only in relation to health issues but to copyright issues as well, relating to access to information (such as the photocopying of textbooks) and the reproduction of CDs and DVDs and software. This resistance to the intellectual property regime even became a quasi governmental policy in certain ministries, such as the ministry of education and the ministry of culture, under Gilberto Gil, who tried to put his own music online for free download, only to be sued by his record company.

Not many countries have generated public debate on these issues. In Spain, nearly 2 million people have signed petitions to do away with the canon, which is a tax on blank media to compensate for revenues presumably lost due to peer to peer file sharing. In Sweden, a political party, the anti-copyright party, was created to run in national elections. In Brazil, the most important site for discussion of these issues is *Cultura e Mercado*, the online forum of a set of local NGOs and think tanks dedicated to promoting the exercise of creativity without barriers, and to this end *Cultura e Mercado* conducts monitoring of government laws and policies and critique of any action on the part of government, business or institutions to limit the access to culture, digital or analogical.

FREE TRADE AGREEMENTS

The major way in which the current intellectual property regime is imposed throughout the world is by means of so-called free trade agreements, particularly with the EU and the U.S., which require harmonization of laws governing trade as well as promoting the elimination of all tariff and non-tariff barriers. The result is usually a weakening of important industries in developing countries, such as corn production in Mexico (which now imports it from the U.S.) and especially of whatever national telecommunications are left in the wake of the frenzied privatization of utilities in neoliberal times. I focus on telecommunications because the deregulation and opening of this sector, in countries like Costa Rica, which has a government company that provides high quality telephone and Internet service at very low cost, is likely to lose out to competition from U.S., Mexican and European telecom conglomerates, eventually raising prices at great cost to Costa Ricans.

It is precisely because of the threat to what is left of Costa Rican social democracy, its public utilities and its protection of the environment, that a huge movement against the United States-Central American Free Trade Agreement (plus the Dominican Republic), CAFTA-DR, emerged, even obligating the current president, Oscar Arias, who favors the agreement, to call a referendum to decide the issue. The mobilization of the *No al TLC* movement was very spirited, and since the major newspapers and television networks endorsed the agreement, much of the activity was done in cyberspace. Julia Ardón, a long time activist, took to the Internet and created one of the most visited blogs in Costa Rica. And Juan Manuel Villasuso pointed to the enormous asymmetries between the U.S. and Costa Rica positions. Aside from the disadvantages of having to compete with subsidized U.S. agriculture, Costa Rica will have to allow for oil exploration in its territorial waters, and it will have to open its telecommunications sector.

Why is that important? All mediated culture will soon be disseminated in digital format, and its mode of distribution will be through the convergence of television, Internet and telephony.[16] Indeed, Latin

---

16. Indeed, the iPhone already integrates all three technologies.

America, like India and other developing countries will soon have most of its media flows through mobile telephony. Why would the president of Costa Rica and his top government proponents of privatizing telecommunications be willing to open the Costa Rican telecommunication sector when soon most profits will be made in that sector? Because they are already partners with foreign telecommunications concerns and stand to reap the profits when the convergence is consolidated, and also to promote those industries in which they have a stake, at the expense of others in which tens of thousands of Costa Ricans will lose jobs. The print, television and radio media have a stake in the YES to CAFTA-DR, as is obvious from the side that they took in the debate. That is one reason why much of the dynamism of the anti-free trade agreement was in the blogosphere.

Let me connect this point about telecommunications to the ones I already raised about copyright and the ability to generate local content. If the TV, radio and print media already cater exclusively to publicity-attracting programming, which is largely from the U.S. and Mexico, and if the copyright regime favors that sector, then it follows that any content that is not commercially viable in the mass media will not be carried. It will necessarily be relegated to second and third class status. And it will be difficult for the public at large to ever get to see or hear it. This is the case with all radio stations except the university-administered public station in Costa Rica. As explained above, my research revealed that 95% of programming comes from the U.S., Mexico and Spain, and only 5% of music heard on Costa Rican radio is generated there. The same can be said about television. The free trade agreement will extend this condition to the digital sphere.

And this situation has an impact on the interest that intellectual activists like Mario Bustos of the Conaie expressed. Interculturality can only be promoted effectively if the different communities that comprise a nation-state can project their values and world views so that they themselves and their co-nationals can get to know each other. The copyright regime and free trade agreements make this even more difficult than it already is. Hence the need for intellectual activism in and about the media and especially the new media, which are the future of all mediated representations.

There are many other issues that I could address (including Indymedia and the Zapatistas), but the basic point should be clear. To conclude, I would like to mention briefly another form of intellectual activism in cyberspace. I am referring to youth culture that takes a more antagonist stand than that of AfroReggae and CUFA, especially in his refusal to work with the entertainment industry.[17] I am referring to intellectual activists like the Chilean Vicente Durán, known as Subverso, whose political rap appears almost exclusively online, and which has generated a storm of controversy in Chile. Rather than a general critique of racism or class oppression, Subverso mentions specific names, and backs up his claims with documentation. His videos are masterful productions of sampled digital culture, sequences taken from the Internet and other sources, without regard for copyright, in order to counter the relatively benign criticisms that Bachelet's administration faces in the press and television (Larraín).

In the video, *Infórmate* or "Inform Yourself,"[18] Subverso blames Bachelet for the near death of Patricia Troncoso, who went on a 111-day hunger strike on behalf of the Mapuche Indians rights, the longest one in Chile's history, and for the death of Mapuche activist and student Matías Catrileo by Chile's Special Police Forces. I referred earlier to the collaborative and solidary character of the new intellectual activism. This is the case in these online networks. In this case, the video *Infórmate* was created collectively by all the people who uploaded the material used on YouTube. This is one of the best composed denunciatory hip hop documentaries that I have ever seen. And these videos reach hundreds of thousands of people, mostly youth, who are engaging this medium more than any other, reading and writing perhaps even more than previous generations, since they have a range of different formats in which to do so.[19] Numerous blogs have also been created in which the viewers debate the significance of the videos and the events portrayed in them. This is a new form of intellectual activism that we cannot afford to ignore.

17. If anything, Subverso's attitude to the entertainment industry is antagonistic. In "El Padrino (SubVerso + Estigma)," he takes the popular variety show host Don Francisco to task for disseminating conformity. See http://www.youtube.com/watch?v=CsKbH76snnY.

18. Subverso, "Infórmate," http://www.youtube.com/watch?v=QWxyOI0mqaM

19. García Canclini elaborates on the multimedia character of reading today in *Lectores, espectadores e internautas*. This is an aspect of intellectual activism curiously absent from the analysis of intellectual work in studies on the "lettered city."

It is often argued, following Horkheimer and Adorno, that the media can only reproduce ideology and as such operate as an instrument of total integration. Faced with the increasing dominance of the mass media, Horkheimer and Horkheimer promoted a strategy of hibernation. If the foregoing examples indicate anything, it is that intellectual activity, not only traditional oppositionality but new forms of advocating change in communitarian and new media, have come alive. This does not mean that they will succeed. A crucial part of the struggle is to promote the elimination of the intellectual property regimes that enable the traditional media to maintain their hold. We cannot afford to only focus on the content of activism; we need to be activist about the juridical regimes that rule over the conduits of expression.

WORKS CITED

ALBRO, Robert. "The Challenges of Asserting, Promoting and Performing Cultural Heritage." *Theorizing Cultural Heritage* 1.1. (2005) Web. <http://www.folklife.si.edu/resources/center/cultural_policy/pdf/Rob Albrofellow.pdf>.
—. "The Culture of Democracy and Bolivia's Indigenous Movements." *Critique of Anthropology* 26.4 (2006): 387-410.
ATHAYDE, Celso and MV Bill. *Falcão: Meninos do Tráfico*. Rio de Janeiro: Editora Objetiva, 2006.
BREGLIA, Lisa. *Monumental Ambivalence: The Politics of Heritage*. Austin: U of Texas P, 2006.
BUSTOS, Mario. "Comunicación, política y cosmovisión." Interview by Daniel Mato, Quito, 13 June 2001. *Colección Entrevistas a Intelectuales Indígenas* (2003) 1, Caracas: Programa Globalización, Cultura y Transformaciones Sociales, CIPOST, FaCES, Universidad Central de Venezuela. Web. <http://www.globalcult.org.ve/entrevistas.html>.
CALHOUN, Craig. "Civil Society/Public Sphere: History of the Concept." *International Encyclopedia of the Social & Behavioral Sciences*. Amsterdam: Elsevier Science, 2001. 1897-1903.
CASTELLS, Manuel. *The Rise of the Network Society.* Malden (MA): Blackwell, 2000.
CHITOȘCĂ, Marius Ionuț. "The Internet as a Socializing Agent of the 'M Generation'." *Journal of Social Informatics*. 5 June 2006. Web. <http://

citeseerx.ist.psu.edu/viewdoc/summary;jsessionid=71F7CF8F9B32E86
AC9F95C929FA4EE06?doi=10.1.1.101.4349>.

CORTEZ, Beatriz. "Hometown Organizations: Las asociaciones de salvadoreños en Los Ángeles y su reto al imaginario social." *Estudios Cen-
troamericanos* 62.703-704 (2007): 467-470.

ESCOBAR, Arturo. "Other Worlds Are (already) Possible: Cyber-Internatio-
nalism and Post-Capitalist Cultures." *Revista TEXTOS de la CiberSo-
ciedad* 5 (2005) Web. <http://www.cibersociedad.net/ textos/articulo.
php?art=18>.

FRASER, Nancy. "Transnationalizing the Public Sphere: On the Legitimacy
and Efficacy of Public Opinion in a Post-Westphalian World." *Theory,
Culture & Society* 24.4 (2007): 7-30.

GARCÍA CANCLINI, Néstor. *Lectores, espectadores e internautas*. Barcelona:
Gedisa, 2007.

GIRARD, Bruce, ed. *The One to Watch: Radio, New ICTs and Interactivity*.
Rome: Food and Agricultural Organization of the United Nations, 2003.
1 September 2009. Web. http://www.fao.org/sd/2003/KN12023_en.htm.

HABERMAS, Jürgen. *The Structural Transformation of the Public Sphere: An
Inquiry into a category of Bourgeois Society*. Cambridge: MIT Press, 1989.

HEBDIGE, Dick. *Subculture: The Meaning of Style*. London: Methuen, 1979.

HANISCH, Carol. "The Personal is Political." *Feminist Revolution, Redstock-
ings.March 1969*. New York: Random House, 1979.

HARDT, Michael and Antonio NEGRI. *Empire*. Cambridge: Harvard UP,
2000.

HORKHEIMER, Max, and Theodor W. ADORNO. Preface to the New Edition.
Dialectic of Enlightenment. Trans. John Cumming. New York: Herder &
Herder, 1972. x.

HUEZO MIXCO, Miguel. (2008) "Los migrantes salvadoreños pasando por
México." Presentation at the *Encuentro Latinidades 2*, Convenio Andrés
Bello & Colegio de la Frontera Norte, Tijuana, 26 Sep., 2008.

Internet World Stats. "Latin American Internet Usage Statistics." 2008.
Web. 3 Jun 2009. <http://www.internetworldstats.com/stats10.htm>.

LARRÁIN, Sebastián. Entrevista con Vicente Durán, Subverso: 'La crítica es
un punto de partida, no de llegada." *El ciudadano* 6 (2008). Web.
<http://www.elciudadano.cl/2008/05/06/vicente-duran-%E2%80%9
Cla-critica-es-un-punto-de-partida-no-de-llegada/>.

LEEDS, Elizabeth. "Rio de Janeiro." *Fractured Cities: Social Exclusion, Urban
Violence and Contested Spaces in Latin America*. Eds. Kees Koonings and
Dirk Kruijt. London: Verso, 2006.

LEMOS, Ronaldo. "From Legal Commons to Social Commons: Developing
Countries and the Cultural Industry in the 21st Century." Oxford: Centre

for Brazilian Studies, 2007. 1 September 2009. Web. http://virtualbib
.fgv.br/dspace/handle/10438/2677.

MARTÍN-BARBERO, Jesús. "A Latin American Perspective on Communica-
tion/Cultural Mediation." *Global Media and Communication* 2.3 (2006):
279–297.

—. "Entrevista a Jesús Martín-Barbero: Jesús Martín Barbero reflexiona
sobre el patrimonio." Universitat de Barcelona. 22 May 2008. Web.
<http://video.google.com/ videoplay?docid=-8595357065325377403>.

MATO, Daniel. "Not 'Studying the Subaltern' but Studying *with* 'Subaltern'
Social Groups, or, at least, Studying the Hegemonic Articulations of
Power." *Nepantla* 1.1 (2000): 479–502.

NEGRI, Antonio. *Negri on Negri. Conversation With Anne Dufourmentelle*.
New York; London: Routledge, 2004.

PLEITEZ, Rafael. "Remesas y su importancia en el desarrollo." Presentation
at the X Foro Interamericano de la microempresa del Banco Interamericano de Desarrollo. San Salvador, 3 Oct. 2007. Web. 7 March 2009
<https://www.bmi.gob.sv/pls/portal/docs/PAGE/BMI_HTMLS/BMI_
PULSO_MYPE_IMG/ CAPITULO%20III%20REMESAS%20Y%
20SU%20IMPORTANCIA%20EN%20EL%20DESARROLLO.PDF>.

PNUD (Programa de las Naciones Unidas para el Desarrollo). *Informe sobre
Desarrollo Humano El Salvador 2005: Una mirada al nuevo Nosotros. El
impacto de las migraciones*. San Salvador: PNUD. Web. <http://www.
pnud. org.sv/migraciones/content/view/8/105/>.

RAMOS, Sílvia. "Youth and the Police." *Boletim Segurança e Cidadania* 5.12
(October 2006): 1-16. Web. <http://www.ucamcesec.com.br/arquivos/
publicacoes/boletim12web_eng.pdf>.

RAPPAPORT, Joanne. *Intercultural Utopias: Public Intellectuals, Cultural
Experimentation, and Ethnic Pluralism in Colombia*. Durham: Duke UP,
2005.

REGUILLO, Rossana. "El lugar desde los márgenes: músicas e identidades
juveniles." *Nómadas* 13 (2000): 40-53.

RIBEIRO, Gustavo Lins. "Internet e a Comunidade Transnacional Imagina-
da-Virtual." *Interciência* 21.6 (1996): 277-287. Web. <http://www.inter
ciencia.org/v21_06/ciencia_tecnologia.html>.

—. 1998. "Cybercultural Politics: Political Activism at a Distance in a
Transnational World." *Cultures of Politics, Politics of Culture*. Eds. Alvarez,
Sonia E. et al. Boulder: Westview P. 325-352.

—. "Global Navigations." (n/d) Web. <http://web.archive.org/web/2005
1224104451/http://www.jhu.edu/~igscph/ribeiro.htm>.

RIBEIRO, Gustavo Lins and Arturo ESCOBAR, eds. *World Anthropologies: Disciplinary Transformations within Systems of Power*. New York: Berg, 2006.

SANCHES, Pedro Alexandre. "Arte na zona de guerra." *Carta Capital* 416. 25 Oct. 2006. Web. <http://pedroalexandresanches.blogspot.com/2006_12_01_archive.html>.

SCHULZ, Markus S. "Modes of Structured Interplay in the Modeling of Digital Futures." *The ISA Handbook in Contemporary Sociology.* Eds. Ann Denis and Devorah Kalekin-Fishman. Thousand Oaks, CA: Sage, 2009. 291-304.

SNYDER, Pete. "How Obama Killed 'Election Day' and Became President." *Advertising Age.* 5 Nov. 2008. Web. <http://adage.com/campaigntrail/post?article_id=132250>.

SOARES, Luiz Eduardo, MV BILL and Celso ATHAYDE. *Cabeça de Porco.* Rio de Janeiro: Editora Objetiva, 2005.

VAL, Ana. "El Salvador." (n/d). Web. 7 March 2009. <http://fis.ucalgary.ca/AVal/321/ElSalvador.html>.

VIANNA, Hermano. "A música paralela: Tecnobrega consolida uma nova cadeia produtiva, amparada em bailes de periferia, produção de CDs piratas e divulgação feita por camelôs." *Folha de São Paulo.* October 13, 2003. <http://www.overmundo.com.br/banco/ a-musica-paralela>.

WARNER, Michael. *Public and Counterpublics.* Cambridge, MA: Zone Books, 2001.

YÚDICE, George. *The Expediency of Culture: Uses of Culture in the Global Era.* Durham: Duke UP, 2003.

GLOBAL REALIGNMENTS
AND THE GEOPOLITICS OF HISPANISM

Abril Trigo

I have always had mixed feelings regarding the all-encompassing field of Hispanism. However, my misgivings became even stronger with the new fashion of Transatlantic Studies, given the relentless compartmentalization of fields of research and the compulsive bidding of new critical paradigms which come and go according to the pressing need to be always on the cutting edge, make an original contribution, and become a star in an academic market driven by planned obsolescence, the ideology of efficiency and reward, and the culture of instant gratification, which dictate the current entrepreneurial ethos of the institutions of higher learning and the intellectual marketplace. So, restrained by skepticism but driven by curiosity, I questioned myself, what is new in Hispanic Transatlantic Studies that makes of it a new critical paradigm, as many advocate?

THE GEOPOLITICAL SHIFT OF AREA STUDIES

My hypothesis is that Transatlantic Studies are the outcome of a dual shift: a geographical displacement provoked by the geopolitical debunking of area studies, and an epistemological rift produced by the new global regime of capitalist accumulation. In the U.S., the geographical shift in the focus from continental regions to oceanic ranges was meant to salvage area studies from their virtual obsolescence, while it represented to European academic circles a golden opportunity to break the hegemony of a U.S.-centered area studies' agenda. The epistemological rift from hardcore, neo-positivistic and developmental social sciences to relativistic, postmodern and postcolonial interculturalism was a response to the economically driven and globally experienced cultural turn. This combined shift, from which Transatlantic Studies emerged, translates profound geopolitical realignments, economic transformations and epistemological quandaries that traverse and make up our global age. As an outcome of this global realignment and Spain's freshly acquired international status, Hispanic Transatlantic Studies adopts this dual shift and adapts it to a renovated Pan-Hispanism. This complicates things further, insofar as it involves the overlapping interests of Spanish capitalism and transnational corporations, so that the first is put to work at the service of the latter under the pretense of a shared cultural tradition, and Hispanic imperial nostalgia becomes an alibi for global geopolitics. As José María Aznar, at that time president of Spain, wrote: "We have an Atlantic call thanks to our geographic position and our relation to America. How do we explain the history of Spain without taking America into consideration?" (*Ocho años* 164). If we accept Joseba Gabilondo's reading of globalization as "the active and ahistorical actualization of history in so far as the latter can be mobilized by capital in order to further expand commodification in the present," we must agree with him that "The Hispanic Atlantic, in its global and post-national/-colonial deployment, constitutes one case of such retrojective mobilization of multinational capital" ("One-Way").

The crisis of area studies brought forth by the fading of Cold War politics, the challenge of feminism, ethnic and cultural studies, and its increasing rebuke as scientific colonialism, was met in Europe and the U.S. by different strategies. While the *Report on the Restructuring of the Social Sciences* written by the Gulbenkian Commission led by Immanuel Wallerstein recommended several innovations in area scholarship, particularly in regard to the opening of the social sciences to interdisciplinary research and the adoption of a global and systematic interpretation of contemporary events, the revision actually started in 1993 with the publication of the influential *The Black Atlantic* by Paul Gilroy, an English scholar of Guyanese ancestry who drew upon cultural and postcolonial studies to rethink the African diasporas in the Atlantic scenario. The Ford and the Rockefeller Foundations, important sources of funding for language and area training since the 1950s, promoted several projects to revitalize area studies, "lest it be supplanted by a vague globalism that avoids place, culture and language specificity. Central to this revitalization effort is the imagining of new geographies – new spatial frameworks that encourage alternative ways of seeing the world" (Lewis and Wiwen 161). The premise of those projects was that border crossings could be accomplished by redrawing area studies around maritime flows. Of course, this idea of the Atlantic as a geopolitical crucible, first envisioned as a domain of inquiry by European historians like Fernand Braudel and Pierre Chaunu, constitutes the strategic foundations of NATO, but eventually would evolve from the study of regional formations to the study of oceanic flows of people, commodities and cultures between different regions. As Thomas Bender will summarize it years later, "Here is the rule – or ought to be – follow the people, the money, the things, and the knowledges wherever they go [...] The resulting history is not a global history; it remains local, regional, thematic, or even national. But it is a history that recognizes a global context, and at one level and in various degrees all histories share in a global history after 1500" (xvii). This is the intellectual and geopolitical bedrock of Transatlantic Studies.

THE POST-THEORETICAL VANTAGE POINT

One of the most noticeable characteristics of Hispanic Transatlantic Studies is its unmistakable theoretical restraint, a premeditated reticence to venture into the advancement of new critical models that responds, sustains Julio Ortega, to a post-theoretical scenario characterized – and he quotes Ernesto Laclau – by "a process of mutual contamination between 'theory' and 'empiria'" ("Post-teoría" 109). Although the ultimate reason for the post-theoretical penchant of Hispanic Transatlantic Studies would be the creation of a more open, horizontal space of transdisciplinary dialogue that would promote new ways of reading texts, genres and contexts, it also evinces some sort of academic cleansing from the theoretical excesses of the 1990s, "a self-derivative critical activism and its redundant academic sequels" which ultimately transformed "major theoretical models into systems of authority, sheer academic power, and mass-mediating fads" (Ortega, "Post-teoría" 109). The question is whether this theoretical shift away from theory is simply a reaction against the over-theorization of the 1990s or a strategic maneuver linked to a specific global design. There is much more in the epistemological scope and the political implications of the post in post-theory, which Ortega construes as a theoretical overcoming of theory through the calculated misreading of Ernesto Laclau, when, as a matter of fact, post-theory designates exactly the opposite, as Laclau himself makes clear in his preface to the volume *Post-Theory: New Directions in Criticism*, where he underlines (and I take the quote where Ortega left it out): "So, although we have entered a post-theoretical universe, we are definitely not in an atheoretical one" (vii). Post-theory, in a sense, would designate a new brand of meta-theoretical discourse.

For this reason, I do not think that Hispanic Transatlantic Studies' embracing of the post-theoretical position can be explained away as a backlash against the political squabbles of the 1990s for a new critical paradigm. As I see it, it is a strategic maneuver in order to adopt a very peculiar vantage point, the vantage point of those who are not against theory but beyond theory, those who have managed to remain fairly unscathed by those academic, institutional and political squabbles, and therefore have the moral and intellectual authority to clean up the rubble and reorganize the field anew. This means, of course, the adoption of a new critical and theoretical paradigm, Transatlantic Studies, which due to its post-theoretical stance, cannot be named or theorized as such. The post-theoretical maneuver makes it possible to postulate a hermeneutic praxis as a new theoretical paradigm without the anxiety of being subjected to critical scrutiny. Thanks to this strategic vantage point, Hispanic Transatlantic Studies can stand as a unique space of transdisciplinary dialogue that doesn't need to be authorized by any critical school, because it surpasses them in a dialogic space, free of normative codes and abusive canons (Ortega, *Presentación* 105). Free at last of theoretical agendas and dogmatic cliques, this democratic and cosmopolitan academic space would be exceptionally qualified for the pursuit of a very ambitious agenda, which ranges from the reexam-

ination of the national in a post-national context; to the redefinition
of globalization as a hybridizing force; and last but not least, to the
reformulation of the "long and unequal exchange between Spain
and Hispanic America, in order to overcome the deplorable division
between the Peninsular and Hispanic American areas, which has become obsolete and perfunctory" (Ortega, "Post-teoría" 113-4).

THE REVIVAL OF HISPANISM

This is a truly daring agenda, whose primary intention is to reunite
and establish anew a worldwide field of Hispanic literary and cultural
criticism. However, one of its perhaps unintended consequences is the
promotion of a new form of Hispanic revivalism, "as Madrid places
itself at the center of international arrangements, the language is reaffirmed as the primary and legitimizing vehicle for intercultural relations, and the expectation of profitable business paves the road for the
reentry of Spanish capitals in the old colonies" (Moraña xix).

Hispanism, according to Joan Ramón Resina, is "the academic
game that sets the rules and arbitrates the practices that endow with
value the cultural memory of and about Hispania [...] An emanation
of empire, Hispanism is the earliest instance of a postcolonial ideology engaged in promoting hegemonic ambitions by cultural means"
("Whose Hispanism?" 160-3). In a word, Hispanism is both an ideology endowed with a geopolitical agenda and a field of research supported by a positivistic discipline, a dual status which perhaps explains
much of its ambiguity and imprecise boundaries: "Is Hispanism, for
instance, limited to Spain, or does it also include Latin America? Does
it primarily focus on literature, or rather on history and culture? Is it
necessary for a Hispanist to be a Hispanophile as well? And if so, does
that imply a love and interest for Spain, for Spanish America, or just
for the Spanish language?" asks Sebastiaan Faber ("La hora" 65).
Despite its elusiveness, most critics tend to narrow it to "the study of
the Spanish language and literature and all things related to Spain,"
according to the definition of the 1936 edition of the dictionary of the
Real Academia Española (Santana 34). In this regard, Hispanists have
tended to be Hispanophiles, affirms Faber ("Economies" 12), which
means that Latin American cultures and, even more so, indigenous

cultures have always been in a subordinate position in the field of Hispanism, whose ideology upholds "the existence of a unique Spanish culture, lifestyle, characteristics, traditions and values, *all of them embodied in its language*; the idea that Spanish American culture is nothing but Spanish culture transplanted to the New World; and the notion that Hispanic culture has an internal hierarchy in which Spain occupies a hegemonic position" (del Valle and Gabriel-Stheeman 6; original emphasis). The denial to Latin America, its indigenous peoples and the regional cultures within Spain of any form of cultural specificity involves a convoluted mystification of Hispanic culture as quintessentially popular, historically authentic and spiritually superior that reifies Spanish neo-imperial ambitions behind a narrow cultural nationalism. This makes Faber conclude that "Hispanism, as a term and a disciplinary paradigm, has long outlived its validity and legitimacy – or, for that matter, its usefulness" ("La hora" 64).

As Resina recalls, "Hispanism arose in the nineteenth century, together with the national philologies, as a compensatory strategy to offset Spain's staggering territorial losses in America" ("Whose Hispanism?" 163). It was the byproduct of a geopolitical defeat and a national crisis, ideologically negotiated through an amalgamation of nationalism, populism, spiritualism, historicism and positivism, so that the lost Spanish colonial grandeur was reformulated in tragic, transcendental and existential terms (Subirats 37).

The history of Hispanism in the U.S. would be even more contradictory, torn apart between its devotion to the cultural splendor of the former Spanish Empire and its allegiance to the hemispheric interests of the emerging U.S. imperialism. This is magnificently captured by James Fernández's "Longfellow's law":

> at the origins of U.S. interest in Spanish is the view that Spanish is an American language, with a history and, most important, a future as such [...] however, this interest in the American language called Spanish [...] was translated in practice into an interest in the language, literature and culture not of Latin America but of Spain. A double displacement would seem to be at work here: from Latin America to Spain and from language/politics/commerce to literature / history / culture (124).

In other words, the popular demand for a second-rate European language deemed necessary to do business with Latin America would foster the academic prestige of Hispanism, despite the fact that the ideology of *Hispanidad* was in great part a reaction against the cultural, economic and political expansion of Pan Americanism. As Faber demonstrates, both the journal *Hispania*, founded in 1918, and *Revista Iberoamericana*, official journal of the *Instituto Internacional de Literatura Iberoamericana* (International Institute of Ibero-American Literature), founded in 1938 under the auspices of Roosevelt's Good Neighbor Policy, always played both cards. The *IILI*, despite being devoted to the study of Latin American literatures (explicitly excluding Spain and Portugal), and openly adhering to U.S. Pan Americanism, would be always tainted by the connotations of the term *Ibero-America*, used as an alternative to the suspiciously Gallic *América Latina*, and by the political ambivalence of adopting an anti-fascist and anti-communist position during the Spanish Civil War (Faber, "Economies" 18-9; "La hora" 70-5). These ambiguities will leave an indelible mark in U.S. Hispanism, since interest in Latin America will be coded for a long time as primarily economic and geopolitical, while interest in Spain would be exclusively cultural (Fernández 133), thus consolidating the prestige of Spanish literature over Latin American texts, and the hegemony of Peninsularist scholars over their Latin Americanist peers.

The defeat of the Spanish Republic in 1939 drove hundreds of intellectuals into exile; many of them, moderate liberals, would end up in U.S. academia, thus strengthening Peninsular Hispanism and counteracting the surge of Latin Americanism during the 1930s. Though this influx of first-rate anti-Francoist intellectuals increased the field's prestige, "it did not significantly change the fundamental conservatism of the discipline, its wariness of politics, or the way it navigated the economies of prestige [...] They tended to espouse a vision of Spain and Spanish culture that was ideologically *hispanista* [...] They celebrated the colonization of the Americas as a triumph for Spain and the whole of humanity, and conceived of Hispanic culture as a source of uniquely 'spiritual' values in an increasingly materialist world" (Faber, "Economies" 23). This notion of Hispanism, so well articulated by Américo Castro, dovetailed with the apolitical aestheticism prevalent in the humanities, and the protection of their turf implied for these Hispanists the exaltation of Spanish culture and history, even though it coincided with Francoist neo-imperial nostalgia. This

ideological investment and the methodological adherence to the positivist national philology founded by Marcelino Menéndez y Pelayo
and Ramón Menéndez Pidal, will make Cold War Hispanism especially unreceptive to the theoretical and methodological revolution
that will shake the humanities and the social sciences, and will deep-
en the future rift between Hispanism's conservative hermeneutics and
the more politically driven Latin American studies, encouraged in the
1930s by the Pan American policies of president Roosevelt and developed since the 1960s under the clout of the Cold War (Faber, "Economies"; Resina "Cold War").

    In view of this history, the challenge raised by Transatlantic Studies
to the current distinction between Latin American and Hispanic studies, and its strategy of building bridges is, at least, problematic. It is
obvious that the distinction between Hispanic and Latin American
studies, which won legitimacy under the Cold War, carries all the ideological biases and geopolitical drawbacks of area studies, according to
which "non-Western areas were analytically the same as Western areas,
but not quite," the difference being explained by the leveling of a presumed universal knowledge and the instrumentation of modernization theory (Gulbenkian Commission 40). We all know very well
that area studies embodied a neocolonial remapping of the world, the
appropriation and instrumentation of knowledge about the so-called
Third World, and the translation of ideological warfare into academic
knowledge, such that the learning of foreign languages, literatures and
cultures became an instrument for national security (Wallerstein 202).
Latin American Studies, born under this geopolitical framework, will
flourish over the next decades, providing the scientific alibis for the
many forms of cultural intervention denounced from Latin America
as scientific colonialism or cultural imperialism (Wallerstein 220-4).
Nevertheless, while promoting the instrumental knowledge of Latin
America, Latin American Studies also bolstered a generation of progressive, anti-imperialist Latin Americanists, who, torn between feelings of solidarity and superiority toward their object of study, had to
recycle themselves and their field anew. Meanwhile, the expansion of
the Spanish language market, alongside an unprecedented migration
of Latin American academics to the U.S. during the 1970s and 1980s,
led to a dramatic growth of Latin American programs. All these circumstances led in the 1980s, precisely when area studies began to

fade, to the virtual emancipation of Latin American studies from the historical hegemony of Hispanism.

In this context, Hispanic Transatlantic Studies could be understood as a reaction against this reversal, and in the words of a Peninsularist, "As a result of these strictures, a 'new field' in 'trans-Atlantic studies' has arisen, permitting 'Peninsularists' to reposition themselves nearer the dominant Americanism" (Resina, "Cold War" 96). Displaced from its long-lasting hegemony, which made possible its identification with Hispanism tout court, indicates Mario Santana (another Peninsularist), Peninsular or Iberian studies must justify its existence in an unstable disciplinary field, thus experiencing a certain degree of Latin Americanization and shifting progressively to the study of the "transatlantic production" (35-6). According to Faber (yet another Peninsularist), the turn to cultural studies and the insertion of "Iberian phenomena into emerging comparative fields, in a transatlantic, European, Mediterranean, or more global framework" offers "Peninsular Hispanism new strategies for shoring up its position within the savage economies of prestige that govern American academia" ("Economies" 28-9). It seems obvious that up to a point Hispanic Transatlantic Studies is a byproduct of the increasing questioning of Hispanism by Hispanists themselves. This complex debate, which in a very simplified version pits Peninsularists in the Anglo-Saxon academy against Peninsularists in Spain, actually unfolds the profound crisis of Hispanism by deploying the psychodrama between U.S. Hispanism, always trying to catch up with the latest theoretical post, and the incestuous endogamy of traditional Hispanism, entrenched in historical philology, or, as Ángel Loureiro put it, between the neurotic conservatism of Spanish Hispanism and the psychotic avant-gardism of Anglo-Saxon Hispanism (34). What is at stake, asserts Resina, is how to turn Hispanism into a venue for the open, plural and equitable coexistence of the many cultures in Spain and Latin America ("Whose Hispanism?" 172). Is this still possible?

The underlying fact is that Latin American and Hispanic literary criticism and cultural studies have become over the years completely divergent fields, which face dissimilar problems, apply different methodologies, involve distinctive theoretical paradigms and demand entirely opposite epistemological and even ontological perspectives regarding global affairs. To promote collaboration and dialogue between these two different fields in order to better understand some complex cultural processes and historical conjunctures is simply reasonable. The colonial societies, cultures and literatures of the New World cannot be understood without taking into consideration their colonial condition, and the same should be said (although is rarely admitted) of the European metropolises. Who can deny the pertinence of a transatlantic perspective for the study of certain periods of intense economic, political, demographic or cultural transactions, such as the literature of exile (e.g. the Republican exiles in Latin America after 1939 or the Latin American refugees in Spain after the 1970s), or certain parallel literary movements (e.g. Latin American *modernismo* and the Generation of '98), or the long-lasting influence of certain journals and publishing houses (e.g. *Revista de Occidente* or Espasa Calpe), or the impact of certain editorial policies (e.g. the important role of Spanish publishers in the induction of the Latin American boom)? However, an approach that is indisputably relevant for certain periods or specific phenomena cannot be indiscriminately applied without serious mystification.

But even more problematic is the adoption of a pan-Hispanic subject position of worldwide scope. How do we convince the Bolivian Aymara, the Peruvian Quechua and the Guatemalan Maya that "the road to freedom runs through Hispanicization," as Manuel Alvar used to say? According to Resina, "Since Hispanism is based on this smug collusion over the pressure that the colonial language continues to exert on native cultures of America *and* of the Iberian peninsula, I can see neither an ethical nor a serious epistemic reason to retain Hispanism as the common disciplinary structure for the transmission of knowledge about Latin America and the Iberian peninsula" ("Cold War" 97).

A Geopolitical Design

Contemporary Hispanic revivalism, which reached its operatic climax during the neo-imperial nostalgia staged during the festivities for the Quincentenary in 1992, cannot be disconnected from the extraordinary expansion of Spanish corporations, their relentless takeover of banks, industries, land and strategic resources everywhere in Latin

America, and their managerial strategy to portray themselves as brokers between Latin America and the European Community. The arrogance, brutality and sense of impunity with which Spanish corporations, such as Telefónica or Repsol, have behaved in Latin America during *La década dorada* (The Golden Decade) (Casilda Béjar), can only be characterized as unscrupulously neocolonial, at a time when Latin American economies were forcefully converted to the neoliberal model. Some deals, such as Iberia's purchasing of Aerolíneas Argentinas, verge on the outrageous. As of 1999 Spain became the largest investor in Latin America after the U.S. Spanish direct investment was highly concentrated in banking, telecommunications, public services, oil and natural gas, and the seven largest Spanish corporations, BBVA, Banco Santander, Endesa, Iberdrola, Unión Fenosa and Repsol YPF had assets worth 283 billion U.S. dollars and serviced 128 million customers (Toral). In most cases, Spanish companies resorted to purchasing state enterprises and pre-existing assets when making their foreign investments. This obviously demonstrates a geopolitical division of areas of influence, by which Spanish corporations became intermediaries between the Latin American markets and global capital, while Latin American migrants flooded Spain. In a sort of *quid pro quo*, the U.S. made it possible for Spanish capital to move freely into Latin America while Spain, under Aznar's leadership, became a staunch geopolitical ally of the Bush administration (Seiglie). Does this opposite flow of capital and bodies show the emergence of a new Spanish imperialism, asks Gabilondo, or is it global capital disguised as Spanish ("One-Way Theory" 92)? Felipe González, the architect of Spanish modernization, wrote in 1999: "We owe Latin Americans so much historically that they have the right to expect us to behave like ourselves, not as the hardened managers of Wall Street" (115).

The virtual monopoly of the Spanish language market, held by a few transnational corporations consolidated in the flourishing Spanish publishing industry, such as Bertelsmann, Vivendi, Grupo Planeta and Santillana, is a case in point of this geopolitical design; the aggressive expansion of the *Instituto Cervantes*, which is modeled after the *Alliance Française,* the British Council, and the Goethe Institute, has branched out in over forty countries with more than 77 centers since its not coincidental inception in 1991, is another. The multiple activities organized and funded by the Instituto, in principle devoted to advance the study of Spanish language and culture throughout non-Spanish speaking countries and to consolidate the cultural bonds between Spanish speaking countries, ultimately promote a global version of Pan-Hispanism under the geopolitical leadership of the Spanish state. As Carmen Caffarel, current director of the Instituto Cervantes, said at the conference "Learning to Export: Cultural Products for the World," Spanish has a growing added-value, and the language which used to be the instrument of missionary zeal has become the tool of business ("El castellano"). The homology captures vividly the main tenets of a coherent design, made apparent in the *Congreso Internacional de la Lengua Española* (International Congress of Spanish Language), organized by the *Instituto* and the *Real Academia Española* (Spanish Royal Academy) in different Latin American cities every three years. The Congress has been held in Zacatecas, Mexico (1997); Valladolid, Spain (2001); Rosario, Argentina (2004); and Cartagena, Colombia (2007). The next one is planned to meet in Valparaíso, Chile, in 2010. Although every congress is focused on a different subject, two distinctive thematic foci seem to traverse them all and converge in the layout of a carefully crafted geopolitical strategy: the celebration and promotion of the cultural and ideological value of Spanish linguistic uniformity, and the appraisal and development of the economic and political value of Spanish language.

Regarding the first issue, Fernando Lázaro Carreter, then Director of the *Real Academia Española*, stated unambiguously in the inaugural lecture to the congress in Seville 1992, "Unity, since not in custody, must be nurtured and promoted. Change, absolutely necessary to keep up with the times, must be homogeneous [...] The Hispanic presence in the world today depends decisively on this linguistic unity [...] the *Real Academia* believes that the time is ripe to intensify the promotion of this not merely aesthetic, but decidedly political cause" ("La Real"). These ideas provoked several critiques at the following congresses. While Octavio Paz would say that "The Spanish of the 20th century would not exist without the creative influence of the American peoples and their diverse histories, psychologies and cultures" which means that "the Spanish spoken and written in Hispanic-America and Spain is many languages, every one distinctive and unique" ("Nuestra"); Gabriel García Márquez would claim the linguistic creativity of popular cultures and oral literatures, which mold "a language that has ceased to fit in its skin long time ago" ("Botella"). Others, like Miguel León Portilla, defended indigenous languages and denounced their historical decimation:

> There are people who believe the disappearance of Amerindian langua-
> ges is inevitable and there is no reason to lament it, since linguistic unifica-
> tion is the ultimate aspiration. But there are others, including me, who
> think that the disappearance of any language impoverishes humanity [...]
> Spanish has been enriched by Amerindian languages, whose study has
> revealed the existence of unknown linguistic categories which demonstrate
> that different linguistic structures yield very diverse worldviews and episte-
> mologies ("El español").

Although the III Congress, whose main topic was "Linguistic Identity and Globalization," allocated one section to the discussion of
"Spanish and the Indigenous communities today," and another to
"Castilian and the other languages of Spain," the denunciation of linguistic colonialism and the defense of indigenous languages galvanized
a confrontation with the message of linguistic and cultural unity
expounded by the organizers. Besides the discreet criticism raised by
Latin American official invitees, like Gabriel García Márquez, Octavio Paz, and Carlos Fuentes, less prominent intellectuals, led by Nobel
Peace Prize winner, Adolfo Pérez Esquivel, organized in Rosario the
parallel counter-congress *I Congreso de laS lenguaS*, which, "In response
to the elitist and policed notion of culture imposed by the *Real Academia* to the III International Congress of Spanish [...] became an open
space of debate that [...] repudiated the hegemony of Castilian over
other languages, as the only language, in a multi-linguistic and pluricultural continent." Moreover, they stressed their differences by stating that "It is not the same thing to speak 'about' the natives than to
speak 'with' the representatives of the native peoples who live and use
their languages" ("Adhesión"). Some literary stars invited to the *III Congreso Internacional de la Lengua Española*, such as José Saramago and
Ernesto Cardenal, also attended the *I Congreso de laS lenguaS*, which
concluded with a declaration denouncing existing colonial relations
that subjugate ethnicities and suppress diversity, and demanding the
right of indigenous peoples to linguistic and cultural self-determina-
tion ("Adhesión").

Even though the study of the economic and political value of Spanish and how better to exploit it has been less controversial and spawned less resistance than the sponsorship of linguistic uniformity, it is probably more symptomatic, because it explicitly involves the strategic development of new cultural markets for Spanish corporations, particularly regarding the publishing industry, television, cinema, Internet, and educational tourism. In 2007, for instance, study-abroad programs attracted 237,000 students to Spain who left 463 million euros to the Spanish economy, although Latin American countries, which enjoy lower costs, pose a serious challenge to this profitable business. Brazil, which has made the learning of Spanish at the secondary level optional, with an estimated market of 11 million students, and the U.S., whose 46 million Latinos comprise the world's third largest Spanish-speaking population, with a buying power near $1 trillion, are among the most sought-after emerging markets. As Enrique Iglesias said at the IV Congress in Cartagena, research on the economics of the language should be encouraged, even though "It is difficult to measure the economic value of a complex human resource which permeates our entire social, cultural, and political reality. But in order to build an Ibero-American Community of growing international importance we must persevere in promoting our linguistic integration" ("El español"). According to some of these studies, the economic value of the Spanish language amounts to 15% of the Spanish GDP; according to others, it involves 16% of the labor market (Constenla). Of course, the more consumers the language has, the higher its political and economic value.

The promotion of Spanish linguistic uniformity, and the exploitation of its economic value, set the foundation for a full-fledged geopolitical strategy, best summarized by King Juan Carlos I in the inaugural address to the III Congress held in Rosario: "Ladies and Gentlemen: the complex phenomenon of globalization brings to the horizon problems that we should not ignore. Many forecast the danger of an unstoppable homogenization which will wipe out all differences [...] From a linguistic point of view it is clear that the same globalization can assist Spanish to expand even further and consolidate itself as an international language" ("Discurso Inaugural"). Or, as the then Director of the *Instituto*, César Antonio Molina, put it, "the 21st century should be the Spanish century" ("Discurso de Clausura"). Nevertheless, this neo-imperial whiff is best made apparent in the historical analogy offered by Jon Juaristi, at that time director of the Instituto, in his closing remarks to the Congress in Valladolid:

> Yes, there is a certain similarity between the historical situation of medieval Castile and our own, as well as an obvious parallelism between medieval Spain and the present Hispanic community. As nowadays, 15th century Spaniards faced the challenges of a technological revolution, a political globalization, and an incipient global civilization [...] Beyond the excesses and injustices of the conquest and the colonial order, Spanish language set the foundations of a civilization in which the dispossessed and the oppressed would use the old Castilian language, enriched with the accents and vocabulary of Amerindian languages, to demand the recognition of their human dignity against the caste system ("Discurso de Clausura").

The economic and symbolic significance of these developments cannot be detached from the ideology of Hispanism that at different times in history has always professed some sort of trans-Atlanticism, as becomes transparent in the words of José María Aznar:

> Spain is interested in obtaining a greater Atlantic projection and in helping Europe to obtain it as well [...] because it would be suicidal not to recover what Braudel called Spain's 'transatlantic destiny.' That's why Spain has to develop a policy of 'special relations' with the Americas [...] Our common history and culture is the best foundation for sharing markets and collaborating in the international arena [...] The opening of markets, the process of privatization, the development of regional economic blocs and the emergence of a middle class who bet on the democratic system have transformed Ibero-America into a highly attractive political, economic, and social scenario (*España* 170-1).

The almost farcical squabble between Hugo Chávez and Juan Carlos I, at the closure of the Ibero-American Summit held in Santiago de Chile in November 2007, in which the provocatively plebeian manners of the mestizo, democratically elected president of Venezuela, who was actually voicing with complete disregard of diplomatic etiquette the resentment of millions of Latin Americans, were shut down by the authoritarian "¡*Por qué no te callas!*" ("Why don't you shut up!")

by the king of Spain, a descendant of the Bourbon house appointed to
the throne by a fascist dictator, is a painful reminder of the subtle and
insidious ways in which colonial relations constantly reappear.[1] Or, as
Gabilondo says, "As the original space of Spanish imperialist expansion into the Americas, the Atlantic is a foundational space and yet,
perhaps because of globalization, it is making a new appearance with a
(post)historical – and theoretical – synergy that we are only now beginning to feel, grasp, and analyze" (Introduction 93).

THE EPISTEMOLOGICAL LOOP

    This is why Hispanic Transatlantic Studies, suffused with His-
panism's trans-historical spiritualism and *de facto* monolingualism,
involve a conservative hermeneutic turn cloaked as radical criticism.
Despite repeated declarations about the need to move "beyond disciplinary and monocultural perspectives" (Kaufman and Macpherson
xix), "there is nothing particularly 'interdisciplinary' or 'border-cross-
ing' in most of these moves, which in fact reinforce the discipline's traditional reliance on the legacy of the empire. Merely inverting the sign
of the discourse and turning the apology of colonialism into postcolonial critique changes nothing, as detractors turn objectively into
accepters" (Resina, "Cold War" 96). Sometimes, the veneer of methodological audacity is no more than a reflex of the philological tradition
of loose historicism, as Faber suggests ("Economies" 26). Of course,
Transatlantic Studies had inspired a good deal of ethnically sensitive
and politically sharp analyses, particularly regarding the colonial period, which cannot be seriously studied without taking into consideration the economic, political, military and cultural flows and blows
between Europe and the Americas. But despite the existence of this
geopolitically sensitive production, and the balanced approach of the
politically conscious Latin Americanists committed to this approach, I
concur with Resina when he affirms that:

> Trans-Atlantic studies as a subspecialty within Hispanism, Franco-
> phone studies as a new focus within French, and similar disciplinary

---

[1] See among others, http://www.youtube.com/watch?v=X3Kzbo7tNLg.

displacements cover legitimate cultural territory, but they are neither more honorable, as their practitioners sometimes imply, nor intellectually broader than the national traditions from which they stem. Nor are they intrinsically multicultural; rather, they tend to reinforce the hegemony of former colonial languages, squeezing out even further the native languages and cultures, which rarely if ever come under such headings ("Cold War" 81).

In fact, this surreptitious repoliticization can be found in the most authoritative definitions of Hispanic Transatlantic Studies, such as the one provided by Julio Ortega, one of its most distinguished advocates:

> ...free from disciplinary genealogies which reduce texts to their origins, and from the liberal bias which entails a subject reduced to the role of victim, either colonial, sexual, imperial or ideological, Transatlantic Studies maps out the European, American and African flows which redefine the monuments of civilization, its modern institutions and its different interpretations. For this reason, more than explaining any particular historical period, this approach gives an account of a transhistorical time traversed by narratives updated over and over ("Post-teoría" 114).

Two interwoven propositions stand out here: the claim to consider subaltern subjects not as victims of European colonization, imperialism, slavery and so on, but as full partners in the development of modern civilization, and the emergence of a transhistorical transatlantic subjectivity. I agree in regard to the liberal bias that led to the over-victimization of the victims and the postmodern celebration of marginality as an epistemological and political vantage point, but we cannot forget that the history of Latin America and Africa as well is indeed a history of victimization, domination, annihilation, exploitation and acculturation. America was part of the modern world since the very beginning, but always in a subservient and subsidiary way. We cannot thin out the intricate European, American and African colonial (and neocolonial) entanglement as simple, harmless, innocent flows of peoples, ideas and cultural artifacts, completely detached of economic structures and political designs. We have to be careful when using politically cleansed expressions such as "dialogical encounters," "contact zones," "cultural exchanges," "dynamic interactions" or "ethnic reciprocity," all notions tainted with cultural anthropology's functionalism. The very notion of a transhistorical time suggested by Ortega empties out history, that is, the historical succession of colonial formations so aptly captured by the term coloniality, originally proposed by Aníbal Quijano in order to refer to the complementary and necessary dark side of modernity and capitalism (*Colonialidad*).

So, why is Ortega so anxious to distance Transatlantic Studies from Postcolonial Studies, as well as from some unambiguously Latin American anti-colonial theories, like dependency theory or Fernández Retamar's Calibanism? It is because he considers, in a clear misreading of postcolonial theory, that "the political paradigm of imperialism and its symmetric notion of center vs. periphery, the dialectics of the master and the slave, and the ethics of otherness have been the dominant hypotheses of postcolonial studies, which entail the notion of a colonial subject deprived of identity by the brutal imposition of modernity" (Ortega, "Post-teoría" 114). As a result, in order to avoid what according to him is a simplistic and reductive interpretation, he proposes to adopt an intercultural point of view, which would allow us to demonstrate that the colonial subject does not always suffer victimization but, on the contrary, is able to negotiate her own limits and participate in a dialogue, not confined to the closure of the master's narrative. According to this, Caliban not only learns how to curse with language, but also how "to know his own limits, affirm his body, represent his own role [and] act out the identity as native that the others have attributed to him, even playing with his name and his evil reputation." Furthermore, "it is thanks to language that he can now take charge of his own mission. Names give him back the island of abundance. He still does not know what to do with this uncertain power, but learning to speak has taught him that the world becomes valuable by virtue of the way it is named [...] The language that he has learned is his first profit from becoming human" (Ortega, *Transatlantic* 35, 47). In other words, according to Ortega, Transatlantic Studies challenges an interpretation which accentuates the monstrosity of the subject in order to denounce her victimization, and portrays instead the subject "in the process of humanization and acquisition of agency" ("Post-teoría", 115). To put it differently, the colonial subject is actually empowered as a sovereign subject when she adopts the culture imposed by the colonizer; Caliban becomes wholly human – or civilized, as Domingo Faustino Sarmiento would have preferred – only after he has learned his master's language. In fact, Ortega's take on postcolonialism doesn't add much to the ideology of Hispanism, which, according to Resina, "operates as if 'the Hispanic World' represented a somewhat variegated but strictly monolingual territory" and subalternity were "the flip side of the cultural law that Hispanism furthers" ("Whose Hispanism?" 161).

However, Hispanic Transatlantic Studies can be conceptualized in entirely different terms, as in the definition provided by Eyda Merediz and Nina Gerassi-Navarro, who put the emphasis in the historical articulation of geographic movements, political power and economic structures: "Transatlantic Studies presuppose an Atlantic that is, to begin with, a geopolitical space that generates its own power structures, which explains why its foremost concern is the connection between imperialism and modernity" (614). The history of the Atlantic, according to this view, is the history of modern capitalism, which is to say the history of European colonialism and Western civilization. The history of the transatlantic trade is the history of the primitive accumulation which made possible the further development of capitalism, only successful by the continuous colonial, imperial and neocolonial expansions. I cannot agree more. Unfortunately, Hispanic Transatlantic Studies are irrevocably tainted by the ideology of Hispanism and the geopolitical designs of Spanish capitalism. Moreover, I am still unconvinced about the disciplinary legitimacy, the theoretical necessity or the strategic convenience of revamping a field that adds so little to already existing fields and is so tainted by historical crimes and ideological deception. It is true, as Resina says, that it covers a legitimate historical and cultural space, but it is also true that that space could be covered as well, as it is actually covered, by other, sometimes not less problematic fields of research, like postcolonial and cultural studies.

Therefore, I have to conclude that Transatlantic Studies (and even more so Hispanic Transatlantic Studies) do not constitute a new critical paradigm, since they rely on paradigms already widely accepted. Nor do they constitute another discipline, since they do not have a particular object of inquiry, nor propose any specific methodology, nor pinpoint a set of specific theoretical problems, all of which they partake with different disciplines and current theories in the academic market. But even more importantly, Transatlantic Studies are the result of a geographical displacement provoked by the geopolitical debunking of area studies, and an epistemological rift produced by the unstable consolidation of a flexible and combined regime of capitalist accumulation. This combined shift, which translates profound geopolitical realignments, economic transformations and epistemological dilemmas that traverse and constitute our global age, is perhaps more striking in Hispanic Transatlantic Studies' revival of the ideology of Hispanism, so confusedly entangled with the overlapping interests of Spanish capitalism and transnational corporations that Spanish cultural and moral hegemony over the Hispanic world becomes an alibi for global economics and international geopolitics.

WORKS CITED

ASOCIACIÓN DE INVESTIGADORES EN LENGUA QUECHUA. "Adhesión de ADILQ al I Congreso de laS LenguaS". Web. 26 March 2009. <http://www.adilq.com.ar/CongresoLenguas.html>.

AZNAR, José María. España. La segunda transición. Madrid: Espasa Calpe, 1994.

—. Ocho años de gobierno. Una visión personal de España. Barcelona: Planeta, 2004.

BENDER, Thomas. Foreword. The Atlantic in Global History, 1500-2000. Eds. Jorge Cañizares-Esguerra and Erik R. Seeman. Upper Saddle River, N.J.: Pearson Prentice Hall, 2007. xvii-xxi.

CAFFAREL, Carmen. "El castellano, un valor en alza." El País. El País Cultural. 17 January 2008. Web. 11 March 2009. <http://www.elpais.com/articulo/cultura/castellano/valor/alza/elpepucul/20080117elpepucul_12/Tes>.

CASILDA BÉJAR, Ramón. La década dorada. Economía e inversiones españolas en América Latina. Madrid: Universidad de Alcalá de Henares, 2002.

CASTILLO, Susan and Ivy SCHWEITZER, eds. The Literatures of Colonial America. Oxford: Blackwell, 2001.

CONSTENLA, Tereixa. "El español, un filón huérfano de prestigio." El País. El País Sociedad. 31 December 2008. Web. 10 March, 2009. <http://www.elpais.com/articulo/sociedad/espanol/filon/huerfano/prestigio/elpepisoc/20081231elpepisoc_1/Tes>.

FABER, Sebastiaan. "'La hora ha llegado.' Hispanism, Pan-Americanism, and the Hope of Spanish/American Glory (1938-1948)." Ideologies of Hispanism. Ed. Mabel Moraña. Nashville: Vanderbilt UP, 2005: 62-104.

—. "Economies of Prestige: The Place of Iberian Studies in the American University." Hispanic Research Journal 9.1 (2008): 7-32.

FERNÁNDEZ, James D. "Longfellow's Law: The Place of Latin America and Spain in U.S. Hispanism, circa 1915." *Spain in America. The Origins of Hispanism in the United States.* Ed. Richard L. Kagan. Urbana: U of Illinois P, 2002. 122-41.

GABILONDO, Joseba. "One-Way Theory: On the Hispanic-Atlantic Intersection of Postcoloniality and Postnationalism and its Globalizing Effects." *Arachne @ Rutgers* 1.1 (2001). Web. 9 March 2009. <http://arachne.rut gers.edu/vol1_1gabilondo.htm>.

—. Introduction. *The Hispanic Atlantic. Arizona Journal of Hispanic Cultural Studies* 5 (2001): 91-193.

GARCÍA MÁRQUEZ, Gabriel. "Botella al mar para el Dios de las palabras." *I Congreso Internacional de la Lengua Española. Zacatecas 1997.* Instituto Cervantes. Web. 26 March 2009. <http://congresosdelalengua.es/zaca tecas/inauguracion/garcia_marquez.htm>.

GILROY, Paul. *The Black Atlantic: Modernity and Double Consciousness.* London: Verso, 1993.

GONZÁLEZ, Felipe. *Memorias del futuro. Reflexiones sobre el tiempo presente.* Madrid: Aguilar, 2003.

GULBENKIAN COMMISSION. *Open the Social Sciences. Report of the Gulbenkian Commission on the Restructuring of the Social Sciences.* Stanford: Stanford UP, 1996.

IGLESIAS, Enrique. "El español, instrumento de integración iberoamericana." *IV Congreso Internacional de la lengua española. Cartagena 2007.* Instituto Cervantes. Web. 26 March 2009. <http://congresosdelalengua. es/cartagena/plenarias/iglesias_e.htm >.

JUARISTI, Jon. "Discurso de Clausura." *II Congreso Internacional de la Lengua Española. Valladolid 2001.* Instituto Cervantes. Web. 26 March 2009. <http://congresosdelalengua.es/valladolid/clausura/juaristi_j.htm>.

KAUFMAN, Will and Heidi SLETTEDAHL MACPHERSON. "Transatlantic Studies: A New Paradigm." *Transatlantic Studies.* Eds. Will Kaufman and Heidi Slettedahl Macpherson. Lanham, MA: UP of America, 2000. xvii-xxiii.

KING JUAN CARLOS I OF SPAIN. "Discurso Inaugural." *III Congreso Internacional de la Lengua Española. Rosario 2004.* Instituto Cervantes. Web. 26 March 2009. <http://congresosdelalengua.es/rosario/inauguracion/ rey.htm>.

LACLAU, Ernesto. Preface. *Post-Theory. New Directions in Criticism.* Eds. Martin McQuillan, Graeme Macdonald, Robin Purves and Stephen Thomson. Edinburgh: Edinburgh UP, 1999. vii.

LÁZARO CARRETER, Fernando. "La Real Academia y la unidad del idioma" *Congreso de Sevilla 1992.* Centro Virtual Cervantes. Web. 26 March

2009. <http://cvc.cervantes.es/obref/congresos/sevilla/apertura/Aper_Laz_Car.htm>.

LEWIS, Martin W. and Karen WIGEN. "A Maritime Response to the Crisis in Area Studies." *The Geographical Review* 89.2 (1999): 161-171.

LOUREIRO, Ángel G. "Desolación y miseria del hispanismo." *Quimera* 138 (1995): 33-36.

MEREDIZ, Eyda M. and Nina GERASSI-NAVARRO, eds. *Otros estudios transatlánticos: lecturas desde lo latinoamericano.* Special issue of *Revista Iberoamericana OK* 75.228 (2009): 605-636.

MOLINA, César Antonio. "Discurso de Clausura." *III Congreso Internacional de la Lengua Española. Rosario 2004.* Instituto Cervantes. Web. 26 March 2009. <http://congresosdelalengua.es/rosario/clausura/molina_c.htm>.

MORAÑA, Mabel, ed. Introduction. *Ideologies of Hispanism.* Nashville: Vanderbilt UP, 2005: ix-xxi.

ORTEGA, Julio. "Post-teoría y estudios transatlánticos." *Iberoamericana* 3.9 (2003): 109-117.

—. Presentación. "Travesías cruzadas: hacia la lectura transatlántica." *Iberoamericana* 3.9 (2003): 105-108.

—. "Los estudios transatlánticos al primer lustro del siglo XXI. A modo de presentación." *Transatlántica: idas y vueltas de la literatura y la cultura hispano-americana en el siglo XX.* Dossier coordinado por Francisco Fernández de Alba y Pedro Pérez del Solar. *Iberoamericana* 6.21 (2006).

—. *Transatlantic Translations. Dialogues in Latin American Literature.* London: Reaktion Books, 2006.

PAZ, Octavio. "Nuestra lengua." *I Congreso Internacional de la Lengua Española. Zacatecas 1997.* Instituto Cervantes. Web. 26 March 2009. <http://congresosdelalengua.es/zacatecas/inauguracion/paz.htm>.

LEÓN PORTILLA, Miguel. "El español y el destino de las lenguas amerindias." *II Congreso Internacional de la Lengua Española. Valladolid 2001.* Instituto Cervantes. Web. 26 March 2009. < http://congresosdelalengua.es/valladolid/inauguracion/leon_m.htm >.

QUIJANO, Aníbal. "Colonialidad del poder, eurocentrismo y América Latina". *La colonialidad del saber: eurocentrismo y ciencias sociales. Perspectivas latinoamericanas.* Ed. Edgardo Lander. Buenos Aires: CLACSO, 2000.

RESINA, Joan Ramon. "Cold War Hispanism and the New Deal of Cultural Studies." *Spain Beyond Spain. Modernity, Literary History, and National Identity.* Eds. Bradley S. Epps and Luis Fernández Cifuentes. Lewisburg: Bucknell UP, 2005. 70-108.

—. "Whose Hispanism? Cultural Trauma, Disciplined Memory, and Symbolic Dominance." Moraña. 160-186.

SANTANA, Mario. "El hispanismo en los Estados Unidos y la 'España plural'." *Hispanic Research Journal* 9.1 (2008): 33-44.

SEIGLIE, Carlos. "Spanish Foreign Direct Investment in Latin America: A Strategy for Reducing Conflict with the U.S." Paper presented at the annual meeting of the *International Studies Association* (Montreal, March 17, 2004). 2009. *All Academic Research.* Web. 20 March 2009. <http://www.allacademic.com/meta/p72854_index.html>.

SUBIRATS, Eduardo. "Tres visiones de América." *Quimera* 137 (1995): 35-39.

TORAL, Pablo. "Spanish Investment in Latin America." FOCAL. Canadian Foundation for the Americas. 2001. Web. 20 March 2009. <http://focal.ca/pdf/Spanish%20investment%20in%20LAC.pdf>.

VALLE, José del and Luis GABRIEL-STHEEMAN. "Nationalism, hispanismo, and monoglossic culture" *The Battle over Spanish between 1800 and 2000.* Eds. Valle, José del and Luis Gabriel-Stheeman. New York /London: Routledge, 2002. 1-13.

WALLERSTEIN, Immanuel. "The Unintended Consequences of Cold War Area Studies. *The Cold War and the University: Toward an Intellectual History of the Postwar Years.* Ed. Noam Chomsky. New York: The New P, 1997. 195-231.

Postscript

Pluralism, Articulation, Containment: Knowledge Politics Across the Americas

Bret Gustafson

In January of 2009, Bolivians approved by referendum a new constitution. The document declares the country a "plurinational state" and inscribes a series of significant changes in law, politics, territorial order, and representation in the country. The constitution was written in a national constitutional convention – by representatives democratically elected from the country's political parties – yet central tenets of the document emerged out of a long history of social movement struggle and intellectual labor. Though approved in a context charged with violent right-wing opposition tactics, the text was backed by the MAS (Movement to Socialism), the party led by recently elected President Evo Morales, an indigenous coca-growers' leader. The preamble, seen in light of Latin American constitutions and constitutional histories, is remarkable. It notes in part that "[We] people this sacred Mother Earth with different faces, and we comprehend from there forward the plurality of all things and our diversity as beings and cultures."[1] Drawing inspiration from indigenous concepts of the multiplicity of knowledges and their rootedness in particular historical

---

1. *Nueva Constitución Política del Estado*: http://www.comunicabolivia.com/ nueva-constitucion-bolivia.

groundings and relationships with natural space, this recognition of plurality marks a radical shift in the official language of law and knowledge in Latin America. Though important for its recognition of indigenous rights, the shift transcends particularly indigenous issues to open space for a wider recognition of what Walter Mignolo has called "epistemic rights" – the right to know as a means of exercising a particular kind of grounded sovereignty, whether of the state itself, or of its constituent peoples. Against its critics, who imagine it to be a turn toward pre-modern theocratic principles, the text is in fact a hybrid – a progressive encounter and epistemic exchange between liberal, indigenous, socialist, and entirely novel concepts of law, rule, and the state. It is this turn toward plurality that Mignolo (this volume) defends in his spirited essay, a turn toward pluralities that is deemed a threat to stability and order by the status quo.[2]

As Catherine Walsh describes in this volume, a similar shift – however tentative – is underway in Ecuador. The country's new constitution, like Bolivia's, has also introduced a 'rethinking' of knowledge in the language of official law. These are shifts that emerge from an indigenous and Afro-descendant political and epistemic "insurgence." As Walsh writes, "one that establishes, builds, and articulates logics, practices, ethics, philosophies, and ways of life and living that interrupt the Western modern, capitalist, colonial design." Without undue romanticization of what are obviously complex processes that will yield years of conflictive debates over implementation in practice, these legal and epistemic shifts are the most visible signs of an ongoing transformation of knowledge production and politics in Latin America. It is clear that these changes – even in the seemingly similar countries of Bolivia and Ecuador – do not represent a monolithic turn, or even an easily characterizable "ideology." They are themselves marked by internal plurality. This fact highlights the pedestrian quality of analyses of journalists and writers like Jorge Castañeda (132-33), who group entire nations and regimes into outmoded categories such as "retrograde" and "populist" or "modern" "left[s]." It also challenges emerging military and security paradigms which criminalize change by viewing all efforts to rethink the state as evidence of bodies and minds

2. I consider the particular issue of "plurinationalism" in Gustafson ("Manipulating").

outside of reason and law.[3] On the contrary, these shifts represent possibilities, ruptures, and interventions that create space for rethinking
and addressing the region's ongoing paradoxes – a history of monocultural nationalism in a region of vast plurality, vast wealth and intense
gaps of inequality, democracy and racial and social exclusion, environmental degradation and an embrace of natural resource extraction and
export, and zones of relative stability alongside regions of bloody war,
violence, and criminality.

An illustrative contrast to Bolivia is Peru. Rather than moving forward on a trajectory of change, Peru appears to return to an authoritarian model of colonial violence and rule that have long characterized
its history. At this writing, the country is immersed in a drama of
modern colonialism. The rush to find and extract oil and other miner-
als has overwhelmed the rule of law and the already fragile system
of rights for indigenous people and other marginal populations in
resource-rich areas. Over 70% of the country's Amazon region is con-
cessioned to multinational oil operations, much of it in ecologically
delicate locations home to indigenous Peruvians (Finer et al.). In
recent years, through a series of legislative moves and decrees, many
unconstitutional, the government of President Alan García has accelerated and facilitated this extractive fever. Indigenous resistance, as
with other forms of community opposition to large-scale extractive
operations, has grown in the past several years. In early 2009, after
receiving little attention in the formal arenas of law, Amazonian indigenous movements turned to other tactics – blocking rivers, seizing
oil fields, and blockading highways. In early June of 2009, the state

---

3. I refer here to legislative actions aimed at criminalizing social movement
protest in a number of Latin American countries by labeling it "terrorism" (El Salvador, Mexico, Chile, among others). I also refer to official U.S. government documents that have in recent years portrayed indigenous movements as "challenges to
governance," "threats to stability" or the potential source of "armed violence," and a
"source of conflict" (see National Intelligence Council, 2000, 2004). These stances
implicitly situate protest of any sort as outside of the law, suggesting that dissent
(and in particular what is termed "communal" types of epistemic alterity) naturally
runs counter to the logic and reason of Western modernity. It should be emphasized
that the knowledge projects discussed herein share little with the kinds of anti-West-
ern epistemic regimes (real or imagined) that have fueled the discourse of "the war
on terror" and its tragic sequiturs.

ordered the military to open fire on a blockade at Bagua, the northern portal to the Amazon region. At least ten indigenous Peruvians were killed and nearly one hundred wounded. Several hundred were detained. Those killed at the blockade were armed only with sticks and stones, unable to defend themselves against bullets. Yet these killings provoked reprisals against the police in other sites, leading to the equally tragic deaths of some 23 officials, though details of the events remain contested (Anaya 6).

Beyond the tragedy of the violence, only the most recent visible sign of deeper histories of exclusion and violence in the region, what is revelatory in relation to the rethinking of intellectuals is how the case reveals stark contrasts to Bolivia and highlights a deeper clash unfolding in the region. On one side is an emerging scenario of change built on the articulatory work of social movements and their various projects of epistemic transformation. On the other rises a politics of containment and retrenchment in defense of existing relations and structures of political and economic power. It is in this space of contestation, not simply between older paradigms of Left and Right, but between a plurality of political-epistemic contests and the entrenched interests of stability over change, that our 'rethinking' of intellectuals in Latin America was undertaken. Knowledge claims – to truth, reason, and the right to ascribe legitimacy to temporal, cultural, social and political-economic orders and imaginaries – are at the heart of these political contests.

In the case of Peruvian oil, cabinet ministers ensconced in Lima, far from the effects of exploration and drilling, argued that oil brought only positive impacts for the nation. From a different space of comprehension, indigenous organizations, speaking from their rootedness in place and experience, decried environmental destruction, political marginalization and social dislocation linked to oil activities. These were processes that not only generated physical effects, but in their link to the procedural exclusion of indigenous Peruvians, politically negated their very existence. Peru's President Alan García contributed to this situation by reasoning that the Amazon and its peoples were outside of the present, beyond the law, and in opposition to progress – a space devoid of people and knowledge, a legitimate object of rational exploitation by and for the country's 'real' citizens. In a 2007 article, García argued in defense of the export of natural resources by suggesting that those who opposed it were "dogs in the manger" (from *perros del hortelano*). The saying derived from Aesop's story of the dog who refused to let the ox eat his straw, nor did it eat it itself, enshrined in the common Spanish saying *el que ni come ni deja comer*. García suggested that indigenous peoples were among the lazy and indolent *perros del hortelano* who were obstacles to resource use afflicted with "ideologies that have been superseded," and whose logic for opposing resource extraction was, 'If I cannot do it, then no one will.' This was a crude recasting of colonial reason in modern developmentalist terms. After the killings at Bagua, García found it easy to say with the support of a mass media characterized by long history of racism against those called *chunchos* ("savages" of the Amazon) that any recognition of indigenous claims not only implied weakness in the face of foreign conspiracies, but a return to irrationality:

> The basic principle of society is order ... [these indigenous] people do not wear a crown, these are not first class citizens *(ciudadanos de primera clase)* [such] that 400,000 *nativos* can say to 28 million *Peruvians*, 'you do not have the right to come here [to the Amazon].' No way. This is a terrible error and whoever thinks this way wants to take us to irrationality, to primitive regression, to the past *(el retroceso primitivo, en el pasado)* (Peru.com, emphasis added).

PLURALISM AND CONTAINMENT: TACTICAL ARTICULATIONS

These cases – Bolivia's novel constitutional turn and Peru's colonial retrenchment– reveal wider patterns of knowledge politics that are at the heart of the contributions to this volume. Specifically, they illustrate what we might call a dynamic of "pluralism" confronting a politics of "containment" – both of which operate through tactical articulations between knowledge production and grounded politics, across multiple geographic and institutional scales of political, social, and cultural life. In what follows I discuss these ideas as a way of thinking about intellectual transformations and highlight how the chapters in the volume illustrate these processes. I comment in particular on two key themes, the linkages between aesthetics, temporality, and race and the geopolitics of knowledge, tied to what Arturo Escobar has called competing modes of "localization" operating through procedures of knowledge production and validation (32).

I will suggest – as evidenced in the interdisciplinary conversation represented herein – that the "rethinking" of intellectuals in Latin America must negotiate multiple scales and forms of intellectual activity and consider how these intersect with multiple modalities of analysis and representation. These are tactical articulations to consider within the social milieu of a myriad of kinds of intellectual labors and actors under study, as well as between these sites and more (and less) distant nodes of more conventional academic production. The expressions of epistemic pluralism and the politics of containment both unfold through such tactical articulations, linkages that transcend boundaries of language, culture, nation, and state, yet which also reground themselves or congeal at particularly grounded nodes of politics that shape and reshape peoples' lives within these deeply politicized spaces of practice. In short, intellectual articulations are political networks.

Hall's formulation of the concept of articulation is generally referenced in relation to the congealment of identity positions in shifting historical and structural circumstances, projects nurtured by and often "articulated" through the work of public intellectuals and social actors, returning cultural production to projects of identity formation. This kind of articulation and mediation by intellectuals of various forms – once lettered elite, vanguardist intellectual, or revolutionary leader, now the think tank actor, movement activist, media commentator, or hip-hop artist – are certainly part of what intellectual politics are about. However, the dislocations and movements described throughout this volume transcend local political arenas and identity projects. These kinds of articulations – as networks – link plural subject positions and epistemic categories through translations, partial appropriations, or selective mimetism that crosses boundaries of the nation, locality, and conventional categories of social and ideological order. These articulations join projects in often ephemeral and contingent ways across different scales and spaces, as suggested by the anthropologist Anna Tsing, rather than necessarily congealing as permanent or durable formations. As inter-epistemic exchanges and translations, these present a challenge to familiar modes of analysis which tend to link positions, subjects, and discourses (language, culture, ethnicity, class) in a more static mode. By this I refer to articulations across intel-

lectual and political arenas and across heterogeneous subject positions
– for example, between global activists and local movements in the
Caribbean and Brazil; between indigenous organizations, spiritual
leaders and foreign linguists in Guatemala; or between neoconserva-
tive D.C. Beltway think tanks and violent urban movements in eastern Bolivia. Many such articulations are described in this volume. To
characterize them as "tactical" acknowledges and draws attention
to their active work of "intervention" – after Moraña in this volume –
in processes of political transformation at multiple scales.

The concept of tactical articulations draws our attention to the
networked character of knowledge production across space and social
locations and leaves us open to engaging intellectual work not only as
the congealment of closed corpus of discourse (or ideology), or the
pursuit of the embrace of a singular ideological stance, but rather
invites us to engage and to analyze spaces and processes of translation
and mediation across epistemically plural communities (c.f. Rappaport, Gustafson, Escobar). Analytically, this entails pursuing an understanding of linkages between multiple forms, media, and contexts of
intellectual production, representation, and practice as these move
across space and time, but also come to ground in specific moments of
transformation – be they in the constitutional convention of Bolivia
or the highways of Bagua, northern Peru.

This rethinking thus entails not rejecting or abandoning existing
paradigms of analysis or political action, but reconsidering them in
relation to emergent and contingent, often uncertain redirections.
This calls for a rupture in our own intellectual labors and analytical
practices – or at least a disposition to rethink them – which parallels
the kinds of ruptures in intellectual and political work that we see in the
region. As such, rethinking intellectuals is a question of rethinking
epistemic "pluralism" – engaging heterogeneity and multiplicity. This
is not a postmodern deconstructive project, but a constitutive one. It
should be as much concerned with novelty and change as it is with
comprehending the politics of epistemic "containment" – the modalities through which power at various scales shapes, silences, or seeks to
domesticate emergent epistemic projects or redirect them toward
familiar and manageable forms.

These comments are a way of highlighting the deeply contested
– and intensely plural – political status of knowledge(s) and transfor-

mations underway across Latin American states and societies. The dissolution of traditional centers of intellectual production (Moraña, this
volume), the erosion of the lettered city as the epistemic center now
challenged by a multiplicity of new media and new voices from the
margins (Mignolo), the eruption from within the literal city itself of
new actors empowered by new technologies as older modes of communication wither away (Yúdice, in this volume); and the disruption
of the category of intellectual itself – which, given no singular meaning in this book – now emerges from within social movements, think
tanks, NGOs, bloggers, media outlets, development agencies, and corporations, as well as a more traditional – yet multifaceted – academy.
Rather than worrying over the categories, this suggests in one sense
that rethinking intellectual production in terms of *movements* – and
tactical articulations – may provide a useful way of rethinking the various *loci of enunciation* and connections between them through which
intellectual work emerges and comes to ground in political action. As
Moraña points out, these shifts are tied to the emergence of new social
actors, the changing form of the public sphere and the juncture of new
technologies of communication with new meanings of once familiar
tropes of *nation, race, class, democracy,* and so on, fundamental political
shifts which may in some contexts represent the unsettling of structural, political, and economic relations of power. These shifts in many
ways, and perhaps paradoxically so, are tied to the relative success of
democratization processes in much of the region.[4]

    In light of this dynamic of tactical articulation across a sphere of
pluralist knowledge politics and the politics of containment, recent

---

4. I say paradoxically because much of the top-down democratization discourse
was linked to projects of political and ideological containment (in the service of
neoliberal doctrine) and the wider project of U.S. hegemony in the region. The trans-
mutation of democratization rhetoric into the harder forms of control – the drug
wars, militarization, and the tacit embrace of non-democratic sectors (as in the case
of Honduras' 2009 coup d'état, to name the most recent) are now questioned by the
democratically elected progressive regimes and their social movement backers. There
was of course also a broader grassroots democratization project underway that
engaged and contested the electoralist and tutelary 'democratization' spearheaded by
elites during the 1990s. These deeply contested forms and meanings of "democracy"
in the region, are themselves part of the ongoing epistemic struggle we discuss here
(see French; Mignolo, in this volume; Paley).

events like the passage of the Bolivian "plurinational" constitution and the tragic violences of Bagua, Peru, are illustrative. On the one hand, the Bolivian constitution – as a constellation and congealment of a multiplicity of alternative knowledge projects that have a long history in the country – represents at one level the insurgent interpellation or "intervention" into the state form by critical intellectual and social movements. It is a pluralist and articulated document, permeated at once by indigenous concepts of "living well" and acknowledgements of indigenous rights to knowledge and autonomy; socialist orientations toward property and the state, and an array of liberal and western understandings of law, democracy, and economy.

In Peru, in the embodied "articulation" of indigenous movements in mobilization on the rivers and highways (along with their multiple national and transnational allies) and in the colonial counterattack of the state (with its own ideological and institutional supports elsewhere, as in the global oil regime), we see how pluralism and containment come to ground. Certain knowledges – the embodied and lived exercise of voice and truth seen on the highways, rivers, and communities of the Amazon – revindicate and express resistant subjectivities. Similar processes can be seen historically (as in the above chapters by Mazzotti, and Acree) or contemporarily (as in Walsh, Mignolo, Yúdice, Maxwell, and Ajpub'). They inevitably challenge and undermine dominant subject positions and institutionalized forms of epistemic production and validation. In doing so they enunciate and articulate new forms of truth, such that their enactments or interventions should themselves be seen as constitutive acts. In response, the colonial stance of containment as voiced by Alan García positions itself as the timeless and placeless voice of ongoing modernization. It is a position perhaps doomed to extinction, but possessed of destructive power in the present, whether in Bagua, Honduras, or Bolivia.

There is therefore novelty and sameness in Latin American intellectual projects, the former represented in an array of unprecedented shifts and articulations, the latter evidenced in the stubborn recourse to violence of a neocolonial form or lingering in older paradigms of absolutist struggle. There is also continuity, such that the current scenario is not one of a postmodern free for all, an epistemic space of creativity, if not chaos, which might be celebrated without concern for social and historical groundings. To speak of epistemic pluralism

requires paying empirical attention to groundings of intellectual projects and agendas in relation to ongoing issues of contention: structural
inequalities magnified by the respatializing of politics – making of
some citizens privileged bearers of possibility and others marginal bodies outside of society and law; the legacies of patriarchal coloniality
that manifest themselves in durable racism and gendered exclusions;
the risks and possibilities of new models of development and democracy linked to new forms of nationalism – all contending with the resurgence of militarized (neo)liberalization projects; the shadow economies
which move drugs, guns, and people; the multiple crises of the urban
milieu; and the ongoing significance of rural struggle now charged
with environmental extraction and resurgent agroindustrial expansion;
and finally, the reconfiguring of the state and the nation against the
premature announcement of the demise of both. It is against this more
familiar backdrop of Latin American economic and social history that
today's intellectual pluralism, heterogeneity, movement, and translocal
articulations must be engaged.

Our conference and this volume thus respond to this conjuncture
through an interdisciplinary and international dialogue tied to an
ongoing rethinking of academic labors as new technologies, challenges, and audiences intensify pressure on the paradigms of university
knowledge production. For U.S.-based academics these realities are
often obscured by attempts to sanitize or detach intellectual work
from grounded processes of change. In fact, drawing attention to these
very real interconnections and articulations, as well as enacting them
in our own practice, is both a starting point and a defining condition
of both distanced academic analysis and grounded intellectual politics
in Latin America today.

RACE AND THE AESTHETICS OF INTELLECTUAL BODIES

There is throughout this volume a recurring recognition of the linkage between knowledge projects and the production of temporalities.
As a theme, temporality intersects a range of cases. Arango's chapter, on
the disjunctures between synchronicity and temporal uncertainty in
intellectual debates over Cuba's past, present, and future is particularly
revelatory in this sense. The issue of temporality and decolonization

– and the framing of postcolonialism – are also central, and in particular a number of chapters highlight the question of race and racism, core components of the coloniality of power (see Mignolo, herein). Race and racial imaginaries are of course linked to the construction of particular kinds of subjects (indigenous peoples and Afro-Latin Americans). But racial imaginaries also penetrate and structure political imaginaries. These include the 'darkening' of Lula, poverty, and populism voiced by Fernando Henrique Cardoso in John French's chapter; the racialization and denigration of populism in the figure of Gálvez' Argentine Calibán (Aguiar); the anti-racist and decolonizing thrust of the Ecuadoran constitution (Walsh); the subtle, in some ways silenced but implicit resistance and negotiation of mestizo (Mazzotti) or Afro-Uruguayan intellectuals (Acree); or the 'whitening' of academic, urban, and 'urbane' labors embedded in the overarching trope of the lettered city, seen critically across a number of these pieces.

This attention to the intersection of temporality and race also highlights the *aesthetic* politics of intellectual work, in many ways the fundamental axis around which struggles of pluralism and containment revolve. As many authors in this volume have pointed out, this is a dismissal of the Other – seen implicitly or explicitly as ugly, undesirable, or outside the frames of acceptable form, genre or style or even the kinds of bodies best suited for articulating modern knowledge claims. Whether these dismissals are couched in critiques of an 'uncouth' Lula, the "filthy and crazy" Negro intellectual (as cited by Acree, herein), young urbanites disrupting the formalities of Chilean presidential power (after Yúdice), of an unruly Chávez who is told to shut up by the King of Spain (after Trigo, this volume),[5] or of indigenous people questioning Western paradigms – all are, at base, epistemic dismissals. The aesthetic can of course be subversive (after Del Sarto), but also works to contain, setting out proper and desirable forms and actors of knowledge, ordering acceptable media, for instance, against the unruly, or 'vulgar' work of those who dissent. All are denials of epistemic

5. At the same event, Spain's Socialist President José Luis Rodríguez Zapatero followed on the King's admonition and echoed this colonial aestheticization of rights to speak and know when he reminded Chávez in a paternalistic and didactic tone that he should "have some respect," since, after all, "forms give being to things" (*las formas dan el ser a las cosas*). See: http://www.youtube.com/watch?v=X3Kzbo7tNLg.

rights. All are also culturally mediated ways to deny the Other the status of what Benhabib calls "epistemic contemporary," that is, one who
is acknowledged as occupying a shared time and space (and right to
know and speak) despite epistemic plurality. This denial that congeals
around the triad of temporality, aesthetics, and race denies the possibility of epistemic encounter, engagement, and exchange. The articulation of pluralities is a challenge to it, the politics of containment make
of this denial a central instrument. It is thus important to account for
an aesthetics of knowledge production and validation procedures, one
that takes into account the ways that the proper and desirable come to
mediate and structure the ascription of legitimacy and truth.

SPATIALITY AND GEOPOLITICS OF KNOWLEDGE

A second related theme that transects these chapters is the connection between knowledge production and the production of space and
spatiality – the varying ways in which social and cultural relations are
constituted by and constitute particular localities. Here a rethinking of
different forms of "localization" (Escobar) can be a useful way of distinguishing articulations of plurality from practices of containment,
and can yield new conceptualizations of older categories like state and
nation, as well as the often underspecified usage of terms like globalization (see Ortiz, this volume).

For instance, Trigo's discussion of Transatlantic Studies and the
notion of Transatlantic Hispanism highlights the articulation between
the theoretical work of academy-based intellectuals and emergent cultural projects that aim to produce new forms of geopolitical and economic hegemony. For Trigo, transatlantic Hispanism centralizes
epistemic, cultural, and linguistic authority (in Spain), while localizing
(or vernacularizing) peripheral places (in Latin America). The vehicle
is primarily a concern for Spanish language unification and normaliza-
tion politics, all of which is directly tied to a particular regime of
political and economic power. This is paralleled by Ortiz' penetrating
analysis of English language dominance in academic labor (especially
the so-called 'hard' sciences). While English is less geographically centralized, its hegemony has structuring effects on knowledge production, creating hierarchies of spaces, subjects, and epistemic practices

– between, for instance, sciences assumed to be unmediated by language and thus best suited to English and social sciences and humanities more rooted in locality and specificity, implicitly suggesting that the former (and the English language) are more valid modes of knowledge production than the latter. This generates a myth of quality that obscures the often parochial and provincial character of English language academic work. In another vein, this brings to the fore the ways that language and knowledge are spatialized and spatializing, and have concrete effects in the distribution of symbolic, economic, and social value. Maxwell and Ajpub's discussion of the centrality of place (often very specific places) and community as anchors of epistemic authority is a crucial counter example to such projects, evidencing a third kind of localization – what Mignolo describes as the "communal" – in which the particularities of place, experience and history become a potential source of knowledge that might recenter and reconstitute communities fragmented by years of genocidal and colonial violence. These spatializing processes and effects – alongside the stubborn persistence of colonial narratives tied to aesthetics, temporality, and race – are core themes, in my reading, that emerge in consideration of Latin American knowledge projects today.

The Missing Intellectuals: Scientists and Neo-Neoliberals

Our volume is of course limited, and leaves room for other explorations of "intellectual" work which offer themes for future reflection. The first is that of science and technology and its expansions into governance and governmentality. The rising prominence of regionally specific scientific labor and knowledge production is addressed herein by Ortiz (on the dilemma of English dominance and the risks of parochial English-centric provincialism) and Yúdice (on the politics of intellectual property). However, there are emergent processes in the region that reflect the new technological power of rising hegemons like Brazil, ongoing situations of dependency or new kinds of colonialism in certain areas of technology and capital (often agro-industrial, as with GMOs), and the imbrications between competing models of development and technological trajectories. This is evidenced, for example, in Brazil, where science linked to resource extraction and energy production (in oil and biofuels) is highly advanced. This is creating a new role for Brazil on the global stage while replicating familiar hierarchies and models of economic production and political power. Can, for instance, the biofuel boom not dramatically reintrench a deeply unequal model of agrarian production (rooted in sugar and soy), thus undermining other political-epistemic projects in the country? On the other hand, will Brazil's new role as a pioneer in offshore drilling (and the technological prowess it reflects) offer transformative social possibilities as Lula's regime argues? A consideration of these emerging articulations of science, technology, and society would also be central to understanding the new politics of intellectual labor in Latin America.

Though touched on in some of the historical contextualizations herein (see, for instance, Aguiar), another issue which merits more analysis is that of the intellectual projects and practices of the powerful. In today's Latin America, these intellectual projects appear to coincide with the dramatic erosion – or active destabilization of – categories of legality, democracy, and rights and the generation of new kinds of de facto powers and politics. The "pink tide" and other contestative projects like the indigenous and Afro movements have generated a reactionary backlash among conservative elites. This intellectual Right – plural, though perhaps less so than the multiple pluralities of alternative knowledge projects described here – is regrouping around a cluster of intellectual agendas and tactical articulations. These are both mimetic of social movements (in presenting themselves in the language of civil disobedience) even as they use sophisticated tactics and abundant resources (like the mass media or new modes of violence) to rethink and redefine lines of legality and propriety in order to counter the wave of popular democracy. This (re)turn to violence accelerates even as progressive movements increasingly appeal to the rule of law, rather than armed struggle, to restructure power relations (c.f., Jan French, among others, in this volume).

Though widely networked in webs linking Europe, the U.S., and multiple points across the America of the South, in many cases these once-powerful actors have lost their formal grip on state power, marginalized by popular democracy, the retreat of development aid, and the breakdown of the neoliberal 'Washington Consensus.' Once claiming the status of oracles, with links to places and figures like Jeffrey

Sachs, Ivy League universities, or Beltway think tanks, prominent intellectuals have retreated to the (still powerful) domain of workshops, local think tanks, NGOs, and media. Many who enjoyed prominence as mainstream intellectuals during the 1990s are now vociferous critics of popular and indigenous projects. Still others have now turned to extralegal and illegal tactics given the outcome of democratic and legislative processes that have brought progressive regimes to power. The harder side of the Right's project, once embodied in state military apparatuses, now delves into the extralegal world of paramilitarism (in Colombia), the organization of urban street thugs or rural civic leagues, and 'land defense committees' (in Brazil, Peru, Bolivia); legalistic (but illegal or anti-democratic) maneuvers for disrupting progressive regimes or criminalizing social movements (as in Chile, Mexico, Peru, and El Salvador), or, as in the recent case of Honduras, the exercise of media-facilitated 'legalization' of a good old-fashioned military coup d'état.

What makes this regrouping of the Right relevant to a wider rethinking of intellectuals in Latin America is their use of networks, media, movements, and claims to truth to mobilize subjectivities and imaginaries in their battle over the present and future. Middle classes, situated as they are between the prospects of mobility and the threat of poverty, are clearly receptive audiences of these projects. Business leaders – many now more loyal to multinational flows than to national economic systems – are also avid supporters, especially in countries with weak or dependent business classes. Some young urbanites, perhaps teetering between a life of poverty in informal labors or criminality as an option for survival, are interpellated by emerging philanthropic NGOs as potential "entrepreneurs," reflecting attempts to resituate the neoliberal project as an urban-centered regional (and deeply aestheticized) process of individual achievement tied to models of personal and geopolitical "autonomy" (from democracy, from the state, or from the poor majority of the *nation*).[6] Understanding how these

6. In Bolivia, for example, this takes the form of the deification of beauty queens and business elites by the urban opposition of the East. Similarly the aesthetic value of the coat and tie (contested by leaders like Evo Morales) is foregrounded in the work of think tanks promoting "liberty" and "free markets" against the unruly threats of the state and poverty (See, e.g., CIPE, among others).

projects also find productive space in the bodies and subjectivities of the region – and in particular among youth – alongside the kinds of progressive youth media projects described, for instance, by Yúdice or the epistemic rediscoveries undertaken by some Maya youth and described here by Ajpub' – is a key task for scholars.

THE DOG IN THE MANGER

At this writing, these networks of the intellectual Right are at work trying to dismantle or contain transformations like those represented in the Bolivian constitution. Even the moderate articulation of plurality, which combines Western and other paradigms of rights and laws, is seen as a grave threat to modernity. In a recent publication, *The Ideology of the 2009 Constitution,* the Bolivian scholar Fernando Molina – collaborator of a think tank called *Fundación Milenio* – critiques the text as a "radicalization of the fragmentary vision of reality (social pluralism)," one that celebrates the environment, health, social welfare, and employment over and above "private property."[7] Rather than seeing this as a creative and transformative intervention, Molina concludes that this "will create a paternalist, prebendal, [and] corrupt State." Against pluralist articulations, a politics of containment. Molina's book was financed in part by the Center for International Private Enterprise (CIPE), a U.S.-based think tank whose initiatives called "Energizing Development" and "Information on Values" financed the publication with funding from the U.S. government by way of the National Endowment for Democracy and USAID.[8] Such are the tactical articulations involved in the production of knowledge, power, and containment.

If we return to Bagua, we also find transformative agendas confronting efforts at containment, as in the figure of President Alan García, who sees the world of truth as a world under threat. For García, this appears to be imagined as a threat against lettered cities occupied by superior races. As he imagined in one interview, Peru was threatened only by its backwards south (of Andean indigenous and "messianic" thinkers), while figures like himself, a "Latin," occupied a space

---

7. See www.fundacionmilenio.org/libros.html.
8. See CIPE and Molina.

of epistemic and political contemporaneity with "Saxons" – both with equal possibilities of leading nation-states toward modernity – despite minor cultural differences.[9] From such a perspective, any rethinking of intellectuals is a threat to modernity and progress. For García, these are interventions by "dogs in the manger" who neither eat, nor let others eat. The phrase has its own history. But beyond Aesop, the Gospel of Thomas and Lope de Vega, García's "dog in the manger" appeared to echo the more recent imperial figure of Winston Churchill. When speaking to the Peel Commission regarding the partitioning of Palestine in 1937 – and questioning Palestinians as dogs in the manger – Churchill voiced a similar kind of reason underlain by the racist logic of temporality:

> I do not agree that the dog in a manger has the final right to the manger even though he may have lain there for a very long time. I do not admit that right. I do not admit, for instance, that a great wrong has been done to the Red Indians of America or the black people of Australia. I do not admit that a wrong has been done to these people by the fact that a stronger race, a higher-grade race, a more worldly wise race to put it that way, has come in and taken their place (cited by Gilbert 120).

President Alan García could easily have said the same of Peru's indigenous citizens (and loosely, he did). It is against such expressions that the rising challenge of Latin America's plural epistemic-political projects unfold. Whether those of urban youth, indigenous movements, the recharged literary intelligentsia, Brazilian lawyers or the activists of Brazil's incipient oil-fueled progressive turn, or the backers of the 'Bolivarian Revolution' in Venezuela, these clearly bear within great transformative potential as well as possibilities of generating new modalities of exclusion. To question dominant paradigms of knowledge is not to embrace alternatives acritically. Nor is it to 'return' – as Alan García might argue – to older ideological projects. Rather, as one of our conference participants suggested, it is to express a willingness to act and think in spaces of uncertainty.

We hope to have acknowledged the significance of this reshaping of an unruly – in the positive sense – and creative public sphere.

9. Washington Post, "A Conversation."

Rethinking intellectuals should lead us neither toward ungrounded utopian cosmopolitanism nor centralizing projects of containment, but toward what Andean indigenous intellectuals might call an *epistemic tinku*. The *tinku* are ritual encounters of exchange that reflect, articulate, and act upon social and political schisms. Though sometimes violent, the *tinku* is not aimed at the elimination or the denial of the other, but at the reproduction of an ongoing inter-epistemic exchange of sociality. The exchange does not preclude mutual transformations but does rely on the dismantling of stark inequalities.

Against the overstated exhaustion of intellectual vibrancy which characterizes accounts of the decade of the 1990s – overstated because it failed to capture the thriving political work fermenting among social movements – intellectual labors in the 21st century are energized by entirely new social, environmental, and political challenges. This calls for a deep questioning of the familiar and a move beyond conventional categories. In many ways the social movements of Latin America, at least partially free of the crude logic of collective armed violence that affects transformative politics in other regions of the postcolonial world, offer an inspiring energy to those willing to embrace possibility and uncertainty. These plural modes of tactical articulation – the connections between intellectual labors of various sorts, translocal modalities of communicative exchange and translation, and intimately grounded and embodied practices that challenge the politics of containment – are at the heart of the region's transformative projects today.

WORKS CITED

ANAYA, James. "Observaciones sobre la situación de los pueblos indígenas de la Amazonía y los sucesos del 5 de junio y días posteriores en las provincias de Bagua y Utcubamba, Perú." *Informe del Relator Especial de Naciones Unidas sobre la situación de los derechos humanos y las libertades fundamentales de los indígenas.* New York: United Nations, 2009.

BENHABIB, Seyla. *The Claims of Culture: Equality and Diversity in the Global Era.* Princeton: Princeton UP, 2002.

CASTAÑEDA, Jorge. "Morning in Latin America: The Chance for a New Beginning." *Foreign Affairs* 87.5 (2008): 126-139.

CIPE (CENTER FOR INTERNATIONAL PRIVATE ENTERPRISE). *Latin American and the Caribbean: Partners for Success,* Annual Report, 2008. Web.

3 August 2009. <http://www.cipe.org/publications/report/2008/CIPE_AR2008_LAC.pdf.>

ESCOBAR, Arturo. *Territories of Difference: Place, Movements, Life,* Redes. Durham: Duke UP, 2008.

FINER, Matt, et al. "Oil and Gas Projects in the Western Amazon: Threats to Wilderness, Biodiversity and Indigenous Peoples." PLoSOne 38.3 (2008): 1-9.

GARCÍA, Alan. "Poner en valor los recursos no utilizados: El síndrome del perro del hortelano." *El Comercio* (Lima, Peru). 28 October 2007. A4. Web. 3 August 2009. <http://www.elcomercio.com.pe/edicionimpresa/html/2007-1028/el_sindrome_del_perro_del_hort.html>

GILBERT, Martin. *Churchill and the Jews: A Lifelong Friendship.* New York: Holt, 2008.

GUSTAFSON, Bret. *New Languages of the State: Indigenous Resurgence and the Politics of Knowledge in Bolivia.* Durham: Duke UP, 2009.

—. "Manipulating Cartographies: Plurinationalism, Autonomy, and Indigenous Resurgence in Bolivia." *Anthropological Quarterly* 82.4 (2009): 985-1016.

HALL, Stuart. "On Postmodernism and Articulation: An Interview with Stuart Hall, edited by L. Grossberg." *Journal of Communication Inquiry* 10.2 (1986): 45-60.

MIGNOLO, Walter. *The Idea of Latin America.* Malden, MA: Blackwell, 2005.

MOLINA, Fernando. *La ideología de la constitución 2009.* La Paz: Fundación Milenio y Center for International Private Enterprise, 2009.

NATIONAL INTELLIGENCE COUNCIL. *Global Trends 2015.* Washington, D.C.: National Intelligence Council, 2000. Web. 3 August 2009. <http://www.dni.gov/nic/PDF_GIF_global/globaltrend2015.pdf.>

—. "Latin America 2020: Discussing Long-Range Scenarios. Discussion paper on the Global Trends 2020 Project," Washington, D.C.: National Intelligence Council. 2004. Web. 3 August 2009. <http://www.dni.gov/nic/PDF_GIF_2020_Support/2004_06_06_papers/la_summary.pdf.>

PALEY, Julia. *Marketing Democracy: Power and Social Movements in Post-Dictatorship Chile.* Berkeley: U of California P, 2001.

PERU.COM. "Presidente Alan García advierte a nativos: 'Ya está bueno de protestas'." *Peru.com.* 5 June 2009. Web. 3 August 2009. <http://www.peru.com/noticias/portada20090605/37781/Presidente-Alan-Garcia-advierte-a-nativos-Ya-esta-bueno-de-protestas>.

RAPPAPORT, Joanne. *Intercultural Utopias: Public Intellectuals, Cultural Experimentation, and Ethnic Dialogue in Colombia.* Durham: Duke UP, 2005.

TSING, Anna. *Friction: An Ethnography of Global Connection.* Princeton: Princeton UP, 2005.

WASHINGTON POST. "A Conversation with Alan García: Interview by Michael Shifter." June 4, 2006.

ABOUT THE CONTRIBUTORS

WILLIAM ACREE is Assistant Professor of Spanish at Washington University in St. Louis. His present research centers on print and popular cultures in nineteenth-century Latin America, especially in the Río de la Plata region. He is coeditor of *Building Nineteenth-Century Latin America: Re-rooted Cultures, Identities, and Nations* (Vanderbilt UP, forthcoming) and *Jacinto Ventura de Molina y los caminos de la escritura negra en el Río de la Plata* (Linardi y Risso, 2008). Acree is currently completing a book that studies the development of print culture and its links to collective identity in Uruguay and Argentina from 1780 to 1910.

GONZALO AGUIAR was a Lecturer in Literary Theory at the Universidad de la República in Montevideo, Uruguay, and is currently a PhD candidate at Washington University in St. Louis. In Uruguay he was recognized by the Ministerio de Educación y Cultura for his work on the poet Alfredo Mario Ferreiro and the Uruguayan Avant-Garde. He has published on Portuguese Inquisition, Portuguese cinema, Argentinean theater, and the relation between intellectuals and power in journals such as *Latin American Theatre Review*, *Hispanic Review*, and *Maguén-Escudo* (forthcoming). His doctoral dissertation is entitled

*Campos magnéticos de la modernidad latinoamericana: una historia int-
electual de Brasil, Argentina y Uruguay (1900-1935).*

ARTURO ARANGO is a Cuban short-story writer, novelist, essayist,
screenwriter, and playwright. His personal anthology of stories *¿Quie-
res vivir otra vez?* appeared in Mexico (UNAM) in 1997. As an essayist, he has been most centrally involved with Cuban literature and
cultural life. Some of these texts have been collected in the books
Reincidencias (Abril, 1989) y *Segundas reincidencias* (Capiro, 2002).
His novels include *Una lección de anatomía* (Letras Cubanas, 1998), *El
libro de la realidad* (Tusquets, 2001), and *Muerte de nadie* (Tusquets,
2004). He is the coauthor of screenplays for *Lista de espera* (2001),
Aunque estés lejos (2003), and *El cuerno de la abundancia* (2008). He is
in the processing of publishing *El viaje termina en Elsinor,* for the
stage; *La Historia por los cuernos,* a collection of essays; and *Usos de
la razón,* a collection of short stories. He is the editorial director of *La
Gaceta de Cuba,* and the Department Head, specializing in screenplays, at the International School of Television and Film *(Escuela Internacional de Cine y Televisión)* at San Antonio de los Baños, Cuba.

JUAN PABLO DABOVE is Associate Professor of Latin American Literature at the University of Colorado at Boulder. He researches the elite
depiction of the diverse forms of rural insurgency labeled "banditry"
in postcolonial Latin American writing. On this topic, Professor
Dabove has published *Nightmares of the Lettered City: Banditry and
Literature in Latin America, 1816-1929* (2007). He is currently completing a book devoted to the same topic from the period of 1931-
2009. Professor Dabove edited *Jorge Luis Borges: políticas de la
literatura* (2008) and is coeditor (with Natalia Brizuela) of *Y todo el
resto es literatura: ensayos sobre Osvaldo Lamborghini* (2008) and with
Carlos Jáuregui of *Heterotropías: narrativas de identidad y alteridad latinoamericana* (2003).

ANA DEL SARTO is Assistant Professor of Latin American literature
and cultures in the department of Spanish and Portuguese at the Ohio
State University. Among her recent publications are *Los estudios culturales latinoamericanos hacia el siglo XXI*, coedited with Alicia Ríos and
Abril Trigo (special issue of *Revista Iberoamericana)* and *The Latin*

American Cultural Studies Reader, also coedited with Alicia Ríos and Abril Trigo, published by Duke UP. She has also published articles on Latin American discourses on criticism (literary criticism, cultural critique, cultural studies), on the interdisciplinary relations between the Humanities and the Social Sciences, on contemporary Latin American women narrative, and on Latin American cinema. She has just finished a book manuscript titled *Sospecha y goce: una genealogía de la crítica cultural chilena,* which will be published in Cuarto Propio, Santiago de Chile.

JOHN D. FRENCH is a Professor of History at Duke University whose specialties include labor and politics in Brazil and the rise of alt-global politics. His most recent books include *Drowning in Laws: Labor Law and Brazilian Political Culture* (2004) and the *The Gendered Worlds of Latin American Women Workers* (1997). "Another World Is Possible: The Rise of the Brazilian Workers' Party and the Prospects for Lula's Government," *Labor: Studies in Working Class History of the Americas* (2005) draws from a current book manuscript entitled *Lula's Transformative Politics of Cunning: From Trade Unionism to the Presidency in Brazil.*

JAN HOFFMAN FRENCH (PhD Cultural Anthropology, Duke University; J.D. University of Connecticut School of Law) is Assistant Professor of Anthropology at the University of Richmond. She has held postdoctoral fellowships at the Kellogg Institute for International Studies at Notre Dame, Northwestern University, and the University of Maryland, College Park. French has published articles in *American Ethnologist, American Anthropologist, The Americas,* and *Political and Legal Anthropology Review.* Her book, *Legalizing Identities: Becoming Black or Indian in Northeastern Brazil* was published by U of North Carolina P in June 2009. Before becoming an anthropologist, French practiced law.

AJPUB' PABLO GARCÍA IXMATÁ is a sociolinguist and level I researcher at the Institute of Linguistics and Education of the Universidad Rafael Landívar, in Guatemala City, Guatemala. Ajpub', who speaks and works in Tz'utujil, Kaqchikel, K'iche, and Spanish, has published widely on Maya languages, linguistics, and epistemologies.

Among others, this work includes a Tz'utujil Grammar, publications on the teaching of Maya languages, and presentations on the mass media and the Maya in Guatemala. He currently works as a professor of linguistics and linguistic issues at various universities in Guatemala City and with the *Academia de Lenguas Mayas,* one of the leading Maya organizations involved in linguistic and epistemic politics. His current work focuses on the politics and practice of Maya epistemologies, efforts that engage academic spheres, Maya religious actors (daykeepers), and Maya cultural movements. He is currently working with Judith Maxwell on a project on the contemporary significance of Maya sacred spaces and on the cultural conflicts and politics related to their use and (non-Maya) appropriation.

BRET GUSTAFSON received his PhD in Social Anthropology from Harvard University (2002) and is an Assistant Professor of Anthropology at Washington University in St. Louis. He is the author, most recently, of *New Languages of the State: Indigenous Resurgence and the Politics of Knowledge in Bolivia* (Duke, 2009) and the coeditor (with Niki Fabricant), of *Remapping Bolivia: Territory and Resources in a Plurinational State* (forthcoming). His research focuses on indigenous movements in Bolivia and on the cultural politics of natural gas and regional transformation in Bolivia and Brazil.

IXQ'ANIL, JUDITH M. MAXWELL holds a BA in TESOL from Justin Morrill College, an MA in linguistics from Michigan State University, and a joint PhD in Linguistics and in Anthropology from the University of Chicago. She began working with Maya peoples in 1973, when she joined the *Proyecto Lingüístico Francisco Marroquín* (PLFM) in Guatemala. Her recent publications include *Kaqchikel Chronicles* (2006) from the University of Texas Press, coauthored with Dr. Robert M. Hill II, *¿La ütz awäch?: Introduction to Kaqchikel Maya Language* (2006), University of Texas Press, with Drs. Walter E. Little and R. McKenna Brown and *Oxlajuj Aj: Kaqchikel Tijonïk* (2006) from Editorial Junajpu' with Dr. Walter E. Little. Building on the *Kaqchikel Chronicles,* and working with modern *ajq'ija'* (cf. Yucatec *ajk'in*), her current research project maps, records and describes the social history of active ritual sites in the Kaqchikel region of *Kaqulew.* Co-construction of knowledge in the academic endeavor is a key theme in her research and teaching. She and her co-directors run a Kaqchikel Language and Culture program in which non-Kaqchikel speakers learn the language, while testing models of "Western" scholarship on the Maya in the crucible of autochthonous intellectual critique.

JOSÉ ANTONIO MAZZOTTI is Professor of Latin American Literature and Chair of the Department of Romance Languages at Tufts University. He is also President of the International Association of Peruvianists since 1996. Prof. Mazzotti has published *Coros mestizos del Inca Garcilaso: resonancias andinas* (1996), *Poéticas del flujo: migración y violencia verbales en el Perú de los 80* (2002), *Incan Insights: El Inca Garcilaso's Hints to Andean Readers* (2008), seven volumes of poetry, and over fifty articles on Latin American colonial literature and contemporary poetry. He has also edited *Agencias criollas: la ambigüedad "colonial" en las letras hispanoamericanas* (2000), *"Discurso en Loor de la Poesía". Estudio y edición, by Antonio Cornejo Polar* (2000), and coedited *Creole Subjects in the Colonial Americas: Empires, Texts, Identities* (2009), *The Other Latinos: Central and South Americans in the United States* (2007), *Edición e interpretación de textos andinos* (2000), and *Asedios a la heterogeneidad cultural. Libro de homenaje a Antonio Cornejo Polar* (1996).

WALTER MIGNOLO is the William H. Wannamaker Professor of Literature and Romance Studies and a Professor of Literature, Cultural Anthropology, and Romance Languages at Duke University. His work focuses on Coloniality and Globalization in Latin America and also Spanish. His publications include *The Darker Side of the Renaissance: Literacy, Territoriality and Colonization* (1995), *Globalization, Civilization Processes and the Relocation of Languages and Cultures, in The Cultures of Globalization* (1998), *Local Histories/Global Designs: Coloniality, Subaltern Knowledges and Border Thinking* (1999), *Globalization and the Borders of Latinity, in The Latin American Perspectives on Globalization,* (2002), *The Geopolitics of Knowledge and the Colonial Difference* (2003), *The Idea of Latin America* (2005), and *Globalization and the De-Colonial Option* (2007).

MABEL MORAÑA is William H. Gass Professor of Arts and Sciences and Director of Latin American Studies at Washington University, St.

Louis, where she teaches in the Dept. of Romance Languages and Literatures and International and Area Studies. She was Director of Publications of the *Instituto Internacional de Literatura Iberoamericana* for 12 years and taught as Visiting Professor at the University of California, Santa Cruz, Harvard, Universidad Andina Simon Bolivar (Quito), UNAM, etc. Some of her latest books are *Crítica impura* (2004), and the coeditions *Coloniality at Large: Latin America and the Post-colonial Debate* (2008), *Colonialidad y critica en America Latina* (2008) and *Revisiting the Colonial Question in Latin America* (2008).

RENATO ORTIZ has a doctorate in Sociology and Anthropology from the *École de Hautes Études en Sciences Sociales*, Paris. Currently he is Professor of Sociology at UNICAMP, Brazil. He has taught also at the universities of Lovaina, Mato Grosso, Campinas (Sao Paulo), at the Latin American Institute, Columbia, the Kellogg Institute at the University of Notre Dame and the National School of Anthropology and History (ENAH) in Mexico. He is the author of *Cultura e modernidade* (1991), *Mundialização e cultura* (1994), *Um outro território: ensaios sobre a mundialização* (1996), *O próximo e o distante: Japão e modernidade-mundo* (2000); *Ciências Sociais e trabalho intelectual* (2002); *Modernidad y espacio: Benjamin en París* (2000), among others.

ABRIL TRIGO is Professor of Latin American cultures and Director of the Center of Latin American Studies at Ohio State University. He is the author, among other titles, of *Caudillo, estado, nación. Literatura, historia e ideología en el Uruguay* (1990), *¿Cultura uruguaya o culturas linyeras? (Para una cartografía de la neomodernidad posuruguaya)* (1997), *Memorias migrantes. Testimonios y ensayos sobre la diáspora uruguaya* (2003), and coeditor of *The Latin American Cultural Studies Reader* (2004). He is currently working on two projects: *Crisis y transfiguración de los estudios culturales latinoamericanos* and *Crítica de la economía político-libidinal de la cultura.*

CATHERINE WALSH is Senior Professor and Director of the doctoral program in Latin American Cultural Studies at the Universidad Andina Simón Bolivar in Quito. Her present work focuses on issues of interculturality, decoloniality and the socio-political and epistemic insurgency of Afro and indigenous and movements. Among her publications are *Interculturalidad, Estado, Sociedad: Luchas (de)coloniales de nuestra época* (2008), "(Post)Coloniality in Ecuador: The Indigenous Movement's Practices and Politics of (Re)signification and Decolonization" (in *Coloniality at Large*, Moraña, Dussel, Jáuregui, eds., 2008) "Shifting the Geopolitics of Critical Knowledge: Decolonial Thought and Cultural Studies 'Others'", (in *Cultural Studies*, 2007), "Afro-Andean Thought and Diasporic Ancestrality" (with E. León) (in *Shifting the Geography of Reason: Gender, Science and Religion*, Banchetti and Headley, eds., 2006), *Pensamiento crítico y matriz (de)colonial* (2005) and "The (Re)Articulation of Political Subjectivities and Colonial Difference in Ecuador: Reflections on Capitalism and the Geopolitics of Knowledge" (*Nepantla*, 2002).

GEORGE YÚDICE, PhD, Princeton University, 1977, is Professor of Latin American Studies and Modern Languages and Cultures at the University of Miami, and was until recently Director of the Title VI Center for Latin American and Caribbean Studies at New York University. He is the author of *Vicente Huidobro y la motivación del lenguaje poético* (Buenos Aires, 1977); *Cultural Policy*, coauthored with Toby Miller (Sage Publications, 2002, in Spanish as *Política Cultural*, Gedisa, 2004); *The Expediency of Culture* (Duke UP, 2004), with versions in Spanish and Portuguese. He has in press or is preparing *Cultura y valor: Ensayos sobre literaturas y culturas latinoamericanas; Música, tecnología y experiencia* (Gedisa, 2007), and *Cultura y política cultural en América Central: 1990 a 2008* (Editorial de la Universidad de Costa Rica). He is also coeditor (with Jean Franco and Juan Flores) of *On Edge: The Crisis of Contemporary Latin American Culture* (University of Minnesota Press, 1992); and coeditor of the "Cultural Studies of the Americas" book series with the University of Minnesota Press.

INDEX IN ALPHABETICAL ORDER

Of related interest

Birle, Peter; Costa, Sérgio; Nitschack, Horst (eds.): **Brazil and the Americas. Convergences and Perspectives.** (Bibliotheca Ibero-Americana, 120) 2008, 237 p.
 * *A view from outside Brazil that seeks to understand how Brazilian society is reponding to the processes of global integration. Also documents the plurality of ways that social actors and analysts interpret the transformations.*

Bremer, Thomas; Fleischmann, Ulrich (eds.): **History and Histories in the Caribbean.** (Bibliotheca Ibero-Americana, 70) 2001, 272 p.
 * *The historical discourse will always consist of a collection of "(hi)stories" which changes in the course of time and with the story teller. This volume presents the diversity of views and interpretations by showing different story tellers.*

Moraña, Mabel (ed.): **Cultura y cambio social en América Latina.** (South by Midwest, 1) 2008, 445 p.
 * *Compilación de análisis sobre cultura contemporánea que parte del cambio social como elemento primordial para pensar la cultura en un momento de conflicto marcado por la transición desde la modernidad al capitalismo tardío.*

Moraña, Mabel; Jáuregui, Carlos A. (eds.): **Revisiting the Colonial Question in Latin America.** 2008, 296 p.
 * *From the configuration of Empire in the colonial period to the multiple facets of modern coloniality, this book offers a challenging approach to the developments and effects of imperial domination and neocolonial rule in Latin American.*

Phaf-Rheinberger, Ineke; Oliveira Pinto, Tiago (eds.): **AfricAmericas. Itineraries, Dialogues, and Sounds.** (Bibliotheca Ibero-Americana, 119) 2008, 224 p.
 * *In their contributions, the authors elaborate on research and cultural practices. For that, they take a closer look at specific regularities by focusing on historical texts, art, literature, music in past and present.*

Santos, Lidia: **Tropical Kitsch. Mass Media in Latin American Art and Literature. Translated by Elisabeth Enenbach.** 2006, 242 p.
 * *Distinguished as the best book in Brazilian Studies by the Latin American Studies Association (LASA).*